CW00524863

Flexibility and Employment Security in Europe

Flexibility and Employment Security in Europe

Labour Markets in Transition

Edited by

Ruud J.A. Muffels

Professor of Socio-Economics and Research Director of the Institute of Labour Studies (OSA) at Tilburg University, the Netherlands

Edward Elgar
Cheltenham, UK • Northampton, MA, USA

Published by
Edward Elgar Publishing Limited
The Lypiatts
15 Lansdown Road
Cheltenham
Glos GL50 2JA
UK

Edward Elgar Publishing, Inc.
William Pratt House
9 Dewey Court
Northampton
Massachusetts 01060
USA

A catalogue record for this book
is available from the British Library

Library of Congress Cataloguing in Publication Data

Flexibility and employment security in Europe : labour markets in transition / edited by Ruud J.A. Muffels.
    p. cm.
 Includes bibliographical references and index.
 1. Job security–Europe. 2. Occupational mobility–Europe. 3. Labor supply–Europe.
I. Muffels, R. J. A.
 HD5708.45.E85F55 2008
 331.25'96094–dc22

2008023875

ISBN 978 1 84720 464 6

Printed and bound in Great Britain by MPG Books Ltd, Bodmin, Cornwall

Contents

Contributors

Ruud Muffels is Professor of socio-economics (labour market and social security science) at the Department of Sociology and research professor at the Institute for Labour Studies (OSA) at Tilburg University. He is also fellow at REFLECT, the Research Institute on Labour Market Dynamics and Flexicurity, and NETSPAR, the Network for Studies on Pensions, Ageing and Retirement. His main research interests deal with labour market dynamics, income distribution and social exclusion, comparative analyses of the welfare state and the socio-economics of ageing. He has published in a wide range of sociological, economic and interdisciplinary journals and co-edited a number of international academic volumes.

Jean-Claude Barbier is research director (CNRS, Sociology) at the Centre d'économie de la Sorbonne, Université Paris I, équipe Matisse. He works on the international comparison of social policies, social protection systems and employment policies. He is also studying the European Employment Strategy, from the point of view of the dissemination of ideas. He conducts research on the epistemological and methodological issues arising from the international comparative stance. He has been active in numerous European networks, including the TLM.net project and its Transwell follow up.

Annelies Debels is researcher at the Centre for Sociological Research at the University of Leuven, Belgium. She finished her thesis on poverty in April 2008. Her research interests include poverty, labour market flexibility, methodology and ageing issues. She has published in international journals on these issues.

Virginia Hernanz is Professor of Economics at the Universidad de Alcalá since 2001. Before, she has been research assistant at the Fundación de Economía Aplicada (FEDEA) and post-doc fellow at Bocconi University. Her main research interests include labour market flexibility, temporary work, working time transitions and training. She has published widely in international journals and book chapters on these issues.

Federica Origo is currently assistant professor at the economics department of the University of Bergamo but previously engaged as a senior researcher at IRS, the Institute for Social Research in Milan. Her main research interests include labour market transitions, non-standard contracts and wage diferentials. She has published in journals on these issues.

Manuela Samek Lodovici is president of IRS, the Institute for Social Research in Milan, where she is also the head of the Labour Market Department. She is also professor of Labour Economics at the Università Cattolica in Milan, at the Università Cattaneo (LIUC) in Castellanza and at the Sociology Department at the Università di Milano-Bicocca. Her main areas of research include the comparative analysis of Labour Market Trends and Labour Regulation Systems and the evaluation of Labour and Equal Opportunity Policies. She has acted as an expert in numerous European networks and has carried out consultancy for the European Commission.

Luis Toharia is professor of Economics at the Universidad de Alcalá since 1980. He has published widely in international journals and academic volumes on a variety of issues among which the measurement of unemployment, flexible contracts, part-time work and labour market transitions. He has served as consultant for many Spanish public institutions, including the Ministry of Labour, the Public Employment Services of Spain and several regions, the regional governments of Catalonia and Andalusía, the National Statistical Institute and the Statistical Institute of Andalucía.

Mieke Booghmans and *Seppe van Gils* are researchers at the Policy Research Centre Work and Social Economy, an applied research institute in the city of Leuven, Belgium. They share an interest in research on labour markets, employment transitions and social security.

Caroline Vermandere is researcher at the department of labour and organisation of the Higher Institute for Labour (HIVA) in Leuven, Belgium. The Institute conducts applied research in the area of labour market, the labour organisation and social security.

Ruud Luijkx is associate professor of Sociology at the Department of Sociology at Tilburg University, Netherlands. He has contributed to international benchmark studies on social mobility and has published widely in international journals and academic volumes in the field of (educational) heterogamy, social inequality, career mobility, labour market transitions and loglinear and latent class analysis.

Markus Gangl is professor of Sociology at the University of Wisconsin-Madison. His main research interests are in labour market dynamics, job mobility and unemployment, and the relationship of labour market processes with patterns of income inequality and social stratification. He has published on these issues in the American Journal of Sociology, the American Sociological Review, the European Sociological Review and other international journals.

Nigel Meager is Director of IES, the Institute for Employment Studies of the University of Sussex in Brighton, United Kingdom. His main research interests include self-employment dynamics, long-term unemployment and European labour market issues in general. He has published widely in a number of European sociological journals and in international academic volumes.

Didier Fouarge studied economics at the Facultés Universitaires Notre-Dame de la Paix (FUNDP) in Namur, Belgium. He holds a PhD from Tilburg University on the topic of poverty dynamics and social policy in Europe. From 1999 to 2007 he was researcher at the Institute for Labour Studies (OSA) and post-doc at Tilburg University. Since November 2007, he is researcher at the Research Centre for Education and the Labour Market (ROA), Maastricht University. His main research interests lie in scientific and applied research on labour market and income dynamics, working times, retirement, income distribution and poverty, and the welfare state. He published in national and international Journals as well as in books with distinguished publishers. For a full CV, see:
< www.roa.unimaas.nl/cv/fouarge/fouarge.htm>.

Govert Bijwaard (PhD) is a post-doctoral researcher at the Econometric Institute at Erasmus University. He got a VENI grant from the Dutch National Science foundation NWO for his study on the Dynamic Economic Aspects of Migration. His research interests include migration, labour econometrics and labour market transitions.

Bram van Dijk is a PhD student at the Tinbergen Institute and at the Econometric Institute at Erasmus University Rotterdam. His research interests include labour market econometrics, human capital, training and working time transitions issues. He has published his work in international journals.

Jaap de Koning is professor of labour market policy at the Erasmus University Rotterdam and director of SEOR, a research institute of the same university. His main research interests are the evaluation of labour market policies, the economics of training, labour market forecasting and education and social economics.

Stephen Ziguras is honorary researcher at the Centre for Public Policy of the University of Melbourne, Australia. He has previously been affiliated as a researcher with the Brotherhood of St. Lawrence in Melbourne. His research interests include labour market policies, social inequality and employment transitions.

Peter Stricker is a researcher at the Centre for Public Policy at Melbourne University, Australia. His main interests deal with labour markets, labour market policies and labour market transitions.

Axel van den Berg is professor of Sociology at McGill University in Montreal, Canada. He has been a Marie Curie Incoming International Fellow at SISWO/Social Policy Research and the Amsterdam Institute for Advanced Labour Studies (AIAS) in 2004 and 2005. His research interests include the sociology of labour markets and the relation between sociology and economics.

Claus-H. von Restorff currently works for the Canadian federal government in Ottawa, while completing his PhD in Economics from McGill University in Montreal, Canada. His main areas of interest are labour market transitions and the importance of various forms of human capital in self-employment.

Daniel Parent is associate professor of Economics at McGill University in Montreal, Canada, holder of a Dawson Chair. He specialises in labour economics and applied econometrics. His current research focuses on the impact of pay-for-performance schemes on wage inequality as well as on employment. He also examines how performance pay affects white–nonwhite wage differentials across the wage distribution.

Anthony C. Masi is professor of Sociology and the Provost of McGill University in Montreal, Canada. He has been a visiting professor in Italy at Bari (1987; 1994) and Pisa (1990), was the Jemolo Fellow in Italian Studies at Nuffield College, Oxford (1993), and from 1996 to 2000 was Visiting Research Fellow at the Italian National Institute of Statistics in Rome. He has published on labour force, industrial policy and the relationship between institutions and economic development in Italy as well as comparative studies of labour market flexibility in Canada and Sweden.

Per Kongshøj Madsen is professor at Aalborg University and director of CARMA at the Department of Economics, Politics and Public Administration. His main research interests include comparative labour market analysis and European employment policy. Since 1997 he has been a member of the European Employment Observatory. He has published widely in journals and international academic volumes on the issue of flexicurity and the Danish flexicurity model.

Preface and Acknowledgements

Flexibility and Employment Security in Europe: Labour Markets in Transition traces how individual workers cope with the increasing dynamics on the labour market and the effects that has for their transition patterns and labour market careers. Through the analysis of unique comparative panel data from 14 European countries during the 1990s up to the early 2000s, and tracking the individuals' career fate over a period of eight years, a number of esteemed authors coming from different origins and angles examine the way workers and governments cope with rising demands to meet the needs for increasing flexibility without endangering income and employment security. They address issues as to whether these changes signal the alleged shift in the employment relationship from 'lifetime employment' to the 'boundaryless' career, as for example the Transitional Labour Market theory contends, and how countries through their institutional set up and policies cope with these changes and try to improve the balance of flexibility and security in their societies. The latter has become a key issue now in the European policy debate under the heading of 'flexicurity' since the EU governments have accepted the principles of 'flexicurity' policies in the Autumn of 2007.

It is common among economists to speak about a 'zero-sum game' or the inevitable trade-offs when viewing the relationship between efficiency and equity to which the flexibility–security issue refers, but the authors contend that such trade-offs can be avoided and that a 'positive sum-game' is conceivable. For that purpose they try to draw lessons from 'best policy practices' with a view to transitional labour market and flexicurity approaches in Australia, Canada and Denmark.

The book is the outcome of a collaborative effort among a set of researchers in ten countries, eight from within and two from outside the EU. The project was funded as a network by the European Commission under the 5th Framework Programme and called the Transitional Labour Market Network (TLM.Net). The Network was coordinated jointly by the University of Amsterdam (Dr. Nick van den Heuvel) and the WZB, Wissenschaftszentrum fur Sozialforschung Berlin (Professor Dr. Klaus Schömann). The contributions in the book form a selection of the papers prepared and presented in workshops and conferences organised in the context of the activities of Work package three of the network: 'Supporting Labour Market Mobility and Dynamics'.

Acknowledgements

The editor is primarily indebted to the authors of the chapters for their invaluable contributions to the substance of the book dealing with the intriguing issue of the relationship between flexibility and security and their cooperation and support during the editing process.

The book hinges on two major socio-economic approaches: 'Transitional Labour Market (TLM)' and 'Flexicurity', the founding fathers of which were members and contributors to the network. The TLM.Net network is therefore much indebted to Professor Dr. Günther Schmid, the inventor of the Transitional Labour Market Model and the instigator of a number of networks and research endeavours preceding this network, who inspired the group on many occasions during the project with his work and ideas. We also want to acknowledge Professor Ton Wilthagen's contribution to the network and this book with a view to his scholarly work on the notion of 'flexicurity' that by the European Commission is currently accepted as the leading principle for European policies in the domain of labour market and social security.

Further we want to express our gratitude to a number of people who contributed directly or indirectly to make the network a success either by acting as invited speakers or discussants at the workshops and conferences held in Amsterdam and Budapest, or by commenting on previous drafts of the papers and the book: Dr. Peter Auer, Dr. Jean-Claude Barbier, Maarten Camps, Professor Axel van den Berg, Professor Gösta Esping-Andersen, Dr. Stephano Cagliarducci, Professor Erik de Gier, Dr. Nick van den Heuvel, Dr. Egbert Holthuis, Dr. Nigel Meager, Professor Dr. Günther Schmid, Professor Albert Tuijnman and Professor Ton Wilthagen.

The editor is also much indepted to Kees Boos for the pleasant cooperation with him in organising the editing process and for painstakingly compiling the typescript. A last word of gratitude goes to the publisher Edward Elgar for the shown trust in the endeavour and for the excellent way they have guided the publishing process and supported the editor and the authors.

Ruud Muffels, March 2008

PART I

Labour Market Mobility and
In-Work Transitions

1. Flexibility and Employment Security in Europe: Setting the Scene

Ruud Muffels

1.1 INTRODUCTION

This book seeks to gain a better understanding of the paradoxical relationship between the alleged need for European labour markets to become more flexible and the way in which national policies pursue this aim without jeopardising existing high standards of income and employment security. The book devotes special interest to the way in which countries opt for different policy routes to cope with the aim of balancing flexibility and security goals in their respective labour market and social protection policies. The idea of policies focusing on balancing flexibility and security goals has become key now in the European social policy debate under the heading of 'flexicurity' (Wilthagen, 1998; Wilthagen and Tros, 2004).

This volume tries to document the differences and similarities of the various labour markets in Europe in coping with the pressures of enhancing the flexibility of its labour markets and simultaneously maintaining employment security. All labour markets confront changing mobility and working patterns albeit to a different extent and complexity causing what is called a diversification or individualisation of careers and life courses.

The book examines in particular the potential trade-offs between economic and social goals translated into the question as to how and to what extent employment regimes in Europe are capable – through their particular institutional design – of attaining fairly high levels of flexibility and employment and income security simultaneously. The book deals with this relationship by examining the role and performance of welfare states and employment regimes for attaining high levels of mobility and flexibility and promoting labour market and social integration simultaneously (European Commission, 2006, 2007; Philips and Eamets, 2007). Another aim of the book is to provide more insight into the underlying factors that might explain why some countries perform better than others and what role specific policies and institutions have played. To find answers to these questions the contributors in this book all try to unveil the particular changes or transitions occurring in the various labour markets, to learn about their medium and longer-term effects and the role of institutions and policies to cushion the adverse consequences of these changes. The latter policy-related issue is addressed by comparing labour market outcomes across countries and regimes and by analysing 'best policy practices' in Australia, Canada and Denmark. In terms of methodology, the book therefore is concerned with the analysis of labour market changes and dynamics, the comparative analysis of countries and welfare states and single country case studies in the form of 'best policy practices'.

The book is the outcome of a collaborative EU project called TLM.Net, under which umbrella a series of books became published (De Koning, 2007a; De Koning, 2007b; Lassnigg et al., 2007)

The innovative aspect of the book apart from its dynamic and comparative treatment of the relationship between flexibility and security is on the role of institutions and policies in explaining transition patterns within work against the backdrop of a rapidly changing societal context due to ageing, individualisation and increasing international competition. These changes affect the so-called 'flexibility–security' nexus (Wilthagen and Tros, 2004) in the various countries and regimes which are markedly different. Particular attention is devoted to the upcoming of new, sometimes precarious or insecure, forms of paid labour and self-employment. One of the major issues dealt with is the contended 'scarring' effect of these new employment forms on the future career in terms of impaired employment chances and wage prospects. In the literature to date the more general question posed is whether these new forms function as 'stepping-stones' into standard jobs or as 'employment traps' or 'dead-ends' from which it is hard to escape (Blank, 1989; Gangl, 2003, 2006; Muffels et al., 2007; Scherer, 2004). There is mixed and incomplete evidence on these 'stepping-stones' versus 'scarring' effects of these new employment forms, such as part-time work, fixed-term contracts and typical self-employment jobs and especially on their longer-term effects for the career which gap we want to fill, at least partly, with the contributions in this book. A second major issue deals with the implications of the rise of new employment forms for the attained level of flexibility and security and for policies confronted with the possible adverse effects of any unbalance that might exist.

1.2 CHANGING WORKING PATTERNS AND RISING INSECURITY

Working patterns have changed in many countries during the last decades especially for women but also for men. This does not imply that the dominant work pattern of men during the life course changed as dramatically as that of women. The majority of men work full-time and because male tenure did not change much in most European labour markets they still tend to work in long tenured jobs. Women work more than ever before and more often in part-time jobs, in short-hours jobs and in temporary jobs. Due to the declining traditional gender role behaviour of women and the rising economic pressures for women to work, they need to develop their own career and though they still carry the largest burden with respect to care they spend more time in the labour market over the life course than ever before. This shift in work attitudes and work behaviour is partly associated with the wake and rise of the 'knowledge economy', demanding people to spend more time in maintaining and renewing their human capital through training and further education during their entire working career (life-long learning).

The influence of socio-cultural changes – irrespective of whether they are due to autonomous cultural shifts or associated with structural socio-economic changes – cannot be denied. Cultural changes refer to what is called the individualisation of society leading to changes in role patterns between men and women and to changing preferences for combining work and leisure and a more diversified career. But also demographic changes associated with these cultural changes play a central role, such as the declining fertility rates, the increasing instability of families due to divorce and separation and population ageing. These cultural and demographic changes have especially affected the working patterns of their younger female counterparts. The usual drop in female participation rates after childbirth tends to be much smaller now for younger women even in countries with a traditionally low participation of women (Stier et al., 2001). Younger women compared to older women therefore participate more in the labour market and work on average longer hours than their predecessors (Fouarge et al., 2006). Male and female careers therefore seem to converge, but women due to their caring roles still face more unstable careers and career interruptions than men (O'Reilly and Bothfeld, 2002).

At the same time the waning of lifetime employment went along with more unstable working careers for men due to the heightened turmoil on the labour market as a result of the internationalisation of the economy or globalisation forces leading to more frequent job changes with more intermittent periods of unemployment, the wake of new forms of temporary work and self-employment. The standard working career of men now seems to be shifting towards a more diverse working career pattern with a richer variety of non-standard work forms: part-time work, small-hours temporary jobs, seasonal work, on-call work, casual work, employment agency work, in- and outsourcing, labour pooling, multi-tasking, job rotation, job sharing, e-working and new forms of self-employment (the freelancer or the self-employed person without personnel). About one in seven workers in Europe are now engaged in a temporary or fixed-term labour contract. Another 20 per cent is engaged in part-time work and an increasing part of these part-timers are working in a small-hours job of less than 15 hours. If we add the growing proportion of people engaged in new forms of self-employment, the sheer size and potential importance of non-standard work becomes clear. All this happened in a few decades but even now we observe a rapid rise in the share of part-time work and some types of self-employment even though temporary work has remained rather stable during the late 1990s and early 2000s in Europe. Nonetheless, the share of workers engaged in 'non-standard' jobs is now at a fairly high level in many European countries questioning the definition of the 'standard' job itself. Below we present some more evidence on the evolution in the 1990s and early 2000s of part-time work and fixed-term contracts.

Trends in non-standard work

Some evidence on the evolution of non-standard work is given in the next three tables showing the evolution of part-time and temporary work in Europe over the last few decades. In Figure 1.1 we depict the evolution of part-time work between 1983 and 2001 for EU15, the Euro area, the US, Canada and Japan. In the EU15 but especially also in Japan the incidence of part-time work has strongly increased whereas it has slowly decreased in the US and remained fairly stable in Canada over this period. For the development between 2000 and 2005 the Employment in Europe 2006 report gives some further evidence (see Figure 1.2). Here we observe rising shares of part-time work in Europe during this period excepting some Eastern European countries.

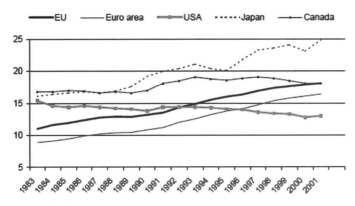

Sources: OECD, Eurostat (Labour force surveys).

Source: Buddelmeyer et al. (2004): The Determinants of Part-Time Work in EU. Countries: Empirical Investigations with Macro-Panel Data, IZA paper, no. 1361.

Figure 1.1 Evolution of part-time work in the EU15, the Euro area, Japan, the US and Canada during the period 1983–2001

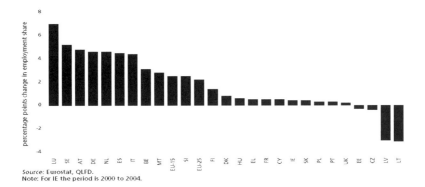

Notes:
BE Belgium, CZ Czech Republic; DK Denmark; DE Germany; EE Estonia; EL Greece; ES Spain; Fr France; IE Ireland; IT Italy; CY Cyprus; LV Latvia; LT Lithuania; LU Luxembourg; HU Hungary; MT Malta; NL Netherlands; AT Austria; PL Poland; PT Portugal; SL Slovenia; SK Slovakia; FI Finland; SE Sweden; UK United Kingdom.

Source: Employment in Europe (2006).

Figure 1.2 Change in the share of part-time employment in total employment between 2000 and 2005

Figure 1.3 depicts the evolution of the incidence of workers with a time-limited contract (temporary or fixed-term contract) between 2000 and 2005. The figures show that compared to the rise in part-time work, a moderate rise in most countries except for Greece and France and the two Anglo-Saxon countries UK and Ireland.

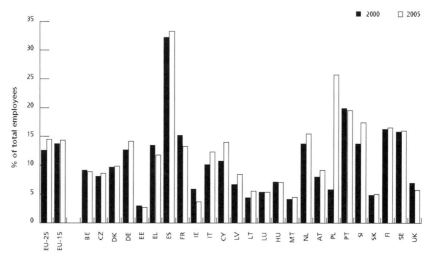

Source: Eurostat, QLFD.

Notes:
BE Belgium's Czech Republic; DK Denmark; DE Germany; EE Estonia; EL Greece; ES Spain; Fr France; IE Ireland; IT Italy; CY Cyprus; LV Latvia; LT Lithuania; LU Luxembourg; HU Hungary; MT Malta; NL Netherlands; AT Austria; PL Poland; PT Portugal; SL Slovenia; SK Slovakia; FI Finland; SE Sweden; UK United Kingdom.

Source: Employment in Europe (2006).

Figure 1.3 Development in the share of employees in fixed-term employment in the EU between 2000 and 2005

1.3 CONCEPTUAL TENETS

To derive hypotheses about factors which explain differences across countries in the way they combine flexibility and security we will build on the most important theories formulated on their relationship as elaborated in the economic and sociological literature: the 'Transitional Labour Market' and the 'Flexicurity' approach. In both approaches the notion of the 'welfare regime' is utilised to explain the observed differences in labour market performance across countries. For that reason we briefly discuss the welfare regime approach and some 'best policy practices' as applied in the last part of the book.

1.3.1 The Transitional Labour Market Approach

One of the theories concerned with the effects of globalisation and the wake of the 'knowledge economy' for national labour markets has been the well-known 'Transitional Labour Market' approach as introduced by Günther Schmid in the mid-1990s (Schmid, 1995). One of the basic premises of the TLM approach is that the adjustment to asymmetric economic shocks is not due to changes in prices or wage levels (wage flexibility) but to the role of wage-setting institutions (minimum wage, wage bargain, employment protection) by adjustment of the labour input itself through 'numerical flexibility', that is, by adapting the size of the workforce. It implies that according to Schmid's TLM approach the diversification and rise of non-standard forms of labour has had the same function as the low wage service jobs in the US. They seem to act as a 'buffer' cushioning the consequences of asymmetric macro-economic shocks due to the whimsicality of the business cycle though at the same time endangering the levels of employment security in society (Schmid, 2000; Schmid and Schömann, 2003). In downturn periods the least protected temporary workers will be the first to be dismissed whereas in upturn periods they are the first to be hired again due to risk-averse employers who are reluctant to employ permanent workers before the economic recovery has proved to last. In the 'normative' interpretation of the TLM model however, 'activating policies' are required to build institutional bridges between unemployment and employment which just as the 'non-standard jobs' can act as a 'buffer' to cushion the unemployment effects of downturn periods but without having the adverse effects in terms of the income and employment insecurity it provides to the workers involved.

The unified theory of Blau and Kahn and the contingent worker

The TLM approach therewith renders an answer to the contested predictions derived from the economic so-called 'unified theory' of Blau and Kahn (2002). This theory predicts that due to the existing wage rigidities in European labour markets as caused by the wage-setting institutions, the adjustment to asymmetric economic shocks will not be through wage flexibility but through high unemployment levels of the low-skilled worker. The knowledge-economy leading to a so-called skill-biased technological change will lower the demand for the low-skilled in favour of the demand for the high-skilled causing downward pressures on real wage levels of the low-skilled and to heightened unemployment risks. Due to the existence of wage rigidities (for example, minimum wage, wage bargain), wages cannot fall because this could lead to the low-skilled workers being expelled from the labour market and higher unemployment risks. The low-skilled are hence the losers in this process. DiPrete et al. (2006) reviewing the evidence for the US and Europe showed that the wage levels of the low-skilled as well as the unemployment rates by skill-level seem to have largely remained stable especially in countries where the wage-setting institutions were strong such as in the small countries of the Netherlands, Norway and Austria and in the larger countries of Germany and France. The authors then try to come up with an alternative institutional explanation. The adaptation process to asymmetric macro-economic shocks will in their view not result in high unemployment levels or in high wage inequality as the 'unified theory' (Blau and Kahn, 2002) predicts, but in reduced employment security due to increasing shares of workers in insecure non-standard jobs.

However, non-standard jobs also impact on the levels of flexibility in a country because they are viewed as a way to circumvent the strict employment protection rules for permanent workers and to render employers the necessary numerical flexibility they need to adapt successfully to the rapidly changing economic conditions due to globalisation trends (Muffels and Luijkx, 2006). Policies in various countries have in the course of time adapted the institutions, for example in France and Spain (see Chapter 4 of Hernanz et al.), to allow for these new forms of flexibility and by doing so paving the way for a rapidly rising 'temporary workforce' especially in the most regulated countries such as in Continental and Southern countries.

The flexibility needs in many regulated European countries have therefore been partly satisfied through the diversification of employment forms by allowing employers to hire this new type of contingent worker. However, it also reduces their employment security since a number of these workers – due to their low skills – have difficulties acquiring a permanent job after being engaged in a temporary job. DiPrete et al. (2006) therefore argue that the adjustment to asymmetric economic shocks in these regulated countries has not been through rising wage-inequality or falling real wages to low-skill workers as in the US nor to changes in the demand of labour by skill-level (unemployment), but 'through the creation of low-adjustment cost/low-security jobs and through the allocation of an increasing large share of low-skilled workers to these jobs'.

The larger wage inequality and decline in real wages in the lower strata in the US was due to lack of supply of high-skilled workers to meet the rising demand caused by the process of skill-biased technological change in the US and to the absence of a floor in the wage building (Acemoglu, 2003). Contrary to the US, Europe was able, through a better functioning education system, to raise the supply of high-skilled workers as the wages were hardly affected. For the low-skilled worker the wage setting institutions had the effect in Europe that the wage level could never fall below the floor set by the minimum wage because even in the lower strata of the labour market wages tend to be rather stable. The authors argue that European labour markets have absorbed skill-biased technological change not by increased unemployment of the low-skilled as the 'unified theory' would predict but by allocating an increasingly large share of low-skilled workers to non-standard jobs. For the same reason they hypothesise 'job security returns to skill in Europe, which parallel rising wage returns to skill in the US' (DiPrete et al., 2006).

The 'trade-off' and 'scarring' thesis
These theoretical predictions tend to argue for a trade-off or 'zero-sum' relationship between flexibility and security. Increases in flexibility seem to occur at the expense of decreases in employment security. The low-skilled worker employed in a 'flexible' contract seems to carry the burden of the consequences of asymmetric economic shocks in terms of heightened unemployment risks.

Also scholars engaged in social stratification research have asked attention for the adverse effects of globalisation trends and the accompanying larger demand for flexibility. They showed that due to social stratification processes particularly in the weakest groups on the labour market, workers with low-skill levels and human capital endowments are increasingly exposed to employment instability and income insecurity (Blossfeld et al. 2006; Breen, 1997, 2004; DiPrete et al., 1997; DiPrete, 2002; Goldthorpe, 2001). The unskilled seem to be entrapped in low-quality jobs acting as 'dead-end' jobs from which it is difficult to escape. For that reason non-standard jobs are sometimes such as in France, but also in some Southern countries (Spain, Italy) viewed upon as 'precarious' jobs as Barbier shows in Chapter 2 of this book. This also refers to the 'scarring thesis' that has now become more popular in academic circles according to which experiences of non-employment, self-employment or employment in low-level jobs have an enduring negative effect on the worker's future career in terms of employment stability and future earnings (Blank, 1994; Booth et al., 2002; Fouarge et al., 2006; Gangl, 2006). Chapters 7 to 10 in part II of this book present more evidence on these 'scarring' effects for temporary work, unemployment, self-employment and part-time work.

1.3.2 The 'Flexicurity' Thesis

However, from a theoretical point of view the necessity of a 'trade-off' relationship between flexibility and security can be contested. There is reason to argue for a mutually reinforcing relationship in which the relationship is characterised by a 'positive sum-game' or 'win–win' situation implying that high levels of flexibility and security can be attained simultaneously (Wilthagen, 1998; Wilthagen and Tros, 2004).

From the evidence presented earlier, one might raise some scepticism about how realistic such an image of an 'ideal world' is in which there are no losers but only winners. However, the idea has founded some ground – though not uncontested – in one strand of the management literature in the realm of organisational sociology where one speaks of the 'new' or 'flexible' employment relationship. This 'new' employee relationship is seen as a consequence of the alleged flexibility trend that is delineated as an ongoing shift 'from lifetime employment to the "boundaryless" career' (Stone, 2005). In this view job security offered through lifetime employment on the 'internal labour market' is substituted by employment security on the external labour market offered through investments in the 'employability' of workers by providing training opportunities raising the 'general' skill-level (Collins, 2005). The underlying hypothesis is that the 'new worker' will change jobs and employers more frequently provided that sufficient investments are made in skill formation during the job. By marketing the newly acquired skills on the external labour market the worker is more capable of safeguarding his or her employment security therewith supporting the 'flexicurity' thesis. From an analytical perspective, the 'flexicurity' concept resembles Streeck's concept of 'competitive solidarity', providing for internal equality and external competitveness, that he sees as the productivist reconstruction of the traditional redistributive solidarity eroded through the growing competition in an internationalising economy (Streeck, 2000).

Defining 'flexicurity' and its dimensions

The notion of 'flexicurity' as coined by Wilthagen (1998) and Wilthagen and Tros (2004) reads as:

> Flexicurity is (1) a degree of job, employment, income and 'combination' security that facilitates the labour market careers and biographies of workers with a relatively weak position and allows for enduring and high quality labour market participation and social inclusion, while at the same time providing (2) a degree of numerical (both external and internal) functional and wage flexibility that allows for labour markets (and individual companies) timely and adequate adjustment to changing conditions in order to maintain and enhance competitiveness and productivity.

In this definition, job security refers to job tenure in a specific job; employment security to remaining in work not necessarily with the same employer; income security to the degree of income replacement due to the loss of work and combination security to the capability to combine paid and unpaid work or social activities during the life course. With the latter addition they connect the flexicurity thesis to life course theory and to the policy issue of the work–life balance.

The relationship between the various dimensions of flexibility and security – the so-called flexibility–security nexus – is represented by Wilthagen's well-known flexibility–security matrix in which his four types of security (job, employment, income, combination) are cross-tabulated to four types of flexibility (external and internal numerical, functional flexibility and pay or wage flexibility). The underlying idea is that countries will have different scores on each dimension of flexibility and security implying different combinations of the 'flexibility–security' nexus. The Danish 'flexicurity' system is, for example, based on the combination of a low level of employment protection or job security (external numerical flexibility), high expenditures on activating labour market policies and a strong focus on in-company 'employability' policies (functional flexibility) safeguarding employment security and high levels of income replacement benefits safeguarding income security (see Madsen in Chapter 13). Standing (1997) extends the security concept by distinguishing seven forms of security, the four of Wilthagen and three new forms associated with the work content or the job quality dimension: 'employability', representation and workplace security. These three security forms are associated with the internal functional flexibility dimension. In Table 1.1 we show how the seven security forms are linked to the various forms of flexibility.

Compared to the TLM approach the 'flexicurity' approach pays heed to the ongoing changes within the 'employment relationship', within firms, on the internal labour market and therefore brings to the fore the so-called 'in-work transitions'. Most of the contributions in this book are concerned with transitions within work although due to lack of company data they are unable to deal with functional internal flexibility and the security attached to it. Therefore, the book is primarily concerned with external flexibility and how that relates to employment and income/wage security.

Flexicurity policies

The idea of a mutually reinforcing relationship between flexibility and security as hypothesised by these theorists has become very popular now in the European social policy debate under the metaphor of 'flexicurity' (European (European Commission, 2006, 2007a; Wilthagen, 1998; Wilthagen and Tros, 2004).

Table 1.1 Classification of types of flexibility and security and their linkage

Type of flexibility	Description/definition	Type of security	Description/definition
Numerical, internal	Working Hours Flexibility (part-time; overtime; multiple jobs)	Job security	Security of employment in current job
	Working Time Flexibility (flexible WT, WT accounts; career breaks, leave options; flexible pensions)	Work–life balance or combination security	Availability of child care relief, working time and care or education leave options according to needs
Numerical, external	Contract flexibility (temp agency; casual; fixed-term; on-call; hours; in-outsourcing; subcontracting; homework; telework; labour pool)	Employment/ contract security	Security of employment and/or contract
Functional, external	Labour force flexibility (knowledge worker; detachment; freelance; advising/consultancy)		
Functional, internal	Labour input flexibility (multi-skilling; multi-tasking; task/job rotation; task/job enrichment)	Employability security	Opportunities to acquire and maintain skills
		Representation security	Protection of collective voice through worker's representation and trade unions/employer organisations
		Workplace security	Safe/Healthy workplaces
Wage flexibility	Wage/Pay flexibility (wage/salary changes; average pay; performance related pay; anciennity pay; group pay; piece work; bonuses)	Wage/Income security	Fair/equal pay Safeguarding income against social risks

Source: Muffels et al. (2007), reworked from Standing (1997) and Wilthagen (1998, 2004).

The underlying idea is that when institutions are properly designed to activate employers and employees to facilitate investments in their 'employability', this will also contribute to a high level of mobility raising the worker's productivity and therewith his employment security. Hence, investments in the 'employability' of the worker are critical to achieving a higher level of mobility and flexibility on the labour market and simultaneously improving the level of employment security. Flexibility and mobility seems not only good to employers; it also allows workers to tune their work and leisure needs better whereas security seems not only good to workers, but also employers benefit from the increased 'employability' of the worker because of the larger commitment and the productivity gains involved.

The flexicurity definition we presented earlier has also been used in the Commission's 2006 and 2007 'Employment in Europe' reports (see Chapter 2, EC, 2006 and Chapter 3, EC, 2007). Though slightly rephrased, this theoretical definition has further been included in the final Communication on 'flexicurity' policies (Commission, 2007a): 'Flexicurity aims at ensuring that EU citizens can enjoy a high level employment security, that is the possibility to easily find a job at every stage of active life and have a good prospect for career development in a quickly changing economic environment'. In the same document it is said that flexicurity 'can be defined as an integrated strategy to enhance, at the same time, flexibility and security in the labour market'. Hence, flexibility and security are seen as two sides of the same coin.

The 'flexicurity' thesis immediately poses a challenge to the various labour markets to create an efficiently operating market with safeguarding the employment security of its actors, so as to arrive at a balanced mix of adequate levels of flexibility and labour market mobility on the one hand and income and employment security on the other. The way the various labour markets are able to deliver such a 'flexibility–security' mix will be path-dependent, as it will be strongly affected by their political, institutional, demographic, socio-economic and socio-cultural roots and heritage. In the same document the Commission argues for 'diversity' rather than 'unity' by stating that due to the large variation in approaches at the country level as well as at the company level a 'one-size-fits-all' approach is unlikely to work. In the Commission's language it is articulated that Europe is 'not opting for a single European model but it allows member-states to follow their own national routes or pathways'. Although the Commission is very clear about which pathways provide better socio-economic outcomes and which worse, it certainly seems unwilling to confront member-states with a 'naming and blaming' exercise that might jeopardise the support for 'flexicurity' policies in Europe.

1.3.3 Welfare Regimes, Policies and Institutions

In both the trade-off and the 'flexicurity' thesis, the role of institutional and policy related factors seems to be of crucial importance. Basically, there are three ways of examining how institutional factors contribute to explain the variation in a country's levels of flexibility and employment security in comparative research. One way is to define classifications or typologies of country clusters based on the elaboration of a set of statistical indicators; another one is to use existing typologies as they are elaborated in the literature and a third one is to look into very specific or concrete policy measures at the country level such as active labour market policy measures and to see how each of them separately and jointly impacts on socio-economic outcomes. In the empirical chapters (Chapters 2 to 9) we will either carefully examine the very specific institutions in each country under scrutiny, such as in Britain, the support to self-employed people, and how it impacts the levels of flexibility and security. In another approach we either use existing classifications like the one developed in the seminal study of Esping-Andersen (1990) or we develop our own classification to view their impact on both dimensions. In addition, we examine in the policy-oriented chapters of part III of the book including some particular case studies: the Canadian reforms of the unemployment system in the 1990s, the 'flexicurity' approach nicely framed by the author as the 'golden triangle' in the Danish system and the Australian active labour market policy reform.

A typology of welfare regimes

In Esping-Andersen's *Three Worlds of Welfare Capitalism* (1990), various forms of 'welfare capitalism' with very dissimilar economic (efficiency) and social (equity) outcomes are considered. These welfare regimes are characterised by their degree of decommodification or the extent by which the state intervenes in the market and the level of social stratification in society. That study has been succeeded by very many others creating more refined classifications of countries (Bonoli, 1997; Ferrera, 1996; Ferrera et al., 2000; Goodin et al., 1999). In the 'variety of capitalism' approach (Albert, 1991; Hall and Soskice, 2001) the focus has been on the modes of co-ordination, the degree to which it is the market which mediates or whether it is the institutions that take up the coordination responsibilities. Albert speaks of the Rhineland versus the Beveridgian or Anglo-Saxon model of capitalism whereas Hall and Soskice distinguish between liberal or unregulated market economies versus regulated market economies. Hall and Soskice's approach is further elaborated by Amable (2003). They all conclude to consider a classification very much alike that of Esping-Andersen: the market based model typified by the US and the UK in Europe;

the social-democratic model typified by the Nordic countries and the Continental model typified by the central European countries, though they add a Mediterranean and an Asian model (Muffels and Luijkx, 2008).

In the literature there seems to be agreement to using a so-called modified Esping-Andersen typology with geographical instead of socio-political labels. This modified typology consists of four types: the Anglo-Saxon, the Nordic, the Central European or Continental and the Mediterranean or Southern regime. A fifth regime type should be added for the so-called transition countries, the former socialist Eastern countries and the three Baltic states, since they do not share many characteristics with the other four regime types. However, since the contributions in this book use data from Continental, Northern and Southern countries only we were not able to say much about the flexibility–security balance in these transition countries (Philips and Eamets, 2007). In Chapter 6 we show how the various European labour markets and regimes perform in balancing flexibility and security goals. A typology has been constructed by elaborating a set of dynamic outcome indicators and by mapping the countries on that set of indicators. The derived classification resembles the modified Esping-Andersen typology though it also revealed a large within-regime variation. The findings showed that the Anglo-Saxon and Nordic regimes are seemingly performing best in balancing flexibility and employment security goals and the regulated Continental and Southern countries worse. The chapter also tries to examine the impact of the institutional features of the various regimes on the flexibility–security balance. The level of employment regulation is not the only thing that seems to count but also the institutional features of the social security system, the wage bargain and the design and content of labour market policies.

Mapping countries on flexibility and security
The European Commission in its two latest 'Employment in Europe' reports (2006, 2007) attempted to map the countries not by using dynamic but primarily static (cross-sectional) institutional and outcome indicators on flexibility and income and employment security. In the 2006 report the focus was on external flexibility and income/security indicators whereas in the 2007 report internal flexibility indicators were also used, in particular when dealing with working-time flexibility, work intensity (long hours) and work irregularity (unusual hours) as well as with internal (work autonomy/complexity) and functional flexibility (job rotation/teamwork).

In the first step a factor analysis, more specifically a principal components analysis, has been executed on the indicators. It shows that there are basically three latent or hidden factors with one factor counting for 46 per cent of the variance. This represents the internal numerical and functional flexibility dimension as represented by the working time flexibility and work autonomy/complexity indicators. This factor is also positively related to the labour market policy and education/training indicators with one numerical flexibility factor (counting for 21 per cent of the variance) that is strongly and negatively associated with EPL but positively with internal working time (numerical) flexibility and a third factor reflecting the other part of the *functional flexibility* dimension, represented by the job rotation and teamwork indicators (counting for 18 per cent of the variance).

The high correlations of the education and training indicators (life-long learning) as well as the labour market policy indicators with the internal flexibility component (working time and work autonomy/complexity) show that investments in the employability of workers also imply that their employment security is better safeguarded. This is also indicated by the positive correlation of job satisfaction and the negative correlation of unemployment and long-term unemployment with this component (EC, 2007, p. 170). The level of income security as indicated by the variable 'reduction in poverty' and work–life balance security (satisfaction with being able to reconcile private life and the career) also shows a high correlation with the first internal flexibility/employability component indicating that the regimes scoring high on internal flexibility/employability also perform better on income and work–life balance security. In the second step the four indicators were used to map the countries on the three dimensions: internal flexibility (D1), numerical external flexibility (D2) and functional flexibility (D3). In Figure 1.4 the results are shown for the mapping on D1 and D2, and D1 and D3, respectively. In both cases the exercise resulted in five regime types: the Anglo-Saxon (UK, Ireland), the Nordic cluster (Sweden, Finland, Denmark, the Netherlands), the Continental cluster (Austria, France, Belgium, Germany), the Mediterranean cluster (Spain, Greece, Portugal but without Italy) and the Central/Eastern Cluster (Hungary, Poland, Czech Republic, Slovakia and Italy).

The classification of countries in these five types resembles to a large extent the modified Esping-Andersen typology. The mapping of countries seems to indicate that the internal flexibility model indicated by strong HRM policies and demanding work tasks but with a large autonomy (Nordic countries) correspond with high levels of internal flexibility and employability and income and work–life balance security (European Commission, 2007, p. 176).

It is also shown that the functional flexibility model with high levels of work intensity and work irregularity and relying strongly on rotation and teamwork but with low autonomy (transition regimes), is associated with negative outcomes in terms of lower levels of internal flexibility and security, and also with lower levels of job satisfaction and health.

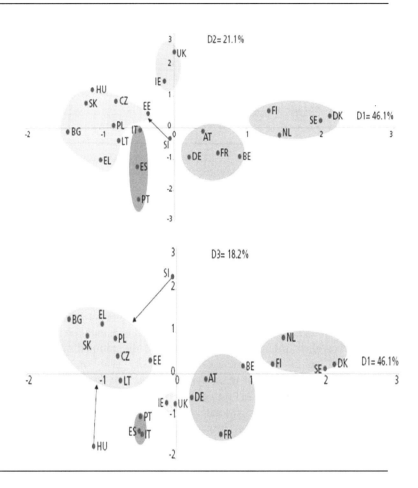

Source: Employment in Europe 2007, pp. 168–77 (European Commission, 2007).

Figure 1.4 Country flexibility/employability and security scores based on the first (D1 = internal flexibility) and second component (D2 = external numerical flexibility) (upper graph) and the first and third (D3= functional flexibility) component (graph below)

Because these analyses are based on correlation analysis and not on causal modelling of transitions and mobility patterns, one needs to be cautious in drawing firm conclusions. We should also keep in mind that the clustering is based on static or rather short-term evidence and on a limited number of institutional indicators only, though the 2007 report provides much more detail on indicators dealing with internal and functional flexibility than the 2006 report. Further, since we are interested in long-term changes we need dynamic evidence on the effect of institutions on transition and mobility patterns and hence on 'outcomes', preferably over the life course. Information on long-term 'outcomes' is not readily available, certainly not if we seek for recent and comparative data covering many countries of the EU (European Commission, 2007; Muffels et al., 2007).

1.3.4 'Best Practices'

The third part of the book is devoted to some particular policy configurations or welfare regimes which are delineated as 'best practices' with a view to transitional labour market and 'flexicurity' policies. These chapters on 'best practices' might contribute to the policy debate since they bring into discussion the so-called 'transferability' issue of specific policy measures from one national context into another. Though, it does so, not in a mechanic way but by taking notice of the particular features and path-dependency of the national systems. In all three chapters an attempt is made to compare the own 'best practice' with the two others especially with a view to the transferability of policy issue. Chapter 13 therefore describes these three 'best practices' in Denmark, Chapter 12 Canada and Chapter 11 Australia.

However, there might be 'best practices' at the national or even regional level from which other countries, regions or policy regimes can learn irrespective of the question to what extent these are transferable to another context. The Danish road of 'flexicurity' very much hinges on the view that 'employability' policies are essential to create a balanced flexibility–security mix. In a recent publication Jørgensen and Madsen discusses the Danish 'flexicurity' system referring to the famous phrase of the Swedish economist Gosta Rehn, when he spoke about 'the security of the wings', referring to the intensive efforts to improve workers' skills and transferable qualifications in order to build a flexible workforce (2007, p.13). But, more than that, the 'flexicurity' approach requires the existence of a high level of trust between the social partners, an atmosphere of cooperation and the acceptance of the responsibility to be adaptive to change as Jørgensen and Madsen argued (Jørgensen and Madsen, 2007).

This dimension of trust has also in the Dutch context been held responsible for the success of the Dutch 'miracle' in the 1990s of creating high levels of employment together with a moderately flexible labour market. In the Dutch context the industrial relations system was built on achieving consensus in the domain of employment and wages. However consensus asks for trust among the social partners and the combination of consensus and trust has certainly been one of the major critical factors in explaining the success of the Dutch 'poldermodel' as it was framed in these years. But it did not last long before the Netherlands entered a deep recession in the early 2000s during which productivity declined and unemployment rates increased fairly quickly. From the mid 2000s, the Dutch economy recovered and started to again experience high levels of GDP growth and low unemployment rates. The impact of trust clearly points to the important role of norms, values and beliefs in explaining the dissimilar levels of success of the various policy regimes in Europe to create a 'high performance' labour market in terms of flexibility and security.

1.3.5 Towards a Conceptual Framework

The question now arises how the various theoretical tenets are connected in the conceptual framework that we will use throughout this book. The two strands in the literature that is, the transitional labour market and 'flexicurity' approach are closely linked while they share the focus on flexibility and security. The 'best practices' in the part III are seen as examples for the way in which TLM and 'flexicurity' policies are institutionally designed. In Figure 1.5 the conceptual framework is depicted.

The research focuses on the flexibility–security nexus in society by studying transitions and mobility patterns between standard work (full-time jobs with open-ended contracts) and non-standard work (that is, part-time jobs, temporary or fixed-term work, a traineeship or a specific form of self-employment). The general idea is to study these in-work transitions in a comparative setting to learn about the effects of institutions on socio-economic outcomes in terms of the attained levels of flexibility and security.

The various contributions in the book therefore deal in particular with the effects of transition patterns on people's future wage and income level, their poverty risk and their labour market participation chances and how these outcomes are mediated through differences in working-time preferences, labour market policies, economic and demographic conditions and labour market settings. These latter factors are assumed as being particularly affected by the international context and changes therein over time. The arrow at the downside of the graph shows that the flexibility–security nexus is studied from a dynamic perspective meaning that it can change over time due to a changing context, changing social norms and changing policies.

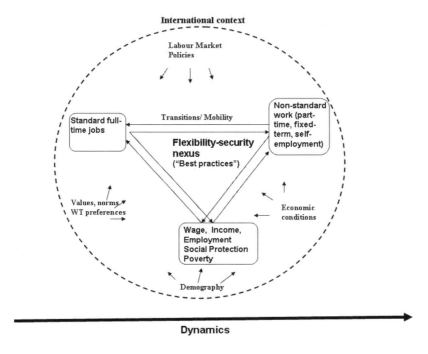

Figure 1.5 The conceptual framework

1.4 OVERVIEW OF THE CONTRIBUTIONS

The book consists of three parts. Part I of the book is devoted to labour market mobility and in-work transition patterns in particular between standard and non-standard jobs. The question to what extent non-standard workers are able to move fairly quickly into a 'standard' job seems at the core of the debate even though it is recognised that the definition of a standard job is changing as well. That also pertains to the issue to what extent these jobs reflect merely the increased flexibility needs of employers and therewith endanger employment security or that they also serve the needs of employees for flexible working times.

Part I starts with the contribution of Barbier in Chapter 2 in which he explains extensively the French debate on the definition and meaning of the notion of 'precarious' jobs or 'précarité' as it is framed in the French political and academic (especially sociological) discourse. He also recalls the inability to arrive at a common understanding of the notion in a European research project a few years ago, illustrating the widely different interpretations of the concept in the European context. He finally makes a plea for elaborating the concept of job quality as a better instrument to reach a common understanding in Europe of what we mean by the adjective 'non-standard' in terms of job quality in dealing with these new employment forms.

In parallel with this debate the question is posed in the following chapters of what the role of these 'precarious' jobs is in modern labour markets: do they fulfil the role of 'stepping-stones' which bridge the gap between work and non-work more easily or do they reflect the precarious position of their occupants entrapped in 'low-level' jobs. In the latter case temporary and fixed-term contracts provide low employment as well as low income security, but also little protection to poverty as Debels argues in Chapter 3. She therefore examines the employment and income security of non-standard workers across Europe using the European Community Household Panel. She also compares the income and employment situation of these workers with the unemployed and the standard worker and looks in more detail to the supporting role of the household context in preventing or cushioning income poverty.

In Chapter 4, Hernanz, Origo, Samek and Toharia discuss in more detail the transition patterns of temporary workers into permanent jobs in Italy and Spain, two southern countries known for the 'insider-outsider' character of their labour markets with relatively large shares of fixed-term or temporary workers. They focus on the transition chances of the so-called 'involuntary temporary workers' – those working on temporary contracts because they could not find a permanent job, who make up 41 per cent and 70 per cent of the total temporary work force in Italy and Spain, respectively.

In Chapter 5, Booghmans, Van Gils and Vermandere do not restrict themselves to the analysis of annual transitions but extend the analysis by focusing on longer-term mobility patterns and career paths of various categories of workers, full-timers, part-timers, self-employed workers and so on. The data they use are rather unique as they are drawn from administrative data sources in Belgium and linked on the basis of the person's unique social administration number. The Scandinavian countries share a tradition in these data sources but they are now also becoming available in some Continental European countries such as Germany, Belgium and the Netherlands. From a methodological viewpoint the contribution is interesting since the authors apply a very interesting technique to distinguish and examine career patterns by constructing a typology of work–life trajectories using sequence data analysis.

Part II deals with the possible 'scarring' effects of non-standard work on the future career. This part starts with the contribution of Muffels and Luijkx in Chapter 6, based on a comparative analysis of the way in which countries are more or less able to maintain a fair balance between flexibility and security. They use the European Community Household Panel data to elaborate on dynamic 'outcome' measures for flexibility and security. For flexibility they use transition indicators on contract and occupational mobility; for employment and income security, they elaborate indicators for changes in employment security (stability in employment position) and income security (reduction in poverty) over time. Dynamic income security is measured by looking at how many people annually moved into or out of poverty as measured by the European 60 per cent median equivalent income threshold. Using these measures they examine the dissimilarities in labour market mobility patterns and the dissimilar way in which these mobility patterns have an impact on flexibility and security levels. The authors also investigate which classification of regime types as explained in the literature fits the differences in mobility patterns best.

In Chapter 7 the issue is raised of how long the scarring effects of unemployment last before people tend to recover from the initial drop in income and reduction of labour market chances. A comparison is made between the evidence on 'scarring' in the unregulated American labour market and the strongly regulated labour markets in Europe. For that purpose he combines American with European data. He uses the 1996 Survey of Income and Program Participation containing work history information for the US and the European Community Household Panel data for Europe covering the period 1994–2001. Gangl discusses in detail the very interesting issue to what extent the existing institutions in the US and Europe with respect to employment protection regulation and the generosity of the unemployment benefit system affect the size of the initial 'scarring' effect and the time it takes to recover from it.

Then in Chapter 8 Meager deals with the 'scarring' effects of self-employment in the UK, an issue that has hitherto received much less attention in the academic and policy debate than the 'scarring' effects of unemployment, part-time work or temporary employment. The UK known as a liberal, unregulated labour market has traditionally had a larger share of self-employment than countries with more regulation though the share of self-employment has traditionally not been that high but it reached its higher level especially in the 1980s. Meager uses the British Household Panel and a longitudinal data set of young people aged 18–30 years, supported to enter self-employment. It allows him to compare this last sample with a matched sample of young people who are not supported to enter self-employment. The research to date is rather scarce but the evidence provided by Meager gives a rather unexpected but interesting picture of the 'scarring' effects of self-employment.

In Chapter 9 Fouarge and Muffels deal with the 'scarring' effects of part-time work. The chapter focuses on the effects of people's decisions in choosing particular combinations of working time and caring duties for the future employment and wage career. They use the European Community Household Panel, but added the Hungarian panel for the period 1992–1997. They focus on the effect of a particular life course event, for example, first childbirth, on the future career. The idea was that 'scarring' effects of part-time work occur because women due to caring duties tend to withdraw fully or partially from the labour market in advance or at birth especially when it is their first child. Because of the career break which might last short- or long-term, women might experience difficulties in recovering from the reduction in participation and wage income. However it might also be that women prefer not to return into a full-time job and that they opt for continuing working in a part-time job because it improves their work–life balance. The chapter therefore looks into the mediating role of working time preferences of women to explaining the effect of first childbirth on future participation and wage incomes.

In Chapter 10, the role of working time preferences for job moves and job satisfaction is further explored. Compared to the previous chapter the aim of this chapter is to acquire a deeper insight into the relationships between working time preferences and working time transitions (job moves) on the one hand and job satisfaction on the other. Due to the unavailability of data in other countries the analyses are limited to the Netherlands. The authors use data from the OSA-labour supply panel for the period 1986–1998 in the Netherlands containing detailed information on working time preferences, job changes and job satisfaction. For examining the impact of job changes on job satisfaction they develop a so-called conditional probit model because that allowed them to correct for sample selection due to the fact that people who are dissatisfied with their job might be more inclined to withdraw from the labour market and not to be observed after the transition.

Part III examines 'best policy practices' in three country case studies, Australia, Canada and Denmark. Australia was for a long time known as the 'wage earners welfare state' (Arts and Gelissen, 2002) but according to the authors Ziguras and Stricker in Chapter 11 have progressed lately into a pure liberal model. The authors use the data from the Australian Household, Income and Labour Dynamics of Australia panel (HILDA) to examine the transition and mobility patterns in Australia and to document the risks of particular groups on the labour market to experience so-called exclusionary transitions. The chapter also looks at the role of part-time work in the observed transition patterns and to what extent preferences for part-time work associated with caring duties and education activities can be fulfilled on the Australian labour market.

According to the authors of Chapter 12, Van den Berg, Von Restorff, Parent and Masi, Canada shares with Australia to some degree the Anglo-Saxon settler society's 'rugged individualism' and the 'residual' approach to the provision of welfare, but it is also clearly different, for example, with respect to the role of the labour movement that was much stronger in Australia. They also argue that both countries however had striking similarities with a view to the Governments' attempts during the early 1990s to put more emphasis on active labour market policies. The authors therefore attempt to compare the country's cases and to learn from them also with a view to the issue of the 'transferability of policies' from one context into the other. The authors discuss extensively the major Canadian Unemployment Insurance reform in the mid 1990s and their effects on access to benefits and on labour market transitions. The idea is that some interesting lessons might be drawn from this major reform in the Australian context as it informs us about the validity of the claims of the transitional labour market approach suggesting that a move from unemployment insurance to employment insurance improves the effectiveness and efficiency of labour market policies.

It sounded a good idea beforehand to learn from the comparison between these two more Anglo-Saxon oriented welfare states with another contrasting case, being the Denmark's celebrated 'flexicurity' model' that according to Van den Berg et al. is currently the toast of policy makers and researchers in Europe and beyond (see Van den Berg et al. Chapter 10). The promises of the 'flexicurity' approach are manifold and ambitious and sketch a world in which there are only winners, calling for some scepticism in advance. In particular, the trade unions have voiced their concerns about the concept and some see it as a Trojan horse designed to abolish job protection for which they have fought so long for with very little security in return (see also (Jørgensen and Madsen, 2007). In Chapter 13 therefore, the Danish road to 'flexicurity' delineated as the 'golden triangle' – a flexible labour market with little protection, a generous system of economic support and active labour market policies especially focused on investments in the 'employability' of workers – is sketched by Madsen but at the same time put into perspective by comparing it with the representatives of two other welfare state regimes: a liberal, the UK and another Scandinavian, Sweden. The question addressed in all three country case studies is to what extent the current labour market situation as well as current labour market policies mirrors the analytical and normative premises of the transitional labour market model especially with a view to combining flexibility with security.

Finally, in Chapter 14 we draw some lessons for future research and policies dealing with the relationship between flexicurity and society and how to improve the balance between them.

REFERENCES

Acemoglu, D. (2003), 'Cross-country inequality trends', *Economic Journal*, **113** (485), F121–F49.

Albert, M. (1991), *Capitalisme contre capitalisme*, Paris: Editions du Seuil.

Amable, B. (2003), *The Diversity of Modern Capitalism*, Oxford: Oxford University Press.

Arts, W. and Gelissen, J.P.M. (2002), 'Three worlds of welfare capitalism or more? A state-of-the-art report', *Journal of European Social Policy*, **12** (2), 137–58.

Blank, R. (1989), 'The Role of Part-Time working Women's Labor Market Choices Over Time', *The American Economic Review*, **79** (2), 295–99.

Blank, R. (1994), *The Dynamics of Part-Time Work*, Cambridge, MA: National Bureau of Economic Research.

Blau, F.D. and Kahn, L.M. (2002), *At Home and Abroad: US Labor Market Performance in International Perspective*, New York: Russell Sage Foundation.

Blossfeld, H.-P., Mills, M. and Bernardi, F. (2006), *Globalization, Uncertainty and Men's Careers. An International Comparison*, Cheltenham, UK and Northhampton, MA, USA: Edward Elgar.

Bonoli, G. (1997), 'Classifying welfare states: a two-dimension approach', *Journal of Social Policy*, **26** (3), 351–72.

Booth, A.L., Francesconi, M. and Frank, J. (2002), 'Temporary jobs: Stepping stones or dead ends?', *Economic Journal*, **112** (480), F189–F213.

Breen, R. (1997), 'Risk, commodification and stratification', *Sociology-the Journal of the British Sociological Association*, **31** (3), 473–89.

Breen, R. (2004), *Social Mobility in Europe*, Oxford: Oxford University Press.

Collins, H. (2005), 'Flexibility and stability of expectations in the contract of employment', *Socio-Economic Review*, **26** (4), 139–53.

De Koning, J. (ed.) (2007a), The Evaluation of Active Labour Market Policies. Measures, Public Private Partnerships and Benchmarking, Cheltenham, UK and Northampton, MA, USA: Edward Elgar.

De Koning, J. (2007b), Employment and Training Policies in Central and Eastern Europe, Amsterdam: Dutch University Press.

DiPrete, T.A., De Graaf, P.M., Luijkx, R., Tahlin, M. and Blossfeld, H.P. (1997), 'Collectivist versus individualist mobility regimes? Structural change and job mobility in four countries', *American Journal of Sociology*, **103** (2), 318–58.

DiPrete, T.A. (2002), 'Life course risks, mobility regimes and mobility consequences: a comparison of Sweden, Germany, and the United States', *American Journal of Sociology*, **108** (2), 267–309.

DiPrete, T.A., Goux, D., Maurin, E. and Quesnel-Vallee, A. (2006), 'Work and pay in flexible and regulated labor markets: A generalized perspective on institutional evolution and inequality trends in Europe and the US', *Research in Social Stratification and Mobility*, **24**, 311–32.

European Commission (2006), *Employment in Europe 2006*, Luxembourg: Office for Official Publications of the European Communities.

European Commission (2007), *Employment in Europe 2007*, Luxembourg: Office for Official Publications of the European Communities.

Ferrera, M. (1996), 'The 'Southern Model' of welfare in social Europe', *Journal of European Social Policy*, **6** (1), 17–37.

Ferrera, M., Hemerijck, A. and Rhodes, M. (2000), 'Recasting European Welfare States for the 21st Century', *European Review*, **8** (3), 427–46.

Fouarge, D., Luijkx, R., Manzoni, A. and Muffels, R. (2006), *Careers of working mothers after first childbirth,* Dublin, Tilburg: European Foundation, OSA-Tilburg University, 35.

Gangl, M. (2003), 'The only way is up? Employment protection and job mobility among recent entrants to European labour markets', *European Sociological Review,* **19** (5), 429–49.

Gangl, M. (2006), 'Scar Effects of Unemployment: An Assessment of Institutional Complementarities', *American Sociological Review,* **71**, (December), 9861013.

Goldthorpe, J.H. (2001), *Globalisation and Social Class,* Mannheimer Vorträge 9, Mannheim: Mannheimer Zentrum für Europäische Sozialforschung, 41.

Goodin, R.E., Heady, B., Muffels, R.J.A. and Dirven, H.-J. (1999), *The Real Worlds of Welfare Capitalism,* Cambridge: Cambridge University Press.

Hall, P. and Soskice, D. (eds) (2001), *Varieties of capitalism: the institutional foundations of comparative advantage,* Oxford: Oxford University Press, 560.

Jørgensen, H. and Madsen, P.K. (2007), *Flexicurity and Beyond. Finding a new agenda for the European Social Model,* Copenhagen: DJØF Publishing Copenhagen.

Lassnigg, L., Burzlaff, H., Rodriguez, M.A.D. and Larsson, M. (2007), *Lifelong Learning. Building Bridges through Transitional Labour Markets,* Apeldoorn Antwerpen: Het Spinhuis Publishers.

Muffels, R., Chung, H., Fouarge, D., Klammer, U., Luijkx, R., Manzoni, A., Wilthagen, T. and Thiel, A. (2007), *Summary Report: Flexibility and Security over the Life course,* Dublin: European Foundation for the Improvement of Living and Working Conditions.

Muffels, R. and Luijkx, R. (2008), 'Labour Market Mobility and Employment Security of Male Employees in Europe: "Trade-off" or "Flexicurity"?', *Work, Employment and Society,* **22** (2), 221–42.

Muffels, R.J.A. and Luijkx, R. (2006), 'Globalisation and Male Job Mobility in European Welfare States', in Blossfeld, H.-P., Mills, M. and Bernard, F. (eds), *Globalisation and uncertainty of men's careers,* Cheltenham, UK and Northampton, MA, USA: Edward Elgar, 38–72.

O'Reilly, J. and Bothfeld, S. (2002), 'What happens after working part time? Integration, maintenance or exclusionary transitions in Britain and western Germany', *Cambridge Journal of Economics,* **26** (4), 409–39.

Philips, K. and Eamets, R. (2007), *Approaches to flexicurity: EU Models,* Luxembourg: Office for Official Publications of the European Communities: European Foundation, 51.

Scherer, S. (2004), 'Stepping-stones or Traps? The Consequences of Labour Market Entry Positions on Future Careers in West Germany, Great Britain and Italy', *Work, Employment and Society,* **18** (2), 369–94.

Schmid, G. (1995), 'Is Full-Employment Still Possible – Transitional Labor-Markets as a New Strategy of Labor-Market Policy', *Economic and Industrial Democracy,* **16** (3), 429–56.

Schmid, G. (2000), 'Transitional Labour Markets. A new European Employment Strategy', in Marin, B., Meulders, D. and Snower, D. (eds), *Innovative Employment Initiatives,* Aldershot, UK: Ashgate, 223–53.

Schmid, G. and Gazier, B. (2002), *The dynamics of full employment: social integration through transitional labour markets,* Cheltenham, UK and Northampton, MA, USA: Edward Elgar.

Schmid, G. and Schömann, K. (2003), *Managing Social Risks Through Transitional Labour Markets: Towards a European Social Model,* Berlin: Wissenschafts-zentrum Berlin, 37.

Schömann, K. and O'Connell, P.J. (2002), *Education, Training and Employment Dynamics*, Cheltenham, UK and Northampton, MA, USA: Edward Elgar.

Standing, , G. (1997), 'Globalization, Labour Flexibility and Insecurity: The Era of Market Regulation', *European Journal of Industrial Relations,* **3** (1), 7–37.

Stier, H., Lewin-Epstein, N. and Braun, M. (2001), 'Welfare Regimes, family-supportive policies, and women's employment along the life course', *American Journal of Sociology*, **106** (6), 22.

Stone, K.V.W. (2005), 'Thinking and Doing – the regulation of workers' human capital in the United States', *Socio-Economic Review*, **26** (4), 121–38.

Streeck, W. (2000), Competitive Solidarity: Rethinking the "European Social Model", in Hinrichs, K., Kitschelt, H. and Wiesenthal, H. (ed.), *Kontingenz und Krise: Institutionenpolitik in kapitalistischen und postsozialistischen Gesellschaften*, Frankfurt am Main: Campus, 245–61.

Wilthagen, T. (1998), *Flexicurity: A new paradigm for labour market policy research*, Berlin: WZB Discussion Paper FS I 98–202.

Wilthagen, T. and Tros, F. (2004), 'The Concept of 'Flexicurity': A new approach to regulating employment and labour markets', *Transfer, European Review of labour and research*, **10** (2), 166–86.

2. There is more to Job Quality than 'Precariousness': a Comparative Epistemological Analysis of the 'Flexibility and Security' Debate in Europe

Jean-Claude Barbier

2.1 INTRODUCTION

Given the normative European Employment Strategy (EES) discourse, it would be crucial to measure to what extent the flexibility of work and of employment relationships[1] and the accompanying forms of security (basically of one's job, income and entitlement to social protection) are compatible and effectively contribute to the promotion of 'quality jobs' as opposed to 'poor jobs'. It is striking that research in economics and sociology has so far shown only limited interest and capacity to take up this task appropriately. For lack of adequate indicators, but also for lack of adequate concepts, it is still really difficult to objectively assess the prevalence of quality jobs across Europe.

It is certainly true that a wide range of increasingly comparable indicators is available now at EU-level. In Laeken in December 2001, in the context of the EES, quality indicators devised by the Employment Committee (EmCo) were adopted by the Council of the EU and they have been used ever since, although their documentation is still far from being homogenous. This was followed by an important communication on the 'quality of work' by the Commission, encompassing a wide range of subjects (European Commission, 2001, Com (2001) 313 final). At the time of writing, it was difficult to assess what sort of influence this approach would eventually retain within the new framework formally adopted on the 12th of July 2005. However, several EG guidelines include explicit references to dimensions related to 'quality in work'.[2]

The research efforts needed to elaborate concepts and notions to treat the question of 'quality in work' appropriately are still largely in front of us. We agree with Dekker and Kaiser (2000) who, stressing the difficulty of reconciling the various notions available, proposed to use the concept of 'non-standard employment', which they next applied on individual-level data in three countries (the Netherlands, the UK and Germany). The purpose of this chapter is to bring into discussion some findings derived from a project[3] which was originally built – admittedly with a strong Latin bias – upon the tentative notion of 'employment precariousness'. The research project examined whether the phenomena, which in France, but also in Spain and Italy, tend to be associated with the notion of the précarité de l'emploi (temporalidad, precarietà del lavoro), took on equivalent forms in the UK and Germany. Denmark was also considered for comparison but it was not a full member country of the project.

Many researchers involved in the project were surprised at being confronted with important definitional issues to the extent that the question of 'what is employment precariousness?' became one of the key research questions in the project (Barbier and Brygoo, 2001; Barbier, 2002c; Laparra, 2004, p. 6). Indeed, it even led to an intellectual debate within the research team, which eventually resulted in the writing of two 'final reports' with quite different conceptual orientations.[4] It unequivocally illustrates: (i) the resilience of the conceptual problem over time and (ii) its close relationship with the more or less implicit, normative debate that takes place in Europe about the consequences of the current trends of labour market flexibilisation. In the end, it appears that there was no agreement possible on a common definition. Part of the team wanted to stick to a specific definition.[5] The definition they used was based on figures on part-time work, fixed-term contracts and self-employment, which they considered as the most important elements of the concept of 'non-standard employment' (Frade and Darmon, 2005, p.109).

Dekker and Kaiser (2000) who eventually opted for a notion of 'non-standard employment' also include part-time employment in their concept, although they remark that it 'can hardly be regarded as being part of the concept of non-standard employment' in the Netherlands (2000, p. 4). Part of the problem to arrive at a clear definition was associated with the lack of appropriate data to cover the substance of the various concepts. The research group was constantly faced with the irreconcilable goals of using the current quantitative data (especially those provided by Eurostat standardised labour market surveys) to elaborate a clear concept that would also fit the normative substance of what is termed in French 'la précarité de l'emploi', in Spanish, 'precaridad laboral' and in Italian, 'precarietà'. All these notions may be easily interpreted as pointing to a common concept of 'quality in work'.

Equally to Dekker and Kaiser (2000, p. 3–4) and the contributors to the Rodgers and Rodgers volume (1989), the group also struggled with the task of separating 'positive' and 'negative' consequences of the current transformation of employment relationships and with the inadequacy of existing data sources, in the context of a highly value-laden debate.

More generally, it is remarkable that most economists trying to understand this labour market transformation seem always to be 'caught' in a situation where the only quantitative tools they can use are either rather limited or flawed. This is the case for instance in the work of Auer and Cazes (2000), in their valuable contribution, when they compare the prevalence of 'temporary' (here meaning fixed-term) jobs and what they call 'long-term employment relationship' contracts.

One of the main conclusions we drew from the project was that the concept of quality, as a comparative notion across Europe, was certainly more appropriate than the inadequate and elusive concept of 'employment precariousness'. How we reached this conclusion forms the subject of the first sections of this chapter. We were able to arrive at the apparently robust conclusion that the 'invention' of the notion of 'precariousness' happened in France and was then spread to other Latin countries. It serves as a key illustration to the debate, for it is important to understand the genesis,[6] before extending the perspective to a broader 'quality in work' comparison, in which we will also be confronted with distinct national value orientations.

2.2 EMPLOYMENT PRECARIOUSNESS: AN IMPOSSIBLE FRENCH DEFINITION SET IN A COMPARATIVE PERSPECTIVE

Contemporary sociologists writing in English analyse the changing world of work from many different perspectives. Much of the current literature has been focusing on the flexibility of work and employment relationships. Related topics, mainly on the 'negative' consequences of flexibility include job insecurity, 'uncertain' careers, deteriorating working conditions and downgraded access to standard social protection. The French sociological debate, often different from mainstream international approaches focuses primarily on the concept of 'précarité de l'emploi' (literally 'employment precariousness'). However, this notion is very difficult to define and translate because, in French sociology as well as in public debate, précarité has taken on various meanings. The ESOPE team was confronted with a key obstacle: how to measure the extent of 'employment precariousness' quantitatively since they had observed that no satisfactory indicator could be elaborated, even in France where the notion originated.

2.2.1 French Précarité: from 'Vulnerable' Families to Society in General

In France, précarité[7] emerged in the political discourse in the late 1970s; the new meaning was unrecorded in earlier dictionaries. It is now widely used by politicians of all persuasions, union representatives, social partners, the press and novelists. Key collective meanings, deeply embedded in French society, are associated with it, as testified by the expressions used by politicians. For instance, in his last meeting in the presidential election campaign in 2002, where he was opposing the extreme-right candidate, Jacques Chirac pronounced a solemn call to resist both précarité and xenophobia. The term précarité is now positioned at the heart of Labour Law (Code du travail), in particular when dealing with the compensation for situations different from the standard employment contract (contrat à durée indéterminée, CDI, a close equivalent of the German Normalarbeitsverhältnis).

For the benefit of non-French readers, it is important to stress that this short overview of the notion concerns only précarité (without adjuncts). One of the findings of the project was that France was the only country using précarité in this very encompassing way. In Italian, precarietà, and, in Spanish, precaridad were, at the time of the research,[8] only used in the context of jobs and employment, as shown below.

In French sociology, Agnès Pitrou (1978a, 1978b) pioneered the usage of the term. She focused on 'precarious families', vulnerable to all sorts of 'incidents'. The precarious families of the 1970s were not standard clients of social assistance; they constituted a significant part of the lower classes, but certainly not an 'underclass' in the American sense (nor an 'Unterschicht', in the sense of the 2006 German debate). Pitrou (1978b, 51–64) mentioned a list of characteristics that, according to her, defines précarité: precariousness or absence of labour market skills, resulting in difficult working conditions and low wages, as well as in the absence of any career prospects; scarce as well as irregular financial resources; unstable or unsatisfactory housing conditions; health problems; uncertainty about the future number of children; relative lack of social contact and a rather precarious family or a couple's life balance. At that time, the employment dimension of precariousness was considered only a minor aspect; mass unemployment was still unknown.

A turning point in the sociology of précarité came with the publication of an article by Dominique Schnapper (1989). Stating that the main issue was not segmentation of the labour market, she theorised the importance of status categories in French society. Rights were attached to particular employment situations, associated with social protection and labour law conditions; jobs with legal or statutory rights included public sector jobs and private, open-ended contracts. Other categories were jobs 'without status' or a 'status derived from employment' consisting mainly of unemployed people and pensioners. Jobs 'without status' were emplois précaires, including 'more or less fictitious jobs', such as employment or labour market programmes for young people (Schnapper, 1989, p. 11). For her, this category also included fixed-term contracts and temporary agency jobs.

Much along the same line, Serge Paugam et al. (1993) endeavoured to assess the number of people in 'precarious' situations in France. They concluded that only 53 per cent of the French active population appeared not to be at risk of any sort of fragilité. From a comparative perspective, the extent of this measure in itself shows how widespread the feeling was among respondents of being at risk. Paugam (2000) extended his definition further in later work. Précarité, he wrote, should be studied along two lines: firstly, the relationship to employment or to one's job, précarité de l'emploi, and here he follows Schnapper's (1989) analysis; and secondly, the relationship to work, précarité du travail ('work precariousness'). With reference to the second dimension of this extended definition, Paugam explains: 'The employee is precarious inasmuch as his employment appears to him to be without interest, badly paid and of little value to the firm' (Paugam, 2000, p. 356).

Finally, in parallel with this continuous broadening of the definition of the concept of précarité to précarité de l'emploi and then précarité du travail, the term précarisation was introduced in the French language, that is the process whereby society as a whole becomes more and more precarious, and basically becomes destabilised. Explicitly drawing on 'regulationist' literature, Robert Castel (1995, 324–6) described a new form of society, la société salariale (literally the 'wage-earner's society') in the Fordist era. For him, society has been structured by the rapport salarial ('wage–labour nexus'),[9] which is a global social relationship. But what we have been confronted with for the last 20 years is the erosion of the wage-earner condition ('l'effritement de la condition salariale') (Castel, 1995, p. 385). Indeed, precarious work is one of, if not the, most important feature of the erosion. New forms of employment (formes particulières de l'emploi, FPE, see Table 2.1) are among the clearest manifestations of this erosion (Castel, 1995, p. 400), but they also affect the core labour force. Hence, job précarisation and unemployment form part of the dynamics of modernisation.

Bourdieu's (1998) analysis is phrased in explicitly normative and political language. For him, précarité is present everywhere in society but most apparent in the case of unemployment. Hence, précarité shows up as one of the aspects of a prevailing condition in society, close to unemployment and exclusion. In his view these situations are the product of a new 'mode of domination', which is underpinned by a generalised state of insecurity. With Bourdieu's explicitly political statements in his previous publications, the proliferating normative and analytical meanings of précarité in the French context seem to concur and merge into an elusive and unclear notion. In this context, only a small number of sociologists have tried to escape from a very pregnant influence and define 'employment precariousness' more precisely. Chantal Nicole-Drancourt (1992, p. 57) is one of them. Taking distance from the vagueness of the term, she also sought to break with an 'alarmist conception' of the integration of young people into the labour market. For her, 'precariousness' should be distinguished from 'precarious employment', because fixed-term jobs could function as an entry into stable employment through sequences of intentional mobility. Secondly, holding a 'precarious job' does not deterministically mean that young people perceive it as being 'precarious'. Thirdly, even being unemployed does not systematically mean being précaire. 'Precariousness' should then be understood differently according to the extent by which a young person wishes to invest in working life or the career, which then leads to make a distinction between two sorts of precariousness: integration and exclusion (Nicole-Drancourt, 1992, p. 66). 'Female flexibility' was primarily a strategy used by firms to oblige women to accept underemployment. This resulted in the general conclusion that precariousness was specific to certain sectors and categories of the workforce, without the overall employment system being destabilised or the 'typical employment relationship' being eroded (Nicole-Drancourt, 1990, p. 192). Yet, the underlying dynamics might eventually lead to a transformation of all social relationships, continuously hindering progress towards greater equality between men and women.

Such a proliferation of meanings for a single notion is certainly bound to hinder its export to other linguistic and social systems. This is all the more likely to be true with no consensual quantitative measure of 'précarité' or 'précarité de l'emploi' emerging in France after 20 years of debate.

2.3 'EMPLOYMENT PRECARIOUSNESS' AND 'JOB QUALITY' IN CROSS-NATIONAL COMPARISON

2.3.1 Is there an Anglo-Saxon Perspective on Precariousness?

From a Gallo-centrist perspective, it is surprising to find that one of the most widely known accounts in international sociology of the current transformation of work pays no attention whatsoever to precariousness. While it specifically addresses the consequences of flexibility on 'character', it ignores the notion as such (Sennett, 1999). In one of the few case studies of American employees and workers Sennett builds his argument upon, he states: 'her identity as a worker is light' (1999, p. 74). The French translator over-translates: 'son identité professionnelle est précaire' (Sennett, 2000, p. 101). But Sennett's object is not 'precariousness' nor 'employment precariousness', and his statistical appendix makes no mention of distinct contracts, about which French sociologists and statisticians are so heavily concerned. A Gallo-centrist perspective on the British labour market also results in astonishment about the fact that this market, whose reputation for flexibility is well established, only harbours a relatively small but stable share of fixed-term contracts (6–7 per cent compared with 13–15 per cent in the French case and 30–33 per cent in Spain, according to Eurostat statistics in the year 2000). A similar feeling of 'cognitive dissonance' exists when the meaning of 'precariousness' is to be confused, as for instance in Robert Reich's (2001) *Future of Success*, with the French meaning. Flexibility, in his work is dominantly associated with social advantage, and when precariousness is used, it is strictly applied to variation in incomes and their structure (Reich, 2001, pp. 94, 253). Sennett and Reich both wrote about changing conditions of work, changing tenure and rising instability of jobs, but no equivalent wording exists in their work for the French term of 'employment precariousness'.

Cross-national comparisons
Both the above examples are typical: for cross-national comparison with the UK or the US, French notions are inadequate; they are also inadequate for Germany and the Netherlands. For the latter country Dekker and Kaiser (2000, p. 4) document that the dominant word used is 'flexibele arbeid' (flexible labour). Only in Italy and Spain does 'employment precariousness' bear resonance and meanings similar to the French. In Denmark the notion of 'precariousness' is unknown. Does this mean that the social phenomena that indirectly gave birth to the Latin notion have no equivalents outside the Latin world? Obviously this should not be taken for granted. In-depth comparisons (Barbier, 2002b, 2005a) can certainly not take empirical phenomena at face value or based on their sheer appearance. They have to be set against the normative and cultural standards within each particular country in its 'societal coherence' (Maurice et al., 1982). A similar requirement determines the analysis of even more universal notions: as Paugam (2005) has shown, 'exclusion' poverty (existing in France or Germany) differs from 'marginalising' poverty (the type of poverty Nordic countries dominantly experience).

Such methodological pre-requisites do not contradict the evidence that national representations are likely to evolve over time and are open to influences from abroad. A case in point is provided in the Anglo-French context. A restricted use of the term 'precarity' has been noted recently. Yet 'precarity' is not an English word, but a barbarism (or Gallicism) featuring in only a few international English publications. Its present limited use can easily be explained by the importation of the French notion by international research groups into Anglo-French research programmes. A handful of international English texts circulated by the European Commission and other EU organisations also contained the word 'precarity', which can be interpreted as the testimony of an interest for the French notion in a wider political debate. Similarly, in the wake of the recent Hartz reforms in Germany (from 2002), the awareness of the existence of precariousness (Prekarität) in Germany has certainly increased also.

Stating that no straightforward statistical measure of 'employment precariousness' was attainable (Laparra, 2004, 15–17), the research confirmed earlier analyses (Rodgers and Rodgers, 1989). One of the indicators most widely used for measuring 'atypical employment' distinguishes 'temporary' from permanent contracts in Eurostat surveys. Despite harmonisation, this distinction has remained highly ambiguous and problematic not only across the five countries studied (Barbier and Brygoo, 2001). Part-time work, another indicator, is frequently used despite the existence of similar flaws which are due to the impossibility to separate 'voluntary' from 'involuntary' part-time work in a cross-national context. If we are to make this kind of comparison, it is still necessary to provide a very detailed qualitative definition of the national concepts used.

National approaches to the quality of employment relationships

In France, the standard employment relationship is CDI, a norm enshrined in labour law since the regulation of the fixed-term contract in 1979. In reality it was gradually regulated through a number of legal provisions from the early 1920s on. Other forms of employment have been considered as 'specific' (formes particulières d'emploi, FPE) or precarious, amounting to a little over 10 per cent of the workforce from the 1990s onwards.

In Spain, the terms 'empleo precario', 'precaridad laboral' and 'temporalidad' are the most widely used ones within the public debate and by the social partners. The 1980 Estatudo de los Trabajadores (the basic law) although amended over the years, is based on the open-ended, full-time contract. From 1980 onwards, collective agreements and regulations came into force with the explicit goal of reducing precariousness and increasing instability. This was, for instance, the aim of the 'Acuerdo interconfederal para la estabilidad del empleo' in 1997. Despite renewed efforts by the present Zapatero government, the temporalidad contract nevertheless still accounts for more than 30 per cent of all contracts.

In Italy, the terms generally used are: 'precarietà del lavoro', 'del impiego', 'del posto di lavoro' and 'impiego precario'. The May 2002 strike in Italy showed that, as in France, the standard employment relationship is considered to be an open-ended contract with statutory protection against dismissal. It is defined in labour law under article 18 of the 1970 Statuto dei

Lavoratori, although only a section of the workforce is covered by this article, mostly within firms having more than 16 employees. In Italy, a recourse to part-time contracts was implemented much later (1997) than in other countries. Employees in a parasubordinati contract (see Table 2.1) who are considered precarious amount to about 10 per cent of all employees. Thus, in the three Latin countries, a more or less explicit consensus prevails, exemplified during social protests, about the fact that a standard job is open-ended and that all others are more or less exposed to 'employment precariousness' of some sort,[10] including involuntary part-time jobs. This was never the case in the UK, and, at the time of the research, also not in Germany.

In Germany, by contrast, Prekarität has only been used recently in academic contexts. At the time of the research an exact equivalent of the term 'employment precariousness' could not be found. Yet, the prevalent social standard was the Normalarbeitsverhältnis, a notion even more deeply entrenched in society than in the other Latin countries. Basic regulations, applying to contracts in Germany, date back to the 1950s, including the principle of full time, open-ended contracts with associated social contributions and social rights. Hence, the reason why 'employment precariousness' was inadequate in the German case did not result from the inexistence of a legal or conventional standard for employment contracts. It was linked to the fact that atypical jobs had traditionally been considered to be marginal jobs, as the expression 'geringfügige Beschäftigung' implies. Marginal jobs (5–6 per cent of the workforce in the late 1990s)[11] which have only recently been upgraded to 'mini-jobs' and 'midi-jobs', were traditionally considered mainly as second or additional jobs for couples. They were gender biased with mostly women being employed in these jobs. Yet, attention has only recently been devoted to certain types of non-standard employment (this is the case for example, quasi-self-employment, Scheinselbstständigkeit).

It is the result of the debate on unemployment and in particular on labour costs and labour market rigidities, and the reforms being implemented (notably the Hartz reform),[12] that a key issue has emerged: will labour market reforms to promote flexiblity affect the quality of employment relationships and potentially, the standard employment relationship indirectly? Marginal job schemes, quasi-self-employment and the new special job schemes for recipients of social assistance could then be seen as functional equivalents for the notion of 'employment precariousness' in the Latin countries. Indeed, the majority of the jobs in these schemes can certainly not be considered to be 'quality jobs'.

In the UK, neither in the academic field nor in the public debate, neither in legislation nor in collective agreements, significant reference was found to the notion of 'employment precariousness'. Despite the existence of a broad conception of what is meant by a regular employment relationship, the UK has no legal equivalent for what exists in the four other countries (see Table 2.1).

Table 2.1 Proxies for 'employment precariousness' across five countries (before 2003)

Notions and items	France	Italy	Spain	Germany	UK
Use of 'employment precarious-ness'	Yes	Yes	Yes	No	No
Key relevant notion	Précarité	Precarità del posto di lavoro	Precaridad laboral (temporalidad)	Unsichereit des Arbeits-verhältnisses	None specified
Normal employment relationship	Permanent contract contrat à durée indéterminée (CDI)	Permanent contract tempo indeterminato	Permanent contract contrato indefinido	Permanent contract Normalarbeits-verhältnis (NAV) (unbefristeter Arbeits-vertrag)	Regular work
Normal legal reference	Code du travail	Statuto dei lavoratori	Estatuto de los trabajadores	Various Gesetze and collective agreements	None
Key job category as cross-national 'functional equivalent'	Formes particulières d'emploi (FPE)	Parasubor-dinati: collaborazione coordinata continuativa; lavoro occasionale; associazione in partecipazione	Trabajo temporal Temporalidad	Geringfügige Beschäftigung Schein-selbstständig-keit Ein Euro-Jobs (from 2005)	Bad / poor jobs

Moreover, the notion of 'atypical' jobs is not well established and used here. Part-time work, which would figure among atypical jobs in other countries, is considered typical or regular in the UK, as it is also in the Netherlands. Implicitly, as embedded in the corresponding regulations, these employment relationships, whatever their duration, are conceived as regular work. Hence, we are left, as in the case of Germany, but for different reasons, with the need to look for functional equivalents. In a pragmatic sense, this means examining very specific situations, for instance zero-hour work contracts and casual employees, and jobs that could potentially be equivalent to 'precarious' jobs, in terms of their characteristics such as 'dead-end' jobs,[13] jobs that yield insufficient pay, poor career prospects and so on.

The inadequacy of the notion of 'precariousness' has a different background in Germany and the UK. In Germany, the main reason why it was inadequate at the time of the research was because employment relationships had, overall, remained more stable and secure than in France, Spain and Italy, where a clear segmentation process occurred on the labour market during the 1980s and 1990s. From the post-war period onwards, it has even been claimed that the broad German policy goal was to create a secure environment, resistant to inequality (Vogler-Ludwig, 2002). In the UK, on the other hand, the research findings identified occurrences of low paid labour and insecure jobs of poor quality, with limited or no career prospects, similar to the situation in the Latin countries (Laparra, 2004). For that reason it is more the social perception of the phenomenon than the actual employment situation that emerges as completely different across countries. And this perception is linked to a different normative system shared in a particular society. Hence, vis-à-vis the notion of 'employment precariousness', the use of 'job quality' has obvious advantages in that it allows for broadening the comparative scope and for constructing more encompassing concepts.

2.3.4 Traditional Indicators, the Five Countries and Denmark

Comparison across national borders led us to prefer the concept of job quality. Admittedly, its current definitions vary across countries and innovation is needed to overcome the relative infancy of the research in this domain. It is not the purpose of the present chapter to delve profoundly into this topic, and other chapters in this book do it using various perspectives (see Chapter 1). Numerous studies are currently being conducted in Europe; one recent example in France is the CERC (2004) report that focused on the French situation but also comprised some comparative data on employment transitions. In the French context where, as we have seen, the concept of précarité has prevailed, the CERC report made a distinction between 'sécurité de l'emploi' (employment security) and 'instabilité de l'emploi' (job instability). Employment security was tentatively (statistically) defined by CERC-experts as the situation of a person who is employed without significant (unemployment) interruption over a given time period.[14] Though narrower in scope, this approach is obviously compatible with the TLM (transitional labour market) perspective, according to which job changes involving an employer's change may not endanger the employment security of the worker over time. 'Job stability' is reserved for the situation of employees who remain in the same employment relationship, that is with the same employer over the same time period.

Before turning to some conclusive remarks, we would like to further illustrate the inadequacy of some often used quantitative Eurostat indicators for exploring the subject of employment quality. Table 2.2 displays three indicators for the five large countries plus Denmark and the Netherlands. Denmark is seen here as the benchmark case for achieving simultaneously high levels of flexibility and employment security. The Netherlands was added in the table, because comparative literature on the 'flexibility and employment security' issue very often stresses the similarities between Denmark and the Netherlands (Wilthagen and Tros, 2003).

Table 2.2 Eurostat indicators on 'non-standard employment' for the late 1990s and mid-2000s (per cent of total employment)

Countries	Temporary employment		Self-employment		Part-time	
	1992	2005	1992	2005	1992	2005
Denmark	10.7	9.8	9.3	6.3	23.0	22.1
The Netherlands	10.4	15.5	15.5	13.7	34.8	46.1
France	10.6	13.3	12.0	8.9	13.1	17.2
Germany	10.5	14.2	9.6	11.2	14.5	24.0
Italy (1993)	6.2	12.3	27.3	24.5	5.5	12.8
Spain	34.2	33.3	19.3	14.4	6.0	12.4
The UK	8.9	5.7	12.7	12.7	22.9	25.4

Source: European Commission, Employment in Europe 2006 and 2004 – from Eurostat Labour Force Surveys.

A first remark concerns the ambiguity of the various notions used. Firstly, 'temporary employment' (or as it is often termed, 'fixed-term contract' employment) is ambiguous because of the widely varying substance of 'temporary' contracts in terms of the level of social protection, employment stability, job security, pay, and so on that it provides.

Additionally, the indicator does not allow for separating different meanings of the word 'temporary'; it includes temporary agency work, seasonal contracts, and so on. In the French case, we showed that among these 'temporary' contracts, a non-negligible number of civil servant jobs[15] were included because their holders were in their trial or probation period (although their chances of not becoming full-fledged workers was negligible). Similarly, fixed-term contracts in the French public sector are included which are very stable and long-term (Barbier and Brygoo, 2001). Secondly, in itself, the status of self-employment does not tell much about the quality of the employment involved.

In certain countries (for example, Italy) a substantial part of the self-employed are in fact quasi-self-employed because their status is de facto that of an employee, yet it is extremely difficult to know what part in which country fits into such a 'quasi-self-employment' category. Thirdly, part-time work is quite typical in certain countries and, in some of them the job quality associated with it is similar to a standard full-time job. So, again part-time can hardly be taken as a serious candidate to measure the quality (or the precariousness) of a job cross-nationally. Moreover, the share of 'involuntary' part time work is extremely difficult to assess in comparative terms.

The case of Denmark provides an interesting case in point, especially when compared with the Latin countries. When one uses the figures in Table 2.2, the share of fixed-term contracts in Denmark, France and Italy does not appear markedly different. However one of the key characteristics of the 'Danish model' that came into debate also in France in 2004 and 2005, is that the quality of most short-term employment relationships does not basically differ from the open-ended or 'permanent' contracts in terms of working conditions, social protection, career prospects, and so on. On the other hand, a high share of fixed-term contracts in Spain and France are of a lower quality (Laparra, 2004). When the European Commission experts compared the quality of jobs, they stressed the fact that the share of 'bad jobs' in Denmark was remarkably lower than in the other member states, while job mobility was higher (Barbier, 2005c). Note that whereas labour markets in Denmark and the UK are considered more flexible than those in most other continental countries, their share of 'fixed-term' contracts is relatively low, and, that, in both countries, the basic quality of a 'fixed-term' job does not differ from a permanent one; what differs extremely is the generous social protection attached to all jobs in Denmark as opposed to the British limited social entitlements. The fact that in both countries 'employment precariousness' is equally unheard of does not mean that their share of high quality jobs is comparable. Danes, who are easily hired and fired, enjoy generous social protection coverage, which, for the low and lower median income groups, generously compensates for the temporary loss of income. Poverty rates are, thus, only slightly different for the employed and unemployed people (Jørgensen, 2002).

2.4 'FLEXIBILITY– SECURITY– QUALITY' REGIMES?

Because cross-national comparison of 'job quality' is still in its infancy, despite important comparative endeavours (Barbier, 2004a) quick-fix comparisons, based on gross (or static) and inadequate statistical indicators, like 'temporary employment' or other proxies such as part-time jobs, are bound to display decisive shortcomings. Rodgers and Rodgers (1989) came to a similar conclusion 15 years ago. To progress further, it is necessary to understand in greater depth the nature and components of what we tentatively proposed to term 'flexibility–security–quality' regimes prevalent in different countries (Barbier, 2002c). This goes beyond the simple treatment of 'flexicurity' as it is often envisaged, as a form of 'trade-off' between labour flexibility for employers and security of employment for employees. In some regimes, labour market flexibility is low and employment security is very heterogeneous across the workforce; in other regimes labour market flexibility is generally high and employment insecurity hidden within particular categories, while hardly any public attention is devoted to the issue of 'job quality'.

The regimes we analyse are based on common if varying societal components: a system of social protection; an industrial relations system; and a particular distribution of employment and activity across the population (resulting into rather stable labour market participation rates by age, class and gender). Interactions between these elements shape the conditions for the adoption of a particular conception of what is standard (or regular) employment, what is a 'quality job' as opposed to a 'bad' or a 'poor' job. The elements above are thus closely linked to a fourth one, that is, normative frameworks based upon common sets of values and norms, valid for a given period, and institutionalised in regulations, collective agreements and social actor's and firms' practices. Indeed, legal regulations and informal or conventional agreements shape the conditions under which equivalent concepts of 'bad jobs' can emerge in a specific national context. Three types of such informal or legal regulations are at stake: those explicitly devised to limit and suppress the negative consequences of employment flexibility or, positively, to enhance the quality of jobs; the policies and regulations that have the same effect without being agreed upon for such an explicit purpose; and those which, on the contrary, enhance or increase employment flexibility and insecurity or downgrade the quality of jobs. A crucial component of the normative systems, which extensively varies across nations, is the notion of a 'suitable job', and the ascription of the quality features which make a job offer acceptable for the workless jobseeker.

These normative systems are legitimated (or de-legitimated) across time. They set the conditions and terms under which a job is (or is not) acceptable or suitable – zumutbar, convenable, adecuado are among the terms used. These norms also determine the characteristics of jobs in terms of their (in)stability, their working conditions, labour standards and wages and the level of employment (in)security they offer. Compromises are made over what is globally 'acceptable' and how norms evolve over time, possibly due to influences from abroad. Relevant social actors agree on such compromises, the traces of which can be observed in the very wording of political discourses used in each particular polity.

The minimum wage provides an interesting case in point here. In the UK, partly because of European standards, the Labour government introduced a national minimum wage in 1997. However, a lower rate was applied for 18 to 21 year olds, and no minimum rate existed for those under 18 until 2004. In France, on the other hand, 'acceptable' rules have been very different for a long time. When, in 1993, Prime Minister Balladur attempted to introduce a minimum wage for the young, demonstrations forced him to withdraw his proposal. Ever since, no government has tried to dispense with the norm that the minimum wage is independent of the age. The 'de Villepin' government suffered a similar defeat when it tried to introduce a different contract for the young that was seen as 'discriminatory'. Of course, in the UK as well as in France, a dominant norm is also compatible with exceptions to the general rule. However, what is important is to really take into account the fact that 'dominant norms' remain very different across countries.

Often, within a country, a large part of the normative framework remains implicit; but, seen in a comparative context, it tends to become explicit. Understanding the notion of 'employment precariousness' in a cross-national perspective, or constructing a more adequate and ambitious notion of employment quality thus entails an in-depth analysis of the standards of acceptability, which diverge significantly across Europe. At a time when new member states have just joined the EU and a few candidate countries are still on the waiting list, it is interesting to note that in some of them, the consequences of flexibilisation often show up under the form of wage flexibility. The nature of the contract seems of little interest for cross-national analysis of the quality of jobs. In terms of employment quality, an extension of the comparative scope to the new member states adds new challenges to an emergent research field.

More generally, in the context of the discussion on 'flexicurity' arrangements and strategies – following-up on the Dutch and Danish experience – it is essential to keep in mind that norms and values always play a crucial role. It is certainly not by accident that the fostering of a consensual culture in Denmark (but also in the Netherlands) – albeit often based on conflictual compromise, as Jørgensen (2002) so aptly demonstrated – has been accompanied by a collective search for more quality in jobs, which is clearly documented in all comparative and benchmarking studies published by the European Commission. The concept of 'job quality', measured along the dimensions set out also in this contribution, undoubtedly plays a significant part in the Danish 'flexicurity' conception (Barbier, 2007). Enlargement is accompanied with increased diversity and it is going to be an additional challenge for the development of the various Open methods of coordination.

NOTES

1. From an interdisciplinary perspective (sociology and economics) we showed that the flexibility of work or labour (understood as a production factor) and the flexibility of employment (understood as a status in the firm and in society) should be clearly distinguished (Barbier and Nadel, 2000).
2. The notion of 'quality in work' is rather confusing. In official documents, it is translated differently according to the language involved, and also the expressions chosen are not exact equivalents (Barbier, 2005a). The Laeken solution was to construct a list of ten dimensions, and to attach indicators to each of them. In the July 2005 Council decision, Guideline 17 reads ' Implement employment policies aiming at achieving full employment, improving quality and productivity at work, and strengthening social and territorial cohesion'; Guideline 21 reads 'Promote flexibility combined with employment security and reduce labour market segmentation, having due regard to the role of social partners'.
3. The European Study On Precarious Employment (ESOPE, 2001–03), a research project funded by the European Commission, DG Research, under Framework Programme 5. The research was coordinated by Miguel Laparra (Navarra University) and dealt with five country case studies: France, Germany, Italy, Spain and the United Kingdom (see Barbier and Lindley, 2002).
4. One 'final' report was posted on the Commission's website at the following URL address: <www.ec.europa.eu/research/social-sciences/knowledge/projects/article_3472_en.htm>. The majority of the team nevertheless decided to post another version, the 'policy report', downloadable at the following URL address: <www.unavarra.es/organiza/esope.htm>. On this latter site, the team explained that the majority has rather agreed on this version with the mention: 'La mayoría de los grupos investigadores consideran el Policy Report como el documento más representativo del enfoque y de los resultados del proyecto'. Unfortunately, the Commission was unable to post two final reports on their website, despite the coordinator's request.
5. Their definition of 'employment precariousness' was: 'a variety of forms of employment established below normative standards, which results from an unbalanced distribution towards and among workers of the insecurity and risks typically attached to the labour market' (Frade and Darmon, 2005, p. 107).
6. A more detailed survey of French research in economics and sociology is available (Barbier, 2002a). See also Barbier (2005b) and Barbier (2004a).
7. One would expect to find a universal meaning for the term précarité when considering the human condition. Human life is quintessentially transitory, which drives humans to pray to God or other divinities. Indeed, the verb 'to pray' comes from the Latin precor and 'precarious' from the Latin precarius. What is precarious is what is uncertain and what can only be obtained from praying. Uncertainty and contingency are at the heart of the human condition. Germany has no substantive, except in specialised language, but all five languages in the ESOPE project had a substantive–adjective pair of Latin origin ('precariousness / precarious'; precarietà / precario; precaridad / precario; précarité / précaire; prekär).
8. It is important to stress that observations made at one period are not automatically valid for a longer time, due to many influencing factors: one is, as will be recalled later, the existence of

cross-national influences (ideas travel easily, notably because of the importance of European forums); another one are the ever changing labour market conditions.
9. On the paradoxical origins of the 'Regulation' theory and its concept of 'wage-labour nexus', see the contribution of Hyman (2005).
10. In March 2006, students and young people, backed by unanimous unions defeated the French government blueprint for a reform of mainstream contracts for the young, which introduced apparent CDI, but with a 2-year trial period.
11. Note that this figure stems from the German internal reports for the ESOPE project: the statistical identification of 'marginal jobs' at that time in Germany was not settled unequivocally.
12. In the last leg of the reform (Hartz IV), fully implemented from 2005 on, the situation emerged to be even more complex, because of the introduction of new 'Arbeitsgelegen-heiten' – dubbed 'ein Euro-jobs' in common parlance – for the recipients of social assistance benefits who are classified as employable.
13. The notion was first used by the European Commission in its Employment in Europe report (2001b, p. 74)
14. A period of one year was conventionally chosen.
15. French civil servants (fonctionnaires) are definitely not considered précaires. France is one of the countries where the differences between the statuses of civil servants and private sector jobs is the highest (Barbier, 2005c).

REFERENCES

Barbier, J-C. (2002a), 'A survey of the use of the term *précarité* in French economics and sociology', *Documents de travail CEE*, n°19, Noisy-le-Grand: CEE, <www.cee-recherche.fr>.

Barbier, J-C. (2002b), 'Conditions d'une comparaison internationale approfondie', *Sociétés contemporaines*, (45–6), 191–214.

Barbier, J-C. (ed.) (2002c), with Brygoo, A., Viguier, F. and Tarquis, F., *Normative and regulatory frameworks influencing flexibility, security, quality and precariousness of jobs in France, Germany, Italy, Spain and the United Kingdom (ESOPE)*, Project Report, Noisy-le-Grand: CEE.

Barbier, J-C. (with Sylla, N.S.) (2004a), *La stratégie européenne pour l'emploi: genèse, coordination communautaire et diversité nationale*, Rapport de recherche n°16, Noisy-le-Grand: CEE.

Barbier, J-C. (2005a), 'When words matter: Dealing anew with cross-national comparison', in Barbier, J.-C. and Letablier, M.T. (eds), *Cross-national comparisons: epistemological and methodological issues*, Brussels: PIE Pieter Lang, 45–70.

Barbier, J-C. (2005b), 'La précarité, une catégorie française à l'épreuve de la comparaison internationale, note critique', *Revue française de sociologie*, **46** (2), avril-juin, 351–71.

Barbier, J-C. (2005c), 'Apprendre vraiment du Danemark?', *Connaissance de l'emploi*, n° 18, juillet, Noisy le Grand: CEE.

Barbier, J-C. (2007), 'Au-delà de la 'flex-sécurité', une cohérence sociétale solidaire au Danemark', in Paugam, S. (dir), *Repenser la solidarité au XXIè siècle*, Paris: PUF, 473–90.

Barbier, J-C. and Brygoo, A. (2001), *A tentative approach to precarious employment in France: preliminary report*, ESOPE Project, Fifth Framework Programme, Noisy-le-Grand: CEE.

Barbier, J-C. and Lindley, R. (2002), 'La précarité de l'emploi en Europe', *CEE 4 Pages*, n° 53, Noisy-le-Grand: CEE.

Barbier, J-C. and Nadel, H. (2000), *La flexibilité du travail et de l'emploi*, Paris: Flammarion. (Version italienne, 2003, *La flessibilità del lavoro et dell'occupazione*, introduzione di L. Castelluci e E. Pugliese, Roma: Donzelli).

Bourdieu, P. (1998), 'La précarité est aujourd'hui partout', *Contrefeux*, Paris: Liber Raisons d'agir, 95–101.

Castel, R. (1995), *Les métamorphoses de la question sociale*, Paris: Fayard.

CERC (2004), *La sécurité de l'emploi, face aux défis des transformations économiques,* rapport n° 5, Paris: CERC.

Dekker, R. and Kaiser, L. (2000), *Atypical of Flexible?* – *How to Define Non-Standard Employment Patterns* – *The Cases of Germany, the Netherlands and the United Kingdom,* EPAG Working Paper 13, Colchester: University of Essex.

European Commission (2001a), *Employment and social policy: a framework for investing in quality,* Com (2001), 313 final, Brussels: Commission of the European Communities.

European Commission (2001b), *Employment in Europe 2001*, Brussels: European Communities.

European Commission (2004), *Employment in Europe 2004*, Brussels: Office for Official Publications of the European Communities.

European Commission (2006), *Employment in Europe 2006*, Brussels: Office for Official Publications of the European Communities.

Frade, C. and Darmon, I. (2005), 'New modes of business organization and precarious employment: towards the recommodification of labour', *Journal of European Social Policies*, **15** (2), 107–21.

Hyman, R. (2005), 'Words and things. The problem of particularistic universalism' in Barbier and Letablier (eds), *Cross-national comparisons: epistemological and methodological issues,* Brussels: PIE Pieter Lang, 191–210.

Jørgensen, H. (2002), *Consensus, Cooperation and Conflict: the Policy Making Process in Denmark,* Cheltenham, UK and Northhampton, MA, USA: Edward Elgar.

Laparra, M. with Barbier, J-C., Darmon, I., Düll, N., Frade, C., Frey, L., Lindley, R. and Vogler-Ludwig, K. (2004), *Precarious employment in Europe (ESOPE), Managing labour Market Related Risks in Europe, Policy Implications,* final policy report, funded by the European Commission, Fifth Framework Programme.

Maurice, M., Sellier, F. and Silvestre, J-J. (1982), *Politique d'éducation et organisation industrielle en France et en Allemagne, essai d'analyse sociétale,* Paris: PUF.

Nicole-Drancourt, C. (1990), 'Organisation du travail des femmes et flexibilité de l'emploi', *Sociologie du travail*, n° 2, 173–93.

Nicole-Drancourt, C. (1992), 'L'idée de précarité revisitée', *Travail et emploi,* n° 52, 57–70.

Paugam, S., Zoyem, J-P. and Charbonnel, J-M. (1993), 'Précarité et risque d'exclusion en France', *Documents du CERC,* n° 109, 3è trimestre, Paris: CERC.

Paugam, S. (2000), *Le salarié de la précarité*, Paris: PUF.

Paugam, S. (2005), *Les formes élémentaires de la pauvreté*, Paris: PUF.

Pitrou, A. (1978a), *Vivre sans famille? Les solidarités familiales dans le monde d'aujourd'hui,* Toulouse: Privat.

Pitrou, A. (1978b), *La vie précaire, des familles face à leurs difficultés*, Paris: Études CNAF.

Reich, R. (2001), *The Future of Success*, London: Heineman.

Rodgers, G. and Rodgers, J. (eds) (1989), *Precarious Jobs in Labour Market Regulation: the growth of atypical employment in Western Europe*, ILO/ International Institute of Labour Studies, Brussels: Free University of Brussels.

Schnapper, D. (1989), 'Rapport à l'emploi, protection sociale et statuts sociaux', *Revue française de sociologie*, **XXX** (1), 3–29.

Sennett, R. (1999), *The Corrosion of Character,* New York/London: W.W. Norton & Co.

Sennett, R. (2000), *Le travail sans qualité*, Paris: Albin Michel.

Vogler-Ludwig, K. (2002), *The German policy approach to combat precarious employment,* ESOPE Project, 5th Framework programme, Economix, München.

Wilthagen, T. and Tros, F. (2003), *The concept of 'Flexicurity': A new approach to regulating employment and labour markets*, paper for the European Trade Union Institute Brussels: 'Conference on 'Flexicurity – conceptual issues and political implementation in Europe', November.

3. Transitions out of Temporary Jobs: Consequences for Employment and Poverty across Europe

Annelies Debels

3.1 INTRODUCTION

Temporary jobs tend to get a double interpretation in labour market research; on the one hand they are considered as 'stepping-stones' towards stable, permanent jobs, while on the other hand they are seen as 'dead-end' jobs in a second-rank career (Booth, Francesconi and Frank, 2002; Korpi and Levin, 2001; Scherer, 2004). From a transitional labour market perspective this is an important difference because temporary work can only be considered a valuable policy tool if it 'encourage[s] transitions across the border of social systems without inducing downward spirals of social exclusion' (Schmid, 1998, p. 2). Therefore, it is essential to assess to what extent temporary work leads to transitions into permanent employment and into non-employment. However, it is equally important, though generally overlooked, to examine the broader consequences of the labour market transitions under study. This chapter aims to fill this gap by studying the poverty consequences of transitions between temporary work and other labour market statuses.

Temporary work can smooth transitions between education, unemployment or inactivity and permanent work in several ways. Employment in a temporary job can give access to internal vacancies in firms. It may also increase the attractiveness of the employees by providing them with work experience and work-related skills. However, working in a temporary job could also hinder the transition into permanent employment. It is sometimes argued that temporary jobs belong to a secondary labour market, from which it is difficult to escape (Korpi and Levin, 2001). Others look upon temporary workers as a reserve army, which is economically useful in prosperous times, but which is laid off as soon as the economic tide is turning (Booth, Francesconi and Frank, 2002). In this more pessimistic view, temporary jobs would rather entail transitions to unemployment or inactivity than in-work transitions, with the risk of inducing downward spirals of social exclusion.

In order to shed light on which of the two meanings attributed to temporary work – that is, the more optimistic or the more pessimistic one – applies, empirical research is needed. To this end, this chapter reviews the existing studies on the transitions out of temporary jobs and tries to add to the discussion with new comparative data and new findings about the role of institutional contingencies across Europe.

The focus on transitions out of temporary jobs can provide some useful information on the in- or exclusive potential of this type of job. At the same time, this focus often leads to an oversimplified classification of transitions into permanent work as 'good' or inclusive transitions and other transitions as 'bad' or exclusive transitions. Such a classification can be misleading for two reasons. The first is that transitions from a temporary into a permanent job do not necessarily reduce social exclusion. As a matter of fact, permanent jobs could just as temporary jobs, entail unfavourable conditions in terms of pay, working and living conditions. The second is that temporary workers may well manage to avoid spirals of downward social exclusion, even without making a transition into permanent employment. There is some evidence that a small number of people even prefers the increased personal flexibility of a temporary job-career above the certainty of a permanent job (Casey and Alach, 2004; Sels et al., 2002).

For these reasons, the traditional focus on labour market transitions alone does not suffice and a broader approach is needed that takes into account the consequences of these transitions for social inclusion. A focus on poverty can be helpful in this respect. The concept of poverty is closely connected to that of social exclusion (for example, Berghman, 1995) and poverty reduction is one of the principal aims of the European Employment Strategy, the European Social Model and the Lisbon-strategy (De Gier and Van den Berg, 2005). Therefore, this chapter deals with two main research questions: (1) to what extent and under which conditions do temporary jobs lead to a transition into permanent employment or into unemployment? and (2) to what extent is a transition from a temporary into a permanent job needed to avoid poverty and to what extent does the transition between temporary work and non-work affect the risk of poverty?

The two-folded research question in this contribution will be addressed from a cross-country comparative perspective allowing assessing the impact of distinct institutional contexts on the employment and poverty prospects of temporary workers. The labour market institutional contexts regulating the structure and volume of temporary jobs differ substantially across countries, which is likely to influence labour market transitions accordingly. In a similar way, poverty might reflect cross-country differences in social security systems and in household composition. To take this into account, a wide range of European countries is selected in the study: Belgium, Denmark, France, Germany, Greece, Italy, Ireland, the Netherlands, Portugal, Spain and United Kingdom. The data used for the analysis include seven waves (1995–2001) of the European Community Household Panel.

The chapter is structured as follows. In the next section, we set out the various meanings of temporary jobs in the public debates at national level. In a subsequent section, we derive hypotheses about the poverty risk attached to certain labour market transitions. The third section starts with describing the European Community Household Panel. It then turns to the definition of our main concepts and variables. Finally, the fourth and fifth sections discuss the outcomes of the empirical analyses and the policy implications to be drawn out of the results.

3.2 THEORETICAL FRAMEWORK

3.2.1 The Double Meaning of Temporary Work

Temporary work refers to those employer–employee relationships without formal guarantees for continuing longer-term employment within the same labour relationship. Examples of such guarantees are arrangements protecting against unfair dismissal, like severance pay, notice periods or dismissal procedures. Temporary work thus embraces a wide range of contracts: not only fixed-term contracts, but also temporary agency work, casual jobs (without contract) and other non-permanent working arrangements.

The extensive hiring and firing regulations inherent to permanent jobs encourage employers to recruit temporary workers. Especially in a context of uncertainty about future economic conditions, temporary jobs offer an attractive alternative to permanent jobs because they permit employers to save on future dismissal costs (Brewster, Mayne and Tregaskis, 1997). Moreover, they render more flexibility for adjusting the staffing levels to changes in market demands without implying the need to maintain peak workload staffing (Houseman, 2001). Temporary jobs may be used to replace workers who are temporarily absent because of sickness, vacation, maternity leave, and so on or to fill positions that are temporary because of the seasonality or the limited duration of the task (Houseman, 2001; Zijl and Budil-Nadvorníková, 2001). Alternatively, temporary workers may be employed to fill positions that are in reality permanent. There could be different reasons to do so. Firstly, uncertainty about the value of the match between worker and job could induce employers to use temporary jobs as an efficient screening device or as a continuation of the probation period before permanently recruiting the worker. Another reason suggested in the literature relates to the lower wage-related costs associated with the employment of temporary workers. Temporary workers often receive lower wages and less generous benefits than permanent workers (Houseman, 2001).

The more pessimistic view on temporary work focuses on the idea that temporary workers belong to a part of the labour force that can be laid off fairly easily when it is no longer needed. This view therefore stresses the negative consequences for the employment security of temporary workers. Theoretical arguments for this perspective can primarily be found in the well-known dual labour market and segmentation theories (Piore, 1975). Essentially, segmentation theory hypothesises that the mobility between the 'primary' (or good) and the 'secondary' (or bad) labour market segment is limited, so that once people occupy a job in either or both segments, their chances of leaving them become very small (Doeringer and Piore, 1971).

The explanations for this segmentation process are manifold. According to insider-outsider theory (Lindbeck and Snower, 1988) temporary workers possess less bargaining power than permanent workers because they are more easily replaced by company outsiders. This inferior bargaining position results in more unshielded, unstable positions and fewer career opportunities for temporary workers within the organisation. In addition, having worked in a temporary job might send a bad signal to employers outside the organisation. Some employers might interpret it as a sign of low productivity, assuming that highly productive workers would already have been offered a permanent position by their previous employers (Korpi and Levin, 2001; Scherer, 2004). Moreover, employers may assume that temporary workers have received less training and investment in human capital during their careers and therefore discriminate against them in primary sector recruiting (Korpi and Levin, 2001). These explanations go one step further than explanations in terms of human capital differences, in the sense that they assume that the sheer employment in a temporary job exerts a negative effect on the transition into a permanent job, over and above the effect of human capital.

While the above arguments emphasise the adverse consequences of temporary work, some authors consider it as a stepping-stone into stable, permanent work. They see temporary jobs as entry ports into the core labour market for young labour market entrants (Scherer, 2004). Yet, for the unemployed or inactive, temporary jobs may fulfil a similar stepping-stone function. Atkinson, Rick, Morris and Williams (1996) distinguish three ways in which temporary employment provides a route into permanent work. First, a temporary job can be used by the employer as an inexpensive screening device for a permanent position. Second, once hired, temporary workers have a better chance of obtaining a permanent position in the firm, because they have better access to insider information about vacancies and also because employers have become better informed about their potential productivity and skills. Third, temporary workers may increase their attractiveness for selection into a permanent position with a different employer. The work experience and skills acquired in the temporary position, as well as the apparent capacity to hold a job send a positive signal to potential employers. In addition, accepting temporary work may help to avoid the stigma of having been unemployed (Korpi and Levin, 2001).

Until now, it was assumed that the initiative to use temporary jobs lies at the demand side. However, it may also stem from the supply side. Temporary jobs may render individuals more flexibility in improving their work–life balance, defined as the capacity of employees to reconcile their working situation with their (changing) personal or private life (Sels et al. 2002). However, empirical research indicates that the importance of the employee's individual choice should not be overestimated, because most temporary workers are more or less forced to work in a temporary job as they are unable to find a permanent job. In Europe, a large share of temporary workers appear to enter their contract involuntarily (European Commission, 2002).[1] This supports the assumption that this form of flexible labour might entail a significant portion of employment insecurity and precariousness.

3.2.2 Temporary Jobs and Poverty

Poverty arises whenever the resources of persons or households are so limited as to exclude them from a minimum acceptable way of life in the country in which they are living (European Commission, 1984). The focus in this chapter is on income poverty, which is defined as a lack of income resources relative to the present needs of the household.

Employment is a determining factor in avoiding individual or household poverty. There is ample evidence that households headed by unemployed or inactive persons face higher poverty risks (Barnes, 2002). Moreover, changes in the employment situation of people (for example being hired or laid-off) appear to be the most important predictors of poverty transitions (Duncan et al., 1993; Oxley, Dang and Antolín, 2000). Therefore, it seems reasonable to assume that people will face lower poverty risks when employed in a temporary job than when they are unemployed or inactive.

It is less clear, however, whether the poverty risk for workers employed in a temporary job is higher than for workers in a permanent job. There is some theoretical literature on the relationship between temporary work and low wage, but it is inconclusive. The theory of compensating wage differentials assumes that the level of pay for a job serves as compensation for the disadvantageous features it might have (Smith, 2003). This leads us to suspect that higher wages will be paid to temporary workers to compensate for the lack of employment security. On the other hand, segmentation and human capital theory predict the opposite, namely that temporary workers are more likely to be employed in low quality and low-wage jobs. Empirical research tends to confirm the latter argument. In several countries, there is a substantial wage penalty for temporary workers compared to permanent workers, even after controlling for differences in individual and job characteristics (Booth, Francesconi and Frank, 2002; Blanchard and Landier, 2002; Gustafsson, Kenjoh, Wetzels, 2003; Kalleberg, Reskin and Hudson, 2000; Mertens and McGinnity, 2004; OECD, 2002; Storrie, 2002). Still, there is also evidence that a significant proportion of temporary workers earn relatively high wages (OECD, 2002).

Furthermore, the relationship between a low-wage job and poverty is less straightforward than it might seem at first sight. This is because two factors can intermediate in this relationship: other income resources and household composition. Sometimes, the low wage is not the only source of income in the household. There might be additional labour earnings from other working household members or the household may receive income from non-labour sources, for example from social or private transfers or from capital gains. On the other hand, a (low) wage that is sufficient for a small household might still lead to poverty in other household contexts, for example with dependent children. In sum, there are two possible ways in which working persons still face a risk of poverty (Strengmann-Kuhn, 2002): (1) a worker with a so-called poverty wage[2] cannot avoid poverty through the earnings of other household members or additional resources or (2) a worker with a sufficient wage falls below the poverty line because of his or her household context. Strengmann-Kuhn (2002) shows that belonging to the working poor is most commonly associated with the household context, and to a lesser extent with low pay. Therefore, differences in the household context between temporary and permanent workers should be accounted for in the empirical part of this study.

Little research has been done on the issue of poverty among temporary workers. Peña-Casas and Latta (2004) demonstrate that poverty is more common among temporary than among permanent workers in most countries of the European Union. However, the question remains whether this relationship still exists after controlling for possibly confounding factors such as individual, job or household characteristics. In other words, if temporary workers make a transition into permanent work, would this mean that their risks of poverty are indeed reduced, also after controlling for these confounding variables?

3.2.3 Temporary Employment in Different Countries

Temporary jobs tend to collect a different meaning across countries because they are institutionalised and enshrined in law in dissimilar ways (see the chapter of Barbier in this book; see also Blanpain and Graham, 2004). In countries, temporary contracts are legally permitted in a restricted number of situations such as when an absent permanent employee has to be replaced, or when there is a temporary peak in the workload or in the case of exceptional work. Next to this, there may be restrictions on the permitted duration of temporary contracts, on the renewal of temporary contracts and on the dissimilar treatment of temporary and permanent employees. In other countries, such as the United Kingdom and Ireland, hardly any of these restrictions exist. Not only the regulation on temporary contracts, but also the regulation concerning permanent contracts may be relevant in this context. Some authors have suggested that the need for temporary contracts is higher when permanent employment is more strictly regulated (Booth, Dolado and Frank, 2002). This would explain the extensive use of temporary labour in countries such as Spain, Portugal and Greece. Similarly, it has been argued that in countries with the strictest job protection regulation (these are the Mediterranean countries) temporary workers have lower chances of obtaining a permanent job, because the labour market is more segmented, whereas the opposite is true for countries where job protection regulation is almost absent (Muffels and Luijkx, 2006).

Regarding the existing differences in poverty risks across countries, the role of the social security system has to be acknowledged. The social security system aims at providing a replacement income when regular labour income is no longer available (Berghman and Fouarge, 1999), so it can be seen as a buffer against a low income. From the welfare states literature, it is well known that countries differ with respect to the welfare institutions they entail. However, these differences tend to cluster into what are commonly known as welfare state regimes.

The most renowned welfare state typology comes from Esping-Andersen (1990), who distinguishes three worlds of welfare capitalism, each characterised by a typical constellation of the relationship between the market, the state and the family. In the Anglo-Saxon regime (for example, United Kingdom, Ireland) where the market plays a central role and state intervention is minimised, social provisions tend to be minimal and selective. In contrast, the Nordic regime (for example, Sweden, Denmark, Finland, Netherlands), being the most decommodified regime, stresses the active role of the state and provides universal and generous public services and benefits. The Continental regime (for example, Germany, France, Belgium, Austria, Luxembourg), assigns a large role to the state in regulating the market while its social provisions are originally shaped according to the traditional breadwinner model. Social provisions are generous, but tied to previous labour market performance. This threefold typology has been criticised by different authors for its neglect of the typical features of the Mediterranean countries, that is, the important role of the family, the immature system of social provisions and the absence of a minimum income guarantee (Bonoli, 1997; Ferrera, 1996). Therefore, we will use a modified Esping-Andersen typology taking into account this fourth Mediterranean regime type, consisting of Greece, Spain, Portugal and Italy. The four regime clusters have also proven successful in explaining differences in flexibility and work security across countries (Muffels and Fouarge, 2002a, b; Muffels and Luijkx, 2006).

3.3 DATA AND OPERATIONALISATION

3.3.1 The European Community Household Panel

For the empirical analysis of this chapter, data from the European Community Household Panel (ECHP) are used. The ECHP is a longitudinal survey based on a standardised questionnaire that was presented each year to a representative panel of households and individuals in every member state of the EU-15. It ran from 1994 until 2001 and covers a wide range of topics such as income, health, education, housing, demographic variables and employment characteristics (Peracchi, 2002).

With a view to the purpose of this chapter, the ECHP is an interesting data source for three reasons. First, because the ECHP deals with both employment and income, it allows investigating of the consequences of working in a temporary job for the level of employment security and poverty. Secondly, as standardised methodologies and procedures are applied in both the data collection and data processing, the ECHP allows comparisons of these relationships between countries. Thirdly, it is possible to construct employment and poverty trajectories of individuals, because the same information is collected each year with the same group of people. This panel design therefore allows studying changes at the micro level.

While the full ECHP spans a period of 8 years; for this chapter only the last seven waves will be used ranging from 1995 until 2001. The reason is the unavailability of the variable indicating whether the employment is temporary or permanent in 1994. The countries included are Belgium, Denmark, France, Germany, Greece, Italy, Ireland, the Netherlands, Portugal, Spain and United Kingdom. For Germany, harmonised data from the GSOEP were used and for the United Kingdom data from the BHPS, because the original ECHP-sample for these countries did not cover the entire period.

3.3.2 Operationalisation of Main Concepts

Contract type: temporary versus permanent job. Temporary work encompasses various labour relationships: temporary agency work, fixed-term contracts, casual jobs without contract and other non-permanent working arrangements. This broad definition is used because in France the distinction between fixed-term contracts and casual jobs is not clearly made. The best solution to deal with this problem is to collapse these categories into one broad category of 'temporary jobs'. Moreover, a too detailed distinction between different types of temporary work would restrict the statistical analyses because of the limited number of cases in each category.

Education. The highest level of education completed will be used as one of the indicators for human capital. The variable has three categories: high, that is, recognised third level education (ISCED 5–7), intermediate, that is, second stage of secondary education (ISCED 3) and low, that is, less than second stage of secondary education (ISCED 0–2).

Received education or training. This indicates whether the person has been in education or training since January of the previous year.

Sector. Six sectors are distinguished: (1) agriculture, extraction and utilities; (2) manufacturing and construction; (3) distribution: transport and sale of goods; (4) business services (financial, management, legal, design, real estate); (5) social and community services (public administration, education, health and social work) and (6) personal services (restaurants and hotels, domestic services, other services). For a further motivation of this operationalisation we refer to Crouch (1999).

Duration of the temporary spell. The duration of the temporary employment spell is constructed using the information on the starting date of the job spell given at the first measurement of the temporary employment spell. It is not called duration of temporary job spell, because the current employment spell is also considered to be continued when there is a change of job or employer, provided that this change does not involve a period of unemployment or inactivity. Where the starting date was missing, imputations have been performed based on the employment calendar information in the ECHP.

Previous unemployment spell. This variable indicates whether or not a person has experienced at least one unemployment spell before the start of the current employment spell, but after 1989.

Unemployment rate. We use gender-specific harmonised yearly un-employment rates by country, provided by Eurostat.

Income poverty. Poverty is operationalised as a dummy variable indicating whether the income is more or less than 60 per cent of the median income, being the poverty line in a particular country. This poverty measure is widely used in current research with the ECHP and other data sources. The income measure is defined as the total yearly net disposable household income, divided by the modified OECD equivalence scale[3] in order to adjust for differences in household size and composition. This equivalised household income is then assigned to each member of the household, hence creating a household income measure at the individual level. We need to create an individual measure because we want to carry out longitudinal analyses and the household is not a stable unit of analysis over time.

To compute the total household income we added all the amounts at the individual level derived from labour, social security and private sources to the amounts of income received at the household level. As income components in the ECHP always refer to income in the previous year, we added the amounts for people living together in the same household in the wave prior to the interview, in order to avoid biased income estimates if household composition changes over time.

Household setting. A distinction is made between persons living in households in which at least one other household member is employed (in a temporary or permanent job or self-employment) and persons living in households in which no other members are working.

3.4 TRANSITIONS OUT OF TEMPORARY WORK

3.4.1 Overview of Empirical Evidence

From the theory, two competing hypotheses were derived about temporary jobs. According to the first they function primarily as stepping-stones into regular work while according to the second they act as employment traps. Researchers have tried to examine this question empirically by viewing the employment status temporary workers end in after a certain period of time or after the end of their temporary job (Booth, Francesconi and Frank, 2002; Contini, Pacelli and Villosio, 2000; D'Addio and Rosholm, 2005; European Commission, 2004; Muffels and Fouarge, 2002b; Muffels and Luijkx, 2006; Remery, van Doorne-Huiskes and Schippers, 2002; Scherer, 2004; OECD, 2002). The following quote from the OECD Employment Outlook (2002, p. 131) provides a good summary of existing research on the topic: 'Depending on the country considered, between one-third and two-thirds of temporary workers move into a permanent job within a two-year time interval, suggesting considerable upward mobility. The other side of the coin is that up to one-quarter of temporary workers are unemployed when interviewed one and two years later'.

Research also reveals that not all temporary workers have similar chances of obtaining a permanent job. These chances depend not only upon individual characteristics such as age, gender, education, but also upon job and employment related characteristics such as sector, firm size and previous unemployment spells (Booth, Francesconi and Frank, 2002, D'Addio and Rosholm, 2005; European Commission, 2004; Muffels and Luijkx, 2006; OECD, 2002).

Moreover, the probability that temporary workers move into a permanent job or become unemployed is different across countries and regimes. In particular, when looking at simple transition rates, Muffels and Fouarge (2002b) demonstrate that temporary workers in the Anglo-Saxon countries are more likely to obtain a permanent job than in the other regimes. The Mediterranean regime performs worst in this respect. Other research seems to corroborate this pattern (Debels, 2004; OECD, 2002). This finding is attributed to the fact that countries with the strictest employment protection regulation tend to be featured by more segmented labour markets (Muffels and Luijkx, 2006). When adopting a multivariate perspective, that is, controlling for many other variables, Muffels and Luijkx (2006) come to similar results: moves into permanent employment are more likely to occur in both the Anglo-Saxon and the Nordic regime and less likely in the Mediterranean regime.

Although exit rates out of temporary jobs have been studied by several researchers, some gaps and uncertainties remain. For instance, it remains to be seen how regimes or countries affect transition rates when other factors are being controlled. Unfortunately, most studies in the field are limited to one or few countries, or they are not aimed at comparing countries. Other approaches are restricted to the male part of the population or differentiate only between regimes and not between individual countries. Further to this, it is useful to compare different specifications of variables and models in order to establish the robustness of the results under different types of assumptions.

3.4.2 A Competing Risks Event History Approach: Method and Model

In order to examine the transitions out of temporary work, a competing risks event history approach is followed. For this purpose, only people aged between 16 and 66 years who reported to work in a temporary job in at least one wave are included in the sample. These persons are followed at the subsequent survey years until their temporary employment spell ends. The employment spell can end due to a transition into permanent work, self-employment, unemployment or inactivity or because of right-censoring (for example if they drop out from the panel or the panel is ended). The model estimated here focuses on transitions into permanent employment and into unemployment as competing risks.[4] A separate model is estimated for men and women. Only the first temporary employment spell of the individual is taken into account. We opt for a discrete-time analysis because the crucial variables are measured at discrete points in time.[5]

The aim of our discrete time hazard rate analysis is to model durations, meaning that the units of analysis are spells instead of individuals, in this case spells of temporary employment. The technique offers two advantages over ordinary logistic regression: it can deal with problems of right-censoring and it can take time-dependent covariates into account (Allison, 1984; Blossfeld and Rohwer, 2002; Yamaguchi, 1991). We use a discrete-time logistic model for competing risks (namely unemployment, permanent and temporary employment) that is defined as the following multinomial logit model (Allison, 2003):

$$\log\left(\frac{P_{ijt}}{P_{i0t}}\right) = \alpha_{jt} + \beta_{j1}x_{it1} + ... + \beta_{jk}x_{itk} \qquad (3.1)$$

where P_{ijt} is the conditional probability that individual i experiences the event j at time t, given that the individual has not already experienced an event. This conditional probability will be called the hazard of experiencing event j. P_{i0t} is the probability that no event occurs at time t to individual i, that is, that the individual remains in a temporary job, and x_{itk} represents the value of the kth covariate of individual i at time t. As such, the covariates are allowed to change over time. In order to control for unobserved heterogeneity, we estimated a second model including an individual random effect.[6] The covariates included in the models are personal characteristics (age, age squared, marital status, number of kids, health status), human capital variables (education, received education or training in the previous year), characteristics of the temporary job (duration, duration squared, full-time job, occupation, firm size, business sector), unemployment history and finally gender-specific unemployment rates and country dummies.[7]

3.4.3 Results: the Hazard of Exiting Temporary Work

The findings from the discrete time hazard rate analysis are presented in Table 3.1. The first two columns give the estimates of the effects on the hazard rate of obtaining a permanent job relative to staying in a temporary job. It appears that the longer men and women work in a temporary job, the higher their chances of moving into a permanent job relative to staying in a temporary job, although this effect slows down again after some time.[8]

Table 3.1 Estimates from a competing-risks discrete-time hazard rate model: effects on the hazard of moving into a permanent job or into unemployment versus remaining in a temporary job (1995–2001)

	Hazard of obtaining permanent job		Hazard of becoming unemployed	
	Men	Women	Men	Women
	Estimate	Estimate	Estimate	Estimate
Age	0.002	0.039	0.007	−0.058
Age squared/100	−0.018	−0.065	0.012	0.077
Education				
Low	ref	ref	ref	ref
Intermediate	0.192**	0.012	−0.169	0.165
High	0.232*	0.163	−0.298*	0.013
Received education or training	0.162*	0.116	0.001	0.015
Marital status				
Married	ref	ref	ref	ref
Never married	0.006	−0.125	0.475**	0.051
Divorced/widowed	−0.049	−0.014	0.514***	−0.006
Number of kids	−0.051	0.018	0.056	0.053
Bad health status	−0.276	−0.271	0.461**	0.345
Duration of temporary job spell	0.011***	0.011***	−0.009**	−0.013**
Duration squared	−0.000***	−0.000***	0	0
Previous unemployment spell	0.068	0.093	1.666***	1.516***
Full-time temporary job	0.303*	0.050	0.032	0.041
Occupation				
Legislators, senior officials, managers	−0.954***	−0.510*	−0.828*	−0.308
Professionals	−0.355*	−0.378**	−0.713**	−0.673***
Technicians, associate professions	−0.032	−0.072	−0.404	−0.119
Clerks	ref	ref	ref	ref
Service, shop, market sales workers	−0.082	−0.108	0.037	0.289*
Skilled agricultural and fishery workers	−0.068	–	0.377	1.085*
Craft and related trade workers	−0.459***	0.042	−0.223	0.799**
Occupation				
Plant-,machine operators, assemblers	−0.086	0.184	−0.196	0.640*
Elementary occupations	−0.483***	−0.218	0.182	0.301*
Firm size				
0–4	−0.409***	−0.179	0.113	0.127
5–49	−0.021	0.115	0.205	0.368
50–499	−0.074	0.078	0.152	0.165
>500	ref	ref	ref	ref

Table 3.1 (Continued)

	Hazard of obtaining permanent job		Hazard of becoming unemployed	
	Men	Women	Men	Women
	Estimate	Estimate	Estimate	Estimate
Sector				
Agriculture and extraction	−0.115	0.082	−0.145	0.081
Manufacturing and construction	ref	ref	ref	ref
Trade and transport	0.069	−0.039	−0.056	−0.118
Business services	−0.051	−0.121	−0.203	−0.213
Social and community services	−0.207	−0.227	0.016	0.101
Personal services	−0.215	−0.428***	0.164	0.180
Public sector	0.059	0.006	−0.282	−0.309*
Unemployment rate	−0.165***	−0.132***	−0.067	−0.064***
Country				
United Kingdom	ref	ref	ref	ref
Denmark	−1.446***	−0.279	−1.262	−0.010
Netherlands	−0.696***	−0.136	−1.414	−0.279
Belgium	−0.619**	−0.339	−0.585	0.164
France	−0.575**	−0.201	0.051	1.010**
Ireland	−0.248	−0.237	−0.415	−0.576
Italy	−0.502**	0.504*	0.034	0.500
Greece	−1.029***	0.192	−0.509	0.851*
Spain	−0.553***	0.888***	0.20	1.401***
Portugal	−1.265***	−0.785***	−0.922	−0.055
Germany	−0.592**	−0.099	0.30	0.777*

Model information	Model for men	Model for women
	N = 8,065	N = 6,519
Deviance D (Difference with saturated model)	D/DF = 0.8541, p = 1.000	D/DF = 0.8868, p = 1.000
Likelihood Ratio (Difference with intercepts only model)	X^2 = 1360.84, p < 0.0001	X^2 = 1074.023, p < 0.0001

Notes:
*** $p < 0.001$, ** $p < 0.01$, * $p < 0.05$; – effect could not be estimated; ref = reference category.

Source: Author's calculations on ECHP-UDB, 1995–2001.

Higher unemployment rates tend to decrease the probability of moving into a permanent job for both sexes. There are also some differences between occupational groups, with both higher (managers and legislators, professionals) and lower professions (craft workers and elementary occupations) displaying lower chances of moving into permanent work (in comparison to clerks). Moreover, some effects increase the odds of obtaining a permanent job only for men, that is, having a high education, having received education or training in the previous year, working full-time or in a big firm; for women these effects appear insignificant. Booth, Francesconi and Frank (2002) and D'Addio and Rosholm (2005) reported similar gender-specific effects. Working in the personal services sector entails significantly lower odds of moving into a permanent job, but only for women. These effects seem very much in line with what is known about them in the literature, and therefore need no further explanation.

Next, we turn to results for the hazard rate of becoming unemployed after having worked in a temporary job. For both men and women this hazard decreases with the duration of the temporary contract.[9] Persons who experienced a previous unemployment spell are more likely to become unemployed again. In addition, men and women in higher occupations (professionals, legislators and managers) exhibit lower risks of becoming unemployed. Because temporary workers in the higher occupations also have a lower hazard of moving into a permanent job, this means that they tend to keep their temporary job longer. This indicates that being engaged in temporary work is not necessarily a bad event, at least not for people in the higher-level occupations. For the lower-level occupations, on the other hand, it leads relatively frequently to unemployment, in any case for women. Temporary public sector workers of both sexes have a comparatively lower chance of moving into unemployment. Furthermore, lower educated men, but not women, have a higher hazard of becoming unemployed after having worked in a temporary job. Education or training in the year prior to the year of exit has no effect. Marriage only seems to play a role for men: those who have never been married or are divorced/widowed have a higher hazard of becoming unemployed. Similarly, a bad health increases the risk of unemployment for men, but not significantly so for women. Finally, rather counter intuitively, we find a negative effect of the unemployment rate on the chance of moving into unemployment. This suggests that when unemployment rates go up, people tend to stay in their temporary job longer. This might reflect the risk-calculating behaviour of people who try to prevent unemployment and therefore stay in their temporary job knowing that the chances of getting a new job quickly after unemployment are lower due to the higher unemployment levels. This effect should be interpreted with caution though.

Eventually, we discuss the results of the country effects. Three general observations stand out. Firstly, there are considerable differences between countries within regime type. Secondly, when controlling for all the variables introduced in the model (including the unemployment rate in a country), the results are different from those reached on the basis of the descriptive transition tables. Thirdly, the institutions in a particular country turn out to have different effects for males and females.

In previous research, the Anglo-Saxon regime performed best in safeguarding the chances of temporary workers to move into a permanent job. Our results suggest that this conclusion is still valid at least for men; all countries perform worse in this respect than the United Kingdom, though Ireland only slightly worse. For women however, the Anglo-Saxon countries are not doing any better than most other countries. Somewhat surprisingly, our findings indicate that compared to British women, female temporary workers in Spain, Italy and Greece exhibit the highest chances of moving into a permanent job. For men, the Anglo-Saxon countries are followed by Italy, Spain, France, Germany, Belgium and the Netherlands. In the other Mediterranean countries, that is, Portugal and Greece, male temporary workers still have the worst prospects of obtaining a permanent job. For men, again rather surprisingly, Denmark occupies the worst position in this ranking.

It must be added though, that the unexpectedly good scores of some of the (Mediterranean) countries regarding transitions into permanent jobs, do not extend to transitions into unemployment. On the contrary, especially in France and Spain, but also in Italy (for men) and Greece (for women), temporary workers tend to show high hazards of becoming unemployed. Germany is also not performing well in this respect. The countries belonging to the Nordic regime, for example, Denmark and the Netherlands, exhibit the lowest chances for temporary workers to become unemployed. But also Portugal, scoring worst in getting temporary workers into permanent employment, shares such a favourable position. Apparently, Portuguese temporary workers display lower transition probabilities into both a permanent job and unemployment, thus remaining longer in their temporary jobs. Finally, while male temporary workers in the Anglo-Saxon countries have the highest chances to move into a permanent job, they also run higher risks of becoming unemployed. For women, the reverse is true: Ireland and United Kingdom show rather low exit rates to unemployment and thus belong to the better performing group of countries for this part of the analysis.

3.5 TEMPORARY JOB TRANSITIONS AND THE RISK OF POVERTY

3.5.1 Poverty across Households and Labour Market Statuses: a Descriptive Account

In the theoretical part of this chapter it was argued that employment status is one of the most important determinants of poverty. This is confirmed in Table 3.2, where poverty rates for temporary and permanent workers, the self-employed, the unemployed and inactive people are displayed for the various countries.

Table 3.2 Poverty rates for temporary and permanent workers, self-employed, unemployed and inactive people within different household contexts, by country (1995–2000)

	No other workers in the household					At least one other worker in the household				
	Tempo-rary	Perma-nent	Self-empl.	Unem-ployed	In-active	Tempo-rary	Perma-nent	Self-empl.	Unem-ployed	In-active
DK	13.4	4.3	19.3	19.6	36	2.7	1	9.4	3.2	6.6
NL	20.2	7.3	23.6	36.7	17.7	5.6	2	16.5	11.9	11.3
BE	17	6.6	24.2	50.6	28.4	3.3	1.9	10.9	11	10.3
FR	28.4	11.9	32.2	56.5	26.4	8.5	2.6	14.5	19.7	17.6
GE	19.4	6.6	11	53.1	20.4	5.5	2.1	7.3	13.2	8.3
UK	26.1	11.9	20.4	64.1	37.8	4.1	2.5	6.6	19.1	12
IR	17.8	7.7	20.4	71.7	56	5.7	2.2	9	13.6	12.3
IT	39.3	13.5	26.3	65.8	24.8	18.7	2.8	15.1	36.1	18.3
GR	22.9	7.2	28.3	43.9	36.5	10.5	2.2	23.7	24	17.9
SP	28.1	8.9	28.5	55	30	8.5	1.7	15.4	23	15
PO	33.9	16	43.5	52.3	47.6	11.8	4.2	28.2	21.2	17.9

Source: Author's calculations on ECHP-UDB, cross-sectionally weighted and subsequently averaged over the period 1995–2000.

As expected, the table demonstrates that unemployed and inactive persons have higher poverty risks than permanent workers, temporary workers and the self-employed. This holds true both for people with and without other workers in the household. Furthermore, temporary workers (and also the self-employed) display substantially higher poverty rates than permanent workers. Consequently, temporary work appears to be somewhere in between non-employment and permanent employment in terms of the poverty risk it entails. There are also considerable differences across countries. Temporary workers in Denmark run the lowest risk of poverty. In the Mediterranean countries, but also in France and the United Kingdom they have the highest risks. Finally, the table demonstrates that the household context matters. Persons living in a household where at least one other person is working, show substantially lower poverty rates than those living in a household where no other members are at work.

3.5.2 Fixed-effects Approach: Method and Model

Next, we deal with the question whether and to what extent a transition from temporary work to any other labour market statuses affects the poverty risk of an individual. For that purpose, we estimated a regression model to explain the poverty risk individuals face. In technical terms, we estimate a so-called 'fixed effect' conditional logit regression model. The main advantage of it is that it enables to control for all potential characteristics of individuals, also for the unobserved ones, if these characteristics are stable over time, such as ability (Verbeek, 2004). The fixed effects model controls for this unobserved heterogeneity because it only takes into account the variability within individuals, not between individuals. Hence, it is more likely to produce unbiased estimates (Allison, 2005).

The model is defined as follows:

$$\log\left(\frac{P_{it}}{1-P_{it}}\right) = \mu_t + \beta_{it} + \alpha_i \qquad (3.2)$$

where P_{it} is the probability that individual i is poor at time t, μ_t is an intercept that varies over time and β_{it} is the vector of covariates which change over time. α_i stands for all the heterogeneity between individuals that is stable over time (Allison, 2005). The time-changing covariates included in the model are age, age square, education, household size and the number of hours worked per week. The independent variable of interest is a combination of household composition (no or at least one other working household member) and activity status (temporary job, permanent job, self-employment, unemployment and inactivity).

It must be noted that the coefficients from this model will have a subject-specific rather than a population-averaged meaning (Zeger, Liang and Albert, 1988). To give an example, they can be interpreted as follows: if a particular subject changes from working in a temporary job to working in a permanent job or self-employment, or becoming unemployed or inactive, how will this alter his or her risks of poverty? This kind of interpretation is exactly what we need with a view to our focus on the poverty consequences of transitions out of a temporary job.

3.5.3 Results: the Poverty Consequences of Transitions

Before commenting on the effect on poverty of transitions between temporary work and other labour market statuses, we argue that the household context of temporary workers is a crucial factor in understanding the risks of poverty. This was already apparent from the descriptive analysis, but is now confirmed also in our multivariate analyses and after controlling for unobserved heterogeneity. Table 3.3 demonstrates that the lack of potential support from other working household members increases the odds of poverty with a factor ranging from 2.4 to 6. This effect is significant in all countries. This finding supports our decision to model the effect of temporary work separately for various household contexts.

Table 3.3 Poverty odds ratio for temporary workers: the odds of poverty when living in a household without other working members, relative to the odds when living in a household with other working members

DK	NL	BE	FR	GE	UK	IR	IT	GR	SP	PO
2.93**	4.05***	2.5*	4.63***	2.68***	6.02***	2.39**	2.29**	2.64***	2.7***	3.2***

Notes:
*** = significant at p < 0.001, ** = significant at p < 0.01, * = significant at p < 0.1.
DK = Denmark, NL = Netherlands; BE = Belgium; FR = France; GE = Germany;
UK = United Kingdom; IR = Ireland; IT = Italy; GR = Greece; SP = Spain; PO = Portugal.

Source: Fixed effects logit model estimated on the ECHP-UDB, 1995–2000.

Table 3.4 presents the poverty odds ratios of being employed in a temporary job compared to occupying another labour market status by country. A first question addressed in this table, is to what extent temporary workers need to make a transition into a permanent job in order to avoid poverty or to escape from it. The answer is most clearly visible when there are no other workers present in the household. In that case, exchanging a temporary job for a permanent job obviously helps to escape from poverty. The risks of poverty are higher in a temporary than in a permanent job. In Germany, these risks are 31 per cent higher while in Belgium they are up to 83 per cent higher. Conversely, in a minority of countries (that is, in Greece, Spain, Portugal and United Kingdom), the changing of contract type does not seem to affect the odds of poverty significantly.

It can be expected that occupying a temporary job will have less detrimental effects in terms of poverty in the presence of other workers in the household, due to the additional income earned by these other worker(s). This hypothesis is confirmed for the 'Nordic' countries, that is, Denmark, the

Netherlands, Belgium, France, Germany and the UK. In these countries, a transition into permanent work is not required to avoid poverty, as long as there are other working members in the household. The income from the other working household members seems to offer sufficient protection against poverty for the temporary worker.

However, in the Mediterranean countries, including Ireland, another mechanism appears to be at work. Despite the presence of other workers in the household, occupying a temporary job rather than a permanent one in these countries significantly increases the risks of poverty. It is possible that the protection offered through the incomes of other household members is weaker in the Mediterranean countries. However, this can only be a part of the explanation, because it cannot explain why the effect of contract type disappears (in Greece, Spain and Portugal) or becomes weaker (in Italy, Ireland) when there are no other working household members in the household. If temporary work is an 'unfavourable' event in terms of poverty risk in these countries, we would expect to find at least increasing poverty risks if there are no other working household members and hence no additional earnings present.

The question thus arises of what might explain the puzzling results for the Mediterranean countries. The findings point to the existence of an unobserved selection effect with respect to the impact of the household context on income poverty. In particular, the findings could be explained by assuming that only temporary workers with a decent income will or are able to form an independent household. In this way, the temporary workers with the highest incomes (and the lowest poverty risk) seem to select themselves into households without other working members and vice versa. As a matter of fact, evidence for this selection effect can be found in the literature on household formation. Indeed, the level of personal income resources are an important factor in explaining young adults' decisions to leave their homes (Avery, Goldscheider and Speare, 1992; Aassve, Billari and Ongaro, 2001). Moreover, Aassve, Billari, Mazzuco and Ongaro (2002) show that the effect of the level of the personal income on leaving the home is very strong in the Mediterranean countries (they do not consider Ireland here), weaker in the Continental regime and almost non-existent in the Anglo-Saxon and Nordic countries. This remarkably fits our findings, suggesting that a selection effect is probably driving the different results across countries.

To summarise, making a transition from a temporary into a permanent job will generally help people in avoiding poverty. However, in the 'Nordic' countries, this effect is no longer present when the individual is living in a household with other working members. In the Mediterranean countries (and Ireland), the reverse pattern can be observed, which is probably due to a household formation selection effect. The only country, for which neither of these conclusions seems to be true, is the United Kingdom. Here we find that a transition between a temporary job and a permanent job will have no significant effect on poverty.

A second question addressed in this section, is whether changing a temporary job for self-employment will influence the risks of poverty. Table 3.4 demonstrates that self-employment entails even a higher poverty risk than employment in a temporary job. This effect is present in almost all countries (except in France, Italy, Germany and UK). Moreover, the effect does not disappear when other working household members are present. On the contrary, it often becomes stronger.

Table 3.4 The odds of poverty when working in a temporary job relative to the odds of poverty in other labour market statuses, within different household contexts, by country

	Temporary vs Permanent		Temporary vs Self-employed		Temporary vs Unemployed		Temporary vs Inactive	
	Other workers		Other workers		Other workers		Other workers	
	No	Yes	No	Yes	No	Yes	No	Yes
DK	1.563*	1.083	0.417*	0.275**	0.744	1.258	0.296***	0.759
NL	1.437*	1.000	0.415**	0.250***	0.726	0.905	0.445***	0.864
BE	1.828*	1.550	0.384*	0.425*	0.486*	0.895	0.600	0.753
FR	1.515*	1.249	0.973	0.320***	0.764	0.718	0.484**	0.592*
IR	1.642*	2.714***	0.582*	0.583*	0.174***	0.735	0.215***	0.813
IT	1.399**	1.973***	0.954	0.821	0.427***	0.606**	0.423***	0.786
GR	1.294	1.302*	0.755*	0.406***	0.445***	0.455***	0.413***	0.452***
SP	1.045	1.606***	0.761*	0.622***	0.341***	0.429***	0.351***	0.466***
PT	1.236	1.758***	0.674*	0.438***	0.392***	0.369***	0.324***	0.429***
GE	1.312*	1.291	0.795	0.672	0.352***	0.733	0.379***	0.91
UK	1.414	1.078	1.062	0.519*	0.633	0.537*	0.676	0.716

Note: *** = significant at p < 0.001, ** = significant at p < 0.01, * = significant at p < 0.1; ns = not significant at p = 0.1; country acronyms are similar to Table 3.3.

Source: Author's calculations on ECHP-UDB, 1995–2000. Results obtained from a fixed-effects logit regression model of poverty conditional on the various labour market statuses and various household contexts, controlling for household size, number of hours worked per week, age, age squared and education level (effects not displayed here).

Eventually, we examine the transitions between temporary work and non-employment. To obtain a temporary job after unemployment or inactivity often means an improvement in terms of the income and poverty risks. The effect is most obvious for moves within households with no other workers: it is highly significant in all countries, except for Belgium and United Kingdom. When other working household members are present, it is still significant in France, Greece, Spain and Portugal. This argument can also be reversed, in the sense that becoming inactive or unemployed after a temporary job spell tends to increase the risk of poverty. Although in Denmark, the Netherlands, France and United Kingdom, moving from a temporary job to unemployment has no significant effect; it increases the risks of poverty in the other countries with a factor of 2 to 5.7, if there are no other household members at work. This effect is particularly resilient in the Mediterranean regime, where unemployment leads to higher risks of poverty even when other working household members are present.

3.6 CONCLUSIONS

Finally, we formulate some conclusions while particularly focusing on the policy implications. The main aim of the chapter is to examine the impact of the various types of transitions out of a temporary job. For policy purposes, it appears important to encourage transitions from temporary jobs into permanent jobs. The findings confirm that these transitions help temporary workers to escape from poverty. However, the findings also indicate that employment in a temporary job is less problematic if it occurs within a supportive household context. Transitions between temporary and permanent jobs appear not to change the risk of poverty significantly when there is another household member at work, at least not in the 'Nordic' countries. For the Mediterranean countries and Ireland, on the contrary, such transitions do reduce poverty whenever other working household members are present. Apparently, household solidarity is not sufficient to absorb the harmful consequences of temporary work in these countries. Hence, the need to stimulate transitions into permanent work turns out to be even stronger in the Mediterranean countries and Ireland. However, for the Mediterranean countries Greece, Spain and Portugal, we found no significant effect on poverty for a transition into permanent work when there are no other working members in the household. This must probably be interpreted as a selection effect through which only temporary workers earning a sufficient income form independent households. We came across evidence in the literature that such a selection effect might be typical for the Mediterranean countries. The latter finding suggests another important policy implication: not being poor is not equal to being economically independent. If temporary workers are economically dependent on other household members, this might limit their freedom of choice with respect to household formation and other demographic decisions.

While transitions into permanent work will often reduce poverty, transitions into self-employment, unemployment and inactivity tend to have the opposite effect, although in some countries this effect is insignificant. These results suggest that, speaking in terms of poverty, people in temporary work are better off than people without work. In other words, offering non-employed persons a temporary job will indeed help to reduce poverty in most countries.

In this chapter, the double meaning of temporary work was confirmed: for some people it leads to unemployment, for others to permanent work. Since we know that a transition into permanent work tends to reduce poverty, it becomes all the more important to find out how these moves can be encouraged. First, a well functioning labour market seems to play a crucial role, because high unemployment rates diminish the probability of obtaining a permanent job. Second, in line with previous research, we find that increasing men's human capital in terms of general education or job-related training raises their chances of moving into a permanent job. Surprisingly however, this conclusion does not hold for women. None of the human capital-related variables appears to exert a significant effect on women's chance of obtaining a permanent job. Sector and occupation-related variables, on the other hand, seem to play a more important role for women to make such a move. In general, the results for men and women seem to be rather dissimilar for quite some other variables as well. This suggests that a different policy will be required for men and women in this matter.

Finally, it is interesting for policy makers to know which countries exhibit best practices regarding their policies to promote poverty reducing job transitions. In the literature on the subject it is commonly agreed that the Anglo-Saxon regime provides the best and the Mediterranean regime the worst chances for temporary workers to obtain a permanent job. Our study suggests that this conclusion must be brought into perspective in at least three ways. First, when controlling for all other relevant factors this ranking of the various regimes is blurred. Second, the country-specific institutions seem to exert very dissimilar effects on the transition probabilities of men and women. Third, a high chance of moving into a permanent job does not automatically imply a low chance of a transition into unemployment. As a matter of fact, after controlling for all relevant determinants (including the unemployment rate), temporary workers in the Mediterranean countries have higher chances of obtaining a permanent job than would be expected on the basis of previous research, although they also display rather high transition rates into unemployment. Moreover, the Anglo-Saxon countries still perform best regarding transition rates into permanent jobs for men, but no longer for women. Nor do the Anglo-Saxon countries perform well with respect to preventing transitions into unemployment. Eventually, it should be noted that even though male temporary workers in the United Kingdom have the highest probability of moving into a permanent job, this will not help a great deal in reducing their poverty risk, as the United Kingdom is the only country in which a transition into permanent work does not significantly decrease poverty.

NOTES

1. For comparison, only 20 per cent of part-time workers enter their position involuntarily.
2. A 'poverty wage' is a wage that would set a worker below the poverty line if he would be living alone.
3. The modified OECD equivalence scale is the number of adult equivalents in the household, defined as 1 for the first adult, 0.5 for each additional adult and 0.3 for each child.
4. Other possible competing risks (that is, self-employment, inactivity) are treated as censored in this model.
5. Nevertheless, an additional control variable was built in using the monthly calendar information in such a way that an interruption of a temporary employment spell in between two survey years is captures in the analyses.
6. The individual random effect is assumed to be independently and identically distributed over individuals, following a normal distribution (Verbeek, 2004). The estimates obtained from this model indicate that the individual random effect is not statistically significant and should be left out of the model. In what follows, only results from the model without unobserved heterogeneity are presented.
7. In a substantial number of cases there was a problem of left truncation, meaning that the individual had already started the employment spell before the start of the observation period. For these cases, we do not have all values for the covariates. Yet, this problem is corrected for by including a variable representing the duration of the employment spell before the start of the measurements (Allison, 2003).
8. These are quite different from the estimates obtained by D'Addio and Rosholm (2005). This is probably because the duration variable in this model accounts for left-censoring, and is therefore measured on a different scale. It can also be due to other differences in the specification of the models.
9. This decrease is probably due to the fact that people with a higher risk of becoming unemployed are selected out of the risk set in the beginning, leaving people with a lower risk of unemployment in the risk set.

REFERENCES

Aassve, A., Billari, F.C. and Ongaro, F. (2001), 'The impact of income and employment status on leaving home: evidence from the Italian ECHP sample', *Labour: Review of Labour Economics and Industrial Relations,* **15** (3), 501–29.

Aassve, A., Billari, F.C., Mazzuco, S. and Ongaro, F. (2002), 'Leaving home: a comparative analysis of ECHP data', *Journal of European Social Policy,* **12** (4), 259–75.

Allison, P.D. (2003), *Survival analysis using the SAS system: a practical guide,* Cary, NC: SAS Institute.

Allison, P.D. (2005), *Fixed Effects Regression Methods for Longitudinal Data Using SAS,* Cary, NC: SAS Institute.

Atkinson, J., Rick, J., Morris, S. and Williams, M. (1996), *Temporary work and the labour market,* Brighton: The Institute of Employment Studies.

Avery, R., Goldscheider, F.K. and Speare, A. (1992), 'Feathered Nest/Gilded Cage: Parental Income and Leaving Home in the Transition to Adulthood', *Demography,* **7** (5), 375–88.

Barnes, M. (2002), 'Social exclusion and the life course', in Barnes, M., Heady, C., Middleton, S., Millar, J., Papadopoulos, F., Room, G. and Tsakloglou, P. (eds), *Poverty and Social Exclusion in Europe,* Cheltenham, Northampton, UK and Northampton, MA, USA: Edward Elgar, 1–23.

Berghman, J. and Fouarge, D. (1999), 'Social protection as a productive factor', *Journal of Social Policy,* **6** (1), 65–82.

Berghman, J. (1995), Social exclusion in Europe. Policy context and analytical framework, in Room, G. (ed.), *Beyond the threshold. The measurement and analysis of social exclusion*, Bristol: The Policy Press, 10–28.

Blanchard, O. and Landier, A. (2002), 'The perverse effects of partial labour market reform: fixed-term contracts in France', *The Economic Journal,* **112** (480), 214–44.

Blanpain, R. and Graham, R. (2004), *Temporary Agency Work and the Information Society,* The Hague: Kluwer Law International.

Blossfeld, H.-P. and Rohwer, G. (2002), *Techniques of Event History Modelling. New Approaches to Causal Analysis,* New Jersey, London: Lawrence Erlbaum Associates.

Bonoli, G. (1997), 'Classifying welfare states: a two dimension approach', *Journal of Social Policy,* **26** (3), 351–72.

Booth, A., Dolado, J.J. and Frank, J. (2002), 'Symposium on temporary work. Introduction', *The Economic Journal,* **112** (480), F181–F88.

Booth, A.L., Francesconi, M. and Frank, J. (2002), 'Temporary jobs: stepping stones or dead ends?', *The Economic Journal,* **112** (480), F189–F213.

Brewster, C., Mayne, L. and Tregaskis, O. (1997), 'Flexible Working in Europe', *Journal of World Business,* **32** (2), 133–51.

Casey, C. and Alach, P. (2004), 'Just a temp? Women, temporary employment and lifestyle', *Work, employment and society,* **18** (3), 459–80.

Contini, B., Pacelli, L. and Villosio, C. (2000), *Short Employment Spells in Italy, Germany and the UK: Testing the 'Port-of-Entry' Hypothesis,* Working Paper Series No. 14. Turin: LABORatorio.

Crouch, C. (1999), *Social change in Western Europe,* Oxford: Oxford University Press.

D'Addio, C. A. and Rosholm, M. (2005), Exits from temporary jobs in Europe: A competing risks analysis, *Labour Economics,* **12**, 449–468.

De Gier, E. and Van den Berg, A. (2005), *Making transitions pay! Towards a European employment insurance strategy (EEIS). A policy analysis based on the EU-project Managing Social Risks through Transitional Labour Markets (TLM.NET)*, Amsterdam: SISWO.

Debels, A. (2004), 'Temporary jobs: segmented security through the labour and welfare system', Paper presented at TLM.Net Conference 'Quality in Labour Market Transitions: A European Challenge', Amsterdam: Royal Netherlands Academy of Arts and Sciences, 25–26 November.

Doeringer, P. and Piore, M. (1971), *Internal Labor Markets and Manpower Analysis,* Lexington: Lexington Books.

Duncan, G.J., Gustafsson, B., Hauser, R., Schmauss, G., Messinger, H., Muffels, R., Nolan, B. and Ray, J.-C. (1993), 'Poverty Dynamics in eight countries', *Journal of Population Economics,* **6**, 215–34.

Esping-Andersen, G. (1990), *The three world of welfare capitalism,* Cambridge: Polity Press.

European Commission (1984), *Council Decision of December* 19, *1984,* Brussels: European Commission.

European Commission (2002), *Employment in Europe 2002. Recent trends and prospects,* Luxembourg: Office for Official Publications of the European Communities.

European Commission (2004), *Employment in Europe 2004,* Luxembourg: Office for Official Publications of the European Communities.

Ferrera, M. (1996), 'The "Southern Model" of welfare in social Europe', *Journal of European Social Policy,* **6** (1), 14–37.

Gustafsson, S., Kenjoh, E. and Wetzels, C. (2003), 'Employment Choices and Pay Differences between Nonstandard and Standard Work in Britain, Germany, the Netherlands, and Sweden', in Houseman, S. and Osawa, M. (eds), *Nonstandard Work in Developed Economies,* Kalamazoo, Michigan, WE: Upjohn Institute for Employment Research, 215–66.

Houseman, S. (2001), 'Why employers use flexible staffing arrangements: evidence from an establishment survey', *Industrial and Labor Relations Review,* **55** (1), 149–70.

Kalleberg, A.L., Reskin, B.F. and Hudson, K. (2000), 'Bad Jobs in America: Standard and Nonstandard Employment Relations and Job Quality in the United States', *American Sociological Review,* **65** (2), 256–78.

Korpi, T. and Levin, H. (2001), 'Precarious Footing: Temporary Employment as a Stepping Stone out of Unemployment in Sweden', *Work, Employment and Society,* **15** (1), 127–48.

Lindbeck, A. and Snower, D.J. (1988), *The Insider-Outsider Theory of Employment and Unemployment,* London: Massachusetts Institute of Technology.

Mertens, A. and McGinnity, F. (2004), 'Wages and wage growth of fixed-term workers in East and West Germany', *Applied Economics Quarterly,* **50** (2), 139–63.

Muffels, R.J.A. and Fouarge, D. (2002a), 'Working Profiles and Employment Regimes in Europe', *Schmoller's Jahrbuch, Journal of Applied Social Sciences Studies,* **122** (1), 85–110.

Muffels, R.J.A. and Fouarge, D. (2002b), 'Employment Regimes and Labour Market Attachment: Evidence from the ECHP', in Muffels, R.J.A., Tsakloglou, P. and Mayes, D.G. (eds), *Social Exclusion in European Welfare States,* Cheltenham, UK and Northampton, MA, USA: Edward Elgar, 51–77.

Muffels, R.J.A. and Luijkx, R. (2006), 'Globalization and male job mobility in European welfare states', in Blossfeld, H-P, Mills, M. and Bernardi, F. (eds), *Globalization, uncertainty and men's careers,* Cheltenham, UK and Northampton, MA, USA: Edward Elgar, 38–72.

OECD (2002), *Employment Outlook 2002 – Surveying the jobs horizon,* Paris: OECD.

Oxley, H., Dang, T.-T. and Antolín, P. (2000), 'Poverty Dynamics in Six OECD Countries', *OECD Economic Studies,* **30** (1), 7–52.

Peña-Casas, R. and Latta, M. (2004), *Working poor in the European Union,* Luxembourg: Office for the Official Publications of the European Communities.

Peracchi, F. (2002), The European Community Household Panel: A review', *Empirical Economics,* **27**, 63–90.

Piore, M.J. (1975), 'Notes for a Theory of Labor Market Stratification', in Edwards, R.C., Reich, M. and Gordon, M. (eds), *Labor Market Segmentation,* Lexington: D.C. Heath and Company, 37–68.

Remery, C., Van Doorne-Huiskes, A. and Schippers, J. (2002), 'Labour market flexibility in the Netherlands: looking for winners and losers', *Work, employment and society,* **16** (3), 477–95.

Scherer, S. (2004), 'Stepping-stones or traps? The consequences of labour market entry positions on future careers in West Germany, Great Britain and Italy', *Work, Employment and Society,* **18** (2), 369–94.

Schmid, G. (1998), *Transitional Labour Markets: A New European Employment Strategy,* Berlin: Wissenschaftszentrum Berlin für Sozialforschung.

Sels, L., Van der Steene, T., Van Hootegem, G., De Witte, H. en Forrier, A. (2002), *Flexibel, zeker? Bevindingen van twee jaar flexibiliteitsonderzoek,* Leuven: KU-Leuven-Steunpunt Werkgelegenheid, Arbeid en Vorming.

Smith, S. (2003), *Labour Economics. Second Edition,* London and New York: Routledge.

Storrie, D. (2002), *Temporary Agency Work in the European Union,* Luxembourg: Office for Official Publication of the European Communities.

Strengmann-Kuhn, W. (2002), *Working Poor In Europe: a partial basis income for workers?* 9th BIEN International congress: Income Security as a Right, Geneva, International Labour Office, September 12–14.

Verbeek, M. (2004), *A guide to modern econometrics,* Chichester: John Wiley and Sons, Ltd.

Yamaguchi, K. (1991), *Event History Analysis,* London, New Delhi: Sage Publications.

Zeger, S.L., Liang, K.-L. and Albert, P.S. (1988), 'Models for Longitudinal Data: A Generalized Estimating Equation Approach', *Biometrics,* **44** (4), 1049–60.

Zijl, M. and Budil-Nadvorníková, H. (2001), *Atypical labour. Flexible labour from the social and employers' point of view,* Amsterdam: Randstad Holding.

4. Dreaming of a Permanent Job: the Transitions of Temporary Workers in Italy and Spain

Virginia Hernanz, Federica Origo, Manuela Samek Lodovici and Luis Toharia

4.1 INTRODUCTION

Recent decades have witnessed a significant increase in the flexibility of most European labour markets. In this context, external flexibility has mainly been exercised through the use of temporary or fixed-term[1] employment contracts (OECD, 1999). In 2003, almost 13 per cent of all employees in the EU was employed in flexible contracts, ranging from 6 per cent in the UK to more than 30 per cent in Spain, with the figure for Italy being just below 10 per cent (European Commission, 2004).

Public support for temporary employment schemes has been driven by their potential for increasing employability and lowering the risk of long-term unemployment. Temporary work should in fact help the unemployed to regain employment and preserve or improve their human capital through work experience, thus reducing the number and duration of unemployment spells that individuals experience while enhancing their probability of finding better (permanent) jobs. Empirical evidence also seems to suggest that employers may use temporary contracts as a way to select and screen future permanent employees (Storrie, 2002; Houseman and Osawa, 2003).

However, it has been argued that the positive effects of temporary employment systems may be offset by costs related to the poor quality of temporary jobs and the limited career opportunities of temporary workers. As far as temporary jobs are characterised by lower wages and impaired working conditions, they signal the consequences of dual labour markets arising from the expansion of temporary work (Lindbeck and Snower, 1991; Saint-Paul, 1996).[2] In terms of labour market and social policy, however, the relevant issue is whether workers with a temporary status are at risk of becoming 'trapped' in that situation or whether they are able to make a transition towards a better, more stable, position. The risk of getting trapped in a temporary status and hence in an impaired economic position over a longer period of time is the kind of risk that the transitional labour markets literature emphasises. Our chapter is entirely devoted to the analysis of that risk.

Hence, the aim of this chapter is fold: first, to shed further light on the transitions of temporary workers into permanent jobs in Italy and Spain, paying specific attention to the transitions of so-called 'involuntary temporary workers' (that is, those working on temporary contracts because they could not find any permanent work) and, secondly, comparing their performance with both, other temporary employees and the unemployed.

The incidence of involuntary temporary employment is extremely high in both Italy and Spain (respectively, 41 per cent and 70 per cent of the total number of temporary workers aged 15–64, in contrast to the 2002 EU average of 34 per cent), despite the different incidence of overall temporary work. This should not come as a surprise, given the costs usually associated with temporary work.

In the European context, both Italy and Spain are thought to have tight labour market regulations, as defined by various indicators of direct firing costs, procedural restrictions to workforce adjustment, and other employment protection features (Grubb and Wells, 1993; OECD, 1999, 2004). They also share the 'Mediterranean' welfare and household model, typified by extended family networks and low female participation rates, as well as significant regional differences between a more developed North and comparatively underdeveloped South. Both countries have also recently undergone de-regulation processes, albeit to different degrees and on different timetables, with a stronger emphasis on the use of fixed-term contracts in Spain, especially in the 1980s, than in Italy. These went on, regardless of the fact that in both countries, the pressing force underlying these changes has been unemployment.

Italy and Spain are characterised by quite similar labour market indicators, such as relatively low participation and employment rates as well as fairly high unemployment rates, especially among women and the young (see Table 4.A.1 in Annex 4.1). Despite the significant improvements that have occurred in both countries' labour markets during especially the latter half of the 1990s, still in 2003 both lagged behind the EU average in terms of standard labour market indicators. However, they differ in regards to the incidence of temporary employment, with Spain ranking first among the EU countries and Italy ranking below the EU average.

Due to the institutional similarities between Italy and Spain, in conjunction with their different policies regarding temporary employment, the two countries are interesting and appropriate cases for studying the transitions of temporary workers into permanent jobs.

This chapter is structured as follows. Section 4.2 highlights the main institutional features of temporary employment regulation in Italy and Spain. Section 4.3 discusses temporary work and the transitions of temporary workers in conjunction with the ongoing 'flexicurity' debate in the European Union, which stems partly from the 'transitional labour market' literature. Section 4.4 presents the empirical model that framed the research and also addresses some related methodological issues. The data used in the empirical analysis are outlined in Section 4.5, where specific attention is paid to the comparability of definitions used in the existing literature. The main results of the study are discussed in Section 4.6 and, finally, in the last section some concluding remarks and relevant policy implications are formulated.

4.2 THE INSTITUTIONAL SETTING

Cross-country analyses usually rank both Italy and Spain among the most regulated labour markets in the world, especially in terms of hiring and firing and rules and regulations with respect to atypical contracts (Grubb and Wells, 1993; OECD, 1999). However, despite the existence of rather strict regulations, the most recent OECD data (OECD, 2004), suggest a substantial decrease in the employment protection legislation (EPL) index for Italy. Although no concurrent shift has occurred in its rating, similar changes have also taken place in Spain. This section will first present the institutional settings of Italy and Spain separately and will then turn to a comparison between the two.

Italy
In Italy, dismissals of individual workers employed with standard contracts (that is, full-time, open-ended contracts) are regulated by the 1970 Statuto dei lavoratori, a law which is extremely restrictive in the case of individual dismissals in medium-large establishments (with more than fifteen employees), because the grounds for fair dismissals are extremely limited, the duration of lawsuit is very long and the probability of having the worker reinstated after a court trial for dismissals is high. In addition, ordinary unemployment benefits for dismissed workers are low and of short duration, which is a further deterrent for dismissals. Less restrictive rules and more generous benefits (such as the Cassa Integrazione Guadagni – CIG – and mobility benefits) have been available since 1991 for collective dismissals (which may be either of a temporary or a permanent nature) due to firms' restructuring or crisis.

Regulation of the labour market has undergone a gradual transformation since the mid 1990s through a series of incremental interventions and decrees. One of the most important changes to emerge in recent years has been the diversification and multiplication of employment contracts, leading to an expansion of temporary employment (including seasonal employment contracts, temporary agency work, youth work-training and apprenticeship contracts) up to 9.8 per cent of total employment. The number of 'independent contractors' (workers midway between dependent and independent work, which combine a high flexibility together with low labour costs) has also been rapidly increasing since the late 1990s, reaching 3.3 per cent of total employment in 2003 (Semenza, 2000; CNEL, 2004). While for dependent temporary workers, regulation is gradually shifting towards greater flexibility in their use, the opposite is true for independent contractors, with recent regulation offering some welfare and employment protection benefits.

As for fixed-term contracts, their use has traditionally been considered a temporary solution appropriate for meeting specific production needs, rather than a tool for reducing unemployment more generally (Samek-Lodovici, 2000). Law 230/1962 regulated fixed-term employment until the introduction of a new legislative decree in the autumn of 2001 (legislative decree 368/2001, which applied the 1999 EU Directive on fixed-term work) and the more recent Law 30/2003 (the so called 'legge Biagi'). Under the former legislation, fixed-term contracts were allowed only in particular cases specifically listed in the law and, since 1987, also in collective agreements. The new legislation greatly reduces the constraints formerly imposed on fixed-term employment, introduces new forms of temporary contracts (such as on-call jobs, job sharing, insertion contracts and staff leasing) and makes its use more flexible for firms. It does not put forward a specific list of cases for which the contract may be used and instead states more generally that workers may be hired on a fixed-term basis 'for technical, productive and organisational reasons or for the substitution of absent personnel'. No maximum duration is envisaged but, in the case of extension, the total duration cannot exceed a period of three years.

Between 1984 and 2003, a specific fixed-term contract that emphasised work-training (known as the 'Contratto di formazione e lavoro', or CFL) was available to young people in Italy. Use of the contract was encouraged through reductions in mandatory social security contributions and the simplification of certain hiring procedures. The contract (and its lower labour cost) was designed to promote on-the-job training for young people, thus enhancing their chances of gaining employment. In practice, however, the training provided to workers was usually poor and most firms used the contract mainly as a means of reducing labour costs, which created negative substitution effects on the hiring of both the young and the low-skilled adult worker (Adam and Canziani, 1998).

Use of CFL contracts started declining in the second half of the 1990s (essentially since the issue of law 196/97), as they were progressively replaced by more convenient fixed-term contracts, such as apprenticeships. In 2003, to avoid sanctions imposed by the European Commission, the CFL contract was transformed by the Biagi law into 'insertion contracts', access to which is limited to specific disadvantaged groups.

Temporary agency work in Italy only became formally allowed in 1997 by law 196/97 (the so-called 'Treu Package', after the name of the Labour Ministry that proposed it). In the case of temporary agency work, it is crucial to distinguish between contracts linking an agency to a user firm (that is, contracts for the provision of temporary work, known as 'contratto di fornitura di prestazioni di lavoro temporaneo') and actual temporary work contracts (contratto per prestazioni di lavoro temporaneo), which bind the agency and the worker. The latter may be construed either as a permanent employment contract or as a fixed-term contract. In the first case, workers remain at the disposal of the agency during periods when they are not assigned to specific tasks or 'missions'. In the second case, the employment contract has the same duration as the 'mission' in the contract for the provision of temporary work. So far, the great majority of temporary agency workers have been hired on fixed-term contracts. According to Italian legislation, temporary agency work is allowed in the cases covered by collective bargaining, the temporary use of skills not provided in ordinary production settings, and the replacement of absent workers. Moreover, in each firm utilising temporary agency workers, their number cannot exceed the percentage of permanent employees stipulated in collective agreements.

Regardless of whether one is engaged in fixed-term employment or temporary work, the principle of equal treatment applies.[3] Fixed-term workers have the right to the same working and pay conditions as standard employees. This means that wage levels for temporary workers must at least be the same as those granted to permanent employees with the same job and level of qualifications. Similarly, non-permanent employees have the right to the same amount of holidays as permanent workers proportional to the time they have worked in the firm. Furthermore, fixed-term workers may benefit from sick leave periods (or other kinds of leave, for instance, maternity leave) within the time limit defined by the duration of their employment contract. Finally, both fixed-term employees and temporary workers are entitled to training designed to prevent on-the-job injuries.

Despite the equal treatment promised by Italian employment legislation, in practice, non-permanent employees may be discriminated against by receiving lower wages or less work-related benefits (such as holiday pay or sick pay) compared to 'permanent' employees. Inferior working conditions are more likely when temporary work is of short duration and/or on a part-time basis. In addition, studies on employment transitions frequently underscore a relation between temporary employment and unemployment, as longer periods of non-employment negatively influence employees' skills, thus reducing the probability of subsequent re-employment (Booth et al., 2002).

Spain[4]

Under Spain's fundamental labour law – the 1980 Workers' Statute (LET or Ley del Estatuto de los Trabajadores) – it is regulated that open-ended contracts are the standard labour contract. Under this law, a worker with an open-ended contract who is dismissed can sue the firm for unfair dismissal followed by a mediation process, where the parties bargain about the amount of severance payment (which implies the firm's recognition that the dismissal was unfair), and, if this turns out unsuccessful (which happened in 30 per cent of the cases only), the case then goes to court, where a final sentence, which might even lead to the reinstatement of workers (although in reality only in very exceptional cases where fundamental rights are violated), is dictated. The fact that only unfairly dismissed workers are eligible for unemployment benefits implies that virtually all dismissals are potentially to be challenged by the workers. This is an extremely complicated setup, the details of which can only be understood from a game-theoretic approach (see Malo, 1998).

Two main exceptions are established to this general rule. First, fixed-term contracts, exempt from the standard procedures for dismissals, are permitted in a number of cases where the nature of the task to be undertaken is temporary (these are known in Spain as 'ordinary' temporary contracts). Secondly, the government has been given the right to create other fixed-term contracts although only as a tool of labour market policy to fight unemployment.

In 1984, a significant change to the law was introduced which, although it did not alter the procedures for permanent workers, did affect the significance of the law for employers as a whole. Essentially, the LET was reformed in order to facilitate the hiring of fixed-term workers, by removing most of the constraints existing before. In addition to various specific contracts (such as training and practice contracts for young people or fixed-term contracts for launching 'new activities'), the key component of the reform was the so-called 'employment-promotion fixed-term contract', which could be used to perform any task, temporary or not. This type of contract could last for a minimum of 6 months and a maximum of 3 years, and could be renewed by 6-month periods up to the maximum of 3 years. Upon expiry, the firm had to disburse severance pay of 12 days' wages per year of seniority, but the worker could not sue the employer. Once the maximum period has been reached, the worker had to be given a permanent contract, and if not the firm could not hire another worker for the same job. Unfortunately, it was obviously very difficult to monitor fulfilment of this requirement; jobs could easily be re-defined in order to circumvent the sanction. An additional feature of this type of contract was that it entitled the beholders to unemployment compensation (at a rate of a 3 months lasting benefit for each 6 months of fulfilling the contract). The enactment of the contract constituted a deep change to Spanish Labour Law, because it allowed to depart from the so-called 'causality principle' (which established that only fixed-term contracts could be used for creating temporary work within the firm). Therefore, the firm could minimise costs by hiring successive temporary workers instead of hiring full-time employees.

From the viewpoint of labour market flexibility the second half of the 1980s, may be termed the 'era of temporary contracts'. Spanish society – that is not only employers and employees, but also society at large – came to realise that traditional permanent labour contracts are becoming less important, and that fixed-term contracts even though they provide employment, are much more 'precarious', that is, they cannot guarantee a minimum standard of living. More importantly, the appearance of temporary contracts on a sizeable scale did not prevent firms from firing permanent workers. In fact, the number of firings remained more or less constant over this period (Malo and Toharia, 1994). This was probably due to the fact that most dismissals involved older workers (and firms), of which many were poorly fit for the ongoing modernisation of the Spanish economy and hence, firms had an interest to replace them with more productive, younger workers.

This situation remained unchanged until 1992, when the use of the employment-promotion fixed-term contract was restricted, and more significantly in 1994, when an extensive labour reform law was passed. Basically, this was an attempt to restore the 'causality principle' in the Spanish Labour Law. In addition, and presumably as a quid pro quo, procedures for firing were restructured in an attempt to reduce the costs associated with them. Economic reasons were more clearly included among the fair grounds for dismissals. In addition, the procedures involved in individual dismissals were altered at various points in an effort to reduce the uncertainty surrounding them. As for collective dismissals, in principle an attempt was made to facilitate their use by reducing the time allowed for the labour market authority to respond to the proposal. However, other more cumbersome requirements (such as the presentation of a 'social plan' for firms larger than 50 employees) were also introduced for firms. A complementary law legalised temporary work agencies, although in a very restrictive way.

New regulations on firing and hiring costs resulted from the 1997 agreement between the social partners. Given the persistent duality that remained between temporary and permanent workers despite the 1994 reforms, the new agreement showed once again a trade-off between more flexibility for permanent and less flexibility for temporary workers. The result was the creation of a new type of permanent contract, with lower severance payments in cases of unfair dismissal, and restricted to workers under 30 or over 45 years, the long-term unemployed, and the disabled. The reform also involved the imposition of stricter conditions on the use of temporary contracts, together with the elimination of employment-promotion fixed-term contracts. The government added various tax incentives to this arrangement by reducing the mandatory employers' social security contributions.

Interestingly, the response of firms to these policies to close the door opened for flexible labour by the 1984 reform was to resort to the 'ordinary' causal temporary contracts, characterised by a much shorter duration and less regulation than the defunct employment-promotion fixed-term contract. As a result, further attempts to restricting the use of ordinary temporary contracts were made. At the same time, further reductions of the costs involved in firing permanent workers were quietly introduced in 2002.[5] Unfortunately, none of these changes has significantly reduced the number of temporary contracts in Spain, nor have they radically reduced the total proportion of employees working under such contracts. Thus, overall, the Spanish labour market over the past ten years seems characterised by the consistent failure of policies to attain what they were designed and implemented for, that is, to minimise the use of fixed-term and temporary employment contracts. Although open-ended contracts have become ever since of a less and less permanent nature, this has not worked as an incentive to shift away from temporary into 'permanent' contracts.

Comparative comments

The history of temporary work in the two countries as described here points towards similar situations in terms of the actual flexibility granted to temporary or fixed-term employment in both countries. In Spain, the legal regulation of fixed-term work has followed a two-way trip over the last twenty years: it was highly deregulated in the early 1980s and remained so for almost a decade, after which a process began of re-regulation aimed at returning to the initial situation. This de-regulation was unique in Western Europe and has to be understood with a view to the extremely high unemployment rate – over 20 per cent – that the Spanish economy attained as of 1984 after ten years of suffering from a severe economic crisis. During this two-way trip process, the costs of firing permanent employees have tended to decrease, both directly and indirectly (recall note 5). While fixed-term work has formally become subject to tighter regulations, in practice it remained as flexible and widely used as ever. In Italy, the process of deregulation has been much more recent and has not been so much focused on the fringe of the labour market as in Spain. However, the use of fixed-term employment has remained significant. This has led, like in Spain, to a substantial growth in the number of temporary workers in the labour market. In Italy, however, the tendency to rely on temporary workers has been much milder than in Spain. In summary, Italy and Spain share the historical origin of being countries with rigid labour markets based on high firing costs and also substantial mobility, though being also dissimilar in terms of the timing and consequences of policies especially with a view to the expansion of dual labour markets (in terms of contract stability).

4.3. FLEXICURITY: WHY CAN FIXED-TERM EMPLOYMENT BE DESIRABLE?

The need to promote the right balance between flexibility and security has become one of the focal points of the European Employment Strategy. For instance, guideline 3 of the 2003 Employment Guidelines (2003/578/EC) aims to promote contractual and working arrangements that support the competitiveness of firms without disregarding the security of employees.

In principle, fixed-term workers have the same rights with regard to working and pay conditions as standard employees (EU Directive on temporary work, 1999). However, suggestions that the flexibility of the labour market need to be increased have blurred the flexibility debate. An increase in flexibility brings about new working patterns, characterised by increased uncertainty for the individual due to more people being confronted with the need to combine spells of employment, unemployment, and non-employment. Wilthagen and Rogowski (2002) stress that the success of flexible arrangements is dependent on how different employment regimes operate in trying to achieve a high level of labour market flexibility, while simultaneously guaranteeing adequate levels of work ('employability') and income security ('social protection'). Following these criteria, they distinguish four employment regimes according to how they combine employment protection regulations and work/income security arrangements. Southern European countries such as Italy and Spain are part of the traditionalist regime that seems to deliver the worst combination as regards 'flexicurity'.[6]

A wide range of studies[7] have focused on transitions from (un)employment into temporary jobs and from temporary jobs into permanent employment. Fixed-term workers are more likely to suffer spells of unemployment (Booth et al., 2002) and periods of inactivity (Gagliarducci, 2004). Additionally, a temporary job obtained after a period of unemployment is more likely to be a dead-end than a stepping-stone towards a more stable position in the labour market (*Employment in Europe*, 2004).[8] Furthermore, the probability of moving into a permanent contract decreases with the length of the job interruption.

Temporary employees are more likely to work in low paid and more high-risk occupations (Hernanz and Toharia, 2006)[9] and to be employed in firms providing training. However, once in these firms, temporary employees have a lower probability to participate in training activities than full-time workers (Albert et al., 2005). Lastly, temporary contracts seem to contribute to delayed family formation and reduced fertility rates (Cebrián et al., 2003).

Therefore, it appears that while temporary employment may be preferred to unemployment (as long as there are no incentives to remain unemployed), for many people it remains a less favourable situation compared to being employed in an open-ended, permanent contract.

Yet, as already mentioned, the micro data suggest that not all temporary workers occupy such contracts involuntary. Transitions to temporary work if they do not disrupt long-term careers have, especially when they are freely chosen by those undertaking them, positive effects on the flexibility of firms without reducing the economic security for workers. For some people, holding a temporary job may exert positive effects as being part of a long-term strategy of training designed to improve individual mobility. The important issue is then whether voluntary temporary workers show a higher probability of becoming integrated into the core of the labour market, thus acting as a sort of catalyst for the emergence of a 'transitional labour market' (TLM), in which employment and economic rewards are distributed across the life course. Comparisons between voluntary and involuntary temporary workers in terms of their transitions to other labour market states is highly relevant to the TLM debate, especially in Southern countries, where TLMs are much less likely to have been developed, at least thus far.

4.4 THE EMPIRICAL MODEL

The aim of this study's empirical analysis was to examine the probability of transition to a permanent employment position depending on, other things being equal, whether an individual was a temporary employee or unemployed at the beginning of the time period being considered.

We can express the so-called 'transition equation' as follows:

$$Y_{it} = \beta x_{it} + \partial TEMP_{it-1} + \varepsilon_{it} \tag{4.1}$$

where Y_{it} is a binary variable, which is equal to 1 if the individual holds a permanent job at time t (0 otherwise), TEMP captures the condition in the labour market at $t-1$ (that is, either temporary worker, $TEMP_{it-1} = 1$, or unemployed, $TEMP_{it-1} = 0$) and X_{it} includes a set of other conditioning variables. We assume that the error term (ε_{it}) follows the usual standard normal distribution.

Note that the model proposed resembles a (quasi-)experimental or evaluation design in which the 'treatment' group is represented by the temporary workers, while the 'control' group is represented by the unemployed. If indeed temporary employment would increase the employability of the individual worker, it might be interesting to evaluate whether temporary work experience can increase the (permanent) employment opportunities of the unemployed.[10] The model may be estimated using a traditional binary choice or dependent variable model (such as in the case of a probit or a logit model). This presumes that the initial state (that is, being either temporary employed or unemployed at $t-1$) is exogenous and that the actual transition can be entirely explained by the observed explanatory variables.

If the initial state is not exogenous, the use of a simple probit estimator will lead to biased estimates of the 'true' effect of the initial state on subsequent transition probabilities. In other words, if the initial state is affected by unobserved heterogeneity that is also correlated with the probability of the transition into permanent employment, the initial state is endogenous with respect to the current employment state (that is, $TEMP_{t-1}$ is correlated with ε_{it} in equation 4.1).[11] This problem may arise when some unobservable factors (such as individual ability, preferences, or motivation) influence both the probability of accepting a temporary job (rather than remaining unemployed) and subsequent performance in the labour market (in our case, the probability of getting a permanent job).

The existence of endogenous (self) selection into specific labour market states/programs is a frequent source of bias in the evaluation literature dealing with non-experimental designs (Heckman et al., 1999).

One way to take the problem of endogenous selectivity into account is to estimate jointly the probability of being in a certain initial state and the probability of the transition into permanent employment (conditional on the initial state), assuming a certain correlation between the unobservable elements in the equations.[12] In our case, we then estimate a bivariate probit model as follows:

$$\begin{cases} \text{TEMP}_{it-1} = \gamma' Z_{it-1} + v_{it-1} \\ Y_{it} = \beta' X_{it-1} + \delta \text{TEMP}_{it-1} + \varepsilon_{it} \\ (v, \varepsilon) \sim \Phi_2(0, 1, \rho) \end{cases} \qquad (4.2)$$

where v and ε are jointly distributed as a bivariate standard normal distribution, with $E(v) = E(\varepsilon) = 0$ and $Var(v) = Var(\varepsilon) = 1$. It follows that the correlation term ρ equals also the covariance between v and ε.[13]

In order to identify the model in equation 4.2, one may rely on its functional form, provided that it is non-linear. Alternatively, it is necessary to identify some exclusion restrictions affecting the initial state (for example, entering the Z vector), without affecting the transition probabilities (once conditioned on the initial state). Information prior to labour market entry (such as parental background) may be candidate instruments (Heckman, 1981).

In this case, finding valid instruments might be quite difficult, since direct information on parental background or complete information on past work and unemployment experience for each individual is not available. However, given the relatively high mobility of the temporary employed (at least with respect to the mobility into other working states), the local supply of temporary jobs by skill level at the beginning of the period is likely to influence the initial probability of being enrolled in a temporary contract (rather than being unemployed). However it should not influence subsequent individual transitions to permanent employment per se, provided that local labour market conditions (through regional unemployment rates) are controlled for. Both the lagged incidence of temporary employment by region and skill level (the latter measured by education level) and the lagged change (the change in the incidence of temporary employment by region and skill level from period $t-2$ and $t-1$) were used as instruments. In Section 4.6 the estimates for the transition models under the assumptions of both exogenous and endogenous sample selection will be presented.

4.5 DATA AND DEFINITIONS

The empirical analysis presented here is based on longitudinal, individual data from the Italian and Spanish Labour Force Surveys (LFS). The most recent waves were used, which cover the period 1999–2002 for Italy and the period 2000–2003 for Spain. Italian data refers to the second quarter of each year, while Spanish data refers to all the quarters.

The LFS is the most comprehensive survey on the labour market and its harmonised structure allows reliable comparisons between EU countries. The unit of analysis is the household in Italy and the dwelling in Spain. More than

75,000 households and 65,000 dwellings respectively, are surveyed in each quarter in each country. The coverage rate of the survey is therefore around 0.36 per cent in Italy and 0.5 per cent in Spain. Table 4.A.2 in Annex 4.1 summarises the main features of the survey in the two countries.

The panel structure is different in the two countries. In Italy, the households rotate according to a 2–2–2-rotation plan, that is, the households are interviewed during two consecutive quarters and are interviewed twice more (in the corresponding two quarters of the following year) after a two-quarter interval. Spanish dwellings remain in the sample for six consecutive quarters. Both surveys allow for the analysis of both quarterly and yearly transitions, but only the latter information has been released in Italy. Consequently, the following results are only based on the year-to-year transitions in both countries.

Definitions
The following empirical analysis is focused on unemployed and temporary employees. The first are identified on the basis of the standard ILO definition,[14] while temporary employees are defined as dependent workers whose contract states a fixed end (determined by objective conditions such as a specific date, the completion of a task, or the return of another employee who has been temporarily replaced). Temporary employment, as defined in the LFS, includes fixed-term contracts, temporary-help workers, seasonal employment and specific training contracts (as long as objective criteria for the end of the contract are clearly stated).[15]

The LFS survey also provides information on the main reason why people enter into a temporary contract. In particular, it pinpoints whether individuals cannot find a permanent job or simply do not want a permanent job. Following international classifications, the first group is categorised as involuntary temporary workers, while all other temporary workers are classified in a residual category, named 'other temporary employees'.[16] According to this definition, around 41 per cent of temporary workers in Italy is involuntarily in a temporary job, compared to 75–78 per cent of Spanish workers.

4.6 MAIN RESULTS

Descriptive statistics
Figure 4.1 depicts the evolution of the incidence of temporary employment in Italy and Spain during the last decade. Temporary employment has been increasing progressively in Italy, going from 6 per cent of total dependent employment in 1993 to around 10 per cent in 2003. This growth has been registered for both males and females, though more pronounced for the latter

group. Despite this trend, the proportion of temporary employment in Italy is still much lower than in Spain, where it is around 30 per cent in 2003.

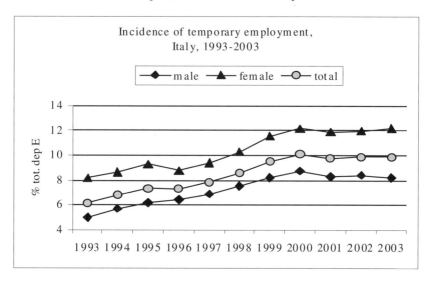

Figure 4.1 The evolution of the incidence of temporary employment in Italy and Spain

Spanish temporary employment reached its peak in 1995, (around 35 per cent) and then started to decline. Female temporary employment has moved down from almost 40 per cent in the mid-90s to 35 per cent in 1998, on which level it remained in the subsequent years. Male temporary employment has shown a steadier decline, from almost 35 per cent in 1995 to less than 30 per cent in 2003. In both countries, the incidence of involuntary temporary employment (that is, the frequency of people working on temporary contracts, because they could not find a permanent job) has been decreasing in the long term, although at a different pace.

In Italy, the share of involuntary workers among temporary employees went down from 52 per cent in 1993–94 to 40 per cent in 1999. It increased to 45 per cent in 2001 and then returned to 40 per cent in 2003. In Italy the long-term decline of the incidence of involuntary temporary employment was mainly due to an overall increase in temporary employment (denominator effect), since for the period under consideration, the number of temporary employees increased steadily (from 464,000 in 1993 to 655,000 workers in 2003). As for total temporary employment, the share of involuntary workers in Spain is much higher than in Italy. For example, nine out of ten workers were involuntarily on temporary contracts in the period from 1993–98. This share has been decreasing since then, reaching its minimum in 2003. Nonetheless, at the end of the period, 3 out of 4 Spanish temporary workers held fixed-term contracts because they could not find a permanent job. Relevant differences by gender did not emerge in either country.[17]

Table 4.1 reports the yearly gross probabilities of unemployed and temporary employees gaining a permanent position during the observation period. Overall, temporary workers are more likely to obtain a permanent job than the unemployed in both Italy and Spain, but the differences in the transition probabilities are much higher in Italy. Almost 42 per cent of the temporary employees in Italy are on permanent contracts one year later, in contrast to 12.7 per cent of the unemployed. In Spain, only 12.8 per cent of the temporary workers are subsequently permanently employed. However, the unemployed do show an even lower transition probability, around 9 per cent. Interestingly, the Spanish unemployed are actually more likely to get a temporary job than a permanent one: more than 39 per cent of the unemployed in Spain are in fact on temporary contracts one year later. On the contrary, in Italy the yearly transition probability from unemployment into a temporary job is much lower than in Spain (and lower than the transition probability from unemployment into a permanent job), around 8 per cent.

A full picture can be obtained by considering the transitions into inactivity (out of the labour force). Again, the differences between the unemployed and temporary workers are higher in Italy than in Spain, but in both countries the unemployed experience higher transitions into inactivity than temporary workers.

*Table 4.1 Yearly transition probabilities for the unemployed and temporary
employees over the period considered*

	Transition probabilities from the moment of observation to one year later — Situation at t (row percentages)				
	Permanent Employed	Temporary Employed	Unemployed	Out of the labour force	Total
Initial state at *t–1*:					
ITALY					
Unemployed					
Full observation period	12.7	7.7	51.4	28.2	100
1999	12.8	7.9	51.3	27.9	100
2000	12.8	7.4	50.4	29.3	100
2001	12.4	7.8	52.9	26.8	100
Temporary employees					
Full observation period	41.8	42.1	6.7	9.3	100
1999	44.1	39.0	7.6	9.2	100
2000	43.4	41.8	5.7	9.2	100
2001	37.3	45.8	6.8	9.6	100
SPAIN					
Unemployed					
Full observation period	9.0	39.2	31.1	20.8	100
2000	6.9	34.1	37.2	21.8	100
2001	9.0	39.0	31.5	20.6	100
2002	8.9	40.5	29.6	20.9	100
2003	11.4	42.7	26.2	19.8	100
Temporary employees					
Full observation period	12.8	51.6	19.7	15.9	100
2000	14.1	58.2	15.7	12.1	100
2001	12.9	52.2	19.6	15.3	100
2002	12.8	50.8	19.9	16.6	100
2003	11.4	45.4	23.7	19.4	100

Source: Labour Force Surveys for Italy, 1999–2002, and for Spain, 2000–2003.

Overall, unemployment seems more persistent in Italy than in Spain (more
than half of the initially unemployed remain jobless one year later in Italy,
which is 20 per cent higher than in Spain), but Spanish temporary employees
seem more likely to become unemployed and less likely to get a permanent
job than their Italian counterparts. Also, the role played in the labour market
by temporary work appears to be very different in both countries. In Italy,
getting a temporary job appears to be quite difficult but once it is achieved

the probability of staying in a permanent job is high. In Spain, however, there appears to be much more movement between unemployment and temporary work. A much lower proportion of temporary workers in Spain obtained a permanent job over our one-year observation window, but the likelihood of staying unemployed during the year is much lower.

Table 4.2 provides more detail by disaggregating the transitions into permanent jobs between involuntary and voluntary temporary workers. The main, striking, result is that in Italy involuntary temporary workers show a lower probability of moving into permanent jobs.

Table 4.2 Transition probabilities from unemployment and temporary employment into permanent employment by initial state, 1999–2002 (Italy) and 2000–2003 (Spain)

	Unemployed	Temporary workers		
		All	Involuntary	Others
Italy	12.7	41.8	38.5	44.4
Spain	9.0	12.8	12.8	12.8

Note: For further details see the full version of the table: <www.siswo.uva.nl/tlm/root_ files/WorkP05-20Dreaming.pdf>.

This result carries over the different breakdowns in Table 4.A.3, although the differences in transition rates between involuntary and other temporary workers are not particularly high.[18] In Spain, the difference between the two groups seems to be insignificant and therefore negligible.

Econometric estimates
Tables 4.3 to 4.5 report on the probit estimates of the models discussed in Section 4.4.[19] Estimates are obtained on the basis of different specifications and using different sets of control factors: personal characteristics (gender, age and education), family characteristics (size of the family and role of the individual within the family), local labour market conditions (regional unemployment rate and the incidence of temporary employment by region and education) and job search behaviour.[20]

Estimates in Tables 4.3 and 4.4 refer to both unemployed and temporary employees. Overall, these estimates show that temporary workers have a significantly higher probability to find a permanent job than the unemployed in both Italy and Spain, even after controlling for personal characteristics, family composition, labour market conditions and job search behaviour.

Nonetheless, the marginal effect of the initial state is much higher in Italy than in Spain; holding everything constant, the probability of getting a permanent job is 20–26 per cent for Italian temporary workers (with reference to the Italian unemployed), while it is only 2–4 per cent for Spanish temporary workers (reference category is the unemployed).

Table 4.3 Transition probabilities into permanent jobs for temporary workers compared to the unemployed (reference); 1999–2002 (Italy), 2000–2003 (Spain): probit estimates of marginal effects (ME)

	Marginal effects for temporary workers (reference: unemployed)							
	Model 1		Model 2		Model 3		Model 4	
	ME	z	ME	z	ME	z	ME	z
Italy	0.26	25.80	0.26	25.70	0.26	25.20	0.20	18.10
Spain	0.04	25.09	0.03	24.60	0.03	24.60	0.02	7.62

Notes: Model 1 controls for personal and regional labour market characteristics. Model 2 is the same as model 1, but age is yet defined in a continuous way instead of in age brackets. Model 3 is the same as model 2, but with inclusion of the family characteristics variables. Model 4 is the same as model 3, but with inclusion of job search behaviour variables. For further details, see the full version of the table: <www.siswo.uva.nl/tlm/root_files/WorkP05-20Dreaming.pdf>.

In both countries, no significant differences seem to emerge between involuntary and other temporary employees. Overall, transition probabilities in Italy are more responsive to both personal characteristics and local labour market conditions than in Spain. For example, being a woman in Italy clearly reduces the probability of obtaining a permanent job, while gender does not seem to be as relevant in Spain where, once controlling for search behaviour, women actually have a slightly higher probability than men to find a permanent job.

Overall, therefore, the results presented in Tables 4.1 and 4.2 are confirmed by the more accurate econometric estimates. When the appropriate controls are taken into consideration, the main trends observed earlier remain the same, that is the probability of achieving a permanent job is higher for temporary workers than for the unemployed. This seems true in both countries; however, the marginal differences between the two groups are much higher in Italy than in Spain. In addition, no significant differences are observed in the transition to permanent jobs in either of both countries between involuntary and other temporary workers. When all the controls are included, Italian involuntary temporary workers have a 23 per cent higher probability of acquiring a permanent job compared to the unemployed; the corresponding figure for other temporary workers is only slightly lower, at 22 per cent. In Spain, the figures are 2.4 per cent for involuntary temporary workers and only 2.5 per cent for other temporary workers.

Table 4.5 adds a further element to the comparison between involuntary and other temporary workers, by focusing on the job characteristics. Estimates on this restricted sample confirm the results reported in Table 4.4

and show that, ceteris paribus, involuntary temporary workers seem not to differ significantly from other temporary workers in terms of the transition probability into a permanent job.

Table 4.4 Transition probabilities into permanent employment for the unemployed, the involuntary and other temporary employed, for Italy (1999–2002) and Spain (2000–2003). Probit estimates of marginal effects (ME), (reference category is the unemployed)

	Italy		Spain	
	ME	z	ME	z
Controls for:				
a) personal and labour market characteristics				
- involuntary temporary	0.295	20.5	0.036	23.79
- other temporary	0.299	27.7	0.039	16.61
b) as a) with family characteristics				
- involuntary temporary	0.291	19.7	0.023	7.61
- other temporary	0.297	26.8	0.024	6.48
c) as b), with searching behaviour				
- involuntary temporary	0.229	16.6	0.024	7.89
- other temporary	0.221	17.0	0.025	6.73

Note: For further details, see full version of the table: <*www.siswo.uva.nl/tlm/root_files/WorkP05-20Dreaming.pdf*>.

Table 4.5 Transition probabilities into permanent employment for involuntary temporary and other temporary employees for Italy (1999–2002) and Spain (2000–2003). Probit estimates of marginal effects (ME), (reference category is the unemployed)

	Involuntary temporary workers (ref: other temporary)					
	Model 1		Model 2		Model 3	
	ME	z	ME	z	ME	z
Italy	–0.02	–1.3	0.004	0.3	0.02	1.2
Spain	–0.0006	–0.2	–0.01	–1.4	–0.01	–1.3

Note: See Table 4.4.

Table 4.6 reports on the relevant results discussed above, taking into account the impact of potential selection bias. Estimates refer to the bivariate probit model as presented in Section 4.4. The model was estimated using the incidence of temporary employment by region and skill level at the beginning of the period and the lagged change in the incidence as identifying restrictions.

Table 4.6 Transition probabilities into permanent employment for the unemployed versus the temporary employed, for Italy (1999–2002) and Spain (2000–2003). Bivariate probit estimates of the marginal effects (ME), controlled for selection bias

	Italy			Spain		
	ME	z*	P>|z*|	ME	z^a	P>|z*|
a) personal labour market characteristics						
Temporary workers (reference: unemployed)	0.35	4.7	0.00	0.0008	0.03	0.98
rho	–0.19	1.2	0.28	0.07	0.77	0.44
b) as a) with inclusion of family characteristics						
Temporary workers (reference: unemployed)	0.33	4.3	0.00	0.0008	0.03	0.98
rho	–0.14	–0.8	0.43	0.07	0.77	0.442
c) as b) with inclusion of search behaviour						
Temporary workers (reference: unemployed)	0.29	6.4	0.00	–0.007	–0.27	0.79
rho	–0.18	3.3	0.07	0.07	0.89	0.38

Notes: * For the rho estimate the Wald test of rho = 0 (chi^2 with 1 degree of freedom). Instruments used in the equation for temporary work are the percentage of temporary workers by education level and region at t–1 and the change in the percentage of temporary workers by education level and region between t–2 and t–1. Instruments are always jointly statistical significant. Complete estimates are available upon request. For further details, see the full version of the table:< www.siswo.uva.nl/tlm/root_files/WorkP05-20Dreaming.pdf>.

When potential self-selection into the initial state is controlled for, the results differ substantially according to the country considered. In Spain, the initial condition appears truly exogenous (the correlation coefficient between the unobservable factors influencing the probability of being in temporary employment and subsequently moving into a permanent job – the rho coefficient in the table – is very small and statistically insignificant).

For Italy however, the estimates seem to confirm the previous results. Once self-selection is controlled for, the probability that a temporary worker will get a permanent job (with reference to the unemployed) is significantly, though only slightly, higher (between 29–35 per cent, against 22–29 per cent using the probit estimates).

The estimates of the correlation coefficient (rho) suggest the existence of a negative self-selection process into temporary employment. In other words, holding other observable characteristics constant, some individuals (who are probably more likely to get a permanent job due to their unobserved characteristics) may prefer to remain unemployed (eventually working in the black economy) and wait for a permanent job rather than accepting a temporary position.21 However, the low statistical significance of the correlation coefficients (particularly in model a and b) indicates that this result should be interpreted with some caution. In any case, it seems to suggest that the probit estimates should be considered at least as a lower bound for the differences between temporary workers and the unemployed with respect to the transition probability into permanent employment.

4.7 CONCLUDING REMARKS

This chapter examined the transitions of temporary workers into permanent employment, focusing on whether temporary work experience could help to escape from unemployment and to prevent long-term joblessness. In the light of the heterogeneity among the temporary workers, specific attention has been paid to the transitions of the so-called 'involuntary' temporary workers (that is, those working on temporary contracts because they could not find a permanent job), by comparing how they fare in terms of moving into permanent jobs with both, the other temporary employees and the unemployed.

The empirical analysis was limited to Italy and Spain, two countries which in comparative socio-economic research is traditionally classified among the so-called 'Southern' or 'Mediterranean' countries, characterised by tight labour market regulation and relatively low benefits, with rather extended family networks and low female participation rates, as well as significant regional differences.

Both Spain and Italy have recently undergone labour market deregulation processes, although to varying degrees and along different time paths, with a stronger emphasis on the use of fixed-term contracts in Spain. Despite their institutional similarities, both countries have implemented quite different policies with respect to temporary employment, therewith exerting rather dissimilar effects on their national labour markets.

In terms of the available opportunities to move into permanent jobs for the unemployed and the temporary employees, the empirical analysis supports two different models. In Italy, the unemployed are less likely to find a job at all than in Spain, but the Italian unemployed are more likely to get a permanent job than a temporary one. Furthermore, temporary employees in Italy have a significant higher probability of getting a permanent job and a relatively low probability of entering unemployment. In contrast, in Spain, the unemployed are more likely to find a temporary job than to remain unemployed, but once working in such jobs they seem to get 'stuck' and not to be able to acquire a permanent job, at least in the short term. Moreover,

Spanish temporary employees are more likely to become unemployed than to get a permanent job.

Our model estimates point out that temporary workers in both countries are actually more likely to get a permanent job than the unemployed, while no significant differences seem to emerge between involuntary and other temporary employees. Nonetheless, the marginal effect of temporary work experience (holding other factors constant) is much higher in Italy than in Spain (0.26 against 0.03). Furthermore, the positive effect of temporary work experience may be slightly higher (at least in the case of Italy) if unobserved heterogeneity is taken into account, suggesting the existence of negative (self-)selection into temporary employment. This may be due to the fact that, holding other observable characteristics constant, some people may prefer to remain unemployed – and to wait for a permanent job – rather than to accept a temporary job. This result seems to confirm that temporary employment can actually enhance, at least in Italy, the likelihood of gaining permanent employment. It therefore seems to imply that temporary workers were not necessarily 'stronger' in terms of labour market chances when they began their temporary job (in terms of unobservable characteristics) than the unemployed but that their chances did improve during the execution of the temporary job due to acquiring work experience that the unemployed lack.

In terms of policy implications, comparative analysis reveals that public support of temporary employment in Spain actually helps individuals out of unemployment, but it does not much help temporary workers seeking to gain permanent employment. The Spanish experience and the policies adopted suggest that this result is not merely due to pure incentive effects (that is, policy support and subsidies bridging the gap between the costs of using temporary and open-ended contracts) but that it rather stems from labour demand effects (that is, production constraints preventing the permanent absorption in the labour market of the entire temporary workforce, regardless of its costs). On the other side, the Italian model shows a more fluid situation with more mobility between temporary and permanent employment, but problems of unemployment persistence are still relevant, despite recent reforms rendering support to flexible and temporary contracts.

In the end a crucial policy issue is the potential combination of the positive effects of the two Southern models. Is it possible to use, or to create incentives that encourage the use of, temporary employment to reduce unemployment, thereby preventing the creation of a dual labour market that causes greater disparities between the working conditions of permanent and temporary workers? Is there a trade-off between unemployment persistence and temporary employment rigidity? Current empirical evidence seems to provide answers in the negative to these questions, but more research and policy efforts are needed in order to improve the performance of the Southern regime in terms of its 'flexicurity' and labour market mobility record.

NOTES

1. In legal terms, a 'fixed-term contract' is an employment relationship of which its terms have been agreed upon by both parties, and which identify a specific date or event (for instance, the return to work of employees on leave, or the end of a construction site) that will determine the end of the employment relation. Temporary contracts may be thought to be a larger category, including temporary agency contracts, seasonal work and training contracts. However, all of these share a fundamental feature: the contract has a limited duration, at the end of which the worker is not entitled to the termination rights granted to standard, open-ended contracts. In most of this chapter, we shall use both terms as synonyms.
2. A rather different issue is to what extent the dual labour market is actually weakened by the emergence of a temporary labour force itself. It could be the case, as it has been argued by several authors (Huguet, 1999; Hernanz, 2003; Toharia et al., 2005), that for Spain demand-side forces seem to explain the wake and growth of a dual labour market and that temporary contracts merely served the development of a secondary segment.
3. The only exception being apprenticeship and insertion contracts which, according to 'legge Biagi', may assign workers up to two qualification levels below those of equivalent standard employees.
4. This section draws on Toharia and Malo (2000); for a more updated view, see Toharia et al. (2005).
5. So quietly that they went unnoticed by the OECD observers who did not mention them in their 2004 calculations mentioned before. However, for some analysts (see for example, Malo and Toharia, 2005), this has been a deeply profound change as it has eliminated, in practice, the need to justify dismissals. If at the time of dismissal the employer makes a deposit of severance payment (at the maximum rate), implicitly accepting its unfairness, no further 'intervening wages' (wages to be paid between the initial date of dismissal and the final court ruling declaring the dismissal fair or unfair) are due. This implies that the means the labour court before had to control and judge the reason of the dismissal have virtually disappeared. The number of dismissals swiftly increased in 2003 and 2004; Malo and Toharia (2005) have calculated that 70 per cent of all dismissals followed the new rules.
6. See Muffels, Wilthagen and Van den Heuvel (2002); Muffels and Fouarge (2004); Muffels, Tsakloglou and Mayes (2002).
7. See, among others Amuedo-Dorantes (2000), Booth et al. (2002), Gagliarducci (2003) and García-Serrano (1998). For an earlier analysis, see Segura et al. (1991).
8. 'Previous labour market status is important in determining the probability of job instability (and therefore of exclusion) implying that past unemployment has a severe penalty on subsequent job tenure. Furthermore, for those individuals entering a temporary job after a period of unemployment, a fixed-term contract is more likely to be synonymous to a dead-end job instead of acting as a stepping-stone' (p. 180).
9. The authors analyse the probability of suffering a work-related accident and find that, after controlling for the job characteristics of workers, the differences between open-ended and temporary workers vanish.
10. A similar framework has already been used in other studies. See, for example, Ichino et al. (2004) for the causal study of temporary help work on the probability of getting a permanent job.
11. This is clear when we further assume that the error term in [1] can be considered as the sum of an individual (time-invariant) specific effect and an orthogonal white noise error: $\varepsilon_{it}=\mu_i + u_{it}$. If the individual specific effect is correlated with the initial state TEMP, then the latter is endogenous in [1].

12. Alternatively, matching estimators (such as Propensity Score Matching) may be used when very rich data sets (in terms of observable individual characteristics, also referred to past labour market history) are available. Unfortunately this is not the case of the data set used in this contribution; for this reason, we prefer to rely on parametric estimators.

13. Remember that: $corr(X,Y) = cov(X,Y)/(\sigma X \sigma Y)$. In this case, $\sigma X = \sigma Y = 1$. Furthermore, the log-likelihood contribution for the i-th individual is given by: $\ln L_i = (TEMP_{it-1} = 1)(Y_{it} = 1)\Phi_2(\gamma'Z_{it-1}, \beta'X_{it-1}, \rho) + (TEMP_{it-1} = 1)(Y_{it} = 0) \Phi_2(\gamma'Z_{it-1}, -\beta'X_{it-1}, -\rho) + (TEMP_{it-1} = 0)(Y_{it} = 1) \Phi_2(-\gamma'Z_{it-1}, \beta'X_{it-1}, -\rho) + (TEMP_{it-1} = 0)(Y_{it} = 0) \Phi_2(-\gamma'Z_{it-1}, -\beta'X_{it-1}, \rho)$

14. Persons in unemployment are those who during the reference week were not employed, but are available to start work within the next two weeks and had actively looked for a job at some time during the previous four weeks. Persons who have found a job that however starts later are also classified as unemployed.

15. In the case of Italy, the so-called 'independent contractors' mentioned in Section 4.2 should be excluded, since they formally are independent workers. However, this type of contract is often used by firms to save on labour costs and independent contractors may actually perform the same tasks as standard employees. Considering that the LFS is based on workers' perceptions of their employment position, it is possible that some of these workers define themselves as temporary dependent workers.

16. In Italy the other temporary employees include also temporary workers on training contracts and on probation period. In both countries it also includes a group of workers on temporary contracts for 'other reasons'.

17. Further characteristics of the temporary employees (involuntary and others) and the unemployed can be observed in Table A.3 in the Annex. The detailed analysis of these characteristics is omitted here for the sake of clarity and brevity.

18. Differences between the transitions into permanent jobs and the searching behaviour of involuntary and other temporary workers in Italy may be due to the fact that in the 'other temporary' category workers are included on training contracts and on probation periods which are usually transformed into permanent contracts.

19. Recall that the dependent variable is a dummy equal to 1 if the individual holds a permanent job one year later, 0 otherwise.

20. Note that searching behaviour may depend also on personal (unobservable) characteristics, such as motivation and ability. In this sense, variables related to searching behaviour may be correlated with the unobservable factors captured by the error term in our model, thus causing a problem of endogeneity. The set of estimates including these variables should then be interpreted with some caution.

21. The role of 'wait unemployment' has been pointed out in the case of southern Italy, where most of the (young) unemployed prefer to wait for a permanent job (preferably in the public sector) rather than accepting a temporary (and often low paid) job in the private sector which may damage their long-term career prospects especially when they are highly educated (Alesina et al., 2001; Dell'Aringa et al., 2004; Barbieri and Scherer, 2003).

REFERENCES

Albert, C., García-Serrano, C. and Hernanz, V. (2005), 'Firm-provided training and temporary contracts', *Spanish Economic Review*, **7**, 67–88.

Alesina, A., Danninger, S. and Rostagno, M. (2001), 'Redistribution through public employment: the case of Italy', *IMF Staff Papers*, **48** (3).

Adam, D. and Canziani, P. (1998), *Partial De-Regulation: Fixed-Term Contracts in Italy and Spain,* Working Paper n° 386, Centre for Economic Performance.

Amuedo-Dorantes, C. (2000), 'Work Transitions into and out of Involuntary Temporary Employment in a Segmented Market: Evidence from Spain', *Industrial and Labour Relations Review*, **53** (2), 309–25.

Barbieri P. and Scherer, S. (2003), 'The pay-offs to education: a North-South comparison', in Checchi, D. and Lucifora, C. (eds), *Education, Training and Labour Market Outcomes in Europe*, Palgrave Macmillan.

Booth, A.L., Francesconi, M. and Frank, J. (2002), 'Temporary jobs. Stepping Stones or Dead Ends', *Economic Journal*, **112** (480), 189–213.

Cebrián, I, Moreno, G., Samek, M., Semenza, R. and Toharia, L. (2003), 'Nonstandard work in Italy and Spain: The quest for flexibility at the margin in two supposedly rigid labour markets', in Houseman, S. and Osawa, M. (eds), *Nonstandard work in Developed Economies*, Kalamazoo, Michigan, WE: Upjohn Institute for Employment Research, 89–129.

CNEL (2004), *Rapporto sul mercato del lavoro 2003,* Roma.

Dell'Aringa, C., Lucifora, C. and Origo, F. (2004), 'Public Sector Reforms and Wage Decentralisation: a First Look at Regional Wage Differentials', mimeo.

European Commission (2004), *Employment in Europe*, Luxembourg.

Gagliarducci, S. (2004), *A multiple-spell analysis of the transition out of precariousness,* Paper presented at 16th EALE Annual Conference, Lisbon.

García-Serrano, C. (1998), *Worker turnover and job reallocation: the role of fixed-term contracts,* Oxford Economic Papers, **50**, 709–25.

Grubb, D. and Wells, W. (1993), *Employment regulation and patterns of work in EC countries,* OECD Economic studies, **21**, 7–58.

Heckman, J. (1981), 'Statistical models for discrete panel data', in Manski, C.F. and McFadden, D. (eds), *Structural Analysis of Discrete Data with Econometric Applications*, Massachusetts: MIT Press, 114–78.

Heckman, J., Lalonde, R. and Smith, J. (1999), The economics and econometrics of active labor market programs', in Ashenfelter, O. and Card, D. (eds), *Handbook of Labor Economics*, Elsevier edition 1, Volume 3, Chapter 31, 1865–2097.

Hernanz, V. (2003), *El trabajo temporal y la segmentación: un estudio de las transiciones laborales,* Madrid: Consejo Económico y Social.

Hernanz, V. and Toharia, L. (2006), 'Do temporary contracts increase work accidents? A micro-econometric comparison between Italy and Spain', *Labour*, **20** (3), 475–504.

Houseman, S.N. and Osawa, M. (2003), *Non-standard work in Developed Economies*, Kalamazoo, Michigan, WE: Upjohn Institute for Employment Research.

Huguet, A. (1999), *La segmentación en el mercado de trabajo español*, Madrid: Consejo Económico y Social.

Ichino, A., Mealli, F. and Nannicini, T. (2004), 'Temporary work agency in Italy: a springboard to permanent employment?', mimeo.

Lindbeck, A. and Snower, J. (1991), 'Interactions between the efficiency wage and insider-outsider theories', Economics Letters, *Elsevier*, **37** (2), 193–6.

Malo, M.A. (1998), *Las indemnizaciones por despido: un problema de negociación*, Madrid: Editorial ACARL.

Malo, M.A. and Toharia, L. (1994), 'Los costes del despido en España', *Revista de economía y sociología del trabajo*, 25–26, 180–92.

Malo, M.A. and Toharia, L. (2005), 'El coste del despido y las reformas del Estatuto de los Trabajadores', in Ruesga, S., Valdés, F. and Zufiaur, J.M. (eds), *Transformaciones laborales en España. A XXV años de la promulgación del Estatuto de los Trabajadores,* Madrid, Ministerio de Trabajo y Asuntos Sociales, 293–311.

Muffels, R.J.A. and Fouarge, D.J.A.G. (2004), 'The role of European welfare states in explaining resources deprivation', *Social Indicators Research,* **68** (3), 299–330.

Muffels, R.J.A., Tsakloglou, P. and Mayes, D. (2002), *Social Exclusion In European Welfare States,* Cheltenham, UK and Northhampton, MA, USA: Edward Elgar, 392.

Muffels, R.J.A., Wilthagen, T. and Heuvel, N. van den (2002), *Labour Market Transitions and Employment Regimes: Evidence on the Flexibility–security Nexus in Transitional Labour Markets,* WZB-discussion papers (Ext. r. no. FS I 02–20), Berlijn: WZB, Wissenschaftszentrum Berlin für Sozialforschung, 37.

OECD (1999), *Employment Outlook 1999,* Paris.

OECD (2004), *Employment Outlook 2004,* Paris.

Rosen, S. (1974), 'Hedonic prices and implicit markets: product differentiation in pure competition', *Journal of Political Economy,* **82** (1), 34–55.

Saint-Paul, G. (1996), *Dual Labour Markets: A Macroeconomic Perspective* Cambridge (Mass.), MIT Press.

Samek-Lodovici, M. (2000), 'Italy. The Long Times of Consensual Re-regulation', in Esping-Andersen, G. and Regini, M. (eds), *Why deregulate labour markets?,* Oxford: Oxford University.

Segura, J., Durán, F., Toharia, L. and Bentolila, S. (1991), *Análisis de la contratación temporal en España,* Madrid: Ministerio de Trabajo y Seguridad Social.

Semenza R. (2000), 'Le nuove forme del lavoro indipendente', *Stato e Mercato,* **58** (1), 143–68.

Storrie, D. (2002), *Temporary Agency Work in the European Union,* Dublin: European Foundation for the Improvement of Living and Working Conditions.

Toharia, L. and Malo, M (2000), 'The Spanish Experiment: pros and cons of flexibility at the margin', in Esping-Andersen, G. and Regini, M. (eds), *Why deregulate labour markets?,* Oxford: Oxford University.

Toharia, L. (dir.), Albert, C., Calvo, J., Cebrián, I., Cruz, J., Herranz, V., García-Serrano, C., Herranz, V., Malo, M.A. and Moreno, G. (2005), *El problema de la temporalidad en España: un diagnóistico,* Madrid: Ministerio de Trabajo y Asuntos Sociales.

Wilthagen, T. and Rogowski, R. (2002), 'Legal Regulation of Transitional Labour Markets', in G. Schmid en B. Gazier (eds), *The Dynamics of Full Employment: Social Integration through Transitional Labour Markets,* Cheltenham, UK and Northampton, MA, USA: Edward Elgar.

ANNEX 4.1

Table 4.A.1 Labour market indicators for Italy and Spain and the EU, 1993 and 2003 (in %)

	1993			2003		
	Italy	Spain	EU15	Italy	Spain	EU15
ALL (aged 15–64)						
Activity rate	58.3	58.5	67.1	61.5	67.3	70.0
Employment rate	52.3	46.6	60.1	56.1	59.7	64.3
Unemployment rate	10.1	18.6	10.1	8.6	11.3	8.1
FEMALES						
Activity rate	41.9	41.0	55.8	48.3	54.8	61.5
Employment rate	35.8	30.7	49.2	42.7	46.0	56.0
Unemployment rate	14.5	24.1	11.4	11.6	15.9	9.0
YOUTH (aged 15–24)						
Activity rate	40.8	42.7	49.6	34.6	43.2	47.2
Employment rate	28.3	25.3	39.4	25.2	33.4	39.7
Unemployment rate	30.1	38.4	20.2	27.0	22.7	15.8
Fixed-term contracts						
(in % of total employment)	6.2	33.0	11.0	9.9	30.6	12.8

Source: European Commission's key employment indicators, derived from Employment in Europe, 2004.

Table 4.A.2 Main features of the Labour Force Surveys in Italy and Spain

	Italy	Spain
Frequency of the results	Quarterly	Quarterly
Reference week	One in each quarter	Evenly spread
Sample unit	Household	Dwelling
Overall sample rate	0.36%	0.50%
Size of the sample (n. households)	75,512	65,000
Stratification	Yes	Yes
Stratifying variables	Region, urbanisation	Region, urbanisation, socio-economic status
Rotation scheme	2 in, 2 out, 2 in	6 waves

Table 4.A.3 Description of the characteristics of unemployed and (involuntary and other) temporary employees for Italy and Spain (% of people in particular category)

	Italy				Spain			
	Unem-ployed	Temporary workers			Unem-ployed	Temporary workers		
		All	Invo-luntary	Others		All	Invo-luntary	Others
Gender								
Males	45.9	50.4	51.8	49.3	42.2	57.0	56.9	57.3
Females	54.1	49.6	48.2	50.7	57.8	43.0	43.1	42.7
Age group								
Up to 24	30.4	23.3	12.4	32.1	26.2	27.8	27.9	27.4
24–29	19.8	19.9	18.0	21.5	19.0	22.7	23.1	21.1
30–39	27.3	28.3	33.4	24.1	26.1	27.4	27.5	27
40–49	13.8	17.9	22.8	13.9	16.9	14.5	14.3	15.3
50 and over	8.6	10.7	13.5	8.4	11.9	7.6	7.2	9.2
Average age (in years)	31.7	33.8	36.5	31.6	33.5	31.8	31.7	32.4
Level of education								
Without education	1.9	1.6	2.7	0.9	6.5	5.0	5.1	4.72
Elementary school	12.3	11.7	16.4	8.1	18.5	16.7	16.6	16.8
Lower-secondary	40.0	34.3	36.6	32.5	32.6	33.9	34.4	31.81
Higher-secondary	33.6	31.8	25.9	36.2	11.2	10.4	9.7	13.2
Further-training (CFP in Italy)	5.9	7.7	6.7	8.5	16.3	17.4	18.1	14.39
University degree	6.3	12.9	11.7	13.8	14.9	16.7	16.2	19.08
Civil status								
Single	58.7	50.2	39.7	58.7	52.2	56.9	57.1	55.7
Married	37.5	46.8	56.6	38.8	42.8	39.1	38.8	40.2
Other (divorced, widow, etc.)	3.9	3.0	3.7	2.4	5.0	4.1	4.0	4.10
Family situation								
Head of the family	21.9	30.9	37.9	25.2	22.4	28.7	28.6	29.3
Spouse	22.6	22.5	25.5	20.0	26.8	17.5	17.2	18.4
Son/daughter	52.6	43.9	33.7	52.3	46.4	48.2	48.6	46.5
Other relative	3.0	2.8	2.9	2.6	4.5	5.7	5.6	5.9

5. Mobility in the Labour Market: Analysing Career Paths using Administrative Data

Mieke Booghmans, Seppe van Gils and Caroline Vermandere

5.1 INTRODUCTION

The theory of the transitional labour market has mobility in the labour market as its centre-point. The analyses of mobility streams on the labour market permit us to map out the dynamic character of the labour market. Günther Schmid's concept of the transitional labour market indicates the range of transitions possible within the labour market (Schmid 1995; Schmid and Gazier, 2002). School leavers enter the labour market as newcomers; pensionable workers leave it; others leave the labour market early; for example through the bridging retirement scheme; some wage-earners withdraw through career breaks and others change jobs. Much has already been said about these dynamics on the labour market (see Chapter 4 of Origo et al., Chapter 6 of Muffels and Luijkx, Chapter 8 of Meager and Chapter 11 of Ziguras and Stricker in this book). But how transitional is the Belgian labour market at this point? Is there much mobility between the different sections of the labour market or not? To answer this question, we investigate the career paths of the full-time employed and the unemployed entitled to a benefit. Which transitions do they make during ten subsequent quarters? The analysis is based on administrative data for Belgium. Great progress has been made in Belgium in that respect with the construction of the 'Datawarehouse Labour Market'. In the Datawarehouse, the main information in the administrative Social Security databases is linked up. All residents known to the Belgian social security instances are contained in the Datawarehouse which makes the data a unique data source for mobility analysis.

5.2 MOBILITY IN THE LABOUR MARKET?

Research based on the Belgian ECHP (European Community Household Panel)-data shows that the career paths of most people on the labour market are characterised by stability (Forrier et al., 2004). Consequently, the conclusion is that the transitional labour market, in which the individual career path is assumed to evolve in a very dynamic way, has still a long way to go.[1] More research based on Belgian survey (ECHP) data shows that certain aspects of a traditional career, such as the security of a fixed contract or a full-time job still dominate the Belgian labour market (Soens et al., 2005). But they also conclude that this traditional model seems to be liable to some erosion. The analyses show that transitional career paths arise. Less stable socio-economic moves such as transitions into unemployment, but also newer, transitional career moves such as job hopping, shifting between full-time and part-time jobs or the transfer into unpaid work, play a role in this. Another conclusion is that these more transitional career paths do not occur at random. There are several personal and labour market specific characteristics that influence such career paths. The Eurobarometer gives some insight in how Belgium is situated in the European picture. The survey on labour market mobility in 2005 concludes that 30 per cent of Belgians older than 35 years never changed employer compared to an average of 25 per cent in the rest of Europe. The average job duration is also longer in Belgium (on average more than 9.5 years) than in Europe (on average 8.3 years). The Eurobarometer also questions the willingness to move. Less than a third of the Belgians believe that changing jobs is a positive change. In Denmark (72 per cent) or Sweden (79 per cent) much more people believe that changing jobs is a good thing. These findings indicate that the level of mobility in the Belgian labour market is quite low. In contrast, an analysis of mobility patterns across regime types in Europe based on a dataset of the European Community Household Panel (1993–1999) shows that Belgium has one of the highest job-to-job mobility rates. This finding was in contrast with the hypothesis. Belgium belongs to the corporate regime type and this regime type is expected to have low mobility rates. The other corporatist regimes showed much lower mobility rates (see Muffels and Luijkx, 2006, 2008).

The main research question concerns the actual level of mobility in the Belgian labour market. Are there substantial transitions between the different sections of the labour market? Or do people still have a more traditional career path characterised by a standard sequence of education, full-time employment and pension? Who has stable career paths and who follows a transitional career path featuring by many interruptions and changes?

This chapter concentrates on describing the incidence of mobility on the labour market using rather unique administrative data (Section 5.2). Two sorts of analyses are conducted. The first one looks at the career paths of the full-time employed (Section 5.3). The second one analyses the career paths of the unemployed entitled to a benefit (Section 5.4). These career paths are clustered into a typology of typical career patterns, to which we can associate different personal characteristics (see also Román and Schippers, 2005).

The availability of statistical data to map out current mobility patterns in the labour market is critical to the future development of the theory of the transitional labour market and the concept of mobility. It is essential to gather adequate information with the help of dynamic statistics to get a clear picture of the different patterns in the labour market especially when the datasets cover such a large number of observations on transitions that surveys generally are unable to provide. Therefore this contribution has another important objective, namely to introduce the features of the Datawarehouse and to discuss the way in which administrative data can be an important tool for analysing mobility in the labour market.[2]

5.3 DATA

5.3.1 Introduction to the Datawarehouse 'Labour Market & Social Protection'

The Datawarehouse 'Labour Market & Social Protection' was set up at the request of several social security institutions and scientists. The objective was to create a database in which certain social data available to the organisations would be permanently linked in order to be more readily accessible for scientific research.[3] The basis for the link is the national insurance number, a unique identification number held by everyone known to the Belgian social security institutions (the number is coded and made anonymous in the Datawarehouse). Individuals are therefore the main statistical unit. Since the characteristics of the job(s) and the employer(s) of the employees are equally included in the Datawarehouse, statistics can also be compiled for the number of jobs or employers. In terms of the labour force, the Datawarehouse consequently includes the majority of the working citizens and a large proportion of the jobseekers in Belgium. The employed people missing from the database are primarily wage-earners working for an employer who are not liable for national insurance contributions to the Belgian state, including cross-border workers. The jobseekers obscured from the Datawarehouse's view are those who do not receive unemployment benefits, neither directly or indirectly. Each participating social security institution offers an extensive list of variables through the Datawarehouse. In addition, a number of 'derived variables' are created, for example the socio-economic position or the number of jobs per person. Since 2003, new administrative sources related to social protection were integrated into the Datawarehouse. Therefore the scope of the Datawarehouse expanded substantially.

5.3.2 Panel on Mobility of Working-age Population (PMWP)

The sample was taken from the labour force on the basis of data from the second quarter of 1998, which is the first quarter the Datawarehouse was created for. The sample population was subsequently followed up each quarter up to and including the third quarter of 2000, which was the most recent quarter available from the Datawarehouse at the time the sample was taken. The PMWP-database does not only allow comparisons between labour market positions at two different moments, but also enables us to construe the course of individual and collective working lives. We will create a typology of career paths of the full-time employed and the unemployed entitled to a benefit. These typologies allow us to measure mobility on the labour market. Questions are dealt with such as: are the career paths characterised by stability or do they show a lot of transitions or mobility?; do people with specific personal characteristics show different career paths? and so on.

5.4 FULL-TIME EMPLOYED THROUGHOUT LIFE

5.4.1 Full-time Employed as a Norm?

Table 5.1 shows that 63.9 per cent of all employed Belgians work as full-time employees. A further 16.6 per cent work as part-time employees and 16.2 per cent are self-employed. In order to make the overview exhaustive, the table also lists 3.2 per cent of employees of whom it is not known whether they are employed full-time or part-time.

A further classification by sex, age and nationality indicates that the proportion of full-time employees is not as high for all groups. For example, the proportion of full-time employees among working men is no less than 73.5 per cent, whereas the proportion among women is much lower, 49.8 per cent, because comparatively more female employees work part-time. The classification by age demonstrates that the proportion of full-time employees is highest in the 25–39 age group and that this proportion drops among higher age groups. The difference is associated with the proportion of self-employed among the employed. After all, the percentage of self-employed is highest in the oldest age group and lowest in the youngest age group. Only a few differences emerge from classifying full-time employees by nationality. The proportion of part-time employees is nevertheless considerably higher among workers from outside the EU, whereas the number of self-employed is rather limited in this group.

Table 5.1 Working population by employment status, sex, age and nationality (Belgium; 2nd quarter 1998)

(%)	Full-time employed	Part-time employed	Employed (% employment status unknown)	Self-employed	Total
Total	63.9	16.6	3.2	16.2	100
Gender					
Males	73.5	4.5	2.9	19.1	100
Females	49.8	34.5	3.8	12.0	100
Age					
15–24 yrs	59.6	22.8	11.0	6.6	100
25–39 yrs	71.1	10.3	3.3	15.4	100
40–49 yrs	65.2	16.0	1.8	16.9	100
50–64 yrs	59.3	12.9	1.7	26.1	100
Nationality					
Belgian	64.3	16.6	3.0	16.0	100
Other-EU-15	59.1	14.6	4.9	21.5	100
Not-EU-15	52.1	23.4	12.1	12.5	100

Source: PMWP-database (Processing Steunpunt WSE).

5.4.2 How do the Careers of Full-time Employees Evolve?

The previous section gave us a static picture of the proportion of full-time employees in the working population of Belgium. We can complement the analysis with a dynamic approach, allowing us to check which full-time employees did or did not remain full-time employed during a particular period (see also Román et al., 2004). For that purpose, we use the PMWP-database. The database enables us to follow these people during ten consecutive quarters in order to collect information about their career. In Table 5.2, we have isolated the full-time employed in the second quarter of 1998 and we followed the group up to and including the third quarter of 2000. This way, we can verify who remains full-time employed during the period and who does not.[4] Of those who do not remain full-time employed, we examine how their career evolved during the studied period.

Who remains full-time employed?

Table 5.2 shows that 75.3 per cent of all full-time employed in the second quarter of 1998 remain full-time employed throughout the entire period. The proportion of men (78.9 per cent) to do so is greater than the proportion of women (67.8 per cent).

By age, a few obvious differences emerge from Table 5.2. The 15 to 24 year olds and the 50 to 64 year olds who are full-time employed in the second quarter of 1998, stand the least chance of remaining in full-time employment for the entire ten quarters (59.0 per cent and 67.8 per cent respectively). With the 25 to 49 year olds (76.2 per cent) and particularly with the 40 to 49 year olds (83.8 per cent), the proportion lies significantly higher. Table 5.2 also shows that immigrants lag behind Belgian nationals. People originating from outside the European Union who were full-time employed in the second quarter of 1998, had considerably less chance of remaining in full-time employment during the entire period (57.0 per cent) than Belgians (76.8 per cent).

Table 5.2 Proportion of full-time employees remaining full-time employed during the entire period, by age, sex and nationality (Belgium; 2nd quarter 1998–3rd quarter 2000)

(%)	Remain in full-time Employment	Others
Total	75.3	24.7
Gender		
Males	78.9	21.1
Females	67.8	32.2
Age		
15–24 yrs	59.0	41.0
25–39 yrs	76.2	23.8
40–49 yrs	83.8	16.2
50–64 yrs	67.8	32.2
Nationality		
Belgian	76.0	24.0
Other-EU-15	67.9	32.1
Not-EU-15	57.0	43.0

Source: PMWP-database (Processing Steunpunt WSE).

Figure 5.1 examines for every earnings group what proportion of full-time employed remains full-time employed from the first quarter for the entire duration of the ten consecutive quarters. Full-time employees in a lower earnings group clearly have less opportunities to remain in full-time employment throughout the entire period. As we look at higher earnings groups, the proportion of people remaining in work throughout the period increases. This effect is valid up to and including the earnings group with average daily earnings of 80 to 90 Euro. The proportion that remains full-time employed is approximately the same in this group compared to the higher earnings groups.

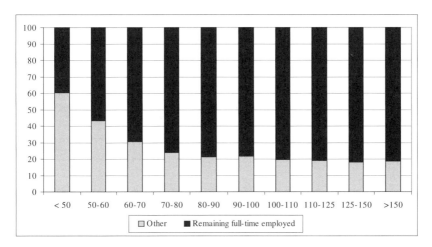

Source: PMWP-database (Processing Steunpunt WSE).

Figure 5.1 Proportion of full-time employed remaining full-time employed during the entire period, by average daily earnings in Euro (Belgium; 2nd quarter 1998–3rd quarter 2000)

And who does not?
Coherent career patterns
In this part, we examine how the careers evolve of those who do not remain in full-time employment. We look at the entire career between the second quarter of 1998 and the third quarter of 2000 of people who were full-time employed in the initial quarter. For our analysis, we choose an 'optimal matching' technique in combination with cluster analysis. The TDA (Transition Data Analysis)-software specifically designed for analysing transition data is used for this analysis. Optimal matching analysis examines which different sequences show a similar course and it reduces the complexity by reducing them to a limited number of groups (a similar approach has been applied for Belgium by Román, 2006). It defines the distance (or difference) between the different sequences. In other words, optimal matching determines the minimal cost to transform one sequence into another. The result of the analysis is a data matrix with the inter-sequence differences (transformation costs). The next step is to carry out a cluster analysis on this cost matrix. An agglomerative hierarchical cluster analysis is

carried out using Ward's minimum. The final step is to analyse these clusters. We were restricted to a maximum of 1,000 different careers. Thus, we did not incorporate all the different career patterns in our analysis. We nevertheless considered the great majority (95.8 per cent) of full-time employed in the first quarter. This percentage is slightly higher among men (96.6 per cent) than among women (94.0 per cent), see Table 5.3.

Table 5.3 Results of the cluster analysis (Belgium; 2nd quarter 1998–3rd quarter 2000)

Cluster	Men (%)	Women (%)	Total (%)
To part-time employment	1.2	7.5	3.2
To unemployment	2.5	4.4	3.1
To self-employment	1.8	0.8	1.5
To not being professionally active	6.7	6.2	6.5
Interruption, but predominantly full-time employed	5.7	7.3	6.2
Always full-time employed	78.9	67.8	75.3
Total	96.6	94.0	95.8
(Residual group)	(3.4)	(6.0)	(4.2)

Source: PMWP-database (Processing Steunpunt WSE).

As already stated clearly, the group that remains in full-time employment throughout the period is by far the largest (75.3 per cent). The division by sex shows that this group is larger among men than among women. Looking at the cluster of workers that did not remain in full-time employment, a few other coherent career patterns emerge; that is, 6.5 per cent moved on to the 'not professionally active' segment of the labour market. The proportion is approximately equal among men and women. Another 6.2 per cent displayed an interrupted career pattern, but nevertheless remained predominantly full-time employed. This is an interesting category while it reflects the thesis of the transitional labour market theory that current employment patterns tend to be associated with more interruptions.

The proportion of this group or cluster is slightly larger among women (7.3 per cent) than among men (5.7 per cent). The latter two clusters show a much higher proportion of women than of men. The share of workers transferring to part-time employment is particularly larger among women (7.5 per cent) compared to men (1.2 per cent), but also the less successful route to unemployment is more prevalent among women (4.4 per cent) than among men (2.5 per cent). Women tend to interrupt their career either by withdrawing temporarily or by reducing hours due to caring duties, for example, after childbirth. A further 3.2 per cent belong to the group transferring to part-time employment and 3.1 per cent end up in unemployment. The last cluster is characterised by a transfer to self-employment. This occurs more frequently among men (1.8 per cent) than women (0.8 per cent).

Further divisions by sex, age, nationality and average earnings per day
Figure 5.2 shows the division by sex in a different way. It examines the proportion of men and women in each individual cluster. The column 'Total' reflects the male–female distribution in the entire sample, enabling us to compare the separate clusters to the average. The figure clearly shows that the proportion of women is significantly higher than the average in the clusters characterised by a transfer to unemployment or to part-time employment. This is also the case, albeit to a lesser extent, for those workers showing an interrupted career pattern. The proportion of women is nevertheless lower in the cluster of the employed moving to self-employment and in the cluster that remained in full-time employment throughout the observed period.

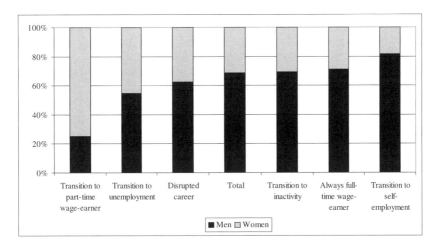

Source: PMWP-database (Processing Steunpunt WSE).

Figure 5.2 Proportion of men and women in each cluster (Belgium; 2nd quarter 1998–3rd quarter 2000)

Compared to the average, the proportion of women is therefore higher in the clusters that lost the connection with the labour market completely (transition to unemployment) or partially (transition to part-time employment, inter-rupted career) and lower in the clusters that remain fully in work (remaining in full-time employment throughout or transferring to self-employment). The general conclusion might therefore be that women tend to depict a much more diverse employment pattern than men.

Before, we already showed that women are not only less likely to work in full-time employment (Table 5.1), but that the proportion of women that remains in full-time employment throughout the studied period is lower than the proportion of men who remain in full-time employment (Table 5.2).

Additionally, it appears from Figure 5.2 that those women who do not remain in full-time employment are more likely to move to an employment position where women are proportionally more represented (the part-time employed, see Table 5.1).

On the other hand, it also appears that men who do not remain in full-time employment are more likely to belong to the cluster of workers moving into self-employment. This also matches the findings in Table 5.1. The proportion of men among the self-employed is after all fairly high.

Figure 5.3 shows the proportion of youngsters in each cluster. It shows that the full-time employed youngsters of the second quarter of 1998 are relatively mobile.

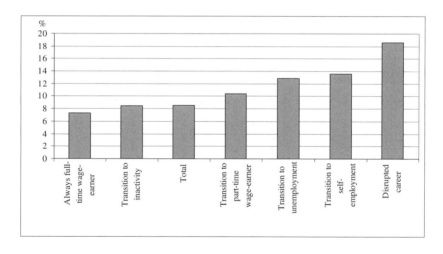

Source: PMWP-database (Processing Steunpunt WSE).

Figure 5.3 Proportion of youngsters (aged 15 to 24) in each cluster (Belgium; 2nd quarter 1998–3rd quarter 2000)

The research of Soens et al. (2005) arrives at the same conclusion. The new transitional career paths are typical for youngsters. They also conclude that job-hopping is more typical for youngsters. Only the mobile group transferring to the 'not professionally active' segment of the labour market contains slightly fewer youngsters than average. Furthermore, the non-mobile group remaining in full-time employment also contains a smaller proportion of youngsters. The first steps of youngsters in the labour market in some cases therefore coincide with a career pattern marked by transitions. For example, the figure shows that the proportion of youngsters in the group with an interrupted career pattern is significantly greater (18.6 per cent) than the proportion of youngsters in the entire sample (8.5 per cent). Additionally, the proportion of youngsters is also greater in the clusters making the transition to self-employment, unemployment and part-time work. This might therefore signal a generation effect suggesting that new generations tend to have a clearly more mobile career patterns than older generations of people.

As we already know, the proportion of employed people in the oldest age group is comparatively low. The older people who are still in full-time employment are also more likely to transfer to the segment of non-working people in the labour market. After all, the proportion of older people in each cluster (Figure 5.4) shows that this group of full-time employed is over-represented in the clusters that leave work temporarily or permanently.

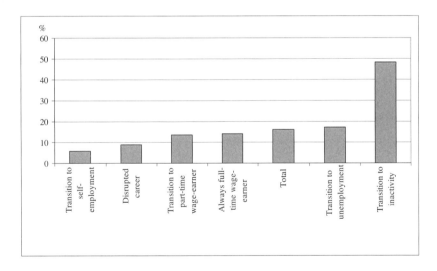

Source: PMWP-database (Processing Steunpunt WSE).

Figure 5.4 Proportion of older people (aged 50 to 64) in each cluster (Belgium; 2nd quarter 1998–3rd quarter 2000)

The proportion of older people is particularly high in the cluster moving to the 'not-professionally active' part of the labour market. The proportion of older people in this cluster amounts to no less than 48.4 per cent, whereas only 16.0 per cent of the entire sample belongs to the oldest age group. A part of this cluster consists of older people taking up retirement, but another part of these older people leave the labour market before the statutory retirement age through early retirement (among other things, the bridging pension). Furthermore, older people in full-time employment are also slightly more likely to become unemployed. The proportion of 50 to 64 years old is after all slightly higher than average in the cluster of people moving to unemployment.

On the other hand, the proportion of older people is always lower in the clusters making a transfer to another employment status, or who remain in full-time employment. Some mobility therefore occurs in the group of the older full-time employed people, but their careers are often characterised by exit out of work instead of a pattern of change to another employment status.

Figure 5.5 shows the proportion of non-Belgians in each cluster.

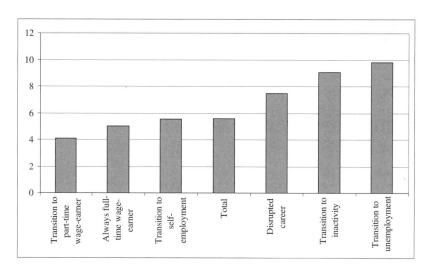

Source: PMWP-database (Processing Steunpunt WSE).

Figure 5.5 Proportion of non-Belgians in each cluster (Belgium; 2nd quarter 1998–3rd quarter 2000)

The presence of a larger than average proportion of immigrants in the clusters of workers who have completely or partially lost their link with the labour market (through a transition into unemployment and not being professionally active or an interrupted career), confirms the weaker position of immigrants on the Belgian labour market. The proportion of immigrants in the cluster of workers moving to unemployment is in particular higher (9.8 per cent) than average (5.6 per cent). Inversely, the proportion of immigrants is lower in the clusters of full-time workers who in the 2nd quarter of 1998 moved to another employment status (self-employment or part-time employment) or who remained in full-time employment. Immigrants with a non-European nationality are much less frequently at work on the Belgian labour market, but when they are in full-time employment, they also have lower chances of remaining in full-time work and are more likely to become unemployed.

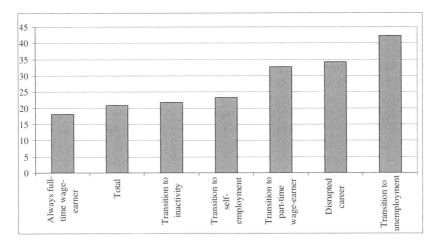

Source: PMWP-database (Processing Steunpunt WSE).

Figure 5.6 Proportion of people in full-time employment in the second quarter, on average earnings below 70 Euro per day in each cluster (Belgium; 2nd quarter 1998–3rd quarter 2000)

Finally, we focus on the full-time employed who on average have low daily earnings. From the analysis in Section 3.2.1, it became clear that the proportion of full-time employed retaining the same employment status throughout the entire period is lower among the employed on low average earnings per day. Figure 5.6 also shows that among the employed who remain throughout the period in full-time employment the proportion of employed with average daily earnings below 70 Euro, is lower than average. The full-time employed in the initial quarter on relatively low average daily earnings are most likely to be found in the cluster of workers moving to unemployment. This group of low earners is furthermore more strongly represented in the cluster of workers with an interrupted career and in the cluster of people moving to the not-professionally active people on the labour market. Those who receive a comparatively low average daily wage are therefore more likely to belong to a group with a less successful career pattern leading to unemployment, not being professionally active or an interrupted career. To reverse the argument we might say that experiences of unemployment, inactivity or employment interruptions tend to be associated with lower average earnings and are therefore not beneficial to the wage career. This is not surprising and corroborates the findings reported in other chapters of this book concerning the 'scarring' effects of unemployment and working in non-standard jobs.

5.4.3 Conclusion

We examined the career paths of full-time employees from the second quarter of 1998 up to and including the third quarter of 2000. Instead of looking at two moments in time, we considered all ten quarters together. It was found that the large majority of workers remain in the same employment status during the ten consecutive quarters. Further disaggregation by sex, age, nationality and average daily earnings confirm this major finding. The fact that so many remain in full-time employment for the entire period gives a strong indication of the homogenous nature of the career patterns in Belgium. After 2000 the economic situation improved. It is possible that this improvement had an influence on the career patterns. More recent studies show however that mobility in the Belgian labour market is still quite low. The analysis on administrative data confirms the conclusions of research based on survey data such as the on the Belgian ECHP-data. The proportion of employees that does not remain in full-time employment throughout the period is only comparatively high among youngsters, people originating from outside the European Union and employees with relatively low earnings. Those who do not remain in full-time employment can be divided into five categories; the first with 6.5 per cent moving to the not-professionally active segment of the labour market over the studied period; another 6.2 per cent has an interrupted career but remains full-time employed for most of the time. A proportion of 3.2 per cent of workers transited to part-time employment and 3.1 per cent moves to unemployment. The fifth group often ventures into self-employment.

5.5 CAREER PATHS OF THE UNEMPLOYED

In the previous analysis we examined career paths of full-time employees. The same analysis can be executed for the unemployed. What are their career paths? What are the characteristics of those who stay unemployed and of those who find a job, be it full-time or part-time? This analysis makes it possible to define profiles of people who tend to be caught in long-term unemployment and of people who will more easily find their way out of unemployment (see also Román and Schippers, 2005).

The same analytical design is used. We select all the unemployed entitled to a benefit in the second quarter of 1998 and follow up their career path until the third quarter of 2000. In other words, the database allows us to follow up persons during 10 successive quarters. The sample is extracted from the labour force and contains 609,971 persons. Of this group, 103,188 individuals are unemployed. Their career path is constructed during 10 quarters using 9 different socio-economic positions (Table 5.4). This results in a large number of different sequences which we can follow over time. The sequences of the unemployed of the second quarter of 1998 vary more than the sequences of the full-time employees. We only allow 1,000 sequences to be examined. In the case of the unemployed, this means that only 87.4 per cent of the sequences are included in the analysis. The sequences that are not included in the analysis are sequences that occur less than five times.

Table 5.4 Socio-economic positions used in the analysis

1.	Unemployed entitled to a benefit
2.	Suspended unemployed
3.	Activation programme
4.	Combination of employee and self-employed
5.	Self-employed
6.	Full-time employee
7.	Part-time employee
8.	Other employees
9.	Inactive

What are the results of the analysis? We found eight different clusters to be distinguished. The people in the first cluster are those who stayed unemployed during the 10 subsequent quarters. The second cluster consists of those who have mainly stayed unemployed, but with some breaks. These breaks deal with work or inactivity. The third group of people finds a part-time job. The people in the fourth cluster became employed in an activation programme. The activation programme (PWA) that is included in the analysis allows long-term unemployed people to practise activities such as household work that due to its nature or their occasional character are not carried out on the regular labour market. The fifth cluster contains people who moved from unemployment into inactivity. The people in cluster 6 start an independent profession. The people in cluster 7 show a somewhat unstable career pattern. It contains people who became employed on temporary contracts. But it also concerns people who worked full-time, but alternated this position with part-time work or inactivity. The last cluster contains individuals who got a job in the observed period as a full-time employee.

Prior to discussing the composition of the clusters, we need to gain a better view on the unemployed population in the starting quarter in order to place the clusters into perspective. Secondly, we will survey the composition of the clusters by sex and age. For the sake of completeness, we include the distribution of the residual group that is excluded from the analysis. Next, we will consider the share of some particular categories in the different clusters. To conclude, we will elaborate on the limitations of optimal matching analysis and on the possible solutions to this.

5.5.1 The Unemployed Population in the Starting Quarter

Before describing the different clusters, we need to have an image of the unemployed population. Table 5.5 shows the unemployed population by sex, age and nationality.

Table 5.5 Unemployed population by sex and age (Belgium; 2nd quarter of 1998)

	Distribution (%)
Sex	
Men	43.5
Women	56.5
Age	
15–24 yrs old	12.9
25–49 yrs old	57.8
50–64 yrs old	29.4
Nationality	
Belgian	86.7
Other EU15	8.5
Non-EU15	4.8
Total	100

Source: PMWP-database (Processing Steunpunt WSE).

In the second quarter of 1998 there are more unemployed women than men. Of all the unemployed, 57.8 per cent are aged between 25 and 49 years, 12.9 per cent are 15–24 years old and 29.4 per cent are 50–64 years of age. The share of older people in the unemployed population is rather high. The definition of unemployment in the PMWP-database is based on the criterion of entitlement to a benefit. This means that, in the PMWP-database, also older people who are exempted from registration for employment are included in the unemployed population, which explains the unexpected large share of unemployed older people. The majority of the unemployed population has the Belgian nationality. Only 8.5 per cent have another European nationality and 4.8 per cent have a non-European nationality.

5.5.2 The Composition of the Clusters

Table 5.6 shows that of all the unemployed in the second quarter of 1998, 48.5 per cent stayed unemployed during the whole period.

Table 5.6 Distribution of the clusters by sex, age (Belgium; 2nd quarter 1998–3rd quarter 2000)

	Total	Men	Women	15–24 yrs	25–49 yrs	50–64 yrs
1. Always unemployed	48.5	51.2	46.5	18.7	40.8	76.8
2. Mainly unemployed	14.7	12.1	16.7	20.3	16.8	8.2
3. Part-time employee	5.7	3.0	7.8	8.8	7.7	0.5
4. Activation programme	0.8	0.2	1.2	0.1	1.3	0.0
5. Inactivity	8.0	7.3	8.5	4.4	6.7	12.2
6. Self-employed	0.9	1.1	0.7	1.3	1.1	0.2
7. Unstable work	1.3	1.7	0.9	2.8	1.6	0.1
8. Full-time employee	7.4	11.0	4.7	15.4	9.0	0.8
Residual group	12.6	12.3	12.9	28.2	15.0	1.1
Total	100	100	100	100	100	100

Source: PMWP-database (Processing Steunpunt WSE).

Another 14.7 per cent stayed mainly unemployed. At first glance, this means that it was not so easy to escape unemployment. Leaving the residual group aside (12.6 per cent), a further 8 per cent became inactive. Only 7.4 per cent of the unemployed found a job as full-time employee and 5.7 per cent as part-time employee.

Compared to women, more men tend to stay unemployed over the whole period, but more women than men were mainly unemployed. Women, however, were more likely to find a part-time job than men. Conversely, men were more likely to find a full-time job than women.

The risk of staying unemployed increased with age. No less than 76.8 per cent of the 50 to 64 years old stayed unemployed during the 10 quarters. The unemployed sector in the PMWP-database included a category of older unemployed individuals who were exempted from registration for employment. In reality, this statute was used as a sort of hidden early retirement scheme. This explains the high percentage of unemployed older people who stayed unemployed or who became inactive. Of the persons of 15 to 24 years old, only 18.7 per cent remained unemployed. However, the youngsters were more likely to be unemployed, but also more likely to find a job as part-time or as full-time employee. Remarkably, 28.2 per cent of the young people of 15 to 24 years were situated in the residual group. We conclude that these career patterns were rather unstable which is a characteristic for the career path of youngsters. They seem to be still making their way in the labour market.

5.5.3 The Share of Specific Groups in Each Cluster

Another way to look at the clusters and their characteristics is to look at the share of certain groups in each cluster.

Men and women
Figure 5.7 shows the share of men and women in each cluster. The clusters on the left-hand side of the total distribution show an over-representation of women. In the clusters on the right-hand side the men are over-represented. As has already been concluded in the first chapter, the total group consists of more women than men. More than 90 per cent of the people employed in the activation programme (PWA) were female. This is not surprising, since it is known that mainly women make use of this activation programme. As expected, the cluster of part-time employees also contained more women than men. It could be that men have more opportunities to be integrated into the labour market. They were over represented in the clusters of the self-employed, the full-time employees and the unstable workers. The last category was always at work, but they could not hold the same position during the whole period of 10 quarters. Rather strikingly, we find that when men are unemployed, they are more likely to stay unemployed for the whole period compared to women, although the difference remains small. This can be explained by the over-representation of men in the group of older unemployed people of which a large part is exempted from registration for employment.

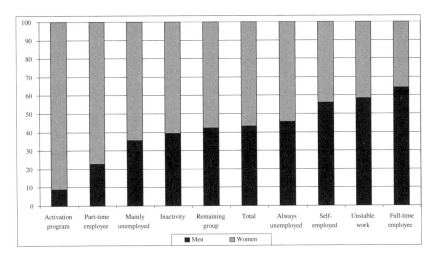

Source: PMWP-database (Processing Steunpunt WSE).

Figure 5.7 Share of men and women in each cluster (Belgium; 2nd quarter 1998–3rd quarter 2000)

Youngsters

As in the previous exercise, we added the total-column for comparison. The persons of 15–24 years are not likely to stay unemployed for a long time, nor are they inclined to become inactive. The share of youngsters in the activation programme turns out to be very small, see Figure 5.8.

The persons of 15–24 years are strongly over-represented in the clusters 'unstable work', 'residual group' and 'mainly unemployed', which are characterised by a rather unstable career pattern. They are still making their way on the labour market, which is sometimes an arduous task. However, they are also over-represented in the clusters which were able to find a job, be it a part-time, a full-time job or employment in an independent profession. In all, the unemployed youngsters generally had a good chance of finding a job, even though it might be a less stable or slightly more precarious one.

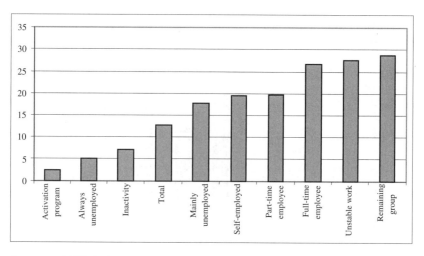

Source: PMWP-database (Processing Steunpunt WSE).

Figure 5.8 The share of youngsters (15–24 years old) (Belgium; 2nd quarter 1998–3rd quarter 2000)

Older people

When we examine the share of the 50–64 year olds in each cluster in Figure 5.9 we observe a well-known pattern.

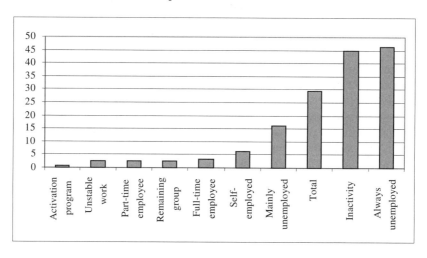

Source: PMWP-database (Processing Steunpunt WSE).

Figure 5.9 The share of older people (50–64 years old) in each cluster (Belgium; 2nd quarter 1998–3rd quarter 2000)

They are clearly under-represented in clusters of people that find their way into work. If an older person is unemployed, he or she is most likely either to stay unemployed or to become inactive. As already mentioned, this can be explained by the inclusion of the older unemployed persons who are exempted from registration for employment. They mostly stay unemployed until they retire.

Non-Europeans

Figure 5.10 shows the share of non-Europeans (EU-15) in each cluster. The first thing that catches the eye is the low share of non-European unemployed that ends up in an activation programme. The figure illustrates the weaker position of non-Belgians on the Belgian labour market. They are over-represented in clusters that stay always or mainly unemployed. If they find a job, it is a rather unstable job. They are under-represented in the clusters that find a job, be it a full-time or a part-time job or working in an independent profession.

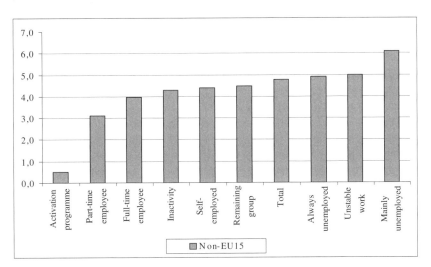

Source: PMWP-database (Processing Steunpunt WSE).

Figure 5.10 The share of non-Europeans in each cluster (Belgium; 2nd quarter 1998–3rd quarter 2000)

5.5.4 Conclusion

A first important conclusion from the analysis of the career paths of the unemployed is that a large proportion (63.2 per cent) of Belgians finds it difficult to escape unemployment. The majority of the unemployed is not mobile on the labour market. Here too, the improved economic situation after 2000 might have changed the pace of these mobility flows. More recent studies however show no evidence of this. Fortunately however, the unemployed already experience more transitions than full-time employees. Approximately 15 per cent of the unemployed makes a transition into work. But also 8 per cent leaves the labour market to become inactive. The traditionally weaker groups on the labour market, such as women, youngsters, older people and people born outside Europe (non-Europeans), show more difficulties in returning to work.

5.6 POLICY CONCLUSIONS

The analysis reported in this chapter leads to the important conclusion that although transitional career paths are existent during the period considered, the traditional career pattern of being steadily employed in a open-ended full-time job is still dominant in the Belgian labour market (see also Román, 2006). Nevertheless, the concept of a transitional labour market could resolve some of the existing problems and policy issues on the labour market. We could ask ourselves if the support of people to facilitate transitions and breaks could, for example, solve the early retirement problem. The Belgian labour market seems characterised by a 'compressed career'. People work very hard between the age of 25 and 49 years, which often leads to burn-out problems at a rather early age. We could argue that relieving the pressures people face during this part of the career by allowing for breaks (for example, through leave schemes) could prevent this from happening. As a result the workers concerned would have more capacity or 'energy' allowing them to work longer and this would contribute to ensure the affordability of the social security system. Until now the research on survey (ECHP) and administrative data could not give a clear answer to this important question. We did find some evidence showing that by allowing for more transitions makes it easier to combine family and working life and would improve hence, the work–life balance. The analysis showed that women, more often than men, make the transition between full-time and part-time work or leave the labour market to take care of children. Policy makers should therefore focus on the facilitation of these transitions so as to avoid adverse consequences at the end of the career by safeguarding support for people to stay active. It is generally believed that facilitating transitions of the unemployed is beneficial to them. The longer people stay unemployed, the lower their chances to recover the links to work and the labour market. Long-term unemployment causes human capital endowments of the unemployed to turn obsolete. Their reintegration into the labour market then passes off with larger difficulty and there is no possibility to gain further work experience. In the end, this could lead to a 'lost generation' issue. Therefore it is important to offer to the unemployed a job very quickly after they lost employment or even better – as the transitional labour market approach suggests – to anticipate unemployment and to prevent them from becoming unemployed and being caught in long-term inactivity. This is what Belgian policy makers focus on in current policy proposals. These are characterised by a 'comprehensive approach' in which unemployment will be tackled both in a preventive and curative way. Every newly unemployed person will be invited to the public employment office to subsequently offer them a new start on the labour market. A special focus will be on the long-term unemployed to support their reintegration on the labour market. Much of what has been proposed might benefit from the ideas developed in the transitional labour market framework which boil down to facilitating transitions and to focusing on preventing people to have their links with the labour market lost and to ask for activating policies to make such policies successful.

NOTES

1. The same conclusion is drawn in Chapter 10 using Dutch survey data.
2. This contribution was possible thanks to the Crossroads Bank for Social Security (Kruispuntbank Sociale Zekerheid – KSZ) and the funding provided by the Flemish Government (VIONA programme, Policy support measure) and from the federal government, POD Science Policy, Agora Programme, Project Quality of Labour. The study has profited from the discussions in the framework of the TLM (Transitional Labour Market)-network being funded by the 5th Frework Programme of the European Commission.
3. The social security institutions involved are the National Service for Medical and Disablement Insurance (Rijksinstituut voor Ziekte- en Invaliditeitsverzekering – RIZIV), the Department of Social Services responsible for child benefit (Rijksdienst voor Kinderbijslag van Werknemers – RKW), the state body responsible for social security of the self-employed (Rijksinstituut voor de Sociale Verzekering van Zelfstandigen, RSVZ), the National Office for Social Security (Rijksdienst voor Sociale Zekerheid, RSZ), the National Office for Social Security for Local and Provincial Authorities (Rijksdienst voor Sociale Zekerheid voor Plaatselijke en Provinciale Overheden, RSZPPO) and the National Employment Office (Rijksdienst voor Arbeidsvoorziening, RVA), the National Health Services (Intermutualistisch Agentschap), the Industrial Accidents Fund (Fonds voor Arbeidsongevallen), the Occupational Diseases Fund (Fonds voor Beroepsziekten), the National Office for Social Integration, Poverty Prevention and Social Protection (POD Maatschappelijke Integratie), the National Office for Pensions (Rijksdienst voor Pensioenen) and the National Register (Rijksregister). The linking takes place at the Crossroads Bank for Social Security (Kruispuntbank Sociale Zekerheid – KSZ); the *Maatschappij voor Meconografie* (SmalS-MyM) is in charge of IT-support, whereas the project will be scientifically supported by the Policy Research Centre Work and Social Economy (Steunpunt Werk en Sociale Economie) and the Point d'Appui Travail Emploi Formation.
4. It is also possible for a full-time employee to move to other full-time employment positiona, but we do not take that into account in this chapter. After all, this person would remain in

full-time employment throughout the period. In other words, job mobility is not considered here. For more information about job mobility, see Stimpson A. and Tielens M. (2004).

REFERENCES

Forrier, A., Heylen, V., Vandenbrande, T., Bollens, J. and Sels, L. (2004), *Arbeidsloopbanen in kaart*, Leuven: HIVA.
Muffels, R.J.A. and Luijkx, R. (2006), 'Globalisation And Male Job Mobility In European Welfare States', in Blossfeld, H.-P., Mills, M. and Bernard, F. (eds), *Globalisation And Uncertainty Of Men's Careers*, Cheltenham, UK and Northampton, MA, USA: Edward Elgar.
Muffels, R. and Luijkx, R. (2008), 'Labour Market Mobility and Employment Security of Male Employees in Europe: "Trade-off" or "Flexicurity"?', *Work, Employment and Society,* **22** (2), 221–42.
Román, A., Fouarge D. and Luijkx, R. (2004), *Career consequences of part-time work: results from Dutch panel data 1990–2001*, Tilburg: OSA-rapport A206
Román, A. and Schippers, J.J. (2005), *To work or not to work: a vital life course decision and how it affects labour careers,* Tilburg: OSA (212).
Román, A. (2006), *Deviating from the standard: effects on labour continuity and career patterns,* Amsterdam: Dutch University Press.
Schmid, G. (1995), 'Is Full-Employment Still Possible – Transitional Labor-Markets as a New Strategy of Labor-Market Policy', *Economic and Industrial Democracy,* **16**, 429–56.
Schmid, G. and Gazier, B. (2002), *The Dynamics Of Full Employment: Social Integration Through Transitional Labour Markets,* Cheltenham, UK and Northhampton, MA, USA: Edward Elgar.
Soens, N., Buyens, D., De Vos, A., Heylen, L., Kuppens, A., Mortelmans, D. en Van Puyvelde, I. (2005), *Belgische loopbanen in kaart: traditioneel of transitioneel?*, Gent: Academia Press.
Stimpson, A. and Tielens, M. (2004), *Mobility in the eEconomy,* STILE report, Leuven: HIVA-KULeuven.

PART II

'Scarring' Effects of Unemployment and
Non-standard Employment

6. Male Labour Market Mobility and Income and Employment Security in Europe

Ruud Muffels and Ruud Luijkx

6.1 INTRODUCTION AND PURPOSE OF THE STUDY

The aim of this chapter is to examine the empirical relationship between flexibility, indicated by the extent of male labour market mobility, and income and employment security in 14 EU countries.[1] In the framework of the European policy debate on this relationship, the notion of 'flexicurity' has gained momentum and departs from the idea that policies might be shaped so as to create a mutually supporting relationship or a synergy between flexibility and employment security (EC, 2007a). In the introductory chapter of this book the contours were already sketched of the current debate and analysis in academic as well as policy circles in Europe on this 'flexicurity' issue. The notion of flexicurity also fits nicely to the normative dimension of the Transitional Labour Market approach promoting a shift from classical 'make work pay' policies to 'make transitions pay' policies (Schmid, 2002, 2006). The aim of such 'activating labour market policies' is to promote employment security (but not necessarily with the same employer) instead of job security (see De Gier and Van den Berg, 2005). In this empirical chapter we focus again on this relationship and build forth on previous studies (see Muffels and Luijkx, 2005, 2006, 2008). We now extend the analyses and broaden our definition of security. With respect to the latter we add the dimension of income security instead of focusing on employment security only. As before we restrict ourselves to male workers because female labour market participation patterns and changes therein over the life course are markedly different compared to men due to interrupted and more unstable working careers which would require a separate treatment. The impact of policies on mobility patterns can be examined in two ways. The dominant approach is to look at the effects of different types of policies as represented by welfare state or policy regimes. Another way is to look at specific and very concrete policy measures and how they affect mobility patterns and careers. Here we focus on the impact of country and regime type though instead of departing from the existing typologies we try to develop our own classification of countries and to examine to what extent that fits to the existing ones; for the impact of specific policy measures we refer to another study (Muffels, 2007).

6.2 BACKGROUND OF THE STUDY

Labour markets in Europe have witnessed during the last decades of the 20th century the wake of a much more diverse pattern of labour contracts, working times and careers over the life course (DiPrete and Nonnemaker, 1997; Schmid, 1995). It has resulted in rising job-to-job mobility on the internal as well as the external labour market, a rising share of workers in non-standard jobs such as part-time, casual and temporary agency work, the rise of short intermittent spells of unemployment or inactivity over the life course and hence of increased re-entry and exit rates out of the labour market during the career.

The so-called de-standardisation of working patterns and life courses has been attributed to structural socio-economic changes associated with globalisation and internationalisation of the economy and to socio-cultural changes associated with the individualisation process (see Chapter 1 of this book).

The internationalisation of the economy and the resulting pressure on employers to adapt the working force more rapidly to changes in aggregate demand (flexibilisation) has increased the turnover on the labour market. In such a context policies aimed at supporting employment security by strict employment protection legislation will have a negative effect on the mobility on the labour market and therewith on economic growth. Strong employment protection will lead to a slowed adjustment process of the labour force to economic shocks signalling a lack of flexibility in the labour market. Institutional economists likewise argue that labour markets that are more tightly regulated, for example, through strong employment protection rules, might not work efficiently owing to the additional transaction costs involves in hiring and firing policies (Addison and Teixeira, 2003; Blanchard and Tirole, 2004; Blanchard and Wolfers, 2000; Nickell, 1997; Nickell, Nunziata and Ochel, 2005). On the other hand policies aimed at increasing mobility by relaxing the employment protection rules might be confronted with increasing unemployment spells especially in downturn periods and especially among the weakest groups, that is, the low-skilled, particularly if there is excess supply of high-skilled workers. Due to skill-biased technical change (Acemoglu, 2002, 2003a, 2003b) the demand for low-skill workers diminishes and that of high-skill workers increases. Because of the wage rigidities in European labour markets this will not result in lower wages of the low-skilled but in higher unemployment or in insecure (temporary) employment, particularly in downturn periods. This will therefore endanger the employment security of the low-skilled.

Also sociologists pointing to the adverse effects of globalisation trends showed that due to social stratification processes particularly the weakest groups on the labour market, workers in low status jobs with low skill levels and human capital endowments are increasingly exposed to rising employment instability and income and employment insecurity (Mills and Blossfeld, 2005; Blossfeld et al., 2006; Breen 1997; Scherer, 2004, DiPrete et al., 2006).

The unskilled therefore might be entrapped either in long-term unemployment or in low-quality jobs acting as 'dead-end' jobs in which people have little prospect for escape. This refers to the 'scarring thesis' according to which experiences of non-employment or employment in low-level jobs as being partly the result of flexibilisation have an enduring negative effect on the workers' future career in terms of employment stability and earnings (Booth et al., 2002; European Commission, 2003, 2007; DiPrete et al., 1997; Gangl, 2003, 2006; Golsch, 2003; Kalleberg, 2000; Muffels and Luijkx, 2006).

Also the changing socio-cultural context deserves particular mentioning here. It causes people to seek more opportunities for working part-time, during flexible working hours, at distant locations, in changing combinations of work, learning and caring responsibilities during the life course and in non-standard labour contracts (European Commission, 2003; DiPrete and Nonnemaker, 1997; Golsch, 2003; Guadalupe, 2003; Kalleberg, 2000; Muffels and Luijkx, 2006, 2008). The shift in preferences is partly explained by changing gender role patterns and particularly by the ageing of the population. It has resulted in a marked increase in female labour force participation and a strongly reduced participation of older cohorts of male and female workers in the last few decades of the former century in nearly every European country. Though we will take the transition patterns of older workers into account, we will not deal with the impact of changing gender role patterns on the transition behaviour of women. For substantive reasons we decided to restrict the analyses to male transition patterns only. The labour market behaviour and transition patterns of women on the labour market are so dissimilar to men's, especially with a view to the underlying causal mechanisms, that a full account of the gender specific transition patterns would require a separate treatment of male and female mobility patterns. Female transition patterns differ for various reasons related to differences in: working time preferences at different stages of the life course due to caring obligations, employment career opportunities, occupations in which they work, their occupational and pay levels. A related argument is more technical and is associated with the larger heterogeneity involved in female working time patterns compared to men especially in a long-term or life course perspective which would complicate the analyses for women further. We therefore decided to start from a more homogenous sample and to focus on male transition patterns.

Due to the aforementioned socio-economic and socio-cultural changes the general view is that the trend to increasing flexibility will jeopardise the attained levels of income and employment protection in Europe. In other words, there will be a negative relationship or a 'trade-off' between flexibility and security. The main question addressed here is therefore whether there is empirical evidence for such a 'trade-off' or that our evidence supports the idea of a 'mutual beneficial relationship', a synergy as the 'flexicurity thesis' presumes (Wilthagen, 1998, 2004).

How is flexibility and income/employment security defined?
Flexibility is understood here in economic terms as the degree to which the labour market is capable of creating opportunities for employers and employees to meet their demands for qualified workers and jobs. A flexible labour market operates efficiently when it exhibits high levels of mobility on the internal (functional flexibility) as well as the external labour market (numerical flexibility) creating more opportunities for employers to adapt the working force to the whimsicality of the business cycle, and for workers and non-employed people to rapidly get the job they are looking for. A flexible labour market means that employers have more leeway due either to lack of institutional constraints or to opportunities offered by the terms of law to adapt the size of the workforce to changes in demand and workers to have more opportunities to find a new job when they want to or when they need to.[2] With employment security we mean in analogy to Wilthagen (2004) remaining in secure employment over time but not necessarily in the same job with the same employer. Employment security is increased when workers are able to escape insecure employment statuses and to move into more secure employment statuses. Income security is defined similarly as remaining income secure over time but not necessarily in the same income position. Income security is increased when people are able to escape poverty by bringing their income above the poverty threshold.

6.3 MACRO-LEVEL HYPOTHESES ABOUT THE RELATIONSHIP BETWEEN FLEXIBILITY AND SECURITY

We will in particular examine the impact of 'welfare regimes' on the relationship between flexibility and income/employment security. We view regime types as an amalgam or a 'regulatory mix' of institutions, law regulations and policies aimed at achieving an efficiently operating labour market without distorting commonly accepted income and employment security levels. The choice of the mix is likely to be different across welfare regimes dependent on their different historical path and economic and socio-cultural roots. The mix itself will consist of a variety of components but according to the literature should include things like the generosity of the benefit systems, the strictness of employment protection legislation (EPL), the features of the industrial relations system, a company's 'employability' policies, wage legislation, the wage bargain and active labour market policies. Before we discuss the empirical results we need to explain how institutions and regime types from a theoretical perspective might affect the relationship between flexibility and security.

In earlier work (Muffels and Luijkx, 2005) we drew a so-called 'flexicurity' quadrant based on the theoretical relationship between labour market mobility (job and contract mobility) on the one hand and income/employment security on the other (see Figure 6.1). In two quadrants there existed a kind of 'trade-off' between flexibility and security in which either mobility/flexibility is high and security low or vice versa. In the other quadrants the values on the mobility/flexibility and security axes are either both high (flexicurity) or low (inflex-insecurity). If we were to draw a scatter plot of the attained levels of flexibility and employment security in Europe, we would expect to find that the countries' scatter points would lie around the 45° lines drawn in Figure 6.1. Either the points would be around the 'flexicurity' line signalling a positive association between flexibility and security, or around the 'trade-off' line signalling a negative association between the two. Such a scatterplot reflecting the country's scores on the attained levels of flexibility and security might show that the countries cluster and that these clusters resemble different so-called welfare regimes.

Trade-off or flexicurity?
The trade-off thesis assumes that a high flexibility attained either through allowing employers more room in hiring workers on fixed-term contracts or through relaxation of the employment protection rules will jeopardise employment security because workers are either temporarily employed or

they can be more easily laid-off or dismissed. This will then also impact negatively on the level of income security.

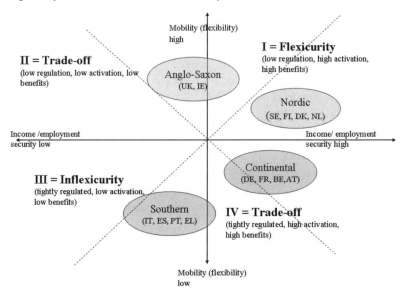

Figure 6.1 The location of regime types in the 'flexicurity' quadrant

However, one may cast doubt on whether such 'trade-offs' need to exist. The idea that flexibility and security are mutually reinforcing has its resemblance in the current European policy and academic debate, known under the heading of the 'flexicurity' thesis ((European Commission, 2003). The 'flexicurity' thesis presumes that a high level of flexibility can go along with a high level of employment and income security provided appropriate investments in the 'employability' of workers are made to assure that workers can move to another job when they need or want to. If employment security is safeguarded, the worker is also more likely to remain income secure. The underlying idea is that a high flexibility not only allows employers to adapt more swiftly to changes in the demand for labour but at the same time to take away the barriers for hiring new workers and by doing so to improve the employment and hence, income security in the longer term. Following this reasoning, there is a synergy between the two concepts. Flexibility and employability are required to eventually attain high levels of income and employment security as well.

In the recently issued final Communication on 'flexicurity' policies the European Commission (2007b) defined flexicurity as follows: 'Flexicurity aims at ensuring that EU citizens can enjoy a high level of employment security, that is, the possibility to easily find a job at every stage of active life and have a good prospect for career development in a quickly changing economic environment'. In the same document it is said that flexicurity 'can be defined as an integrated strategy to enhance, at the same time, flexibility and security in the labour market'.

Regime types

In the area of the labour market and the welfare state, Esping-Andersen's classification of 'the three worlds of welfare capitalism' (1990;1996;1999) is still the 'golden standard' and by far the most influential. That study has been succeeded by many others creating more refined classifications of countries for example, by adding a 'Southern' model to take account of the particular role the family plays in these regimes (Albert, 1991; Bonoli, 1997; Ferrera, 1996; Hall and Soskice, 2001; Amable, 2003).

We therefore use such an amended version with the Southern welfare states (Spain, Portugal, Greece and Italy) as a distinct cluster (Goodin et al., 1999). The UK and Ireland belong to an Anglo-Saxon or liberal cluster, although Ireland does not fit neatly in this regime type.[3] Countries like Germany, France, Belgium, Austria and Luxembourg are believed to belong to a continental or corporatist type of welfare state with the Netherlands and the Scandinavian welfare regimes (Denmark, Finland, Sweden) to the Nordic regime.

The Nordic regime is presumed to attain a high level of institutional flexibility in the labour market (absence of strong employment protection legislation) and at the same time to provide enhanced income/employment security due to generous benefits, collective agreements aimed at maintaining a high employment level, and active or activating labour market policies. It might pay a cost as a result of its efforts to keep their least productive workers at work and to maintain a generous benefit system. The Anglo-Saxon regime is presumably strong on the flexibility part (low employment protection), but weak on the income/employment security part (ungenerous benefits, no active labour market policies and little employment protection). While the Continental regime might not perform particularly well as regards labour market flexibility (strong employment protection) it does fairly well in terms of safeguarding income/employment security due to generous benefits and active labour market policies. Although generalisations are risky, the Southern European familialistic regime might combine a low level of flexibility (strong employment protection) with a low level of income security due to low benefit levels and low levels of employment security for outsiders (segmented labour market aimed at protection of insiders). There is no regime that perfectly fits in the 'flexicurity' quadrant, though the Nordic and Anglo-Saxon regime come closest to it. The location of the four welfare regimes on the flexibility–security axes might be as the one drawn in Figure 6.1.

6.4 MICRO-LEVEL HYPOTHESES

In addition to the macro-level factors, our hypotheses also deal with micro-level factors, which are assumed to have a common impact on mobility and employment security patterns of individuals across all countries. The rationale to consider micro-level factors to explain mobility and employment security patterns at the individual level stems from a broader theoretical framework.

Life course theory
The first hypothesis is related to the impact of the life course on mobility. For that purpose we have taken notice of demographic variables such as marital status and the number of children. According to the male breadwinner thesis we expect that due to higher economic needs, married or cohabiting people make more frequently upward moves, and less frequently downward moves on the labour market than singles or separated people.

For similar reasons we expect the number of children to have a different effect on men's mobility patterns than on women's. It is well-known that women tend to work less or drop out of employment due to generally taking up most of the caring duties involved in raising children. Because men are still less involved in caring we suspect that the more children a household contains, the more economic need there will be for the male head to work or to make a career. Hence, we expect that males with children tend to work longer hours than singles or married men without children. A similar but smaller effect might be expected for males with children (either in-living or not) who are divorced or separated.

Human capital theory
The second hypothesis deals with human-capital theory. We assume that the more human capital endowments people possess, either obtained through formal schooling or through training on-the-job, the better the opportunities are to acquire a job on the labour market or to move to a better paid job offering a higher wage or better wage career prospects.[4] These human capital variables signal the skill-level and work experience of the job seeker, but also the returns to employers' investments in further education and training. We further contend that age – apart from its effect on acquired skills and experience – has a separate effect on job mobility for two reasons. The first has to do with the firm-specific nature of the human capital that is built up during the stay at the firm that will cause mobility to slow down with increasing age. The second has to do with the employer's selective hiring and firing policies revealing a preference for younger workers since investments

in human capital are expected to pay off in the longer term. It implies that the older unemployed people are, the less easy it is to re-enter into work.

Also health status is supposed to affect the value of the human capital a worker possesses. A bad health lowers the value of someone's productivity and human capital endowments. It means that the likelihood of getting a better job is higher and of getting a worse job is lower for workers with bad health.

Economic Resources

A third hypothesis deals with the level of economic resources available in the household that is likely to affect mobility. Therefore we take account of measures that indicate the households' financial resources to make ends meet, such as net household equivalent labour income (corrected for purchasing power parities differences) and non-labour household income consisting of social security income and income from wealth. The proposition is that the more resources are available in the household, the less need there is to work or to search for better (paid) jobs, for which reason mobility is likely to be lower than in the case where such resources are lacking.

Social stratification theory

Following the social stratification theory the fourth hypothesis deals with belonging to a particular occupational class and how that affects a person's mobility path over the career. The underlying reason to include occupational class is that it independently from education level also signals skill-level and wage differences and hence, impacts on the mobility chances to other jobs. However, due to data limitations of the ECHP we were not able to use the well-known and extended EGP-classification scheme of social-class occupations (Erikson and Goldthorpe, 1992). The ECHP allows only a very crude approximation of the original Erikson and Goldthorpe scheme, which will be used here. The variable is included also to take account of so-called ceiling and bottom effects indicating that upward mobility chances are higher at lower levels of the class distribution and downward chances higher at higher levels of that distribution.

The employment relationship

The employment relationship is likely to exert a strong effect on internal as well as external mobility patterns (see Collins, 2003; Stone, 2005). The panel data contain little information on the demand side of labour though some information on job characteristics is available. Apart from occupational class these are the number of weekly working hours, industrial sector and firm size. The weekly number of hours is likely to affect mobility because workers seek jobs with longer hours because it renders them more career opportunities and more income/employment security. Therefore the shorter current working hours are, the more likely it is for workers to move into another job. We also expect that the unemployed prefer jobs with longer working hours especially for males who have no caring duties at home. Next we assume that the more protected a sector is and not affected by shocks on the labour market, the less likely it is for the workers in this sector to experience an involuntary move into another job or into non-work. Because the public sector is generally considered a stable sector that is neither affected strongly by international market pressures nor by severe economic shocks, there is reason to expect less volatility. We also included a dummy for the primary sector. Firm size is included because the larger the firm the lengthier the job ladder and the more opportunities workers have to make an upward or downward move on the internal labour market. Although we do not know whether it is a move on the internal or the external labour market, we suspect firm size to affect labour market mobility. We also assume that job seekers prefer jobs in larger firms because they are likely to provide better career opportunities.

Economic cycle
Finally we suspect that the economic cycle exerts a significant impact on mobility chances. In the upswing stage of the economy we expect more upward moves into better labour market positions and less downward moves into worse positions, whereas in a period of slowdown the reverse holds. During the 1990s, all countries were in the upward stage of the economy that succeeded the recession taking place in the early 1990s. Therefore we expect positive signs of the year dummy parameter effects for upward moves and negative signs for downward moves. Since the economy grows in this period at a higher speed each year, we expect the year dummy parameters to increase over time.

6.5 DATA AND MEASURES

6.5.1 Data

We use the data from the European Community Household Panel (ECHP) covering fourteen countries of the European Union. Sweden was excluded from the sample.[5] For substantive reasons we restricted our sample to male persons of working age, that is, men between 16 and 65 years of age. The reason is that the labour market behaviour and transition patterns of men and women on the labour market are so dissimilar especially with a view to the underlying causal mechanisms that a full account of the gender specific transition patterns would require a separate treatment of male and female mobility patterns. Female transition patterns differ for various reasons related to differences in: working time preferences at different stages of the life course due to caring obligations, employment career opportunities, occupations in which they work, their occupational and pay levels and so on. A related argument is more technical and is associated with the larger heterogeneity involved in female working time patterns compared to men especially in a life course perspective which would complicate the analyses for women further. We weighted the data and calculated adjusted longitudinal weights. These were calculated as the product of the cross-sectional weights and the inverse of the survival probabilities between two consecutive waves. The weights were in a second step adjusted to take account of the differences in population and sample sizes across countries. The ECHP contains information on the type of labour contract, on occupation (2-digit ISCO 1988-code) and the branch of industry (NACE). Unfortunately, hardly any information is available on the function the worker occupies and the work tasks he performs, or on the employer. Therefore, there is a lack of information on multi-tasking and on job-to-job mobility as far as it involves an employer's change. We focus on year-to-year changes in employment contract, labour market status and occupational class. The dependent variables are defined using the information as reported for the preceding calendar year in each of the eight waves we used from 1994 to 2001. For estimation we pooled the information for the seven transition rates for each individual in the sample. We consider changes in status positions between year t and year $t+1$. The independent variables are all measured at time t. The total number of observations in the seven year-by-year transition panel data sets is 384,209. Because of the clustering of transitions over time and the clustering of individuals over countries we used robust estimation of the model parameters and their standard errors.

6.5.2 Measures

Outcome measures
The standard approach is to use static institutional measures such as the level of employment protection to map countries on a flexibility–security scale (for example, EC, 2007a) whereas we focus on developing and applying dynamic outcome measures. Institutions might restrain or promote flexibility but in the end social and economic conditions determine what countries achieve in terms of flexibility or mobility and security levels (see also Muffels, 2007). We apply two outcome measures for contract and occupational class mobility and two for employment and income security, respectively.

Occupational mobility (OM)
The first measure uses the information on the change in occupational class across two years as a proxy for job-to-job mobility. Occupational class is also a good proxy for wage differentials because by focusing on occupational mobility we also take – at least partly – wage mobility into account. A move into a higher occupational class is considered an upward move and a move into a lower class a downward move. Workers staying in the same class might still experience a so-called lateral move because they might change their job without changing occupation for which reason our measure underestimates to some extent the amount of job mobility in society. OM is the sum of upward (OM_{up}) and downward mobility (OM_{down}):

$$OM = OM_{up} + OM_{down} \qquad (6.1)$$

Contract mobility (CM)
The second measure deals with the mobility between different types of contracts (permanent, temporary, self-employment), which we label as contract mobility. The ECHP contains information on whether workers are occupied in a permanent job, a non-standard contract (temporary job, a casual job or another job with a different kind of contract) or a self-employed job. Using the information on the transitions between origin and destination contract status across two years we can calculate the number of workers moving from one of these contract types into another. *CM* is therefore the sum of the mobility between various contract types (CM_{od}) weighted with the share of workers with respect to their origin contract status as percentage of all employed people (ρ_o^e):

$$CM = \sum_{o=1}^{O} \sum_{d=1}^{D} \rho_o^e CM_{od} \qquad (6.2)$$

where o = origin state; d = destination state; O;D = number of origin; destination states; o: 1 = permanent job; 2 = temporary contract and d: 1 = permanent job; 2 = temporary contract; 3 = self-employment.

Occupational and contract mobility are treated as separate outcome indicators for the level of flexibility in a country. The sum of occupational and contract mobility weighted with the share of people in employment as percentage of the population between 16 and 65 years (ρ_e) is called the labour market flexibility or mobility measure M:

$$M = \rho_e (CM + OM) \qquad (6.3)$$

where ρ_e is the share of people in employment.

After multiplication with 100 the *M* measure ranges from 0 to 100 per cent. If *M* is 0 per cent nobody changes occupations or contracts. If it is 100 per cent everybody has changed either from occupation or from contract. The average value for *M* for the 14 countries is 6.73 per cent ranging from 1.74 per cent in France to 11.2 per cent in the UK and 11.6 per cent in Belgium.

Dynamic employment security (ESD)
Dynamic employment security at the individual level is measured by changes in employment security due to changes in the employment status of a person. If a person during two consecutive years enters a permanent job or self-employment from either non-work (unemployment or inactivity) or from a temporary contract, his employment security is increased and if he leaves a permanent job and moves into a temporary contract, self-employment or into non-work his employment security is reduced. It implies that people moving into early retirement after employment are included in our exit rates but early retired people who re-enter employment also show up in the entry rates. We also treated those who stayed in the same status as entries or exits into employment security. We treat workers staying employed across two years as entries because their employment security is improved. From the literature we know that due to path dependency the likelihood to be employed the next year is known to be higher for people already employed. However, for not-working people staying out of work for another year we know that path-dependency effects will impair their chances to re-enter a job and to become employment secure for which reason they are treated as exits into less security. This allows us to define the *ESD* (dynamic employment security) measure as the weighted average of the 'entry' and 'exit' rates, weighted with the shares of the different types of workers with respect to their origin employment statuses in the population of 16 to 65 years (ρ_o):

$$ESD = \sum_{o=1}^{O} \sum_{d=1}^{D} \rho_o \, Entry_{od} - \sum_{o=1}^{O} \sum_{d=1}^{D} \rho_o \, Exit_{od} \qquad (6.4)$$

where o = origin state; d = destination state; $O;D$ = number of origin; destination states; o: 1 = permanent job; 2 = temporary job; 3 = out-of-work; d: 1 = permanent job; 2 = temporary job; 3 = self-employment; 4 = out-of-work.[6]
After multiplication with 100, dynamic employment security ranges between −100 per cent and +100 per cent. If it is −100 per cent it means that nobody has a job and all people moved out-of-the-labour market. If it is +100 per cent it means that everybody acquired a job and that nobody stayed non-working. In our sample the average score is 34 per cent ranging from 15 per cent in Italy to 52 per cent in the Netherlands.[7]

Dynamic income security (YSD)
The dynamic income security measure is defined as the change in income security across two years. The *YSD* is calculated as the average annual proportion of people in a country for the seven years of observation that were able to improve their income security level minus the proportion of people that saw their income security reduced. Income security is improved if people stay out of poverty or escape from it across two years. Income security is reduced if people stay in poverty or become poor. For poverty we use the 60 per cent threshold of the median equivalent income, as it is the one now primarily used in reports of the European Commission.[8] In formula:

$$YSD = \sum_{o=1}^{O} \sum_{d=1}^{D} \rho_o Exit_{od} - \sum_{o=1}^{O} \sum_{d=1}^{D} \rho_o Entry_{od} \qquad (6.5)$$

where $o,d = 1$ (poor) or 0 (non-poor). Dynamic income security ranges between −100 per cent and +100 per cent. If it is −100 per cent it means that all the non-poor entered poverty and nobody escaped from poverty; if it is +100 per cent it means that all poor people escaped from poverty but nobody entered poverty. In our sample the average YSD score is 60 per cent ranging from −25 per cent to 88 per cent across countries.

6.6 MODELS FOR EXPLAINING MOBILITY PATTERNS

6.6.1 Four Models

We estimated multinomial logit models to explain the mobility patterns[9] for different occupational classes and for each of the three origin employment states. The underlying idea is that if people make transitions it involves a choice for the destination state they want to move to, dependent on the origin state. However, choices are constrained due to lack of capabilities or opportunities to move, for example, from a temporary job into a permanent job or from non-work into self-employment. Therefore we take the current status of people and estimate the transition probabilities from that origin state into the various destination states. We distinguish three origin states only excluding self-employment because of the low numbers of transitions and the problems involved in assessing self-employment status though we included movements into self-employment.[10] Then we examine the mobility into various destination states: a temporary job, a permanent job, self-employment and non-work or inactivity.

The probability of moving from the origin state (permanent job, temporary contract, non-participation) into either of the four destination states (including self-employment), as compared to staying in the origin state being the reference group, is given by the following equation:

$$P(y = d) = \frac{\exp\left(\sum_{k=1}^{K} \beta_{dk} x_k\right)}{1 + \sum_{d=1}^{D-1} \exp\left(\sum_{k=1}^{K} \beta_{dk} x_k\right)} \tag{6.6}$$

with d = destination state and D = 4 (the number of destination states, one acting as reference group) and K the number of explanatory variables x.

We estimated four models:

- Model I deals with occupational class mobility. This is the mobility from a current occupational class position at t into another position at $t+1$. We used the occupational class variable in the user database of the ECHP containing only four categories: professional worker; upper manual worker; low white-collar worker and lower manual or personal service workers. Because the scheme is essentially non-hierarchical, the ranking of the four classes is based on the calculation of the median hourly wage level in each category for workers working at least 15 hours a week.[11] Using this ranking we are able to make a distinction between lateral (staying in the same class), upward and downward job mobility.

- Model II and III deal with contract and exit (from work to non-work) mobility. Model II examines the mobility from a temporary contract (origin state) into a permanent job, into unemployment/inactivity or into self-employment (destination states). Model III examines the mobility from a permanent job into self-employment, a temporary contract or unemployment/inactivity. The reference category is staying in a temporary contract in Model II and staying in a permanent job in Model III.

- Model IV examines (re-)entry mobility, the mobility from non-work into a permanent job, a temporary contract or into self-employment. The reference category deals with persons staying out of work.

6.6.2   Operationalisation of the Model Variables

Life course
We included a limited number of life course related variables like age, number of children and marital status (married, divorced/separated, single). These variables show to what extent transitions are affected by particular life course events.

Human capital
We included education level and employment and unemployment history. Education level is transformed into three dummies: (1) primary education; (2) lower and medium level of vocational training plus high school, and (3) higher vocational training and university. The lower and medium level of vocational training is considered as the reference category. Because the information on tenure in the ECHP is rather poor, we included a proxy which we called work experience. It covers the number of years that have passed after the worker has reached the age of 18 and after he has started the first job. We therefore were able to account for the different length of the schooling period before the first entrance on the labour market. Though we lack complete information on unemployment history, we have been able to partially predict for the different length of the unemployment spells during the career. For that purpose, we have used the information on whether people had experienced an unemployment spell in the five-year period preceding their current job.

Subjective health
We have included a dummy for bad health, which is a subjectively assessed measure for one's personal health situation.

Job characteristics
Weekly working hours are the total number of actual working hours a worker had usually worked throughout the past calendar year as being asked at the interview date. The information on the industrial sector is derived from the two-digit NACE-code, which was recoded into four dummies for the primary sector, the services/trade sector, the industrial sector and the public sector. Firm size reflects the number of employees in seven classes in the firm where the worker was working at the date of the interview (0; 1–4; 5–19; 20–49; 50–99; 100–499; 500+).

Income variables
Household labour income is the summation of the annual net labour incomes of all persons between 25 and 65 years in the household in the calendar year prior to the interview year. Non-labour income is the net household income from social security transfers and/or from wealth (excluding income from imputed rent). Incomes are deflated and made comparable across countries using the purchasing power parities as calculated by Eurostat (1996) for the various countries and for different years.

Ceiling and bottom effects

We have taken account of ceiling and bottom effects by including the initial occupational class position, divided into four classes, in the job mobility model.

Economic cycle

We included year dummies to account for economic cycle effects. The reference year is the first year of the observation period. In Table 6.A.1 of Annex 6.1 the summary statistics of these variables are given.

6.7 MOBILITY PATTERNS BY COUNTRY AND REGIME TYPE

In Figure 6.2, we depict the attained levels of labour market mobility M (sum of occupational and contract mobility) and dynamic employment security (ESD), by country and regime type. The relationship turns out to be positive for these 14 countries but appears rather weak as is shown by the drawn regression line and the low level of explained variance ($R^2 = 0.07$).

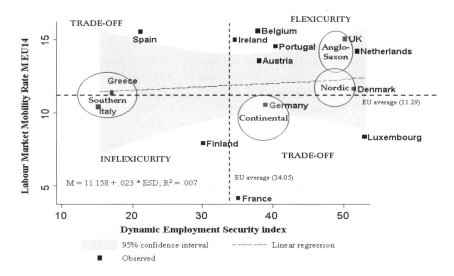

Figure 6.2 The empirical relationship between labour market mobility and dynamic employment security, by country and regime type (in per cent)

The European Union's average for each measure is indicated by a straight line. The highest labour market mobility rates are observed in Spain,

Belgium, Ireland and the United Kingdom. Lower mobility rates but still above the EU average exist in Austria, the Netherlands and Portugal. The German figures are just below the Union average. Low mobility rates are observed in Finland, France, Italy and Greece. The picture shows that the anticipated pattern by regime type is only weakly confirmed. The Anglo-Saxon or liberal countries UK and Ireland indeed show the highest labour market mobility rate and the Continental countries (France, Germany, Luxembourg) as the lowest. On the other hand we observe the Southern countries (Italy, Greece, but especially Spain) exhibiting higher mobility rates than we contended. The high mobility rates in the Anglo-Saxon countries confirm our conjectures, but the ones for the Southern countries are slightly inconclusive.

Further inspection shows that in Southern countries the share of non-standard employment in total employment is high and that they have a high level of contract mobility due to high transition rates of workers in temporary jobs and of workers moving between paid and self-employment, even though the likelihood of moving from a non-standard into a permanent job is rather low. The explanation is that Southern countries have much stricter employment protection rules, a segmented labour market and a large informal sector, whereas the Anglo-Saxon labour markets are much less regulated and therefore exhibit much more job-to-job mobility. While workers can be laid off more easily, there is also less need to circumvent the protection rules seen in the Southern regime by employing temporary workers (see Chapter 4). The highest level of contract mobility is indeed attained in Spain and Greece. It seems that workers keep moving around between different temporary jobs or between paid and self-employment.

It should be noticed that the large variation in labour market mobility within the various regime clusters is much larger than we anticipated. The Belgian and Portugese figures for labour market mobility appear to be very different from the figures for the other countries in their natural regime type, respectively the Continental and the Southern regime. Also the Finnish figures are worse than we expected. The Finnish economy fared not particularly well in this period, for which reason it exhibits low mobility and security. On the other hand, Spain exhibits high levels of mobility that is likely due to the favourable economic conditions tempting workers to change jobs. The high level for Spain is partly explained by the high level of contract mobility due to a large share of workers moving between fixed-term contracts and self-employment (informal economy) not being able to acquire a permanent job. A similar pattern is observed for Greece but at lower levels.

Viewing the employment security figures, we observe again some irregularities, such as Portugal showing a much better record than we expected beforehand setting it apart from the other Southern countries.

Again, Finland's record being below the Union's average is slightly at odds compared to the high level of employment security in the other Nordic countries. The results for the other Nordic and the Southern countries are in line with our expectations, with the first group exhibiting the highest employment security and the latter group showing by far the lowest. The outcomes for the Anglo-Saxon countries is surprising because we suspected that these countries due to their high level of flexibility would have to pay a price through a significant lower level of employment security but the costs turned out to be low. The Nordic countries behave as expected, but the results show that they pay a price for their high level of employment security through a slower mobility rate.

With respect to the relationship between labour market mobility and dynamic income security using the YSD measure as explained before, we depict in Figure 6.3 the results again.

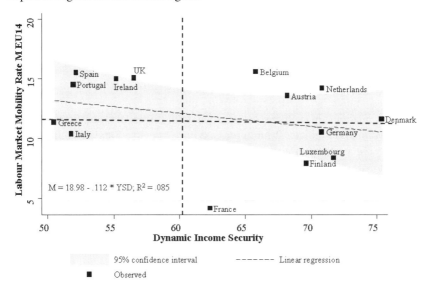

Figure 6.3 The empirical relationship between labour market mobility and dynamic income security (YSD), by country and regime type (in per cent)

The relationship is now negative for these 14 EU countries but again rather weak ($R^2 = 0.08$). The results are only for a few countries different from the earlier picture. The Anglo-Saxon countries (UK and Ireland) seem to perform worse now with respect to safeguarding income security compared to their achievements in safeguarding employment security. The other countries including the Southern countries behave rather similar to the earlier results. In general it seems that there are more countries now showing a 'trade-off' relationship between mobility and income security than in the former case dealing with employment security.

6.8 RESULTS ON MODEL ESTIMATIONS OF LABOUR MARKET MOBILITY

6.8.1 Occupational Mobility

In Table 6.1 we present the findings of our model estimations for occupational mobility (OM). It has to be noted that the coefficient estimates in the multinomial model represent – after exponentiation – relative probabilities or odds ratios. This means that the effect should always be compared with the effect for the reference category. In model I for downward occupational mobility, the coefficient for the dummy variable low education is significant and equal to 0.440. The odds ratio equals the exponent value of it, which is 1.55. This means that the odds for the low educated worker to move downwards into a lower-level job are 55 per cent higher compared to a worker with an intermediate education level. Since we are less interested in these odds ratios than in the strength and the significance of each coefficient we present here the coefficient estimates only.

The relationship with age is U-shaped, both for upward and for downward occupational mobility. With increasing age, occupational mobility slows down. The positive effect for age squared indicates that beyond a particular age threshold both, upward and downward mobility increase again.[12] Upward mobility at a higher age is more likely to occur just before retirement age (at 59 years), whereas downward mobility is likely to occur somewhat earlier at 49 years) either due to demotion on the job or to moving to a lower level job with another employer or into self-employment. The number of children has a significant positive effect on downward and a significant negative effect on upward mobility. These results are interesting, since the effects are well documented for women, but rarely reported for male workers. It appears that just like women and contrary to what we had expected, male labour market behaviour is also affected by childrearing duties. There is no separate effect of marital status on occupational mobility.

Human capital
The education variables demonstrate a strongly significant effect on upward and downward mobility. Low education exerts a strong positive effect on downward mobility into lower-level jobs and a negative effect on upward mobility into higher-level jobs. A high education has the reverse effect; it strongly increases the chances for upward moves and lowers the likelihood of

Table 6.1 Multinomial model for explaining occupational class mobility (reference group is staying in the same occupational class)

Origin		Model I: Occupational class	
	Destination	Downward mobility	Upward mobility
Life course			
Age		−0.168***	−0.026
Age squared/100		0.125***	0.030
Number of children		0.055**	−0.062**
Marital status (ref. = single)			
Married		−0.059	−0.043
Divorced/separated		0.043	0.106
Human Capital			
Education (ref. = intermediate)			
Low education		0.440***	−0.460***
High education		−0.579***	0.302***
Unemployment history		0.484***	0.039
Work experience		0.046***	−0.018***
Socio-economic characteristics			
Bad health		0.077	−0.043
Personal non-labour income		−0.004	0.003
Other labour income HH		−0.004***	0.005***
Non-labour income other HH members		0.002	0.007***
Job characteristics			
Number of working hours		−0.009**	−0.004
Occupational Class (1 = low to 4 = high)		0.973***	−1.161***
Sector (ref. = industry/services)			
Primary sector		0.544***	−0.031
Public sector		−0.356***	0.142**
Firm size		−0.021	0.016
Regime type (ref. = Continental)			
Anglo-Saxon		0.451***	0.933***
Nordic		0.190	0.649**
Southern		0.473	0.492*
Year dummies			
1995		0.294	−0.117
1996		1.642***	1.526***
1997		1.253***	1.010***
1998		1.072***	0.670***
1999		1.463***	1.011***
2000		1.401***	1.065***
Constant		−3.393***	−0.287

Notes: Asterisks denote significance of coefficients: *** 1%, ** 5%, * 10%. The mobility measure is four category occupational class. Coefficients from multinomial logit regressions, relative to lateral move (N = 102,823), Pseudo R^2 = 0.138. Coefficients are effects relative to reference category. The base year is 1994. Sample: males aged 16–64 in all countries.

Source: ECHP, 1994–2001.

downward moves into lower-level jobs. These results are consistent with the human capital predictions and support our hypotheses about the differential impact of the knowledge economy on the demand for low and high skilled labour.

Work experience
Work experience might partly already be covered by age and partly by the experience of unemployment in the last five years. Nonetheless, it exerts a strong positive effect on downward and a strong negative effect on upward mobility, showing that career steps are apparently taken in the early career and not in the later career when demotion is more likely to occur. Also the unemployment history variable has a strong positive effect on downward mobility supporting the 'scarring' hypothesis of unemployment experience.

Socio-economic characteristics
Poor health appears insignificant and does not harm upward mobility nor lead to more downward mobility, at least not in the short term contradicting our prior conjectures though the coefficients have the expected signs.

The income variables show that the joint income of other household members acts as a buffer against downward moves and seems to improve the likelihood of upward career moves.

Job characteristics
The longer the working hours, the less likely it is for workers to move downwards on the career ladder. These results confirm our expectations.

We now turn to our occupational class variable, which accounts for ceiling and bottom effects. The results seem to confirm the existence of these effects. The higher the occupational class level of the worker, the more likely to experience a downward career move and the less likely to experience an upward move. The reverse also holds, implying that the lower occupational class is, the fewer chances workers have to move downwards and the more chances to move upwards.

The dummies for the primary and public sector (the reference group being industry and services) confirm our conjectures. Workers in the primary sector are more likely to move downwards whereas public sector workers are less likely to move downward and more likely to move upward in the career. Firm size has no significant effect on occupational mobility though the signs have the expected direction.

Regime type
We are particularly interested in the effect of policy regimes on mobility. The findings show that the Anglo-Saxon regime exhibit in both models

significantly more upward and downward mobility than the Continental regime acting as the reference category but also compared to the Nordic regime. This is fully in line with our presumptions. Note also the stronger effect for upward career moves than for downward moves in this regime type. Remarkably though, there is also more downward and upward mobility in the Southern regime though the effect is less significant than in the former case. The effect for upward mobility is much weaker in this regime than in the Anglo-Saxon countries.

Economic cycle
Eventually, we turn to the economic cycle effects, which are all positive indicating that in a period of economic upturn the likelihood of downward, as well as upward mobility increases.

6.8.2 Results on Labour Market Mobility

In Table 6.2, we report on the model estimates for labour market mobility: the mobility from a permanent job, a temporary job or non-work (origin states) into any other status (destination states). Staying in the origin state is the reference category in all models.

Life course
The relationship with age turns out to be U-shaped again; mobility decreases initially with age, but after a certain age threshold, mobility increases. This is likely to be due to the attractiveness of exit routes through early retirement, unemployment or disability because of which older workers tend to move out of the labour market at early ages.[13]

This is true for all three models, as shown in Table 6.2. For the mobility from a temporary into a permanent contract this age threshold is such (49 years) that workers in such contracts better not stay too long, while they have fewer opportunities to find a permanent job later in the career. Start-ups into self-employment after having worked in a permanent or temporary contract seem more likely to occur in the midst of the career (threshold is 44 years).

Regarding the number of children in a household, we find that it has a significant negative effect in Model III on the transition from a temporary contract into self-employment and it reduces the likelihood of re-entry from non-work into a permanent job (Model IV). The latter effect is known for female workers with caring duties but not for male workers. Regarding marital status we find that married men are less likely than singles to move out of the labour market after being engaged in paid work in either a permanent or a temporary job, but also more likely to re-enter from non-work into paid work. The economic needs implied with being married and having a family seem to

Table 6.2 Multinomial models for explaining the mobility patterns for workers in permanent jobs (model II), in temporary contracts (model III) and non-working (model IV)

Origin		Model II: Permanent job			Model III: Temporary contract			Model IV: Non-work		
Destination		Flexible Contract	Self-employment	Non-work	Permanent Job	Self-employment	Non-work	Permanent job	Flexible contract	Self-employment
Life course										
Age		−0.188***	0.025	−0.302***	0.071**	0.055	−0.158***	0.316***	0.193***	0.410***
Age squared/100		0.214***	−0.015	0.418***	−0.097***	−0.074**	0.234***	−0.498***	−0.368***	−0.550***
Number of children		−0.006	0.047	0.011	0.044	−0.249***	0.073	−0.121***	−0.017	0.080
Marital status (ref = single)										
Married		−0.085	−0.068	−0.350***	0.054	0.975**	−0.312***	0.632***	0.574***	0.167
Divorced/separated		−1.145***	0.146	0.063	−0.368	1.371***	−0.038	0.060	0.477*	−0.071
Human Capital										
Education (ref = Intermediate)										
Low education		0.067	−0.023	0.034	−0.414***	−0.282	−0.087	−0.396***	0.026	−0.142
High education		0.045	0.121	−0.113**	−0.185**	0.348	−0.249**	0.383***	0.514**	0.727**
Unemployment history		0.768***	0.205***	0.603***	−0.370***	−0.647***	0.182	−0.042	0.573***	−0.196
Work experience		0.001	−0.019**	−0.004	0.005	0.002	−0.015	0.026**	0.036*	0.021**
Socio-economic characteristics										
Bad health		−0.057	0.209	0.908***	−0.254**	0.27	0.689***	−1.293***	−0.840***	−0.709***
Personal non-labour income		0.022**	0.034***	0.017***	−0.023*	−0.05	0.007	−0.060***	−0.061***	−0.051
Other labour income HH		0.003	−0.001	−0.006**	0.007***	0.009	0.001	−0.002	−0.004***	−0.007
Other non-labour income HH		−0.005	−0.014***	0.005	−0.001	−0.004	0.001	−0.022***	−0.007	−0.025
Job characteristics										
Number of working hours		0.008*	0.038***	−0.009***	0.009**	0.029***	−0.018***			
Occ. Class (1= low to 4 = high)		−0.146***	0.288***	−0.095	0.026	0.033	−0.162***			

Table 6.2 (Continued)

Origin	Model II: Permanent job			Model III: Temporary contract			Model IV: Non-work		
Destination	Flexible Contract	Self-employment	Non-work	Permanent Job	Self-employment	Non-work	Permanent job	Flexible contract	Self-employment
Job characteristics (continued)									
Primary sector	0.140	0.294	0.077	-0.503***	0.741***	-0.056			
Public sector	0.236	-0.547***	-0.444***	-0.471**	0.333	-0.120			
Firm size (1 = small to 7 = large)	-0.159***	-0.465***	-0.100***	0.015	-0.364***	-0.082***			
Regime type (ref = Continental)									
Anglo-Saxon	-0.942***	0.267	-0.229***	0.777***	1.311***	0.253	0.392***	-0.152*	0.445
Nordic	-0.019	0.403***	-0.278***	0.333	0.481	-0.585**	0.021	0.443***	-0.254
Southern	0.062	0.905***	-0.193**	-0.493**	0.533***	-0.782***	-1.000***	0.023	0.542**
Year dummies									
1995	-0.073	0.021	-0.201						
1996				-0.052	0.019	0.039	-0.142	-0.296***	0.059
1997	-0.275	-0.242*	-0.177**	0.235*	-0.009	-0.111	-0.090	-0.079	0.101
1998	-0.178	-0.139	-0.167	-0.019	-0.599***	-0.148	0.180	0.033	0.053
1999	0.286	-0.281*	-0.465**	0.01	-0.022	-0.194	-0.029	-0.040	0.147
2000	0.218	-0.092	-0.311**	0.062	-0.087	-0.159	0.006	0.005	0.021
Constant	1.095**	-5.486***	3.339***	-1.430*	-4.264***	3.698***	-5.808***	-4.461***	-9.926***

Notes: Asterisks denote significance of coefficients: *** 1%, ** 5%, * 10%. Coefficients from multinomial logit regression, relative to staying in origin state being the reference group (n = 78,612 in Model II; 12,423 in Model III and 53,026 in Model IV), Pseudo R^2 = 0.088 in Model II; 0.069 in Model III and 0.151 in Model IV. Base year is 1994 (Model II, IV) and 1995 (Model III). Due to autocorrelation the year dummies for 1995 (model III), 1996 (Model II) and 2000 (Model II) and 1995 (Model IV) are removed. Non-work means unemployment or inactivity (disability, education, training, housework). Sample: males aged 16–64 years in all countries.

Source: ECHP, 1994–2001.

157

motivate men to remain in work. For the same economic reason divorced men seem less likely to move to a temporary job after occupying a permanent job but more likely to accept a temporary job when non-working than single men.

Human capital

Education level exerts a strong effect in all models. Low education increases the likelihood of a transition from a permanent job into non-work or into a temporary contract. It also decreases the chance of a transition from such a temporary contract into a permanent contract and into self-employment.

These results confirm our expectations that the knowledge economy aggravates the weaker position of the low-skilled worker in the labour market. The low-skilled not only lack opportunities to obtain a regular job, but also to set up their own business. These results show that people with low-level education are more likely to stay in a temporary contract rather than moving into unemployment because they have little opportunities to move into a permanent job or into self-employment. However, we also find positive effects of a high education level on moves from a permanent job into a temporary contract and negative effects on opposite moves, contesting our prior expectations. Both of these results might point to the attractiveness of particular types of non-standard contracts for highly educated, high skilled professional workers. It might also mean that they can afford to wait longer for the 'ideal' job to arrive before they decide to accept a permanent job offer. However, in the model of transitions out of non-work, a high education level has a strong positive effect on moving into either a flexible or a permanent contract. When high-skilled workers are unemployed they seem more likely to accept any job offer.

Part of the effect of work experience is already captured by age. The results show that work experience has a negative effect on the transition from a permanent job into self-employment and strong positive effects on moving out of non-work into a temporary or a permanent contract.

Past unemployment experience raises the likelihood of a move from a permanent job into self-employment or a temporary contract but also of withdrawal from the labour market altogether. It also reduces the likelihood of obtaining a permanent job after having worked in a temporary contract and of moving from such a contract into self-employment. Again, this provides support to the 'scarring' thesis of unemployment experience. However, it also raises the likelihood of moving out of inactivity into employment. This unexpected outcome might be due to the effect of a longer work experience of these formerly unemployed people raising their chances for re-entry into paid work. It also shows that future mobility into secure jobs is obviously path-dependent.

Socio-economic characteristics

We first included health and contended that it reduces the productivity of a worker and therefore harms someone's employment security on the labour market. Poor health indeed appears to strongly raise the likelihood of becoming unemployed or to withdraw from the labour market after occupying a temporary or a permanent job. It also strongly reduces the chance to escape inactivity and to re-enter any kind of a job (Model IV). For the same reason, poor health inhibits the move from a non-standard job into a permanent job. This corroborates the results of many other studies.

We included personal non-labour income but also net household labour income and non-labour income of the other household members in the models. The non-labour income of the household – be it the personal or the income of others in the household – seems to exert a disincentive effect on staying in work (Model II) or gaining work (Model IV). Other labour income has a different effect and seems to act as an insurance against the loss of a permanent job or an involuntary move into a temporary job.

Job characteristics

We included occupational class level in the models presented here as an additional indicator for skill-level. We had anticipated that due to the knowledge economy, the larger demand for high-skilled workers would also improve the labour market's chances of higher occupational class workers. The results confirm this, showing that the higher the occupational class, the less likely it is for worker to move from a permanent job into unemployment or inactivity or to move into a temporary contract.

However, we also find that the higher the occupational class level of temporary contract workers, the less likely to move into a permanent job. This might again either signal the better quality of the non-standard jobs these higher-skilled professional worker occupy or that the higher skilled can afford to wait before accepting a permanent job offer.

As we already contended, the longer the hours are in the current job, the less likely it is to move out of a permanent or temporary job into unemployment or inactivity. The longer working hours are, the more likely a temporary worker starts his own business or moves into a permanent job.

With respect to sector, we contend that workers in the shielded public sector are less likely to be dismissed from a permanent job. This is confirmed by the data. We also find unexpectedly that temporary workers in the public sector have lower chances to move into a permanent job. Workers in the primary sector are less likely to find a permanent job but more likely to start up a business when they work in a temporary job.

Viewing the results by firm size, we find strong significant effects of firm size on mobility. The larger the firm the employee works for, the less chance there is to lose one's permanent job and to move into either a temporary job, unemployment or inactivity (Model II). We also find that the larger the firm, the less likely for a temporary worker to start up their own business (Model III). It appears that working in a large company has a similar effect on people's behaviour as working in the public sector, that is, it improves the employment security, for which reason people envisage strong barriers to engage in risky market activities.

Regime type
The exit from a permanent job (Model II) into a temporary contract or into non-work and hence into less employment security is significantly lower in Anglo-Saxon regimes compared to the Continental regimes. But even the Nordic and Southern regimes perform better in preventing people moving out of the labour market and becoming employment-insecure. On the other hand, improvements in terms of employment security by switching from a tempo-rary into a permanent contract (Model III) occur more often in Anglo-Saxon countries and much less likely in Southern countries. The expectations we had with respect to welfare regimes seem to be confirmed. Politicians might especially be concerned with getting people out of work into permanent employment (Model IV) and these transitions are more likely to occur in the unregulated Anglo-Saxon regimes than in the strongly regulated Southern and Continental regimes. Business start-ups by people out of work occur more often in Southern countries compared to the Continental ones. This resembles the larger share of self-employment and informal jobs in these countries.

Southern countries and particularly Anglo-Saxon countries also perform better in inducing temporary workers to become self-employed (Model III) compared to Continental regimes (the reference category). The findings for the Southern regimes confirm what we found earlier; that workers in temporary contracts, mostly young workers, tend to shift into self-employment if the door to a permanent job is closed, pointing again to the segmented labour market and the significant role of the informal economy.

Economic cycle
Viewing the results for Model II, it turns out that a number of year parameters are significantly negative though a clear trend cannot be observed. It shows that during this economic upturn period, there are reduced chances to lose one's permanent job. The findings for Model III and Model IV look different as a lot fewer parameters are significant, and showing again no clear trend over time.

6.9 CONCLUSIONS AND DISCUSSION

Due to globalisation working in tandem with the wake of the knowledge economy and the ongoing demographic and socio-cultural changes, labour markets witnessed a much more diverse pattern of labour contracts, working times and careers over the life course resulting in rising mobility patterns and more unstable jobs. The general view is that the trend to increasing mobility or flexibility will jeopardise the attained levels of income and employment security in Europe. The main question addressed is therefore whether there is a 'trade-off' between flexibility and security or a mutually reinforcing relationship known as the 'flexicurity' thesis. We calculated dynamic outcome indicators for flexibility and income and employment security and mapped the countries on the so-called 'flexibility–security' quadrant. We were particularly interested in the role institutions play to affect the balance between the two and for that purpose we explored the performance of the various regime types to balance flexibility and security goals in society. We estimated transition state models to explain the observed mobility patterns across Europe. We included the well-known regime classification of Esping-Andersen in our models because it was shown that it still functions fairly well in explaining differences across countries in the observed labour market mobility patterns.

We found that labour market mobility patterns widely diverge across countries and across regimes. There is more employment stability in Nordic and Continental countries and more mobility in Anglo-Saxon and in Southern countries. The mobility is particularly high among people working in non-standard jobs and among non-employed people. The Southern countries exhibit the lowest mobility rates of temporary jobs to permanent jobs due to their segmented labour markets. With respect to the achieved balance between flexibility and income/employment security the results showed that the unregulated Anglo-Saxon and moderately regulated Nordic regimes achieve a much better balance of flexibility and security, albeit for the Nordic regimes with a small efficiency (less mobility) loss and for the Anglo-Saxon with a small loss in employment and especially income security, than the highly regulated labour markets of the Continental and Southern countries. These findings provide a warning against too much regulation that might lead to a segmented labour market protecting insiders at the expense of outsiders and therewith endangering mobility as well as security.

The models we tested contain a number of other explanatory variables such as life course and human capital variables, socio-economic characteristics, job characteristics and economic cycle or year dummies.

The relationship with age exhibits an U-shaped pattern, first decreasing up to a certain age threshold and then rising again due to exit from the labour market due to unemployment, early retirement or disability. We also found, surprisingly, significant effects of life course variables such as the number of children in the household, suggesting that as is the case for women, for men caring obligations are a barrier to making a career. The child penalty for men is partly offset by a marriage premium. Married workers seem to have better career perspectives than single workers. We find support for the impact of the 'knowledge-based economy'. We concluded that the more human capital endowments workers possess the more opportunities there are to improve one's position on the labour market. Low educated workers appear particular sensitive to downward moves or moves into insecure jobs, which underpins our supposition about the adverse impact of the knowledge economy on the career opportunities of this group.

Our results further show that workers in large firms due to a larger internal labour market are less likely to drop out and to become unemployed or inactive. Working in a shielded sector not being strongly affected by market instability such as the public sector, means that people have better chances to move upwards on the job ladder and lower chances to move downwards.

Eventually, we examined the impact of economic cycle effects and the results show that in an upswing period, as most countries were experiencing during the 1990s, people have lower chances to drop out and higher chances to step in.

We used the ECHP having an eight-year window that is much too short to assess regime type changes over time. However, the analyses indicate that institutional differences are rather stable and that they do shape dissimilar outcomes across institutional settings in this period.

Our analyses were further restricted to male transition patterns although we know that female employment patterns are much more volatile and diverse than those of men. To take full account of the gender specific transition patterns, would require a separate treatment taking account of many specific influencing factors related with working times, caring roles, childcare policies, social stratification, gender wage gaps and so on. This is one of the primary challenges we have to take up in future research.

If the wake of the knowledge economy is indeed detrimental to the employment opportunities of the low-skilled there is reason to believe that over time, labour markets will be faced with more employment instability and more inequality in the distribution of career chances among workers according to skill level. But even if this proves to be true, there is still a positive side to the story. The countries observed here show quite dissimilar results in terms of maintaining the 'flexicurity' balance. The findings signal that particularly the Anglo-Saxon and Nordic countries appear quite successful, notwithstanding the economic pressures they face and with a small cost in terms of either flexibility or security, in maintaining the precious balance between economic and social goals, between flexibility and security. The main policy lesson to be learned is that a 'one-size-fits-all' approach is likely to be ineffective since countries seem to follow their own specific pathways and demonstrate in this respect 'unity in diversity' showing that there is not one world of welfare but many.

NOTES

1. The chapter is an extended and more elaborated version of an earlier paper as published in Muffels and Luijkx (2008). The analyses also take the aspect of income security instead of only employment security into account.
2. No distinction is made between voluntary and forced moves because what matters is that workers and employers have opportunities to respectively find a job when needed or to adapt the work force to changing demands. The economic rationale is that it improves the worker's careers and raises employment because employers are less reluctant to hire workers.
3. Ireland shares the liberal feature of a low level of employment protection but looks very different when viewing a number of other indicators. It shares the corporatist feature of an active labour market policy and the corporatist 'breadwinner's state' characteristic of a low female employment rate. In terms of familial characteristics, it looks more like a Southern welfare state. Ireland seems to be a *hybrid* type of welfare state that does not fit into any of the 'ideal-typical' welfare states. In order to avoid the inclusion of Ireland as the only example of a hybrid type, it was decided to keep it under the liberal heading.
4. The method to include the aforementioned explanatory variables as proxies for the unobserved reservation and offered wages follows human capital theory (Becker, 1975; Mincer, 1974)
5. Sweden is excluded because the data contain only cross-sectional information and no panel data (see Clémenceau and Verma, 1996).
6. In the *ESD* measure, o and d include unemployment and inactivity whereas in the *CM* measure they include employment only.
7. Information on the calculated mobility and security measures averaged over the 7 years of observation by country and regime type is available upon request from the authors.
8. The equivalence scale used for standardisation of the household income is the so-called modified OECD scale (1 for the head, 0.7 for the partner and 0.3 for children).
9. Another way is to use the monthly calendar information and to estimate event history models. However, information in the ECHP is not very precise in terms of the exact duration of each spell over the year and we lack information on the value of the time-varying covariates at the start of the spell.
10. We did not condition on the origin state of self-employment because of the quality of the ECHP data regarding the assessment of self-employment, of which the quality also varies a lot across countries.
11. Calculation of hourly wages on the weighted data shows, that highest mean wages for those working at least 15 hours a week, are observed for professional workers, (€ 12.03), next highest for low, white collar workers (€ 8.25), then for upper manual workers (€ 7.44) and lowest for lower manual and personal services workers (€ 6.53).
12. The age thresholds are in all models calculated with the work experience variable left out, while that variable already partly captures the effect of age. The threshold values in Model I are 57 years (upward mobility) and 49 years (downward mobility).
13. The threshold values (in number of years) are: for model II, 56 (into non-work), 50 (into temporary contract) and 49 (into self-employment); for Model III, 49 (into permanent job), 53 (into non-work) and 49 (into self-employment) and for Model IV, 43 (into permanent job), 44 (into temporary contract) and again 44 (into self-employment).

REFERENCES

Acemoglu, D. (2002), 'Technical change, inequality, and the labour market', *Journal of Economic Literature,* **40** (1), 7–72.

Acemoglu, D. (2003a), 'Cross-country inequality trends', *Economic Journal,* **113** (485), F121–F49.

Acemoglu, D. (2003b), 'Patterns of skill premia', *Review of Economic Studies,* **70** (2), 199–230.

Addison, J. T. and Teixeira, P. (2003), 'The economics of employment protection', *Journal of Labor Research,* **24** (1), 85–129.

Albert, M. (1991), *Capitalisme contre capitalisme,* Paris: Editions du Seuil.

Amable, B. (2003), *The Diversity of Modern Capitalism,* Oxford: Oxford University Press.

Becker, G. (1975), *Human Capital: A Theoretical and Empirical Analysis, with special Reference to Education,* New York: National Bureau of Economic Research.

Blanchard, O. and Tirole, J. (2004), 'Redesigning the employment protection system', *De Economist,* **127** (1), 1–20.

Blanchard, O. and Wolfers, J. (2000), 'The role of shocks and institutions in the rise of European unemployment', NBER WP 7282, and Harry Johnson Lecture, *Economic Journal,* **110**, March, 1–33

Blossfeld, H.P., Mills, M. and Bernardi, F. (2006), *Globalisation, Uncertainty and Men's Careers,* Cheltenham, UK and Northampton, MA, USA: Edward Elgar.

Bonoli, G. (1997), 'Classifying welfare states: a two-dimension approach', *Journal of Social Policy,* **(26)** 3, 351–72.

Booth, A.L., Francesconi, M. and Frank, J. (2002), 'Temporary jobs. Stepping Stones or Dead Ends', *Economic Journal,* **112** (480), 189–213.

Breen, Richard. (1997), 'Risk, commodification and stratification', *Sociology,* **31** (3), 473–89.

Clémenceau, A. and Verma, V. (1996), 'Methodology of the European Community Houshold Panel', *Statistics in Transition,* **2**, 1023–62.

Collins, H. (2005), 'Flexibility and stability of expectations in the contract of employment', *Socio-Economic Review,* **26** (4), 139–53.

De Gier, E. and Van den Berg, A. (2005), *Making Transitions Pay! Towards a European Employment Insurance Strategy (EEIS),* Final Policy Report of the EU Thematic Network on Managing Social Risks through Transitional Labour Markets (TLM.NET), Amsterdam: SISWO/Social Policy.

DiPrete, T.A., Goux, D., Maurin, E. and Quesnel-Vallee, A. (2006), 'Work and pay in flexible and regulated labor markets: A generalized perspective on institutional evolution and inequality trends in Europe and the US', *Research in Social Stratification and Mobility,* **24**, 311–32.

DiPrete, T.A., De Graaf, P.M., Luijkx, R., Tahlin, M. and Blossfeld, H.P. (1997), 'Collectivist versus individualist mobility regimes? Structural change and job mobility in four countries', *American Journal of Sociology,* **103** (2), 318–58.

DiPrete, T.A. and Nonnemaker, K.L. (1997), 'Structural change, labour market turbulence, and labour market outcomes', *American Sociological Review,* **62** (3), 386–404.

Erikson, R. and Goldthorpe, J.H. (1992), *The constant flux: a study of class mobility in industrial societies,* Oxford: The Clarendon Press.

Esping-Andersen, G. (1990), *The Three Worlds of Welfare Capitalism,* Oxford: Polity Press/Blackwell.

Esping-Andersen, G. (1996), *Welfare States in Transition: National adaptations in global economies,* London: Sage Publications.

Esping-Andersen, G. (1999), *Social Foundations of Post-Industrial Economics,* Oxford: Oxford University Press.

European Commission (2003), *Employment in Europe 2003*, Luxembourg: Office for Official Publications of the European Communities.

European Commission (2007a), *Employment in Europe 2007*, Luxembourg: Office for Official Publications of the European Communities.

European Commission (2007b), *Flexicurity Pathways. Turning hurdles into stepping stones,* Final report of the European Expert Group on Flexicurity, Brussels, 41, available at: <http://ec.europa.eu/>.

Eurostat (1996), *European Community Household Panel (ECHP): Survey methodology and implementation,* Luxembourg: Office for Official Publications of the European Communities.

Ferrera, M. (1996), 'The "Southern Model" of welfare in social Europe', *Journal of European Social Policy,* **6** (1), 17–37.

Gangl, M. (2003), 'The only way is up? Employment protection and job mobility among recent entrants to European labour markets', *European Sociological Review*, **19** (5), 429–49.

Gangl, M. (2006), 'Scar Effects of Unemployment: An Assessment of Institutional Complementarities', *American Sociological Review*, **71** (December), 986–1013.

Golsch, K. (2003), 'Employment flexibility in Spain and its impact on transitions to adulthood', *Work Employment and Society,* **17** (4), 691–718.

Goodin, R.E., Heady, B., Muffels, R.J.A. and Dirven, H.-J. (1999), *The Real Worlds of Welfare Capitalism,* Cambridge: Cambridge University Press.

Guadalupe, M. (2003), 'The hidden costs of fixed term contracts: the impact on work accidents', *Labour Economics,* **10** (3), 339–57.

Hall, P. and Soskice, D. (eds) (2001), *Varieties of capitalism: the institutional foundations of comparative advantage*, Oxford: Oxford University Press, 560.

Kalleberg, A. L. (2000), 'Nonstandard employment relations: Part-time, temporary and contract work', *Annual Review of Sociology,* **26**, 341–65.

Mills, M. and Blossfeld, H.P. (2005) 'Globalization, uncertainty and the early life course. A theoretical framework', in H.P. Blossfeld, E. Klijzing, M. Mills and K. Kurz (eds), *Globalization, Uncertainty And Youth In Society*, 1–24. London, New York: Routledge.

Muffels, R.J.A and Luijkx, R. (2005), *Job Mobility and Employment Patterns across European Welfare States. Is there a "Trade-off" or a "Double Bind" between Flexibility and Security,* (TLM.NET 2005 Working Paper No. 2005–12), Amsterdam: SISWO/Social Policy Research.

Muffels, R.J.A. and Luijkx, R. (2006), 'Globalization and male job mobility in European welfare states', in Blossfeld, H-P, Mills, M. and Bernardi, F. (eds), *Globalization, uncertainty and men's careers,* Cheltenham, UK and Northampton, MA, USA: Edward Elgar, 38–72.

Muffels, R. (2007), 'Roads of "Flexicurity" in Europe: How (un)equal are they?', in Jørgensen, H. and Madsen, P.K. (eds), *Flexicurity and beyond. Finding a new agenda for the European Social Model,* Copenhagen: DJØF Publishing, 215–43.

Muffels, R.J.A and Luijkx, R. (2008), 'Labour Market Mobility and Employment Security of Male Employees in Europe: "Trade-off" or "Flexicurity"?', *Work, Employment and Society*, **22** (2), 221-42.

Nickell, S. (1997), 'Unemployment and labour market rigidities: Europe versus North America', *Journal of Economic Perspectives,* **11** (3), 55–74.

Nickell, S., Nunziate, L. and Ochel, W. (2005), 'Unemployment in the OECD since the 1960s: What do we know?', *Economic Journal,* **115**, 1–27.

Scherer, S. (2004), 'Stepping-stones or Traps? The Consequences of Labour Market Entry Positions on Future Careers in West Germany, Great Britain and Italy', *Work, Employment and Society,* **18** (2), 369–94.

Schmid, G. (1995), 'Is Full-Employment Still Possible – Transitional Labour-Markets as a New Strategy of Labour-Market Policy', *Economic and Industrial Democracy*, **16** (3), 429–56.

Schmid, G. and Gazier, B. (2002), *The Dynamics of full-employment through Transitional Labour Markets,* Cheltemham, UK and Northampton, MA, USA: Edward Elgar.

Schmid, G. (2006), 'Social Risk Management through Transitional Labour Markets', *Socio-Economic Review,* **4** (1), 1–32.

Stone, K.V.W. (2005), 'Thinking and Doing – the regulation of workers' human capital in the United States', *Socio-Economic Review,* **26** (4), 121–38.

Wilthagen, T. (1998), 'Flexicurity: A new paradigm for labour market policy research', *WZB Discussion Paper FS*, Berlin, **I** 98–202.

Wilthagen, T. and Tros, F. (2004), 'The concept of "flexicurity": a new approach to regulating employment in the labour market', *TRANSFER-European Review of Labour and Research*, **10** (2), 166–86.

ANNEX 6.1

Table 6.A.1 Model variables and summary statistics (mean)

Variables	Description	Mean
Life course		
Age	Age in years	39.5
Age squared/100	Age squared divided by 100	17.4
Number of children	Number of children below 16 years of age in the household	0.51
Married	Dummy for being married	0.57
Divorced/separated	Dummy for being divorced or separated	0.05
Education		
Education level	1. primary education; 2. lower and medium level of vocational training plus high school (reference category); 3. higher vocational training and university	2.15
Low education	Dummy for low education	0.38
High education	Dummy for high education	0.24
Unemployment history	Dummy for whether people experienced an unemployment spell in the five-years preceding the current job (1=yes; 0=no)	0.20
Work experience	Number of years passed since the worker started his first job. Hence, it is corrected for the different length of the schooling period before first entrance on the labour market	20.9
Socio-economic characteristics		
Bad health	Dummy for bad health, which is a subjectively assessed measure for one's personal health (1 = in bad health; 0 = not in bad health)	0.07
Personal non-labour income	Incomes are deflated and made comparable across countries using the purchasing power parities (ppp) as calculated by Eurostat for the various countries. Personal net non-labour income in 1000 euros per year	2.57
Other net labour income In household	Net household labour income of other household members is the summation of the annual net labour incomes of all other persons between 25 and 65 years in the household in the calendar year preceding the interview year, ppp corrected, in 1000 euros per year	6.48

Table 6.A.1 (Continued)

Variables	Description	Mean
Socio-economic characteristics		
Net non-labour income in household	Net non-labour household income is the net household income from social security transfers and/or from wealth (excluding income from imputed rent), ppp corrected, in 1000 euros per year	10.91
Job characteristics		
Number of working hours	Weekly working hours are the total number of actual working hours a worker usually worked throughout the past calendar year	43.61
Primary sector	Dummies for industrial sector as derived from the two-	0.05
Service sector	digit NACE-code, recoded into two dummies for the	0.16
Industry	primary sector and the public sector. Reference	0.24
Public sector	category is industry plus services	0.13
Firm size	Firm size measuring the number of employees in seven classes in the firm: (0; 1–4; 5–19; 20–49; 50–99; 100–499; 500+)	3.95
Occupational class	To take account of bottom and ceiling effects we included the initial occupational class position consisting of either three categories as in Model I, or four categories as in the Models II, III and IV (1 = low, low manual, 2 = upper manual, 3 = low white collar, 4 = high, professional)	2.8
Regime type		
Anglo-Saxon	Dummies for regime type: Anglo-Saxon, Nordic,	0.16
Nordic	Southern, Continental (reference)	0.07
Continental		0.44
Southern		0.33
Dummies		
Year dummies	We included year dummies to account for economic cycle effects. The reference year is the first year of the observation period (1994 for all models except for model III, that is, 1995)	

7. Unemployment and Worker Career Prospects: a Cross-national Comparison

Markus Gangl

7.1 INTRODUCTION

Experiences of job loss and unemployment are clearly among the unpleasant facts of economic life. As industries expand and shrink, as businesses grow and collapse, as employment relationships between individual employers and workers come and go, some workers inevitably find themselves caught 'in the wrong place, at the wrong time' (Leonard, 1987). And relative to continuous employment, resulting unemployment spells are likely to create significant psychological, social and, last but not least, economic costs to the affected workers. With respect to the latter, unemployment experiences may bring significant financial stress in the short term as unemployed workers may spend some time searching for reemployment, as non-employed household members will not be able to make up for the lost income immediately, and as welfare states will typically protect less than full earnings through unemployment insurance or social assistance programs (see for example, Hauser and Nolan, 2000). Furthermore, there may be significant longer-term costs whenever past unemployment experiences contribute to sustained reductions in individual earnings capacity, that is, whenever workers' future employment and earnings prospects are significantly diminished due to unemployment.

Clearly, workers' total economic cost of unemployment comprises both short-run costs of income losses during unemployment spells and potential long-term costs due to any reduction of workers' earnings potential associated with unemployment. To complement the many earlier analyses that have documented the first component, the income level and income packages available to the unemployed, the analyses in this chapter focus on the second component and seek to document empirical and cross-nationally comparable evidence of unemployment scarring in twelve European countries and the United States. In doing so, the contribution capitalises on the fact that panel data necessary to estimate post-unemployment scarring has recently become available for European Union countries, so that researchers are now in a position to complement the existing evidence on unemployment scarring from US data with respective evidence for European countries that often exhibit institutional structures that are quite different from the US labour market.

Against this background, this chapter is bluntly empirical in orientation to begin with. Using US and European panel data for the second half of the 1990s, this contribution seeks to establish the extent of unemployment scarring on both workers' employment prospects as well as subsequent earnings in thirteen Western countries.[1] Having individual panel data for about five years at our disposal, we can also assess whether scarring effects are largely temporary and tend to dissipate over time or whether scarring is of a more permanent nature, at least over the first couple of years following unemployment. To arrive at credible estimates of the causal effect of unemployment on workers' subsequent careers, we empirically implement a non-parametric difference-in-differences matching estimator that controls for relevant worker covariates, yet that does not require to rely on any explicitly parametric regression model to produce effect estimates and that is at the same time robust to any stable unobserved differences between the unemployed and continuously employed workers. As the empirical analysis will provide evidence of significant cross-national differences in the extent of unemployment scarring, we also conduct an explorative analysis on some institutional correlates of scarring. With the institutional variation available in our country sample, we specifically focus on the impact of employment protection legislation and unemployment insurance systems on unemployment scarring. The following section summarises the theoretical background of these analyses. Section 7.3 describes the data and the statistical methodology, whereas the empirical results are discussed in Section 7.4. Section 7.5 provides a summary and formulates some conclusions from the analyses.

7.2 UNEMPLOYMENT SCARRING AND LABOUR MARKET INSTITUTIONS

Existing empirical evidence leaves little doubt about the fact that unemployment experiences indeed have persistent effects on workers' subsequent careers. Hence unemployment is not merely the transitory spell of non-emploment between two jobs, but rather that it often results in a sustained deterioration of workers' employment prospects, future job quality and post-unemployment earnings. Particularly for the US labour market, empirical evidence on unemployment scarring is by now abundant. Ruhm (1991), using

PSID (Panel Study of Income Dynamics) data on workers displaced during the mid-1970s, reports displacement effects of about eight weeks more unemployment relative to comparable non-displaced workers in the year of displacement, but going down to about four weeks in the following year, and returning to a level of perhaps one week by four years post-displacement. Earnings scars appeared equally pervasive, yet unlike for re-employment prospects, earnings losses were found to largely persist over time. According to the study, initial earnings losses amounted to as much as 16–18 per cent relative to earnings of comparable non-displaced workers, and little of those losses were in fact recouped by workers up to four years after job loss.

Over the years, Ruhm's results have been replicated quite a number of times, using different datasets and for more recent years. Based on 1974–1986 administrative data for Pennsylvania, Jacobson et al. (1993) similarly obtained evidence of significant earnings losses up to 25 per cent of quarterly earnings that were only partly recovered during the first six years following job loss, whereas employment rates rebounded much more quickly to their expected levels. In a series of papers based on Displaced Worker Survey data, Farber (1993, 1997) arrived at similar conclusions for nationally representative samples. Employment rates are substantially reduced immediately after displacement, but quickly rebound afterwards, whereas earnings losses of some 10–15 per cent have been much harder to recover – during either economic downturns in the early or the recovery periods of the late 1980s and 1990s. Stevens' (1997) analyses of long-term earnings losses in fact emphasise that workers' earnings do not return to their expected level even a full decade after displacement. Brand (2004) uses data from the Wisconsin Longitudinal Study for an even longer observation window and finds evidence of persistent earnings losses even up to 15 years post-displacement.

While the US data thus clearly suggests significant and persistent penalties to unemployment, evidence on the longer-term implications of unemployment in other countries is only beginning to become available. For sure, it is already well-known that unemployment spells in themselves are often longer in Europe than in the US labour market (for example, Machin and Manning, 1999). With respect to longer-term scarring, recent evidence for British workers largely seems to coincide with the earlier US studies. For example, Gregory and Jukes (2001) estimate earnings losses of some 15 per cent for British men in the late 1980s and early 1990s, and as for US workers, these earnings losses largely persist even some years after the original spell of unemployment. Arulamapalam (2001) arrives at similar conclusions with respect to wage scarring among British men during the 1990s, yet even finds that initial wage losses of about 6–8 per cent even continue to increase up to 14 per cent in the third year post-unemployment, and only weakly rebound afterwards.

In sharp contrast to the results for Britain, there is good evidence that unemployment scarring is much less pronounced for German workers. Despite the fact that unemployment duration is larger for German workers than among both US and British workers, recent studies by Burda and Mertens (2001) and Couch (2001) report earnings losses well below or at least at the lower bound of scarring observed for either Britain or the United States. Using administrative data, Burda and Mertens (2001) estimate wage losses of displaced workers at about 3 per cent, and Couch (2001) provides the slightly higher estimate of a 6.5 per cent average earnings loss from survey data. Both estimates also fit well with the observation of DiPrete and McManus (2000) that German workers had fully recouped these (small) earnings losses three years after a job loss, whereas US workers showed no significant earnings losses only after more than seven years in their data. In fact, Layte et al. (2000) provide related evidence that may suggest less significant unemployment scarring in other European countries as well; in their analysis of repeat unemployment, past unemployment had strong effects on workers' future unemployment in Britain and Italy, but not for Swedish and Dutch workers.

7.2.1 Unemployment Scarring and the Institutional Regulation of Labour Markets: Two Conjectures

Evidently, the scant empirical evidence available to date suggests that unemployment scarring in Europe may qualitatively differ from, or even be less pronounced than scarring in the US labour market. In fact, this is all the more plausible since the institutional regulation of most European labour markets sharply deviates from the US case of an unfettered labour market and weak institutional protection of workers through either strong unions, significant employment protection legislation or an extensive welfare state. The institutional variation represented in this study's country sample is illustrated by selected indicators of cross-national differences in labour market institutions in Table 7.1.

As evident from these indicators, from a Continental European perspective it is the United States and Britain – that is, precisely those two countries for which there is consistent evidence of significant unemployment scarring to date – that represent the outlier cases of largely unregulated labour markets. Clearly, the United States, the United Kingdom and, perhaps to a lesser extent, Ireland are unique in terms of the limited role of trade unions, the near absence of employment protection legislation and relatively weak unemployment insurance systems that combine limited access to benefits, relatively modest benefit levels and little spending on active labour market policies.

*Table 7.1 Labour markets and institutions in the United States and 12
Western European Countries, late 1990s*

	Average GDP growth 1995–2000	Standardised unemployment rate 1995	Union coverage rate	Strictness of Employment protection legislation	Unemployment benefit coverage rate	Unemployment benefit net replacement ratio	Active labour market policy: expenditure on training (% of GDP)
United States	2.64	5.6	16	0.7	39.2	0.577	0.040
United Kingdom	2.71	8.6	35+	0.9	43.2	0.677	0.062
Ireland	8.78	12.2	(45)	1.1	65.9	0.575	0.145
Denmark	2.22	7.1	75+	1.5	78.4	0.810	0.734
Finland	4.08	15.5	90+	2.3	85.7	0.800	0.460
Germany	1.41	8.1	75+	2.6	81.7	0.695	0.376
Austria	2.45	3.7	95+	2.1	69.8	0.673	0.142
Belgium	2.23	9.3	90+	2.5	80.7	0.702	0.168
France	1.89	11.6	90+	2.8	80.2	0.784	0.300
Greece	2.45	9.1	(30)	3.5	35.5	0.494	0.100
Italy	1.74	11.5	80+	3.4	24.4	0.447	0.006
Spain	3.31	22.7	75+	3.1	46.6	0.751	0.144
Portugal	3.67	7.2	75+	3.7	35.6	0.822	0.068

Source:
1. OECD Main Economic Indicators, geometric means. 2. OECD Main Economic Indicators. 3. OECD (2004), Table 3.3, average of 1990 and 2000 data; (.) trade union density data for Greece and Ireland. 4. OECD (1999a), Table 2.5, version 2. 5. Proportion of unemployed workers receiving unemployment compensation during an unemployment spell, late 1990s, Survey of Income and Program Participation, 1996 Panel (US), and European Community Household Panel, UDB Waves 1–8 (European countries). 6. OECD Benefit Systems and Work Incentives, 1997 data, average ratio across four family types and two earnings levels. 7. OECD Employment Outlook, average figures for 1995–99.

In contrast, the Continental European countries, broadly speaking, are similar to each other in terms of a very significant role of unions in the labour market, yet countries clearly differ both in terms of the strength of the unemployment insurance system and with respect to their approach toward employment protection legislation. Quite obviously, the Scandinavian or Nordic model – exemplified by Denmark and Finland in the following – combines flexible labour markets with near universal access to generous unemployment benefits and significant investment in worker retraining. France,

Germany, Belgium and the Netherlands, that is, the Continental European countries narrowly defined, share a tradition of strong unemployment insurance with the Nordic countries (though perhaps being less strong on active labour market policies), yet exhibit significantly stronger regulation of labour markets through employment protection legislation (see Büchtemann, 1993).

In turn, employment protection is even stronger in Southern Europe, yet compared to both the Nordic and Continental European countries unemployment insurance is much less encompassing, much less generous (particularly in Greece and Italy) and weak on retraining. In sum, the country sample of this analysis comprises countries with quite different approaches to protecting (unemployed) workers through either employment protection legislation, unemployment insurance or both.[2]

Economic models of search and matching in the labour market offer some guidance on potential consequences of such cross-national differences in labour market institutions (Pissarides, 2000). In fact, some partial predictions seem quite obvious from much theoretical and empirical research. Unemployment insurance (UI), for example, can be seen as a search subsidy that raises workers' reservation wages and hence reduces outflow rates from unemployment, but improves post-unemployment job match quality (see Burdett, 1979; Acemoglu, 2001). In addition, time limits on benefit eligibility, strict monitoring of worker job search or the administration of systems of active labour market policies combining activation, counselling and retraining are elements of modern unemployment insurance systems which seek to reduce potential disincentive effects of benefits while improving on workers' reemployment prospects at the same time. Furthermore, unemployment insurance may have effects on unemployment inflow in the first place, as insurance coverage should ease job turnover and economic restructuring (Mortensen, 1990). So far, there is reasonably good empirical evidence on many of these partial predictions – see for example, the review of Holmlund (1998) on unemployment duration effects, and Addison and Blackburn (2000) or Gangl (2004a) on evidence of positive UI effects on post-unemployment earnings. However, the answer to the question of the aggregate impact of a strong UI system on labour market outcomes is far less evident so far as the existence of offsetting partial effects makes our predictions theoretically ambiguous.

Roughly the same situation applies in the case of employment protection legislation (EPL). Theoretically and empirically, it is fairly evident that employment protection reduces labour market dynamics (Bertola, 1999; Bertola and Rogerson, 1997; for empirical evidence see Garibaldi, 1998) and creates economic rents for incumbent workers (Lindbeck and Snower, 1988). Hence, there is the positive effect of EPL of reduced overall unemployment inflow, which perhaps also implies a concentration of unemployment on more marginal groups – that is, the non-white, non-male, non-prime age, non-core workers – for whom unemployment may generate comparatively fewer economic costs (Esping-Andersen, 2000; Kletzer and Fairlie, 2003). However, it may well be that these effects are outweighed by prolonged unemployment duration in low-turnover labour markets or when firing costs are high and employers adopt more risk-averse hiring practices that may further disadvantage the unemployed (for example, Canziani and Petrongolo, 2001; Gangl, 2004b). Again, the aggregate effect of these offsetting mechanisms is theoretically ambiguous, as is the question of how EPL provisions might interact with the structure of unemployment insurance systems. To get an idea of the respective economic effects, we need to turn to empirical analysis.

7.3 DATA AND STATISTICAL MODELING

For obtaining empirical evidence on the extent of unemployment scarring in Western economies, the analysis in this chapter relies on panel data for the second half of the 1990s. More specifically, data is combined from the 1996 Panel of the Survey of Income and Program Participation (SIPP) and the 1994–2001 waves of the European Community Household Panel (ECHP) study. As a result, the subsequent analysis is based on work history data for the United States and 12 Western European countries, including Germany, Denmark, Belgium, France, the United Kingdom, Ireland, Italy, Greece, Spain, Portugal, Austria and Finland.[3]

   To achieve cross-national data comparability, the SIPP data has first been adjusted to reflect the ECHP design that – like the PSID, for example – has the annual panel interview as its building block. In consequence, five equally-spaced 'interview' months were arbitrarily defined for the SIPP (months 4, 15, 26, 37, 48), and data on incomes, earnings, wages, employment status and other variables was extracted as of these time points. The data for the non-selected months was discarded, except in constructing monthly employment status information between interviews similar to the employment status calendar data available in the ECHP. As a result, the cross-national database used in the analysis consists of up to eight consecutive observations (five in the case of the SIPP) on individual wages, monthly earnings and current employment status plus monthly information on individual employment status between survey interviews.

   At each survey interview, respondents' employment status is recorded as well as, for those employed, real hourly wages (deflated to 2000 national currency units), industry, occupation, usual hours of work, and tenure with current employer. Also, the data provides information on individual gender, race (available in the SIPP only), level of education and age, the latter being used to construct a measure of potential labour force experience (both the SIPP and the ECHP lack full employment biography data that would give measures of actual labour force experience). In addition, unemployment experience is measured from both current employment statuses at the time of the survey interview and, to detect spells completed between interviews, the monthly status calendar data. Finally, the sample has been restricted to workers and employees aged 25–54 years in order to arrive at a cross-national comparison of the impact of unemployment among mid-career workers. In total, this leaves us with between 400–2,000 observations of unemployed workers and about 6,500–20,000 control cases per country in the ECHP data. The larger SIPP panel results in a total sample of 2,450 workers experiencing a spell of unemployment and close to 60,000 control cases of continuously employed workers.

7.3.1 Estimating the Scar Effects of Unemployment

To estimate the causal effect of unemployment on workers' subsequent careers, a nonparametric difference-in-differences kernel matching estimator is estimated for the average treatment effect on the treated (ATT; see Heckman et al., 1998; Heckman et al., 2003; Imbens, 2004; see for example, Rosenbaum, 2002; Winship and Sobel, 2004 for more general introductions to matching methods). This approach to estimating causal effects combines the advantages from nonparametric statistical estimation underlying all matching methods with the fixed-effects approach to differencing out unobserved (but individually stable) heterogeneity between unemployed workers and the control group of workers who did not experience unemployment at a given time in a given country.[4]

The essence of any matching algorithm is to define a treatment and a control group relative to some causal factor of interest – in this case workers experiencing an unemployment spell between time point T and $T+1$ – and to adjust for any background differences between them by matching on the propensity score, that is the estimated likelihood of treatment given the observed covariates. Whenever the chosen design allows the analyst to defend the assumption of conditional independence between exposure to the causal factor (unemployment) and outcomes, the comparison of outcomes in the treatment group (workers experiencing unemployment) to the adjusted outcomes for the control group (continuously employed workers) plausibly supports causal statements about the impact of unemployment on workers' subsequent work histories (see the more general discussion in Winship and Morgan, 1999; Winship and Sobel, 2004).

In providing longitudinal information, panel data offer rich options to adequately control for pre-unemployment differences between workers actually experiencing unemployment and workers not experiencing unemployment at a given point in time between T and $T+1$. In particular, panel data provides pre-test observations, that is, information on workers' careers prior to experiencing unemployment. With these, we can control for differences in earnings trajectories or job stability already prior to unemployment and in addition to standard covariates like gender, race, education or industry and occupation of the worker's last job. Since economic adjustment processes may well begin before actual unemployment incidence (see Ruhm, 1991, Jacobson et al., 1993; Stevens, 1997), pre-test observations are essential in order to control for potential pre-unemployment differences in career trajectories between workers – the so-called Ashenfelter's dip phenomenon (Ashenfelter, 1978). In the subsequent analysis, we hence include gender, race, education, labour force experience at T, industry, occupation, current tenure and current log real wage at T as well as dynamic measures of occupational and industrial mobility between $T–1$ and T, employment status at $T–1$ and trends in hours of work and log wages between $T–1$ and T in the probit model that estimates the propensity score. To match comparable workers from the treatment and control samples, we conduct a kernel matching stratified by survey wave for each country (see Heckman et al., 1997, 1998).

The dependent variable of the analysis is individual employment status and the change in log real monthly gross earnings relative to $T–1$ at time points $T+1$, $T+2$ and $T+3$, years after unemployment incidence. Since the whole analysis is conditioned on employed workers at time T, all analyses actually rest on conditional difference-in-difference (DID) estimators of the average treatment effect of unemployment on the treated workers (ATT), and are thus robust to stable unobserved heterogeneity between the unemployed and comparable workers not experiencing unemployment. Since the available panel data is quite limited, the chosen observation window of two pre-test and (a maximum of) three post-test observations seemed the optimal compromise between adequate covariate control and substantively interesting outcomes. With employment and earnings data up to three years after unemployment incidence, we can compare the short- and medium-term consequences of unemployment across countries. Unfortunately, an empirical comparison of any longer term effects is beyond the scope of the current data.

7.4 EMPIRICAL RESULTS

7.4.1 Scar Effects of Unemployment in Thirteen Countries

As the first step in the analysis, Table 7.2 provides the key empirical results on unemployment scarring in Western countries. More specifically, Table 7.2 reports three pieces of evidence relevant to address the role of unemployment in generating inequality in workers' labour market trajectories. To begin with, the first column of Table 7.2 gives estimates of unemployment incidence rates, which are the workers' risk of experiencing a spell of unemployment in any given year. The remaining columns give different estimates of the consequences of such an experience. First, there is the causal (ATT) effect of unemployment on workers' subsequent employment prospects, with Table 7.2 having results from immediate ($T+1$ year) to more mid-term ($T+2$, $T+3$ years) effects. This evidence is supplemented by empirical estimates of unemployment scarring in terms of post-unemployment earnings, given that workers have secured re-employment. Again, there are results for both immediate ($T+1$ year of labour force experience) and somewhat longer-term ($T+2$, $T+3$ years) effects of unemployment on earnings. For presentation purposes, the countries have been loosely classified into liberal (US, UK, IRE), social-democratic (DK, FI), conservative (GE, AT, BE, FR) and Southern European welfare regimes (GR, IT, ES, PT), following Esping-Andersen (1990, 1999), Gallie and Paugam (2000) and others.

Clearly all three pieces of evidence – unemployment incidence rates, re-employment prospects and wage scarring – are required to describe the role of unemployment for inequality in the labour market. In terms of unemployment incidence rates alone, however, the evidence of Table 7.2 supports the perhaps surprising conclusion that it was in the three liberal regimes – the US, the United Kingdom and Ireland – where workers experienced the lowest level of labour market risk during the second half of the 1990s. In these three countries merely some 4 per cent of all workers experienced an unemployment spell from one year to the next (with some of these workers may have experienced even two or three of course).

Among the, broadly speaking, Continental European countries it is only Belgium and Portugal where workers enjoyed similarly low rates of unemployment incidence during the period, whereas unemployment incidence was at rates between 5–6 per cent for practically all other European countries. Spain is the clear outlier case in this respect, with labour market turbulence at an astounding incidence rate of 11 per cent on average.

Table 7.2 Unemployment experience and workers' subsequent careers in the United States and 12 Western European Countries, late 1990s

	Average annual rate of unemployment	Average causal effect (ATT) of unemployment on workers' probability of employment			Average causal effect (ATT) of unemployment on the change in workers' log real monthly earnings		
		T+1	T+2	T+3	T+1	T+2	T+3
United States	0.042 (0.001)	–0.414** (0.021)	–0.139** (0.016)	–0.117** (0.017)	–0.201** (0.038)	–0.100** (0.040)	–0.089* (0.045)
United Kingdom	0.037 (0.002)	–0.297** (0.028)	–0.090** (0.032)	–0.032 (0.028)	–0.122** (0.032)	–0.113** (0.031)	–0.085* (0.036)
Ireland	0.036 (0.002)	–0.177** (0.037)	–0.025 (0.041)	–0.017 (0.039)	–0.043 (0.043)	–0.036 (0.060)	–0.035 (0.068)
Denmark	0.057 (0.002)	–0.240** (0.033)	–0.022 (0.032)	0.058 (0.030)	–0.047* (0.020)	–0.077** (0.025)	–0.060* (0.026)
Finland	0.057 (0.002)	–0.213** (0.029)	–0.018 (0.031)	–0.057 (0.034)	–0.044 (0.032)	–0.060 (0.041)	–0.067 (0.045)
Germany	0.056 (0.001)	–0.552** (0.014)	–0.274** (0.017)	–0.168** (0.018)	–0.052** (0.017)	–0.052** (0.020)	–0.040 (0.024)
Austria	0.058 (0.002)	–0.148** (0.025)	–0.020 (0.023)	0.022 (0.026)	–0.043* (0.022)	–0.053* (0.024)	–0.049 (0.033)
Belgium	0.033 (0.001)	–0.348** (0.035)	–0.130** (0.043)	–0.027 (0.036)	–0.145** (0.045)	–0.111** (0.041)	–0.096* (0.048)
France	0.056 (0.001)	–0.370** (0.019)	–0.167** (0.023)	–0.103** (0.028)	–0.089** (0.026)	–0.086* (0.035)	– 0.110**
Greece	0.059 (0.002)	–0.226** (0.024)	–0.070** (0.023)	0.008 (0.028)	–0.032 (0.022)	–0.043 (0.030)	–0.033 (0.035)
Italy	0.053 (0.002)	–0.258** (0.020)	–0.087** (0.025)	–0.053* (0.022)	–0.036* (0.016)	–0.025 (0.021)	–0.039 (0.029)
Spain	0.109 (0.002)	–0.185** (0.015)	–0.015 (0.015)	0.016 (0.020)	–0.051** (0.011)	–0.039* (0.016)	–0.013 (0.022)
Portugal	0.042 (0.001)	–0.349** (0.024)	–0.160** (0.024)	–0.102** (0.027)	–0.030 (0.026)	–0.014 (0.026)	–0.023 (0.024)

Notes: Workers aged 25–54. ATT estimates based on stratified kernel matching of treatment and control cases. Kernel matching is based on the Epanechnikov kernel using a bandwidth of one half the standard error of the predicted propensity score. Standard errors in parentheses (exact binomial standard errors for unemployment incidence rates, bootstrap standard errors based on N=100 replication samples in case of ATT estimates); * $p < 0.05$, ** $p < 0.01$.

Source: Survey of Income and Program Participation, 1996 Panel; European Community Household Panel, UDB Waves 1–8.

Evidently, for workers in the United States, Ireland and the United Kingdom, the risk of actually experiencing a spell of unemployment was considerably below that of workers in most Continental European countries during the late 1990s. However, findings of low unemployment incidence in particular countries do not necessarily provide accurate guidance on where to expect relatively small effects on the subsequent careers of the affected workers. For example, despite the long US economic boom of the 1990s that resulted in historically low rates of unemployment incidence, the US has continued to be a country where the experience of unemployment leaves a significant imprint on workers' career paths. First, despite a booming economy, American workers experiencing unemployment have faced considerable difficulties in finding new employment, both immediately after job loss but also during the following years. At time $T+1$, that is, on average, by some 6 months after unemployment incidence, the employment rate of displaced workers in the United States is more than 40 percentage-points below the yardstick provided by the employment rate among comparable (that is, matched) US workers who have experienced continuous employment or at least no spell of unemployment between T and $T+1$. In fact, this difference in employment rates continues to remain strongly negative (−14 per cent and −12 per cent, respectively) even by two to three years after unemployment incidence, so that post-unemployment difficulties to secure employment are not limited to a short, merely transitory period of individual adjustment, but persist over a considerable period of time in the careers of US workers.

Clearly, the data of Table 7.2 do not simply reflect unemployment duration narrowly defined, but are also likely – especially at points $T+2$ and $T+3$ – to tap into post-unemployment differences in job security, the evidence points to the conclusion that employment difficulties for the unemployed arise from difficulties to find new jobs in the first place in conjunction with sustained difficulties to find reasonably stable jobs for quite some time after the initial job loss (see related evidence in Stevens, 1997). Obviously, employment rates among workers experiencing unemployment were far from what they should have been, even three years after unemployment incidence.

Furthermore, the jobs regained by the unemployed clearly do not match those that were lost before. In fact, the average unemployed worker in the US loses about 20 per cent of her pre-unemployment monthly gross earnings in the short term, that is, in her first ($T+1$) post-unemployment job. During the second and third year post-unemployment, she will typically be able to recover somewhat and actually partly recoup these large initial losses. Yet, on average, her earnings loss amounts to a full 10 per cent by $T+2$ and still 9 per cent by $T+3$, with few signs of any further strong upward trend. In consequence, unemployment has a significant negative impact on workers' ability to earn their living in the US labour market.

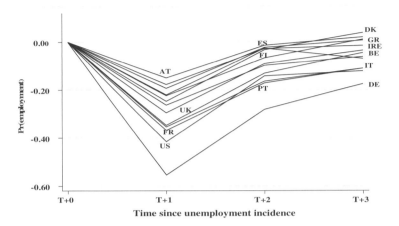

Note: Workers aged 25–54, ATT estimates.

Source: See Table 7.2.

Figure 7.1 Unemployment and workers' subsequent employment prospects, by elapsed time since unemployment incidence

As evident, unemployment experiences imply lower earnings potentials due to both more limited and more insecure employment prospects as well as considerably diminished earnings prospects. In addition, the data strongly suggests that unemployment scarring may be far from transitory, at least up to about three years after unemployment incidence and maybe more evidently so in case of earnings than with respect to employment prospects. In sum, the empirical findings on the US case closely match those of the earlier economic literature (for example, Ruhm, 1991; Jacobson et al., 1993; Farber, 1993, 1997; Stevens, 1997).

As the cross-national comparison clarifies, however, unemployment scarring is not limited to the US case of a largely unfettered labour market, but is pervasive in European Union countries with often quite different labour market structures as well. The extent of cross-national similarities and differences is perhaps best judged graphically. Figure 7.1 for example, re-expressing the ATT effect estimates on employment, shows fundamental similarities in workers' employment prospects after an unemployment spell across countries. Everywhere, there is evidence of a V-shaped pattern, with apparent difficulties to secure employment right after unemployment incidence *(T+1)* that by and large dissipate afterwards (by *T+2* and *T+3*), however. On the other hand, the severity of unemployment scarring clearly differs across countries and there are many European countries where unemployment generates smaller scar effects on employment prospects than in the United States. In countries like Austria, Ireland, but also in Spain, Finland, Denmark or Greece, the $T+1$ employment penalty is around −20 per cent, that is, at about half the United States case only, and employment rates often fully return to those of comparable continuously employed workers by $T+2$ or $T+3$. Belgium, France and Portugal are perhaps the European countries showing a profile that resembles the US case in Figure 7.1, and there is actually but one European country, Germany, where workers are clearly facing even greater difficulties in finding (stable) re-employment than is true for US workers.

Moreover, US workers also find themselves on the high end of the scale if unemployment scarring is measured from workers post-unemployment earnings. Figure 7.2 again provides data from Table 7.2 in graphical form. Evidently, post-unemployment earnings trajectories of US workers are quite distinct from those of most European workers. The experiences of US workers are unique with respect to the drastic earnings losses by $T+1$ followed by a quick partial recovery by $T+2$ and $T+3$. However, even by $T+2$ or $T+3$, US figures for earnings losses in the order of 10 per cent are only matched by equally large losses among workers in three European countries: the United Kingdom, Belgium and France. Interestingly, earnings penalties are at best half as large – typically in the order of 3–5 per cent – in all other European countries (see similar results for Germany in for example Burda and Mertens, 2001; Couch, 2001). And, again consistent with earlier research by Ruhm (1991), Jacobson et al. (1993) and Stevens (1997) on US and Arulampalam (2001) on British data, in contrast to results for workers' employment prospects, it seems that unemployment scarring in terms of earnings is quite permanent and hence leaves the affected workers at a persistent disadvantage relative to continuously employed workers. Of the 13 countries in this analysis, only the US, Britain, Belgium and Spain show reasonably robust evidence of any upward trend in workers' earnings, that is, only in these four countries workers' earnings are (at least slowly) recovering over time (again, cf. related results in Ruhm, 1991; Stevens, 1997; Arulampalam, 2001). However, the United States, Britain and Belgium – that is, the selfsame countries with the single exception of Spain – are also those countries where unemployment inflicts the most significant scars in terms of earnings losses, especially in the short-term at workers' first post-unemployment ($T+1$) jobs.

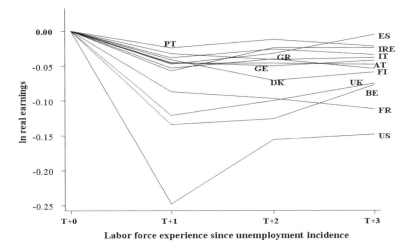

Note: Workers aged 25–54, ATT estimates.

Sources: See Table 7.2.

Figure 7.2 Unemployment and subsequent real earnings, by post-unemployment labour force experience

7.4.2 Cross-national Differences in Unemployment Scarring: an Explorative Analysis

The above empirical evidence on sizeable cross-national differences in unemployment scarring calls for an attempt to provide a more systematic country comparison. The empirical data is certainly suggestive of strong scarring effects in liberal economies – the United Kingdom and the United States as prime examples – as well as in, broadly speaking, continental welfare regimes like Belgium, France, Germany or Portugal. Starting from this first impression, the analyses intend to summarise and synthesise some of the main results of the cross-national comparison. As far as possible, the approach will suggest a particular reading of the above evidence in terms of the relationship between labour market institutions and unemployment scarring. Obviously, with an N of 13 country cases only, this cross-national analysis cannot be conducted solely with an eye on statistical hypothesis testing. Rather, the analyses will employ statistical tools primarily to describe and summarise empirical patterns evident in the cross-national data and aims to reconcile these with the above hypotheses on the impact of labour market institutions. Since 'N = 13' provides little statistical power to firmly adjudicate between competing hypotheses, the exercise is deliberately held at a purely descriptive level and significance testing is not a primary concern. For the sceptical reader, standard significance levels are reported nevertheless. [5]

That said, it is perhaps worthwhile to first summarise the basic results on unemployment scarring in a very general and concise form. To that end, Table 7.3 provides the matrix of Pearson correlation coefficients between the seven indicators of unemployment scarring used before. There are three pieces of evidence that seem to stand out of this exercise. First, unemployment incidence rates show a consistent positive correlation with all six ATT estimates discussed before. That is, for this particular sample of Western economies and the particular observation window of the late 1990s, higher labour market turbulence (as indicated by a higher unemployment incidence) is associated with lower unemployment scarring in terms of either employment prospects or earnings.

Table 7.3 Pearson correlations for unemployment scarring measures

	Unemployment incidence rate	ATT Employment			ATT Real earnings	
		T+1	*T+2*	*T+3*	*T+1*	*T+2*
ATT Employment *T+1*	0.299					
ATT Employment *T+2*	0.303	0.960**				
ATT Employment *T+3*	0.286	0.846**	0.861**			
ATT Earnings *T+1*	0.371	0.431	0.284	0.283		
ATT Earnings *T+2*	0.347	0.289	0.135	0.020	0.823**	
ATT Earnings *T+3*	0.474	0.329	0.232	0.215	0.733**	0.881**

Note: Positive ATT parameter estimates are equivalent to limited unemployment scarring. N = 13. Statistical significance level at * $p < 0.10$, ** $p < 0.05$.

Source: See Table 7.2.

Potentially, this positive correlation might simply imply that high turnover generates a strong compositional effect on inflows into unemployment so that the average worker under high turnover conditions is somebody with generally better labour market prospects than the average worker under low turnover (for example, Anderson and Meyer, 1994). That is, the observed correlation would not necessarily be inconsistent with the fact that job search will be more difficult for all workers during periods of intense structural change in the economy. But whatever the actual causes and mechanisms behind it, the empirical regularity remains that high turnover countries of the late 1990s also tended to be those countries where scarring was less pronounced for the average unemployed worker.

Second, Table 7.3 also suggests that cross-national differences in the degree of scarring by-and-large persist over time (though, perhaps, getting somewhat smaller in magnitude). The correlation between ATT estimates on employment measured at different time points – T is 0.85 and above, and with respect to earnings scarring, correlations are still in the order of 0.75 and higher. That is, in countries where unemployed workers experience above average scarring in terms of either employment or earnings in the short-term $(T+1)$ are also those countries where unemployment scarring is strongest in the medium term at $T+2$ and $T+3$.

And, thirdly, the cross-national comparison provides evidence that both dimensions of scarring are systematically related to each other. The correlation between ATT estimates on employment and ATT estimates on earnings is positive in general. In particular, speedy re-employment seems crucial for avoiding large earnings losses; the cross-national correlation between employment scarring at $T+1$ and ATT estimates on earnings is in the order of 0.30 to 0.40, whereas the other correlations are some 0.10 points below.

Since the different estimates of scarring are consistently positively correlated, that is, mutually reinforcing, it seems plausible to form a composite index of the extent of unemployment scarring in any particular country as a shorthand summary. In particular, the following analysis uses:

$$SI = une\ incidence \times \prod_{k=1}^{3} \frac{1}{1 + ATT_{Employment\_T+k}} \times \prod_{k=1}^{3} \frac{1}{1 + ATT_{Earnings\_T+k}}$$

as a multiplicative index of unemployment scarring. The fact that different aspects of unemployment scarring have empirically reinforcing effects is reflected in the multiplication of the seven components, that is, that scarring is largest whenever there is high unemployment incidence, high and persistent scarring on employment as well as high and persistent scarring on earnings. Next, two versions of this scarring index (SI) will be used.

One version capturing overall scarring is a weighted index with the unemployment (une) incidence rates as weights, as given by the equation above, and a second index, referred to as conditional scarring that consists of the two product terms of ATT, estimates but does not weight them with the unemployment incidence rate. In substantive terms, the latter conditional index represents scarring given unemployment incidence whereas the weighted overall index captures cross-national variation in overall career risk due to unemployment, which includes the likelihood of experiencing an unemployment spell in the first place.

With this, we can finally try to shift the evidence in favour of systematic institutional correlates of unemployment scarring. Table 7.4 provides estimation results from a series of regressions that relate cross-national variation in unemployment scarring to structural and institutional sources.

Average GDP growth over the 1995–2000 period and (where applicable) unemployment incidence rates are included in the regressions to capture essential differences in economic environments across countries. Across all specifications, and for both the two composite indices of unemployment scarring and their constituent parts, there is good evidence that GDP growth reduces scarring for the average worker, as does (perhaps for compositional reasons) high unemployment incidence.

While these effects consistently show the correct sign, parameter estimates often fail to reach acceptable levels of statistical significance.

With respect to the impact of institutions on unemployment scarring, Table 7.4 provides two slightly different model specifications. For each dependent variable, model 1 reports estimates of regime differences between the Anglo-Saxon, Nordic, Continental and Southern European (residual) models of welfare capitalism. Alternatively, the dummy variables indexing regime clusters are replaced with explicit measures of national labour market institutions – in particular, strictness of employment protection and generosity of unemployment insurance – in the second specification.

In terms of regime differences, overall unemployment scarring (in the sense of overall career risk to the average worker) was lowest in the two Scandinavian countries, about equal in Southern Europe and Anglo-Saxon regimes and highest in the Continental welfare regimes. This outcome is partly related to the fact that liberal regimes have clearly seen the lowest unemployment incidence rates during the late 1990s (column 2), whereas conditional scarring among those workers actually experiencing unemployment is low in Northern and Southern Europe, but quite considerable in continental and Anglo-Saxon countries (column 3). Interestingly, the latter finding is reflected in lower unemployment scarring on both employment and earnings prospects in Northern and Southern Europe (columns 4–7). The main difference between continental and Anglo-Saxon regimes is that considerable scars result from low re-employment prospects in the former and considerable earnings scars in the latter.

We can re-express these findings more explicitly in terms of concrete institutional correlates of unemployment scarring. As the straightforward regime comparison suggests that the effects of employment protection and unemployment benefit system might be interdependent, the second regression specification includes the OECD index of strictness of employment protection; an index of worker decommodification through the unemployment benefit system as well as an interaction term between the two.

Table 7.4 Growth, turnover, institutions and unemployment scarring in the late 1990s, OLS regressions

	Overall scarring index	Unem-ployment incidence rate	Conditional scarring index	ATT Employ-ment *T+1*	ATT Employ-ment *T+2*	ATT real earnings *T+1*	ATT real earnings *T+2*
Model 1							
GDP growth	−0.011	−5.3e-5	−0.239	0.031	0.016	0.016	0.010
	(0.009)	(0.004)	(0.154)	(0.021)	(0.013)	(0.008)*	(0.004)**
Incidence rate	–	–	−0.061	0.015	0.014	0.001	−1.7e-7
(x 100)			(0.151)	(0.020)	(0.013)	(0.007)	(0.004)
Regime type							
Anglo-Saxon	ref	ref	ref	ref	ref	ref	ref
Nordic	−0.020	0.019	−1.043	0.090	0.064	0.100	0.030
	(0.048)	(0.019)	(0.849)	(0.115)	(0.073)	(0.041)**	(0.022)
Continental	0.019	0.012	−0.158	0.007	−0.036	0.082	0.035
	(0.046)	(0.018)	(0.786)	(0.106)	(0.068)	(0.038)*	(0.021)
Southern	−0.008	0.027	−0.961	0.059	−0.005	0.113	0.072
	(0.042)	(0.017)	(0.816)	(0.110)	(0.071)	(0.040)**	(0.022)**
Intercept	0.144	0.039	3.729	−0.501	−0.214	−0.200	−0.131
	(0.052)**	(0.020)*	(1.050)**	(0.141)**	(0.091)**	(0.051)**	(0.028)**
R^2	0.312	0.304	0.504	0.423	0.501	0.65	0.729
Model 2							
GDP growth	−0.010	−0.001	−0.201	0.026	0.015	0.010	0.009
	(0.007)	(0.004)	(0.116)	(0.016)	(0.010)	(0.005)*	(0.003)**
Incidence rate	–	–	−0.162	0.024	0.020	0.005	0.003
(x 100)			(0.116)	(0.016)	(0.010)*	(0.005)	(0.003)
Institutions							
EPL strictness	−0.054	0.007	−1.316	0.123	0.074	0.096	0.040
	(0.032)	(0.016)	(0.532)**	(0.073)	(0.047)	(0.024)**	(0.016)**
UI decom-	−0.043	2.7e-4	−0.961	0.101	0.077	0.057	0.012
modification	(0.026)	(0.013)	(0.425)*	(0.058)	(0.037)*	(0.019)**	(0.012)
EPL x UI	0.020	2.2e-4	0.417	−0.044	−0.033	−0.022	−0.006
interaction	(0.010)*	(0.005)	(0.168)**	(0.023)*	(0.015)*	(0.008)**	(0.005)
Intercept	0.262	0.036	6.784	−0.792	−0.429	−0.391	−0.188
	(0.091)**	(0.046)	(1.56)**	(0.215)**	(0.137)**	(0.071)**	(0.046)**
R^2	0.507	0.162	0.648	0.575	0.633	0.787	0.764

Note: UI decommodification index calculated as UI coverage rate x UI replacement ratio x 10. N = 13. Statistical significance level at * $p < 0.10$, ** $p < 0.05$.

Source: See Table 7.2.

As with the regime comparison, the evidence on the impact of institutions is again quite consistent across the different composite and specific measures of unemployment scarring. According to the data, scarring can be reduced through either strict employment protection or generous benefit support. However, the interaction term shows a clearly counteracting effect – which implies that countries relying on both protective mechanisms simultaneously tend to neutralise the positive effect that either institutional arrangement has on its own. In effect, unemployment scarring for workers in Continental Europe is not that different from the experiences of workers in the liberal Anglo-Saxon world.

These implications of the regression results may perhaps best be understood by a (simplified) visualisation. Figure 7.3 provides two scenarios that serve to illustrate the findings. Both panels display residual unemployment scarring (conditional index, after partialling out cross-national differences in GDP growth and unemployment incidence rates) by EPL strictness and unemployment insurance decommodification. In the first scenario, we distinguish between strongly and weakly decommodifying unemployment benefit systems and a regression line is fitted between scarring and employment protection separately for each regime cluster.

Evidently, employment protection lends itself to lower scarring in countries with weak unemployment benefit systems, but sharply increases scarring in countries with strong unemployment insurance systems. Parallel results are evident from Panel (b) that holds employment protection constant and describes the relation between scarring and unemployment insurance; generous unemployment insurance decreases scarring in unregulated, more flexible labour markets, but increases scarring in more regulated ones.[6] As evident from the regression results in Table 7.4, this interaction effect between employment protection and unemployment insurance is evident for all measures of unemployment scarring other than unemployment incidence itself.

Other than this key substantive finding, what also seems remarkable about the second regression specification is that institutional effects are again stronger for conditional scarring, that is, they more strongly affect reemployment and earnings prospects of workers actually experiencing unemployment. Obviously, respective results on overall career risk due to unemployment are weaker because European countries exhibiting worker-supportive institutions have also been experiencing higher unemployment incidence than the liberal economies of the US, the United Kingdom or Ireland. Furthermore, the explicit measures of the various institutional arrangements clearly improve the regression fit relative to the regime dummies, and also lead to more precise estimates for the institutional contrasts. This seems to suggest institutional differences within regime clusters by-and-large work in the same direction as the institutional contrasts between regimes, so that the more sophisticated specification – at the same – time strengthens the statistical model as well as the substantive conclusions.

(a) UI decommodification fixed

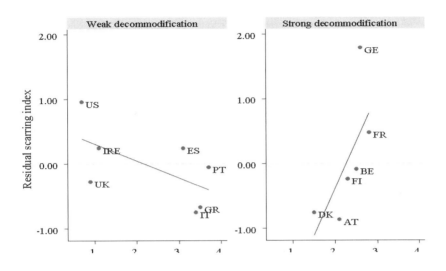

(b) EPL strictness fixed

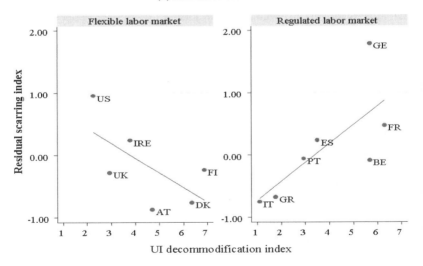

Notes:
Residual conditional scarring index – adjusted for GDP growth and unemployment incidence rate – plotted against strictness of employment protection and generosity of unemployment insurance. OLS lines fitted separately by subgroup.

Figure 7.3 Unemployment scarring and labour market institutions

7.5 SUMMARY AND CONCLUSIONS

Unemployment represents a veritable career risk to workers because unemployment experiences entail economic costs in terms of diminished employment prospects and less favourable post-unemployment earnings trajectories. The empirical evidence presented in this study first of all confirms earlier studies on US data that have stressed significant unemployment scarring in the American labour market. Even under conditions of the long economic boom of the mid-1990s, US workers experience significant difficulties in finding stable reemployment after an unemployment spell and more often than not, re-employment is associated with considerable earnings losses in addition. Like in earlier studies, it was found that workers' employment prospects recover fairly quickly, yet those average post-unemployment earnings losses of American workers remain in the order of 10 per cent even after three years of subsequent employment.

Moreover, the cross-national comparison clearly showed that considerable unemployment scarring is also pervasive in European countries that often exhibit labour market structures quite different from those of the United States. For example, workers' earnings losses in Britain or France are not far below those experienced by American workers, and unemployed workers in Germany experience even more sustained difficulties to find re-employment than American workers (who may find jobs easily, but are perhaps equally likely to lose them again). However, there is also considerable heterogeneity in the extent of unemployment scarring among European Union countries. Unemployment scarring in Britain, France or Germany may not be altogether too different from the US experience, yet in many European countries – notably in Scandinavia and Southern Europe – workers experience much lower economic costs of unemployment. The cross-national comparison reveals that labour market institutions may have a significant role to play in this as both generous unemployment insurance and strict labour market regulation were found to be correlated with low unemployment scarring. However, the interesting twist of the story is that, empirically, only those countries do well that rely on either employment protection legislation or generous unemployment benefits to protect workers' earnings capacity across spells of unemployment. The Continental European regimes combining labour market regulation with generous benefits actually see no less unemployment scarring than the liberal economies that lack extensive worker protection through either regulation or insurance.

The current study has done and could do little to probe further into some plausible mechanisms that may be underlying the reported findings, or even to come up with very specific policy recommendations. Evidently, generous unemployment insurance systems can contribute to reduce scarring despite the disincentive effect brought about by generous transfers. Obviously, benefit effects on productive job search behaviour, extensive job search support, counselling and monitoring, but also appropriate active labour market policies that typically complement generous unemployment insurance systems in Europe are able to counter any negative impact of prolonged unemployment duration. Similarly, labour market regulation seems effective in improving workers' economic fortunes, even as unequivocal evidence of lower unemployment incidence in regulated markets, maybe the primary effect to be expected, did not materialise in this particular data of the late 1990s. So perhaps compositional effects on the structure of unemployment inflow, indirect effects on recruitment patterns or simply more rigid wage structures may be elements to explain why regulation may actually help workers. What seems clear from the analysis, however, is that the twofold protection of workers' economic fortunes through both unemployment insurance and employment protection does not lead to an equally doubled protection from unemployment scarring – but rather achieves no better results than the unfettered labour markets of Anglo-Saxon liberal market economies. Apparently, worker adjustment to economic dynamics – through geographical, occupational or industrial mobility – is part of the parcel of successful behavioural responses to unemployment. In consequence, successful institutional design requires a careful balance between social protection and economic flexibility requirements in order to mediate workers' cost of economic change. Clearly, further and more specific empirical evidence is warranted in order to support and refine the conclusions offered from the present study.

NOTES

1. The contribution has been part of the European Science Foundation ECRP project 'Human Capital Effects of the Welfare State'. The author gratefully acknowledges support by the German Science Foundation (Deutsche Forschungsgemeinschaft, contract GA 758/2–1). The SIPP data has been provided by the US Bureau of the Census, Washington D.C., and Eurostat, Luxembourg, kindly provided access to the ECHP UDB. This contribution has also profited from the collaboration with researchers in the framework of the Transitional Labour Market Network which was funded under the heading of the Fifth Framework Programme of the European Commission during the years 2003–2006. Of course, neither institution bears any responsibility for the use made of these data, nor the inferences drawn by the author.
2. Unsurprisingly, these country contrasts closely resonate classifications commonplace in the institutional literature, for example, Esping-Andersen's (1990, 1999) liberal, social democratic, conservative and Southern European welfare regimes (see also Leibfried and Pierson, 1995), or Gallie and Paugam's (2000) classification of liberal/minimal, universal, employment-centred and sub-protective regimes. Below, we will report empirical results based on both regime clusters and explicit institutional measures.
3. Due to data problems, the remaining EU-15 member states (the Netherlands, Luxembourg and Sweden) had to be excluded from this study. Also, note that the ECHP sample

deliberately includes additional years of data, mostly in order to boost available sample sizes relative to those of the SIPP. Restricting the ECHP sample to the 1995–99 time period covered in the 1996 SIPP panel produces little change in the estimates of (cross-national differences in) unemployment scarring. Inevitably, however, smaller sample sizes would result in inflated standard errors, especially in conjunction with the nonparametric statistical model to be used below.

4. This count potentially includes multiple (panel) observations of the same worker in either the treatment or the control group. In the estimation of the causal effect of interest, however, stratification by survey wave ensures that individuals do not appear simultaneously in the relevant treatment and control samples.
5. From the perspective of statistical inference, one should perhaps add further that the reported standard errors and hypothesis tests are anticonservative because they ignore sampling error in the country-level estimates. If one indeed wanted to insist on appropriate statistical inference with an $N = 13$ country cases, one could employ multilevel modelling for the purpose, although it seems doubtful that standard techniques would produce efficient estimates with the low number of country level units available. In order to focus on the substantive conclusions that emerge from the cross-national comparison, the following is deliberately kept at a rather descriptive level.
6. Observant readers will have noticed that Figure 7.3 provides but a simplified approximation to the reported OLS results. Inevitable differences occur since independent variables have not also been controlled for GDP growth and unemployment incidence rates in Figure 7.3 and because the simple contrast depicted is equivalent to a dummy-coded regime-switching interaction that requires holding constant the second institutional feature whereas the original regression specification exploits the full range of institutional (co)variation. However, Figure 7.3 is easier to communicate without inducing distortions in the main substantive conclusion. Sceptical readers are invited to replicate these results by combining the data of Tables 7.1 and 7.2 in their own analyses.

REFERENCES

Acemoglu, Daron (2001), 'Good jobs versus bad jobs', *Journal of Labor Economics*, **19**, 1–21.
Addison, John T. and Blackburn, McKinley L. (2000), 'The effects of unemployment insurance on post unemployment earnings', *Labour Economics*, **7**, 21–53.
Anderson, Patricia M. and Meyer, Bruce D. (1994), *The Extent and Consequences of Job Turnover*, Brookings Papers on Economic Activity 1994/2, 177–236.
Arulampalam, Wiji (2001), 'Is Unemployment Really Scarring? Effects of Unemployment Experiences on Wages', *Economic Journal*, **111**, F585–F604.
Ashenfelter, Orley (1978), 'Estimating the effect of training programs on earnings', *Review of Economics and Statistics*, **60**, 47–57.
Bertola, Giuseppe (1999), 'Microeconomic Perspectives on Aggregate Labour Markets', in Ashenfelter, Orley and Card, David (eds), *Handbook of Labor Economics, Volume 3C*, Amsterdam: Elsevier, 2986–3028.
Bertola, Giuseppe and Rogerson, Richard (1997), 'Institutions and Labor Reallocation', *European Economic Review*, **41**, 1147–171.
Büchtemann, Christoph F. (1993), *Employment Security and Labor Market Behavior: Interdisciplinary Approaches and International Evidence*, Ithaca, NY: Cornell University Press.
Brand, Jennie E. (2004), *Enduring Effects of Job Displacement on Career Outcomes*, Madison: University of Wisconsin, Department of Sociology.

Burda, Michael C. and Mertens, Antje (2001), 'Estimating Wage Losses of Displaced Workers in Germany', *Labour Economics,* **8**, 15–41.

Burdett, Kenneth (1979), 'Unemployment insurance payments as a search subsidy: A theoretical analysis', *Economic Inquiry,* **17**, 333–43.

Canziani, P. and Petrongolo, B. (2001), 'Firing costs and stigma: A theoretical analysis and empirical evidence on micro data', *European Economic Review,* **45**, 1877–1906.

Couch, Kenneth A. (2001), 'Earnings Losses and Unemployment of Displaced Workers in Germany', *Industrial and Labor Relations Review,* **54**, 559–72.

DiPrete, Thomas A. and McManus, Patricia A. (2000), 'Family Change, Employment Transitions, and the Welfare State: Household Income Dynamics in the United States and West Germany', *American Sociological Review,* **65**, 343–70.

Esping-Andersen, Gøsta (1990), *The Three Worlds of Welfare Capitalism,* Cambridge: Polity Press.

Esping-Andersen, Gøsta (1999), *Social Foundations of Postindustrial Economies,* Oxford: Oxford University Press.

Esping-Andersen, Gøsta (2000), 'Who is harmed by labour market regulations? Quantitative evidence', in Esping-Andersen, G. and Regini, M. (eds), *Why Deregulate Labour Markets?,* Oxford: Oxford University Press, 66–98.

Farber, Henry S. (1993), *The Incidence and Costs of Job Loss: 1982–91,* Brookings Papers on Economic Activity, Microeconomics 1993, (with discussion), 73–132.

Farber, Henry S. (1997), *The Changing Face of Job Loss in the United States, 1981–1995,* Brookings Papers on Economic Activity, Microeconomics 1997, (with discussion), 55–142.

Gallie, Duncan and Paugam, Serge (eds) (2000), *Welfare Regimes and the Experience of Unemployment in Europe,* Oxford: Oxford University Press.

Gangl, Markus (2004a), 'Welfare States and the Scar Effects of Unemployment: A Comparative Analysis of the United States and West Germany', *American Journal of Sociology* **109**, 1319–64.

Gangl, Markus (2004b), 'Institutions and the Structure of Labour Market Matching in the United States and West Germany', *European Sociological Review,* **20** (3), 171–81.

Garibaldi, Pietro, 1998, 'Job Flows Dynamics and Firing Restrictions', *European Economic Review,* **42** (2), 245–75.

Gregory, Mary and Jukes, Robert (2001), 'Unemployment and Subsequent Earnings: Estimating Scarring among British Men 1984–94', *Economic Journal,* **111**, F607–F25.

Hauser, Richard and Nolan, Brian (2000), 'Unemployment and Poverty: Change over Time', in Gallie, Duncan and Paugam, Serge (eds), *Welfare Regimes and the Experience of Unemployment in Europe,* Oxford: Oxford University Press, 25–46.

Heckman, James, Ichimura, Hidehiko and Todd, Petra (1997), 'Matching as an econometric evaluation estimator: Evidence from evaluating a job training programme', *Review of Economic Studies,* **64**, 605–54.

Heckman, James, Ichimura, Hidehiko and Todd, Petra (1998), 'Matching as an econometric evaluation estimator', *Review of Economic Studies,* **65**, 261–94.

Heckman, James, Tobias, Justin L. and Vytlacil, Edward (2003), 'Simple Estimators for Treatment Parameters in a Latent Variable Framework', *Review of Economics and Statistics,* **85**, 748–55.

Holmlund, B. (1998), 'Unemployment insurance in theory and practice', *Scandinavian Journal of Economics,* **100** (1), 113–41.

Imbens, Guido W. (2004), 'Nonparametric estimation of average treatment effects under exogeneity: A review', *Review of Economics and Statistics,* **86**, 4–29.

Jacobson, Louis, LaLonde, Robert and Sullivan, Daniel (1993), 'Earnings Losses of Displaced Workers', *American Economic Review*, **83**, 685–709.

Kletzer, Lori G. and Fairlie, Robert W. (2003), 'The long-term costs of job displacement for young adult workers', *Industrial and Labor Relations Review,* **56**, 682–98.

Layte, Richard, Levin, Henrik, Hendrickx, John and Bison, Ivano (2000), 'Unemployment and Cumulative Disadvantage in the Labour Market', in Gallie, Duncan and Paugam, Serge (eds), *Welfare Regimes and the Experience of Unemployment in Europe,* Oxford: Oxford University Press, 153–74.

Leibfried, S. and Pierson, P. (eds) (1995), *European Social Policy,* Washington, DC: Brookings Institution Press.

Leonard, Jonathan S. (1987), 'In the Wrong Place at the Wrong Time: The Extent of Frictional and Structural Unemployment', in Lang, Kevin and Leonard, Jonathan S. (eds), *Unemployment and the Structure of Labor Markets,* Oxford: Blackwell, 141–63.

Lindbeck, A. and Snower, D.J. (1988), *The Insider-Outsider Theory of Employment and Unemployment,* London: Massachusetts Institute of Technology.

Machin, Stephen and Manning, Alan (1999), 'The causes and consequences of long-term unemployment in Europe', in Ashenfelter, Orley and Card, David (eds), *Handbook of Labor Economics,* Volume III, Amsterdam: Elsevier, 3085–139.

Mortensen, Dale T. (1990), 'A structural model of unemployment insurance benefit effects on the incidence and duration of unemployment', in Weiss, Yoram and Fishelson, Gideon (eds), *Advances in the Theory and Measurement of Unemployment,* London: Macmillan, 57–81.

Pissarides, Christopher A. (2000), *Equilibrium Unemployment Theory*, Cambridge, MA: MIT Press.

Rosenbaum, Paul R. (2002), *Observational Studies*, New York: Springer.

Ruhm, Christopher J. (1991), 'Are Workers Permanently Scarred by Job Displacement?', *American Economic Review*, **81**, 319–24.

Stevens, Ann H. (1997), 'Persistent Effects of Job Displacement. The Importance of Multiple Job Losses', *Journal of Labor Economics*, **15**: 165–188.

Winship, Christopher and Morgan, Stephen L. (1999), 'The Estimation of Causal Effects from Observational Data', *Annual Review of Sociology,* **25**, 659–707.

Winship, Christopher and Sobel, Michael E. (2004), 'Causal Inference in Sociological Studies', in Hardy, Melissa and Bryman, Alan (eds), *Handbook of Data Analysis,* Thousand Oaks: Sage Publications, 481–503.

8. Self-employment Dynamics and 'Transitional Labour Markets': some more UK Evidence

Nigel Meager

8.1 INTRODUCTION

This chapter looks at the potential contribution of self-employment to the dynamics of modern, transitional labour markets (TLM), building on previous work by the author (Meager and Bates, 2002). The question we are concerned with is whether self-employment transitions have a positive or negative effect on labour market dynamics. On the positive side, do they: help to keep people attached to the labour market that might otherwise fall out; offer entry routes to people who might otherwise not get into the labour market or improve the career trajectories of people who might otherwise end up in social exclusion or low wage traps? Or, on the negative side, are they associated with worse outcomes than other kinds of transitions, with low wages, social exclusion and so on?

The chapter reviews and adds to the evidence on these issues for the case of the UK. The UK is of some interest because of its unusual trajectory of self-employment in the last two decades. Additionally, it presents an interesting example of an economy which is, on the one hand, relatively favourable to self-employment entry (because of its liberal regulatory regime, a deregulated capital market, the unusual structure of its housing market and so on); and on the other hand an economy in which the institutional infrastructure to mitigate negative effects of the wider extension of self-employment (for example, through appropriate pension and social security arrangements, training and education regimes) is relatively under-developed.

The chapter starts with an account of the recent history of aggregate self-employment in the UK. It follows with a look at the previous evidence on what is known about self-employment transitions and their implications. Next we supplement this with some new data analysis, of two types:

- Further analysis of the British Household Panel Survey (BHPS), providing evidence on factors influencing self-employment flows during the 1980s and 1990s in the UK. In particular, we recognise the heterogeneity of self-employment and model transitions into and out of different occupational segments of self-employment.
- Analysis of a longitudinal data set of disadvantaged young people (aged 18–30) supported to enter self-employment. This enables us to compare the labour market trajectories of this group with those of a matched sample of young people not supported to enter self-employment, and to examine the impact of self-employment spells on subsequent labour market experience.

8.2 SELF-EMPLOYMENT IN THE UK: AGGREGATE TRENDS

Dramatic changes in UK self-employment occurred in the 1980s (Meager, 1998, Taylor, 2004) with the level and rate of self-employment almost doubling from 1.8 million (7 per cent of those in work) to 3.5 million (13 per cent of those in work). This unprecedented growth in self-employment (following decades of decline or stagnation) was not shared with other European countries (Meager, 1993). Also striking was the fact that self-employment in the UK grew continuously during this period, independently of the economic cycle, undermining simple causal interpretations of the relationship between the economic cycle and the overall stock of self-employment, in terms of 'unemployment-push' (Meager, 1992). The picture during the 1990s was rather different; following a decline in the recession of the early 90s, self-employment grew again over 1992–95, reaching a new peak before declining markedly over the period 1996–2001 (a period of strong overall employment growth). Since 2001, self-employment has again been on an upward trajectory. As in the 1980s, there is no clear relationship between self-employment and the economic cycle (Figure 8.1). As Meager (1992) and others note, this is not surprising, since the cycle acts independently on self-employment inflows and outflows (for example, growing unemployment may have a 'push' effect on inflows to self-employment, but an economic downturn also reduces business survival rates increasing self-employment outflows); the net effect on trends in the stock of self-employment is indeterminate a priori.

Also relevant is the high degree of heterogeneity among the 'self-employed' in official statistics, a fact often overlooked in traditional economic studies on self-employment (which model self-employment as a single ideal type: an independent 'entrepreneur' or small business proprietor).

As many authors point out, self-employment encompasses a wide range of working modes of different degrees of autonomy, some of which conform much more closely than others to the 'entrepreneur' of the economic models. It is, therefore, implausible to model the relationship between the economic cycle and self-employment as a single aggregate, when that aggregate is composed of diverse parts, each responding differently to changes in the economic and institutional environment.

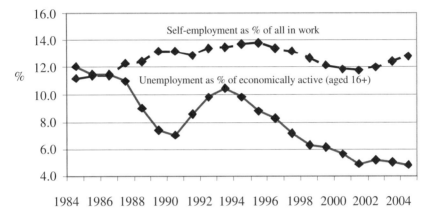

Source: Office of National Statistics – Labour Force Survey (seasonally adjusted data, Spring quarters).

Figure 8.1 Self-employment rate and unemployment rate (UK), 1984–2004

This variety is evident, for example, when looking at self-employment trends by occupation, shown in Figure 8.2 (for the 1990s and early 2000s). Most notable is the fall in managerial self-employment rates, a marked trend also observed in other UK data sets (Knight and McKay, 2000). One hypothesis is that this reflects increasing diversity in the self-employed, with a relative decline in the proportion that sees itself as small business proprietors, and a growth in the proportion working in their own profession, but on 'their own account' rather than for an employer. More straightforward to interpret is the recent decline in self-employment rates among craft and related occupations. This coincides clearly with the decline in self-employment in the construction sector (discussed later).

Bearing in mind this diversity within the self-employment total, what explanations emerge from the research literature for the recent trends in UK self-employment? For the 1980s, there is a consensus (Acs, Audretsch and Evans, 1992, Meager, 1993) that no single factor explains the unusual growth in UK self-employment. Throughout the period, the UK experienced higher inflow rates to self-employment than comparable European countries, and recent work with household panel data (Taylor, 2004; Meager and Bates, 2004) confirms that the 1980s growth was driven by changes in the inflow rate (rather than changes in the duration of self-employment spells). These increased inflow rates were, in turn, influenced by several factors, some of which were common to other countries during that period (for example, government policies designed to encourage business start-up or to support the unemployed to enter self-employment (Meager, 1996) although these were rather larger in scale in the UK in the 1980s than in many other countries).

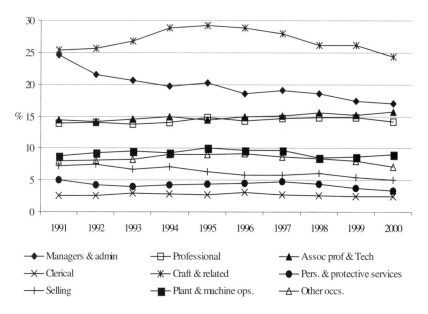

Source: Labour Force Survey (Spring quarters; data not seasonally adjusted).

Figure 8.2 Self-employment rates by occupation; UK 1991–2000

Other factors, however, were distinctive to the UK. In particular: the faster shift from manufacturing to service employment (with higher densities of self-employment) in the UK than elsewhere; the contracting out of service functions by large employers, and the growth in sub-contracting, franchising, and privatisation of public services, were all particularly marked in the UK (particularly in the construction sector, where there was an unprecedented growth in self-employment as 'disguised wage employment', Nisbet, 1997; Winch, 1998; Nisbet and Thomas, 2000); a less restrictive regulatory framework for business start-up in the UK than in many continental economies (Meager, Kaiser and Dietrich, 1992); and a highly deregulated market for financial capital (growing home ownership and rapid house price inflation, facilitating equity withdrawal, contributed to an environment in which it was relatively easy to raise financial capital for business start-up).

Turning to more recent periods, there appears less agreement in the literature regarding the fall in self-employment during the period 1996–2001. Meager and Bates (2004) point out that inflow rates to self-employment and outflow rates from self-employment were both higher during the 1990s than during the 1980s, but outflow rates grew faster than inflows. The sectoral and occupational patterns described above, provide a partial possible explanation, in particular, the period saw a big fall in self-employment in construction, reflecting a campaign by tax and social security authorities to clamp down on 'bogus' self-employment in this sector (Green, 1998; Briscoe, Dainty and Millett, 2000). It is also possible that recent changes in corporation tax regimes provided an incentive for sole traders and self-employed people to incorporate their businesses (and become employees of their own companies), a possible explanation for the decline in self-employment in 'managerial' occupations (Figure 8.2 above), although lacking hard evidence, this remains a hypothesis. These changes appear to have had a one-off impact, however, and since 2001, self-employment resumed its upward trend.

8.3 THE 'SCARRING' EFFECTS OF SELF-EMPLOYMENT ON FUTURE CAREERS IN THE UK: SOME 'STYLISED FACTS'

We have seen that during the 1980s and 1990s the UK experienced growing rates of transition into and out of self-employment. Self-employment became a state which more people (and different types of people) experience at some stage during their working life. What does this mean for the future labour market career of the individuals affected? Overall, the UK findings to date, focusing on the impact of self-employment spells on income levels (Meager and Bates, 2002) are not overly supportive of the case for self-employment exerting a 'positive' impact on the future career and as such being a 'good' transition according to the transitional labour market perspective (TLM). The data show that average self-employment incomes are similar to those of employees, but self-employed earnings are much more polarised than the employee wage distribution (Meager, Court and Moralee, 1996) with larger shares on very high and very low incomes.

Once personal characteristics are controlled for, however, being self-employed significantly increases the likelihood of very low earnings. In contrast, being self-employed does not significantly increase the likelihood of very high earnings (Meager, Court and Moralee, 1996).

Despite increased likelihood of low income while self-employed, panel data (Meager and Bates, 2002) suggest little 'scarring effect' of self-employment once individuals move into wage employment (this contrasts with recent findings for the USA, however; see below). For those still in the labour market, income levels can recover from the impact of spells of low-income self-employment.

Data on lifetime work histories (Meager, Court and Moralee, 1996), however, show that self-employment experience does impact on the incomes in later life of a sample of people aged 55–69. Once other factors are controlled for, self-employment experience is a predictor of very low incomes in later life, but not of very high incomes. Further the ex-self-employed with low incomes in later life tended also to have lower levels of savings and pension entitlements. These findings being supportive of the 'scarring' thesis were challenged by Knight and Mackay (2000), who note that having been self-employed does not reduce average income after retirement, but the key point relates not to average income, but to the dispersion of incomes. Self-employment experience leads to higher probabilities of being in the top and the bottom of the income distribution in later life, but only in the latter case is that association explained by having been self-employed, rather than by other factors.

A tentative conclusion is that a flexible, liberal labour market regime such as the UK may be better at guarding against the short-term 'scarring' effects of self-employment experience on income levels, than in guarding against its long-term 'scarring' effects. Being self-employed raises one's chances of very low income, but this effect does not carry over into wage employment after leaving self-employment; over the lifetime, however, the presence of self-employment spells in the previous work history does increase chances of poverty, low savings levels and poor pension entitlement in later life.

Before turning to our empirical evidence, it is worth noting some interesting findings from another liberal labour market regime (the USA). Williams (2000) using longitudinal US data also shows that self-employment experience produces a significant earnings penalty on return to wage employment (but this effect is present only for women). More recent US panel data analysis (Bruce and Schuetze, 2004), finds that, relative to continued wage employment, short self-employment spells reduced average earnings on returns to wage employment (by 3–11 per cent for men), and that a self-employment spell increases the probability of subsequent unemployment by 3–10 per cent, and of part-time employment by 10–30 per cent. They suggest that their observed negative effects, compared with previous US work reflect not only methodological differences, but also their specific focus on short spells of self-employment (within a five-year window). Bruce and Schuetze argue that their findings raise important questions about the value of self-employment schemes to support unemployed people in starting their own businesses (we consider some data relating to such a self-employment measure in the UK next).

8.4 FURTHER EVIDENCE: SELF-EMPLOYMENT TRANSITIONS BY OCCUPATION

We extend the modelling of self-employment entries and exits in the UK using data from the BHPS, coupled with retrospective work history data (from the 1992 and 1993 waves of the BHPS); our combined data set covers the period 1980–99. Fuller details of the data set, and earlier versions of our analysis are set out in Meager and Bates (2004).[1]

The models in Table 8.1 examine inflows to self-employment for all people and for three occupational groups. The findings show that being female significantly reduces the likelihood of self-employment entry, a familiar finding from earlier research. In the multinomial model modelling self-employment entry in three occupational groups, the gender effect applies to all three, but is weaker in higher occupational groups. The penalty of being female is smallest in the flow to professional self-employment, and greatest in the flow to unskilled self-employment. Age has a consistent effect in all models, confirming previous research; the relationship is curvilinear, with the likelihood increasing, and then falling with age. Education is an important influence on inflow probabilities. In the aggregate models, those with higher qualifications have more chance of becoming self-employed (although the effect is not always significant, and the probability does not increase monotonically with education).

The occupational models show a more coherent pattern; for inflows to professional self-employment, there is a monotonically increasing relation-ship with education level. For skilled self-employment inflows, the highest entry probability is among those with intermediate qualifications, while in the case of inflows to unskilled self-employment it is those with higher qualifications who have a lower entry probability.

Prior unemployment strongly (and positively) influences self-employment entry in all models. Similarly, prior economic inactivity has a positive impact on inflows (although the effect is weaker than that of unemployment, and found only in the skilled self-employment model). Among those employed prior to self-employment, occupational status exerts an effect; that is, professional employees are more likely to enter professional self-employment, skilled employees more likely to enter skilled self-employment, and both groups significantly less likely to enter unskilled self-employment.

Flexibility and Employment Security in Europe

Self-employment transitions do not act as a mechanism for mobility between occupational groups within an individual's working life.

Table 8.1 A logit model of self-employment entry and a multinomial logit model of entry by occupational group (1980–1999)

Models	Logit		Multinomial logit by occupation					
	Entry		Professional		Skilled		Unskilled	
	Coef.	s.e	Coef.	s.e	Coef.	s.e	Coef.	s.e
Gender (ref: male)								
Female	–0.748***	0.078	–0.326***	0.115	–0.827***	0.124	–1.545***	0.193
Age								
Age (18 yrs = 0)	0.060***	0.011	0.067***	0.017	0.053***	0.016	0.084***	0.026
Age squared	–0.001***	0.000	–0.001***	0	–0.002***	0	–0.002***	0.001
Education (CASMIN) (ref: 1ab)								
1c/2a	0.017	0.252	0.582	0.394	0.046	0.334	–0.588	0.717
2b	0.351***	0.100	0.866***	0.195	0.171	0.154	0.423**	0.181
2c	0.618***	0.121	1.366***	0.213	0.526***	0.178	0.199	0.26
3a	0.490***	0.102	1.321***	0.187	0.370**	0.161	–0.088	0.224
3b	0.481***	0.138	1.562***	0.22	–0.356	0.294	–1.360**	0.628
Employment status before self-employment entry (ref: unskilled employee)								
Professional employee	0.099	0.111	0.689***	0.173	–1.158***	0.306	–2.119***	0.362
Skilled employee	–0.081	0.100	–0.576***	0.189	0.739***	0.179	–1.636***	0.222
Unemployed	1.467***	0.116	1.181***	0.217	1.886***	0.21	0.592***	0.23
Economically inactive	0.526***	0.115	0.125	0.209	0.996***	0.217	–0.079	0.24
Employment status before self-employment entry (ref. primary, manufacturing, utilities also including those not in the labour market)								
Construction	1.212***	0.134	0.305	0.286	1.438***	0.175	1.138***	0.321
Traditional services	0.439***	0.109	0.456***	0.166	0.029	0.202	0.571**	0.239
Transport and communications	0.081	0.177	0.120	0.261	–1.530***	0.589	0.469	0.295
Financial and business services	0.453***	0.123	0.455***	0.151	–0.126	0.292	0.853***	0.312
Other services	–0.005	0.112	–0.399***	0.156	0.082	0.179	0.220	0.295

Table 8.1 (Continued)

Models	Logit		Multinomial logit by occupation					
	Entry		Professional		Skilled		Unskilled	
	Coef.	s.e	Coef.	s.e	Coef.	s.e	Coef.	s.e
Father self-employed (ref: father not self-employed)								
Father self-employed	0.335***	0.094	0.215**	0.13	0.445***	0.158	0.415*	0.219
Father professional employee	0.134	0.097	0.369***	0.140	0.084	0.068	–0.509**	0.259
Father skilled employee	0.049	0.084	0.068	0.138	0.126	0.021	–0.169	0.169
Father other	0.034	0.126	0.021	0.210	0.109	0.173	–0.186	0.255
Constant	–5.411***	0.147	–7.220***	0.286	–6.225***	0.238	–5,681***	0.311
No. observations	103,564		94,082					
Wald c^2 (degrees of freedom)	0.042		994.69					
Pseudo-R^2	481.88		0.080					
Log likelihood	–5,910.37		–6,642.10					

Note: * $p < 0.10$, ** $p < 0.05$, ***$p < 0.01$.

The previous sector of employment influences self-employment entry, although it is not clear whether this reflects sector-specific experience gained in wage employment, or greater opportunities to become self-employed in certain sectors. The gender model (not shown here) indicates that it only holds for men. Compared with people who are inactive or employed in the primary or manufacturing sectors, people employed in financial and business services, traditional services, and (especially) construction, are more likely to enter self-employment. The construction effect is expected, given the particular characteristics of UK construction, discussed in Table 8.1. (Table 8.1 shows that the effect is concentrated among skilled and unskilled workers.)

Many previous studies find that parental self-employment has a positive impact on self-employment inflows. Our models are consistent with this inter-generational transmission of self-employment propensity, which is likely to relate to social capital as well as to financial capital and the role of inheritance. Our gender models record the effect for both men and women, but Table 8.1 shows that it applies only to entry to skilled and unskilled self-employment, and not to professional self-employment. Entry to professional self-employment is, however, influenced by the broader occupational background of the father having a father in professional employment which increases the likelihood of entry to professional self-employment (and reduces the likelihood of entry to unskilled self-employment).

Table 8.2 shows similar models for self-employment outflows. The effect of gender is particularly marked in the case of professional and skilled self-employment. Self-employed women in these occupations are more likely to exit self-employment (alongside the earlier findings of lower entry propensities, this helps explain aggregate female self-employment rates remaining persistently lower than those of men).

In all the models, outflow propensities decline with age, although the relationship is curvilinear, and the propensities start to rise again in the older years (a retirement effect). Together with the results for self-employment inflows, this suggests that the stability of self-employment increases with age; as individuals get older (up to a certain age), they are more likely to enter self-employment, and more likely, having entered, to remain in self-employment. This is consistent with the hypothesis that older individuals are more likely to have accumulated financial and human capital which is relevant both to self-employment entry, and to survival in self-employment.

Table 8.2 Logit model of exit from self-employment and multinomial logit model of exit by occupational group (1980–1999)

Models	Logit		Multinomial logit by occupation					
	Exit		Professional		Skilled		Unskilled	
	Coef.	s.e.	Coef.	s.e	Coef.	s.e	Coef.	s.e
Gender (ref: male)								
Female	0.509***	0.08	0.634***	0.109	0.512***	0.168	0.331	0.229
Age								
Age (18 yrs = 0)	–0.070***	0.014	–0.071***	0.022	–0.055***	0.022	–0.088***	0.028
Age squared	0.002***	0	0.002***	0	0.001***	0	0.002***	0.001
Education (CASMIN (ref: 1ab)								
1c/2a	0.374	0.232	0.021	0.356	0.424	0.33	1.036**	0.48
2b	0.287***	0.096	0.217	0.192	0.324**	0.141	0.202	0.186
2c	0.538***	0.109	0.572***	0.186	0.632***	0.164	0.454	0.309
3a	0.268***	0.089	0.262	0.163	0.22	0.147	0.306	0.224
3b	0.444***	0.135	0.464***	0.184	0.448	0.352	–0.243	0.947
Occupation in current self-employment (ref: unskilled)								
Professional	–0.330***	0.118	N/a	N/a	N/a	N/a	N/a	N/a
Skilled	–0.070	0.112	N/a	N/a	N/a	N/a	N/a	N/a

Table 8.2 (Continued)

Models	Logit		Multinomial logit by occupation					
	Exit		Professional		Skilled		Unskilled	
	Coef.	s.e.	Coef.	s.e	Coef.	s.e	Coef.	s.e
Industrial sector of current self-employment spell (ref primary, manufacturing, utilities also includes those not in the labour market)								
Construction	0.118	0.115	1.092***	0.424	–0.018	0.144	0.108	0.271
Traditional services	0.386***	0.116	0.478**	0.196	0.728***	0.201	0.135	0.266
Financial and business services	0.646***	0.134	0.792***	0.206	0.585**	0.268	0.621	0.392
Other services	0.317***	0.116	0.459**	0.195	0.308	0.192	0.076	0.341
Father self-employed (ref: father not self-employed)								
Father self-employed	–0.200***	0.081	–0.370***	0.12	–0.025	0.136	–0.024	0.218
Social background of father (ref: father unskilled employee)								
Father professional employee	–0.017	0.093	–0.074	0.131	–0.100	0.179	0.093	0.275
Father skilled employee	0.065	0.080	–0.133	0.144	0.116	0.121	0.283	0.177
Father other	–0.100	0.110	–0.136	0.211	–0.070	0.167	–0.185	0.233
Constant	–1.708***	0.192	–2.106***	0.332	–2.036***	0.271	–1.235***	0.376
No. observations	9,356		4,213		3,633		1,510	
Wald c^2 (degrees of freedom)	162.23[19]		80.52[17]		84.36[17]		35.16[17]	
Pseudo- R^2	0.024		0.029		0.031		0.027	
Log likelihood	–3,639.43		–1,620.15		–1,357.27		–638.73	

Note: * $p < 0.10$, ** $p < 0.05$, ***$p < 0.01$.

Qualification level has a positive impact on outflows, mainly among professional occupations. Taken together with the inflow findings this suggests increasing dynamism of (professional) self-employment with increasing educational level; the low qualified are less likely to enter this kind of self-employment, but more likely to remain in it when they do. As noted in Meager and Bates (2004), the UK is unusual in this respect, and similar analysis for some other advanced economies suggests increasing stability of self-employment with qualification levels. It is possible that self-employment among highly qualified people in the UK is perhaps less stable than elsewhere, due to the 'flexibilisation' of some professional labour markets in the liberal market regime of the UK.[2] Such an explanation is hard to square, however, with the outflow data in Table 8.2 showing that the professional self-employed are less likely to exit than skilled or unskilled employees. Turning to sector, the models show that compared with primary, manufacturing and construction self-employment, employment in the other sectors (services of various types) is less stable, with higher exit rates.

Finally, the models confirm that parental self-employment not only increases the chances of entry to self-employment, but also reduces the outflow probabilities. Over and above this effect of a self-employed father, however, there seems to be no effect of the father's social or professional status on the likelihood of exit.

What does this tell us about the 'positive' or 'scarring' effects of self-employment transitions in a TLM framework? First, the results reinforce existing evidence on the role of personal characteristics. Thus they confirm persistent gender effects; that women are less likely to enter self-employment, and female self-employment is less stable than male self-employment, raising questions about the potential of self-employment transitions as a 'positive' career step for women (at least without institutions or measures to help sustain them in self-employment). Further, inflow propensities increase and outflow propensities decrease with age throughout most of the working life, suggesting that accumulation of financial and human capital with age facilitates entry to self-employment and protects against exit, in turn raising questions about self-employment transitions as a positive career move for younger people who may lack such financial and human capital (we present in the next section of this chapter evidence from a UK measure to encourage young people's transition to self-employment).

The findings on social mobility and educational background are interesting from a TLM perspective. At aggregate level, the familiar relationship of previous studies is observed: parental self-employment predicts self-employment entry and survival. Inter-generational transmission of skills, attitudes (and possibly financial resources) is found in the literature as an explanation for the homogeneity and stability of self-employment. However, recent work suggests that this traditional homogeneity has been breaking down in recent decades. Our analysis, disaggregating the self-employed by occupation confirms greater heterogeneity at this level. Thus parental self-employment is a predictor of entry into unskilled and skilled self-employment, but not of entry into professional self-employment. For the latter, educational level and general parental social background are more influential. So, for some types of self-employment, the influence of parental self-employment is moderated through other aspects of social and educational background. At the professional level, self-employment appears to be a labour market segment open to those without a family background of self-employment, if they nevertheless have a high level of education and/or a professional family background. It is much less clear that self-employment is a vehicle for upward or downward social mobility, between or within generations. Parental social background exerts a strong influence on entry to professional self-employment. Equally, looking at an individual's own trajectory, it is clear that there is a strong relationship between the prior occupational status, and the status in self-employment. The potential of self-employment acting as a transitional vehicle for improving the individuals' labour market position is not confirmed by our evidence. Despite the growing heterogeneity of self-employment and increasing rates of transition into and out of self-employment (Meager and Bates, 2004), the role of social background remains very important in determining those transitions (the main exception being in professional occupations), as does prior occupational background.

8.5 DO SUPPORTED SELF-EMPLOYMENT SPELLS RAISE EMPLOYABILITY?

A key aspect of the role of self-employment in transitional labour markets is the effect of self-employment spells on subsequent labour market experience, and on the human capital of the individuals affected. One potential justification of self-employment schemes targeted at the unemployed (Meager, 1996), is that even if the businesses quickly 'fail', the experience of self-employment will enhance their subsequent labour market chances (measured by employment probability or earnings, for example). Such enhancement might be direct (that is, self-employment adds to their human capital) or indirect (for example self-employment has a signalling effect to potential future employers).

We have already cited evidence from UK research on life-cycle impacts of self-employment spells, suggesting that such experience can have negative impacts on incomes in later life, as well as US evidence that the impact of short-term self-employment spells on incomes and job-finding chances are also negative. We now throw some further light on these questions using UK data, collected as part of an evaluation of a self-employment scheme targeted at unemployed youth (fuller details of the evaluation can be found in Meager, Bates and Cowling, 2003).[3]

The research followed participants over time,[4] comparing their experience with a matched group of young people, who had not been supported to enter self-employment. A preferred methodology for the evaluation would have been to look at the counterfactual through a control group of people eligible for but denied that support (allocation to the control group would be ideally be random under such an approach). This experimental approach[5] was not possible, as it was necessary to work with an existing sample of self-employed people supported through the scheme. Instead a quasi-experimental approach was adopted, with a comparison group, matched on a range of characteristics to those in the 'treatment group' (the self-employed entrants). Our preferred approach was to construct a comparison group from the eligible population via 'propensity score matching' but this was not possible in the present case, due to the absence of a database of a clearly defined group of the population who are eligible for the self-employment measure, to use as a sample frame.[6] The approach chosen, therefore, was to draw a comparison group from an existing database, offering a reasonable basis of comparison with the sample of self-employment entrants in the scheme. The comparison group was drawn from the JUVOS[7] database of unemployed people, an administrative database of the UK public employment service.

As is common in such approaches, practical considerations limited the number of variables on which matching could be undertaken to three. Inevitably with such a matching process, unobserved heterogeneity in the sample gives rise to issues of selection bias. However, the survey method involved the collection of a range of data on observable characteristics (including motivational and attitudinal variables commonly hypothesised to contribute to unobserved heterogeneity in studies of this type). Despite this, however, it is likely that there remain other unmeasured factors, which are influential both on the likelihood of a young person seeking support from the self-employment scheme, and on their future labour market outcomes. We consider the possible implications of this later in this chapter.

An initial sample of 2,000 participants was surveyed three times at ten month intervals. The comparison sample (1,600 respondents) was selected to fall into the same age range (18–30) as the participants, and matched on three criteria; gender, region and employment status at the date when the matched person in the participant sample entered self-employment.

Table 8.3 Sample structure

	Participant sample	Comparison sample
Wave 1: Mar/Apr 2000	Telephone survey: 2,002 respondents	(retrospective data: 1,600 respondents)
Wave 2: Jan/Feb 2001	Postal survey, with telephone follow-up: 1,332 (identifiable) respondents	Telephone survey: 1,600 respondents
Wave 3: Nov/Dec 2001	Telephone survey: 872 respondents	Telephone survey: 925 respondents

Table 8.3 shows some survey attrition between waves, which introduced response bias into successive survey waves of the survey, so the data for waves 2 and 3 of the participant sample, and for wave 3 of the comparison sample were weighted to compensate for this bias.[8]

The overall survival rate in self-employment of the participants was 88 per cent at wave 1 (March/April 2000), 68 per cent at wave 2 (Jan/Feb 2001), and 65 per cent at wave 3 (Nov/Dec 2001). The wave 1 cohort consisted of a representative cross-section of participants who had started in the scheme in the previous 24 months, so by the time of wave 3, the longest self-employment spells were of nearly four years duration. Taking account of the variable durations of the wave 1 cohort, the data suggest that the survival rate declines steadily to around 70–75 per cent 18 months after self-employment entry, after which the curve flattens out for another 18 months, beginning to decline again as the sample approach their third anniversary of start-up. By the time they approach their fourth anniversary, the survival rate is 50 per cent (Figure 8.3).

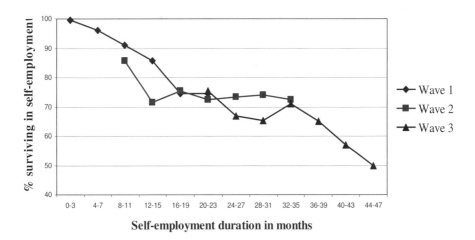

Figure 8.3 Survival rates by duration since self-employment entry (waves 1 to 3)

Multivariate analysis of these survival rates (using logistic regression and Cox regression models: see Meager, Bates and Cowling, 2003 for details), shows that the factors influencing survival are:

- *personal characteristics*: white participants have higher survival rates than non-whites as do participants with a family background of self-employment, older participants, and those with intermediate level qualifications.
- *attitudinal factors*: running counter to some notions of 'entre-preneurial' behaviour, 'risk averse' individuals record significantly higher survival rates than risk-neutral or risk-living individuals.[9]
- *business characteristics:* start-ups in the distribution, catering and transport sectors enjoyed lower survival rates than those in other sectors; similarly businesses dependent primarily on a local market were less likely to survive than those with wider geographical reach.
- *support through the start-up scheme:* self-reported dead weight was strongly and positively associated with survival. This reflects a paradox in the design of self-employment schemes, well documented in the literature (Meager, 1996), namely that such schemes typically record high deadweight, and the most effective strategy to reduce it (targeting the scheme on the most disadvantaged groups) tends to reduce survival rates. In the present case, the form of funding received under the scheme was also relevant, with those receiving grant rather than loan funding having lower survival rates (the scheme administrators appeared to target grants on the most disadvantaged participants). The amount of funding received is positively (but weakly) associated with survival rates; a stronger positive influence, however, is the receipt of personal support from a 'mentor'. The regressions suggested that this effect was mainly apparent at wave 1, suggesting that such support is particularly important in the early months of self-employment.

We now turn to comparisons between the experiences of the participant sample and the comparison sample on indicators relating to subsequent labour market experience, namely: a) employment status; and b) earnings. Two types of comparison are made:

- In some cases (when looking at earnings trajectories), it is appropriate to compare outcomes for the entire participant sample with those for the entire comparison sample.
- In other cases (when looking at subsequent employment status) it is appropriate to compare outcomes for 'non-survivors' from the participant sample (for example, those who have left self-employ-ment), with those of the comparison sample.

Turning to the multivariate analysis, Table 8.4 contains the model estimates exploring differences between employment outcomes in the two samples at wave 3. The model shown is a multinomial logistic model, based on the comparison sample and participant non-survivors at wave 3. It looks, for the combined population, at the likelihood of being self-employed, unemployed or inactive. In each case, this is assessed relative to the likelihood of being in waged employment. A key explanatory variable in the model is the dummy variable identifying which sample the respondent is drawn from, picking up the 'effect' of scheme participation.

Table 8.4 Multinomial logistic regression estimates of employment outcomes: participant and comparison samples at wave 3

| | Multinomial logistic regression (reference category: dependent employment) | | | | | |
| | Self-employed | | Unemployed | | Inactive | |
	Coef.	P>|z|	Coef.	P>|z|	Coef.	P>|z|
Sex (male = 1)	–0.48	0.18	0.35	0.05	–0.71	0
Age of respondent in years	0.01	0.9	0.07	0.01	–0.06	0.06
Disability (disabled =1)	–0.09	0.85	–0.07	0.76	0.73	0.01
Ethnic origin (ethnic minority = 1)	0.36	0.53	0.73	0.01	0.04	0.9
Either parent been self-employed? (yes = 1)	0.94	0	0.04	0.83	0.18	0.4
Ever self-employed before? (yes = 1)	1.22	0.01	0.07	0.83	0.62	0.07
Marital status (single, living alone = 0)						
Single, living with parents	0	1	–0.48	0.01	–0.22	0.4
Married/cohabiting	0.25	0.55	–1.26	0	0.65	0.04
Separated/divorced	0.49	0.74	–0.01	0.99	0.74	0.32
Dependent children (yes =1)	0.26	0.57	0.64	0.02	0.38	0.19
Housing tenure (renting/free = 0; home owner/mortgage = 1)	0.20	0.64	–0.55	0.05	0.23	0.36
Attitude to risk (risk taker = 0)						
Risk neutral	–0.21	0.6	0.54	0.05	0.14	0.65
Risk averse	–0.23	0.67	0.74	0.01	0.34	0.32
Age at leaving education in years	–0.03	0.71	–0.04	0.31	–0.02	0.65

*Table 8.4 (Continued) Multinomial logistic regression estimates of
employment outcomes: participant and comparison samples at wave 3*

	Multinomial logistic regression (reference category: dependent employment)					
	Self-employed		Unemployed		Inactive	
	Coef.	P>|z|	Coef.	P>|z|	Coef.	P>|z|
Highest qualification (NVQ 5 or equiv. = 0)						
NVQ 4 or equiv.	0.14	0.89	0.3	0.67	0.77	0.3
NVQ 3 or equiv.	0.41	0.67	0.10	0.90	1.61	0.03
NVQ 2 or equiv.	0.15	0.88	0.83	0.26	1.01	0.18
Below NVQ2	0.94	0.38	0.68	0.36	0.83	0.31
No qualifications	0.74	0.51	1.21	0.11	0.96	0.24
South West	0.28	0.68	−0.44	0.29	−0.26	0.63
West Midlands	−0.47	0.54	−0.38	0.32	0.07	0.89
East Midlands	−0.06	0.94	−1.29	0.01	0.28	0.63
Eastern	0.30	0.70	−0.50	0.27	−0.46	0.42
Yorkshire and the Humber	−0.08	0.91	−0.09	0.82	−0.05	0.92
North West	−0.01	0.98	−0.39	0.33	0.25	0.62
North East	−1.24	0.15	−0.32	0.44	−0.12	0.83
Previous activity (employed=1)	0.16	0.65	−1.13	0	−0.55	0.01
Amount of funding from scheme (£ x 100)	0.01	0.21	0.02	0.13	0	0.79
Sample (comparison sample = 0, participant sample = 1)	1.29	0.01	−0.96	0.01	0.39	0.40
Constant	−3.57	0.14	−2.05	0.12	−0.57	0.71
N (of cases)	1,056					

Source: Meager, Bates and Cowling (2003).

The table shows that, controlling for the other factors, being in the participant sample significantly increases the likelihood of self-employment at wave 3, and reduces the likelihood of unemployment. It makes no difference to the likelihood of being inactive. Other variables with significant influence in the model are in line with prior expectation. Thus the only other variables with a significant (positive) influence on the likelihood of self-employment are parental self-employment and prior self-employment experience (both variables well-established in the literature as influences on self-employment propensities).

Turning to look at earnings outcomes, Table 8.5 tracks net (post-tax) earnings of the survivors and non-survivors (in work) in the participant sample, and those in work in the comparison sample. Most interest centres on what has happened by wave 3. It is clear that those in the participant sample who remain in their (scheme-supported) self-employment contain, by far, the largest concentrations of extremely low earnings. There is less difference between the distributions of earnings of non-survivors and those in the comparison sample but, on balance, it appears that the non-survivors' sample exhibits a more polarised distribution than that of the comparison sample, with higher proportions in both the highest and lowest earnings categories.

Table 8.5 also summarises wave 3 earnings distributions of the three sub-samples, presenting, in each case, mean and median earnings. It confirms, on both measures, that those surviving in scheme-supported self-employment have the lowest earnings at wave 3. Looking at non-survivors in work, median earnings are very similar to (slightly higher than) that of working members of the comparison sample, but looking at mean earnings the non-survivors group is much higher than that of the comparison sample, reflecting the greater polarisation of earnings among non-survivors.

Table 8.5 Levels of earnings and mean and median earnings per week of all those in employment/self-employment in the participant and comparison sample at wave 3

	Participant sample (%)		Comparison sample (%)
	Still in supported self-employment	'non-survivors'	
Level of earnings per week	Proportion in category		
Less than £100 per week	41.6%	15.8%	10.8%
£100–£299.99 per week	34.3%	48.5%	64.1%
£300 or more per week	10.0%	13.4%	6.3%
N of cases (unweighted)	578	184	570
Earnings per week			
Mean	158.7	246.6	184.5
Median	100.0	179.1	173.1
N of cases (unweighted)	449	142	463

Source: Meager, Bates and Cowling (2003).

Once again, however, in order to look at the impact of participants' self-employment experience on subsequent earnings, a multivariate approach is required. For this, the two samples were again merged, and earnings equations estimated (based on the self-employed and employees across both samples).

Table 8.6 reports two earnings equations. The first focuses on all self-employed respondents at wave 3. The measure of earnings used here is the logarithm of net weekly earnings. Model 2 considers the logarithm of net weekly earnings among employees.

Estimation of these earnings equations requires us to consider sample selection issues. The problem can be summarised as follows. Respondents choose self-employment (or wage employment) over other alternatives. We observe only the earnings from those entering self-employment (or wage employment) over those alternatives. If those entering self-employment (or wage employment) have a propensity to earn more than those who do not, then the sample of observed earnings will be biased upwards.

Table 8.6 Earnings equations: wave 3 self-employed and employees (participant and comparison sample)

| | Self-employed | | Employees | |
| | Model 1: Weekly earnings | | Model 2: Weekly earnings | |
	Coef.	P>|z|	Coef.	P>|z|
Sex (male = 1)	0.04	0.74	0.24	0
Age of respondent in years	−0.04	0.85	0.09	0.35
Age squared	0	0.78	0	0.36
Disability (disabled = 1)	0.05	0.78	−0.08	0.28
Ethnic origin (ethnic minority = 1)	0.29	0.17	−0.23	0.02
Region (London = 0)				
South East	−0.24	0.43	−0.15	0.22
South West	−0.35	0.14	−0.26	0.03
West Midlands	−0.23	0.33	−0.14	0.24
East Midlands	−0.15	0.56	−0.06	0.74
Eastern	−0.3	0.24	−0.18	0.14
Yorkshire and the Humber	−0.33	0.18	−0.36	0
North West	−0.28	0.23	−0.18	0.09
North East	−0.08	0.74	−0.15	0.23
Attitude to risk (risk-taker = 0)				
Risk neutral	0.04	0.78	−0.07	0.27
Risk averse	−0.05	0.77	−0.02	0.81
Age at leaving education	−0.01	0.7	0.02	0.1

Table 8.6 (Continued)

	Self-employed		Employees	
	Model 1: Weekly earnings		Model 2: Weekly earnings	
	Coef.	P>|z|	Coef.	P>|z|
Highest qualification (NVQ 5 or equiv = 0)				
NVQ 4 or equiv.	0.03	0.93	–0.32	0.03
NVQ 3 or equiv.	0	0.99	–0.38	0.01
NVQ 2 or equiv.	0.06	0.86	–0.4	0.01
Below NVQ2	0.26	0.46	–0.39	0.03
No qualifications	0.53	0.16	–0.53	0
Sector (primary and utilities = 0)				
Manufacturing and construction	–0.01	0.93	0.05	0.61
Distribution, catering, transport etc.	0.03	0.86	–0.11	0.26
Business and financial services	–0.05	0.78	0.15	0.16
Public admin, education and health	0.46	0.09	0.04	0.68
Other services	–0.08	0.59	–0.13	0.24
Previous activity (employed=1)	0.41	0	0.11	0.02
Mentoring support in wave 3 (yes = 1)	–0.10	0.28		
Amount of funding from scheme (£ x 100)	0.01	0.02	0	0.34
Sample (comparison sample = 0, participant sample = 1)	–2.18	0	–0.36	0.05
Constant	8.76	0	3.31	0.02
N = cases	377		516	

Source: Meager, Bates and Cowling (2003).

The sample selection models assume that whether or not earnings are observed depends upon an underlying selection equation (for an overview see Heckman, 1979).

Table 8.7. contains the selection equations used for the earnings models, showing the sample selection term (λ), and ρ, indicating the correlation between the unobserved component of the earnings equation and the unobserved component of the selection equation. A significant value of ρ would vindicate the use of a sample selection model, as the standard regression estimator would have yielded biased results. The Chi^2 test suggests that ρ is significant in the two self-employment earnings equations, but not in the wage employment equations. There is, therefore, some justification for adopting this technique.

Table 8.7 Probit selection equation for models on weekly earnings of the self-employed and the employees

	Self-employed		Employees	
	Model 1		Model 2	
	Coef.	P>|z|	Coef.	P>|z|
Either parent been self-employed? (yes = 1)	0.09	0.10	−0.10	0.05
Ever self-employed before? (yes = 1)	0.05	0.47	0.18	0.04
Marital status (single, living alone = 0)				
Single, living with parents	0.16	0.02	0.21	0
Married/cohabiting	0.09	0.23	0.10	0.20
Separated/divorced	−0.18	0.33	−0.43	0.05
Dependent children (yes = 1)	0.06	0.41	0.09	0.26
Sex (male = 1)	0.05	0.44	−0.01	0.89
Age of respondent in years	0.01	0.93	0.05	0.58
Age squared	0	0.95	0	0.52
Disability (disabled = 1)	−0.2	0.05	0	0.96
Ethnic origin (ethnic minority = 1)	−0.26	0.05	−0.2	0.04
Sample (comparison sample = 0, PT sample = 1)	1.53	0	−0.96	0
Housing tenure (renting/free = 0; home owner/mortgage = 1)	0.23	0	0	0.99
Region (London = 0)				
South East	0.13	0.44	0.27	0.08
South West	0.07	0.66	0.34	0.01
West Midlands	−0.09	0.53	0.27	0.05
East Midlands	−0.06	0.72	0.21	0.19
Eastern	0.03	0.85	0.26	0.07
Yorkshire and the Humber	0.03	0.83	0.18	0.19
North West	0.05	0.75	0.22	0.10
Attitude to risk (risk-taker = 0)				
Risk neutral	0.06	0.49	−0.04	0.60
Risk averse	0.03	0.75	−0.09	0.27
Highest qualification (NVQ 5 or equiv. = 0)				
NVQ 4 or equiv.	0.2	0.22	−0.22	0.12
NVQ 3 or equiv.	0.09	0.6	−0.17	0.25
NVQ 2 or equiv.	0.05	0.77	−0.23	0.10
Below NVQ2	0.01	0.95	−0.26	0.09
No qualifications	−0.25	0.19	−0.47	0
Sample Selection Term (λ)	−1.13		0.51	
Probability of Independence between earnings and selection model ($\rho = 1$)	$Chi^2(1) = 46.38$		$Chi^2(1) = 0.28$	

Source: Meager, Bates and Cowling (2003).

The key findings from the models are:

- *Personal and related characteristics:* the effects of sex on weekly earnings are not significant among the self-employed but are significant among employees. However, it is possible that the association between sex and earnings is significant because men are more likely to be working in full-time employment (when hourly earnings are considered in model 4, the sex variable is no longer significant). Among other personal characteristics, age, disability and attitudes to risk were not significant determinants of earnings. Ethnic origin is significant (in model 3) in the expected direction, but this does not affect self-employed earnings.

- *Educational and career background:* there is no clear relationship between self-employment earnings and qualifications at wave 3, or between earnings and the age at which the respondent left full-time education. However, there is a 'qualification effect' among employees. Relative to employees reporting NVQ level 5, those with lower level or no qualifications had lower incomes. In all cases except that of hourly earnings among employees, those in employment immediately prior to self-employment entry had higher earnings than those who entered from unemployment or inactivity.

- *Business and related characteristics:* There is no regional earnings effect for the self-employed, although a London effect is apparent for employee earnings. There is no clear relationship between industrial sector and earnings among self-employed workers, although among employees, those engaged in business-related services or public administration had higher hourly incomes, relative to employment in primary industries.

- *Effects of scheme participation:* the model contains three variables to capture the potential influence of the scheme: (1) whether the respondent is from the participant sample (received financial support via the scheme); (2) whether the respondent received 'mentoring' support via the scheme; and (3) the amount of funding the respondent received from the scheme. Among the subsequently self-employed, there is a positive association between earnings and the amount of scheme funding received. However, it is striking that respondents from the participant sample had lower levels of self-employment weekly earnings than their comparison sample counterparts. Unfortunately, it is not possible to determine whether the differences in earnings between the self-employed in the two samples relate to unobserved aspects of respondents' personal characteristics, their 'human capital' or the nature of their businesses. As the 'sample' variable is not statistically significant (or barely significant at 95 per cent) in the models for employee earnings, however, it is tempting to hypothesise that the variables included in the self-employment models capture a fair proportion of the differences in personal characteristics and human capital across both groups. It may, therefore, be that unobserved business characteristics are responsible for differences in self-employment earnings between the two groups.

The association between 'mentoring' received via the scheme and the subsequent earnings of the self-employed is, counter to initial expectation, negative and statistically significant. The causation is difficult to determine, but we can hypothesise that the self-employed in greatest need of support (for example because their businesses were the least successful) might also have been more likely to have been offered continuing mentoring guidance by the scheme administrators.

To conclude this part of the chapter, we have already noted the need for some caution in making comparisons between the labour market outcomes achieved by the participant sample (who had participated in the self-employment scheme), and those achieved by the comparison sample who had not entered self-employment through the scheme (and who were matched with the participant sample on a number of characteristics). This need for caution arises because of the possibility of selection bias. Despite having controlled for differences in a large number of observed personal, educational and other characteristics, it is possible that some unobserved characteristics distinguish participants in the two samples which may also be relevant to subsequent labour market outcomes. It is plausible, for example, that there are attitudinal or motivational differences between the two groups (although it should be noted that our surveys did attempt to address this by collecting some self-reported attitudinal data relating, for example, to respondents' attitudes to risk-taking). It is also plausible, however, that in so far as such differences are relevant to subsequent labour market success, that they would lead us to over-estimate rather than to under-estimate scheme impact. This is because attitudes or motivations which are favourable to joining a self-employment scheme and setting up a small business are likely also to be favourable to labour market success, and in comparing labour market outcomes between the two samples there is a risk that we attribute differences in outcomes to scheme participation, when they are in fact due to the higher level of motivation and so on among scheme participants.

Despite this likelihood that any bias is likely to operate in favour of finding a positive scheme impact (where there is none), or in favour of over-estimating the size of such impact, it is notable that the analysis finds no evidence that participation in supported self-employment schemes has any significant impact on subsequent employment or earnings chances (it is, of course, possible that some longer-term impact might exist, beyond the three waves of our survey). The analysis shows that among those who leave (supported) self-employment after a short spell, there is no evidence that their subsequent overall chances of being in work are any higher than their counterparts in the comparison sample.

Similarly, having been in self-employment through the scheme does not enhance subsequent earnings levels as an employee, once they leave self-employment. Rather the results suggest that those in the scheme are worse off than the comparison sample while in their self-employment spell, and no better off (or possibly worse off) than those in the comparison sample after their self-employment spell.

8.6 CONCLUDING REMARKS

Our review of some of the previous UK evidence on the impacts of self-employment spells on careers and income levels in the short-term and over the lifecycle, supplemented with more recent work of our own with UK panel data, does not suggest that such spells (at least in the relatively unregulated UK environment) are likely to make a major positive contribution to enhancing those careers and income levels, and suggests some scepticism regarding the promotion of self-employment as a policy tool within a TLM framework.

The UK evidence shows that the self-employed are highly polarised in economic welfare terms, with a much more dispersed income distribution than is the case among employees. Once other factors are controlled for, moreover, the self-employed have a higher likelihood of falling into the lowest decile of the labour income distribution. Short-term scarring effects in income terms are limited, however, in the sense that after entry to wage employment recent self-employment spells do not appear to impair income prospects, compared with those who have not had such spells (some recent US evidence does, however, suggest a scarring effect, with a significant negative impact of short self-employment spells on subsequent earnings). There are, nevertheless, longer-term effects, and having had spells of self-employment during the working lifetime is a predictor of very low incomes in later life (close to, or beyond retirement age). This effect is, moreover, compounded by those with self-employment experience having poorer prospects than their employee counterparts in terms of their likelihood of having built up savings, or occupational/private pension entitlements during their working lives.

Our own work, presented here, shows persistent gender effects in self-employment flows: that is women are less likely to enter self-employment and less likely to survive in self-employment than men. Similarly young people are less likely to enter self-employment and less likely to remain in self-employment than older people. Most striking, however, are the negative results with regard to self-employment as a vehicle for social or occupational mobility. Despite the growth in self-employment, and the greater dynamism of self-employment, having had a self-employed parent remains one of the strongest and most consistent and statistically significant predictors of entry to, and success in (survival in) self-employment. Our occupationally disaggregated results show that this inter-generational transmission of self-employment propensities applies particularly to the self-employed in semi- and unskilled occupations. In higher skilled (professional occupations), parental background is also a predictor of self-employment entry, but in this case it is parental occupational background (also in the different professions) that acts as a predictor. Our findings do not suggest that, in the UK context at least, self-employment transitions are a vehicle for upward (or downward) social mobility, either within or between generations.

Finally, as far as self-employment measures are part of an active labour market policy framework for disadvantaged groups are concerned, our UK findings presented here do not support those who have argued that, irrespective of their business survival rates and indirect job creation impacts, self-employment schemes for disadvantaged/unemployed beneficiaries can be justified in terms of their subsequent positive impacts on 'employability'. This reinforces the somewhat sceptical conclusions from the US studies referred to in the chapter, regarding the potential of self-employment spells and supported self-employment as positive mechanisms within a transitional labour market framework. What remains to be seen (offering perhaps a future research agenda), is whether these kinds of results from the relatively un-regulated liberal UK/US policy regimes, would also apply in other countries which both place greater restrictions on self-employment entry, but which may also offer more effective support mechanisms for those entering or moving through self-employment.

NOTES

1. Similar modelling of inflows to and outflows from self-employment, using BHPS data, can also be found in Taylor (2004). In contrast to Taylor, however, we model the flows at a greater level of occupational disaggregation, to reflect the high degree of heterogeneity among the self-employed.
2. Other research (see, for example: Smeaton, 2003; Fraser and Gold, 2001; Dex et al., 2000) notes the growth of professional freelancers in information technology-related or media occupations.
3. The evaluation was funded by the UK Department for Work and Pensions; the analysis and interpretation in the present paper are the author's own.

4. Three waves of data were collected and by the third wave, the oldest businesses in the sample were four years old, and the youngest just over two years old.
5. See Heckman and Smith (1996) for a summary of experimental and non-experimental designs to evaluation (which also point out a number of significant disadvantages to approaches based on random assignment).
6. See Bryson, Dorsett and Purdon, 2002, for a description of propensity score matching methods of constructing a comparison group in evaluation studies.
7. JUVOS (the Joint Unemployment and Vacancies Operating System Cohort) is a 5 per cent sample of claims for unemployment-related benefits.
8. The weighting used logistic regression models, run on the data from the previous wave, estimating the effect of a wide range of variables (including individual characteristics, business characteristics, trading status of the business and so on). These models enabled the estimation of the probability (p) of an individual participating in wave 2 (or wave 3), given that they had participated in wave 1. Having estimated p, the weights to be applied to the data for wave 2 (or wave 3) were calculated as the inverse of this probability ($1/p$) for each case in the dataset.
9. The survey included questions to assess participants' perceptions of attitudes towards risk, asking whether they 'positively enjoyed taking risks', 'took risks where necessary', or 'avoided taking risks, wherever possible'.

REFERENCES

Acs, Z., Audretsch, D. and Evans, D. (1992), *The determinants of variations in self-employment rates across countries and over time*, WZB Discussion Chapter FSIV, Berlin: Wissenschaftszentrum für Sozialforschung, 92–3.

Briscoe, G., Dainty, A. and Millett, S. (2000), 'The impact of the tax system on self-employment in the British Construction Industry', *International Journal of Manpower,* **21** (8), 596–613.

Bruce, D. and Schuetze, H. (2004), 'The labor market consequences of experience in self-employment', *Labour Economics,* **11** (5), 575–98.

Bryson, A., Dorsett, R. and Purdon, S. (2002), *The Use of Propensity Score Matching in the Evaluation of Active Labour Market Policies*, DWP, Research Working Chapter no. 3, London: Department for Work and Pensions.

Dex, S., Willis, J., Paterson, R., Sheppard, E. (2000), 'Freelance Workers and Contract Uncertainty: The Effects of Contractual Changes in the Television Industry', *Work, Employment and Society,* **14** (2), 283–306.

Fraser, J. and Gold, M. (2001), 'Portfolio workers': Autonomy and Control amongst Freelance Translaters', *Work, Employment and Society,* **15** (4), 679–98.

Green, B. (1998), 'Survey reveals effects of fewer self-employed', *Construction New,* **5**, November, 6–7.

Heckman, J. (1979), 'Sample Selection Bias as a Specification Error', *Econometrica,* **47**, 153–61.

Heckman, J. and Smith, J. (1996), 'Experimental and non-experimental Evaluation', in Schmid G, O'Reilly, J. and Schömann, K. (eds), *International Handbook of Labour Market Policy Evaluation*, Cheltenham, UK and Brookfield, US: Edward Elgar.

Knight, G. and McKay, S. (2000), *Lifetime Experiences of Self-Employment*, DSS Research Report No. 120, London: Department of Social Security.

Meager, N., Kaiser, M. and Dietrich, H. (1992), *Self-Employment in the United Kingdom and Germany,* London, Bonn: Anglo-German Foundation for the Study of Industrial Society.

Meager, N. (1992), 'Does Unemployment Lead to Self-Employment?', *Small Business Economics*, **4** (2), 87–103.

Meager, N. (1993), *Self-employment and labour market policy in the European Community*, WZB Discussion Chapter FSI 93–201, Berlin: Wissenschaftszentrum für Sozialforschung.

Meager, N., Court, G. and Moralee, J. (1996) 'Self-employment and the distribution of income', in Hills, J. (ed.) *New Inequalities: The changing distribution of income and wealth in the United Kingdom*, Cambridge: Cambridge University Press.

Meager, N. (1996), 'Self-Employment as an alternative to dependent employment for the unemployed', in Schmid, G., O'Reilly, J. and Schömann, K. (eds), *International Handbook of Labour Market Policy and Evaluation*, Cheltenham, UK and Brookfield, US: Edward Elgar.

Meager, N. (1998), 'Recent trends in self-employment in the UK', *European Commission, Employment Observatory, SYSDEM Trends,* **31**, Winter.

Meager, N. and Bates, P. (2002), 'From Salary Workers to Entrepreneurial Workers?', in Schmid, G. and Gazier, B. (eds), *The Dynamics of Full Employment: Social Integration through Transitional Labour Markets*, Cheltenham, UK and Northampton, MA, USA: Edward Elgar.

Meager N., Bates, P. and Cowling, M. (2003), *Business start-up support for young people delivered by the Prince's Trust: a comparative study of labour market outcomes*, DWP Research Report no. 184, Leeds: Department for Work and Pensions.

Meager, N. and Bates, P. (2004), 'Self-Employment in the United Kingdom during the 1980s and 1990s', in Arum, R. and Müller, W. (eds), *The Re-emergence of Self-Employment*, Princeton: Princeton University Press.

Nisbet, P. (1997), 'Dualism, flexibility and self-employment in the UK construction industry', *Work, Employment and Society*, **11** (3), 459–80.

Nisbet, P. and Thomas, W. (2000), 'Attitudes, Expectations and Labour Market Behaviour: The Case of Self-Employment in the UK Construction Industry', *Work, Employment and Society*, **14** (2), 353–68.

Smeaton, D. (2003), 'Self-employed workers: calling the shots or hesitant independents? A consideration of the trends', *Work, Employment and Society*, **17** (2), 379–92.

Taylor, M. (2004), 'Self-employment in Britain: When, who and why?', *Swedish Economic Policy Review*, **11** (2), 141–173.

Williams, D. (2000), 'Consequences of self-employment for women and men in the United States', *Labour Economics,* **7** (5), 665–87.

Winch, G. (1998), 'The growth of self-employment in construction', *Construction Management and Economics*, **16**, 531–43.

9. Part-time Work and Childbirth in Europe: Scarring the Career or Meeting Working-time Preferences?

Didier Fouarge and Ruud Muffels

9.1 INTRODUCTION

One major aspect of the transitional labour market approach is its interest for the consequences of the ongoing individualisation process on the way people behave on the labour market. One important consequence of that is that women seek to develop their own career and tend to work more hours than they used to in the past. A second consequence is that due to women's increasing participation they desire more options to be able to combine working and caring duties. In general it seems that people want more leeway to adapt their labour supply to changing conditions over the life cycle and to improve their work–life balance. The TLM approach devotes particular interest into the role of life events such as childbirth, on the way people behave on the labour market and how they seek to improve their work–life balance. In this chapter we focus on the effect of people's decisions in choosing particular combinations of working time and caring duties on the future career. We use the European Community Household Panel but added the Hungarian household panel to analyse the short and medium-term effects of the various types of combinations of part-time work and care breaks on the occupational career[1]. The Hungarian panel has been added to include at least one of the transition countries from the East. Transition countries are particularly interesting to study because part-time labour is a rather new phenomenon in these post-socialist countries. In particular, we try to assess the effect of part-time employment on the probability of being employed full-time later in their career. Finally, we specifically assess the effect of a major life event – childbirth – on the future labour market participation and income position of females. Regression models on the changes in working time owing to the career break are used to examine the future income and employment effects across countries. The major question deals with the contended negative or 'scarring' effect of part-time work on the future employment and wage career (see in particular Chapter 7).

The chapter is structured as follows. In Section 9.2, we discuss the background of the research and our research questions. Section 9.3 discusses the data used and the selection of the main dependent variables. Descriptive results for part-time employment, transitions from part-time work and motives for working part-time are reported in Section 9.4 and model estimates in Section 9.5. Section 9.6 reports on the effect of childbirth on the labour market participation of young women, both in terms of the participation decision and the number of hours worked, while the effect of childbirth on labour market income is studied in Section 9.7. The main findings are summarised in Section 9.8.

9.2 BACKGROUND AND RESEARCH QUESTION

9.2.1 Previous Research

The incidence of part-time employment varies considerably for male and female workers as well as across countries of the EU. According to data from the Labour Force Survey, in 2005, 7.5 per cent of European male workers were employed in a part-time job, but this percentage varied from as low as 1.3 per cent in Slovakia to as much as 22.6 per cent in the Netherlands. For females the rates of part-time employment were higher. More than a third of employed women are working in a part-time job. Again, that percentage is lowest in Slovakia (4.1 per cent) but largest in the Netherlands (75 per cent). These numbers suggest that across Europe, people chose different combinations of working time and caring duties. These choices turn out to be very different both across gender and across countries.

In the literature, much attention has already been devoted to part-time employment and its consequences for participation later in the working life, but also on its consequence for future income. Although some authors have suggested that part-time jobs could be a springboard towards full-time jobs (Blank, 1989), there is little evidence that this is indeed the case in Europe. Recent studies for European countries have shown that most females who do work part-time are not so likely to move into a full-time job (O'Reilly and Bothfeld, 2002; Buddelmeyer et al., 2005). Furthermore, a Dutch study shows that also in the 'first part-time economy of the world' employees still experience a lower wage and social status as a consequence of part-time employment even several years after they have returned into a full-time job (Román, Fouarge and Luijkx, 2004).

Childbirth has also been shown to affect the participation decision of working mothers. Due the increased time squeeze after childbirth, mothers have a higher tendency than fathers to withdraw from the labour force (Dekker et al., 2000). Several studies, however, have illustrated the importance of institutional arrangements in keeping mothers in paid employment. In countries where the supply of female-friendly institutions (for example childcare) is higher, females have a higher probability of remaining in paid employment (Kenjoh, 2003; Gornick et al., 1998; Uunk et al., 2005). Furthermore, in such countries women seem more likely to work more hours (Van der Lippe, 2001).

9.2.2 Research Question and Expectations

Here we deal with four main research questions. They pertain to the effect of caring and part-time employment on future employment opportunities and to the effects of childbirth on the employment and wage career. With respect to the latter, we firstly investigate to what extent part-time employment has a 'scar effect' on employment later in the career, that is, we investigate to what extent part-timers workers have lower opportunities to move on to full-time jobs, conditional on their preferences and their life cycle phase. Secondly, we investigate the effect of childbirth on the decision to withdraw or to stay in the labour market and to choose for a certain number of weekly working hours. By doing so, we are able to compare the number of hours worked pre- and post childbirth. Thirdly, we examine the income consequences of childbirth.

From the existing literature on the subject we have derived some expectations about the effects we are likely to find:

1. Following the 'scarring' theory we assume that to the extent that working part-time has an adverse or 'scarring' effect on employment opportunities later in working life, part-time workers are expected to have a lower probability to be employed full-time later in the career than full-time workers.
2. Following human capital theory (Becker, 1964), we assume that part-timers build up less human capital during their part-time career and therefore are more likely to make a transition into non-employment.
3. For the same reason we contend that part-time employment reduces the probability of subsequent full-time employment, though we also presume that the longer people work part-time the more human capital has been built up and the smaller these effects tend to be as time passes.
4. If neo-classical economic theory has a bearing for women's labour supply decisions (Becker, 1981), we might assume that the price of leisure is lower due to the costs involved in caring because of which women choose to work part-time. In that case part-time work is associa-

ted with personal preferences for working fewer hours due to caring and not a 'scarring' phenomenon for which reason we might predict that the transition into full-time employment is less likely to occur.

5.   Also according to neo-classical thinking, if the costs of caring are high, for example, due to the lack of sufficient income support through public policies, childbirth is expected to result in a reduction of labour market income caused by the reduction in participation – which is then only partly compensated by the public income transfers (mainly child benefits), see Uunk et al. (2005).

9.3. DATA AND MAIN DEFINITIONS

9.3.1 Panel Data

For this chapter, we have used the data from the European Community Household Panel (ECHP), supplemented with the panel data for Hungary to acquire some idea on how dissimilar the results are for different parts of Europe with a different background and tradition in part-time work. The ECHP contains panel data (repeated measurement among the same sample of people) for 14 EU countries. For the UK, Germany and Luxembourg the ECHP contains two sources of information: ECHP-specific panel data, and panel data from the three national panels.[2] For these countries, we use the latter source. For all but three countries, data are available for the years 1994–2001. For Austria and Luxembourg we have data from 1995, and for Finland the data start in 1996.

Hungarian panel data have been matched to the ECHP in a way that comparability of the variables used is ensured. The Hungarian data come from the CHER database (Consortium of Household Panels for European Socio-Economic Research), and were directly derived from the Hungarian Household Survey (HHS). Data are available for the years 1992–1997.

The data is organised as a pooled person-year file, with one record for each person at each point of interview. For the analysis, we retained only people of working age (18–64). For the analysis of the effect of childbirth on labour market participation, however, we focus on the age group 18–45. Our dataset includes some 100,000 respondents aged 18 to 64 per wave across 15 countries. It includes 60,000 to 76,000 people aged up to 45 years old per wave.

9.3.2 Main Variables

Labour market status
The number of hours worked per week (in the main and additional jobs) is reported in the datasets used. This will be the main variable on which we

define labour market participation. In the analyses, we make a distinction between non-participation, part-time employment, and full-time employment. Non-participants are people working zero hours. It includes the unemployed, the disabled, as well as respondents who are currently not looking for a job. Small part-time jobs are defined as jobs of 1 to 14 hours per week.[3] Part-time workers are respondents who are working 15–34 hours per week. Full-time workers are people working at least 35 hours per week. The variable is described in Table 9.1.

Table 9.1 Labour market status according to the number of hours worked in pooled data file, (absolute numbers and percentages)

	N	%
Does not work	314,946	38.3
1–14 hours	19,685	2.4
15–34 hours	75,820	9.2
35+ hours	412,661	50.1
Total	823,112	100

Source: ECHP, 1994–2001 (Eurostat); HHS, 1992–1997 (TARKI).

Income

The effect of care on income is assessed by looking at the respondents' wage and non-wage income before and after childbirth. All incomes are expressed in purchasing power parities (PPP) as calculated by Eurostat in constant 2000 prices in order to ensure cross-country comparison. Total personal income refers to the annual net income from employment, private and public transfers. Wage income refers to the total net income from employment, while public transfers are the sum of all transfers paid to the individual such as unemployment and disability benefits, pensions, child or family allowances and so on. All incomes are measured in the year prior to the interview date. Except for France, all amounts are net of taxes and social security contributions. The hourly wage is measured by dividing the previous year's income by 52, and then by the number of hours worked per week the previous year (at the time of last year's interview).

Life course phase

Over time people experience a number of demographic transitions:; for example leaving home, getting married, having children, getting divorced or separated and so on. To account for these different phases of the life course, we define a life course phase variable that accounts for the household structure, the presence of children, and the age of the youngest child. The variable is self-explanatory and is described in Table 9.2.

Childbirth

We construct a dummy variable for childbirth by comparing the number of children across waves. We define childbirth as the event that a new child enters the household, that is, when the number of children younger than 16 in wave t is larger than in wave $t-1$.

Table 9.2 Life course phase, absolute number and the distribution of households in the pooled data file (absolute numbers and percentages)

	N	%
Couple no child*	278,881	33.7
Couple youngest child 0–5	117,264	14.2
Couple youngest child 6–16	155,113	18.7
Single no child*	218,335	26.4
Single youngest child 0–5	10,914	1.3
Single youngest child 6–16	47,705	5.8
Total	828,212	100

Note: *No child between the age of 0 and 16.

Source: ECHP, 1994–2001 (Eurostat); HHS, 1992–1997 (TARKI).

9.4. DESCRIPTIVE RESULTS

9.4.1 Incidence of Part-time Employment

The labour market status of males in the 15 countries included in our analysis is depicted in Figure 9.1. The data relate to the latest year available in the data: 1997 for Hungary and 2001 for all other countries. Figure 9.2 presents similar data for females. In both figures, the countries are sorted according to the inactivity rate.

Of all countries included, the labour force participation of males is lowest in Hungary and France.[4] High employment rates (80 per cent or more) are found in Austria, the UK, Denmark, Luxembourg and the Netherlands. It is clear from this figure that part-time jobs are not popular among males, with the exception of the Netherlands perhaps where more than 10 per cent of males are employed for less than 35 hours a week. The picture for female labour participation in Europe is very diverse; more than half the females of working age are not employed in France, Hungary and the Southern countries Spain, Greece, and Italy. The large incidence of part-time employment in total employment, for example, in the Netherlands, is also reflected in Figure 9.2.[5] The differences across countries, again, are substantial.

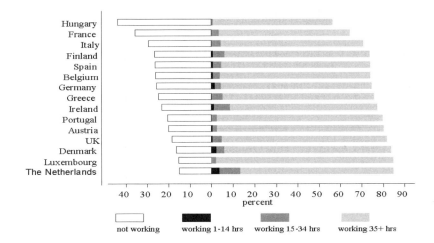

Note: *1997 data for Hungary.

Source: ECHP, 1994–2001 (Eurostat); HHS, 1992–1997 (TARKI).

*Figure 9.1 Labour market participation of males (18–64), 2001 (%)**

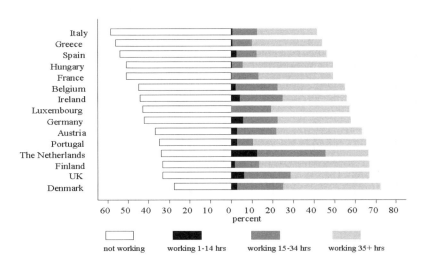

Note: *1997 data for Hungary.

Source: ECHP, 1994–2001 (Eurostat); HHS, 1992–1997 (TARKI).

*Figure 9.2 Labour market participation of females (18–64), 2001 (%)**

Although small part-time jobs remain a limited phenomenon even for females in most EU countries, a significant proportion of females in Ireland, the UK, Germany and especially the Netherlands do work in such jobs. With the exception of Greece, Portugal, Spain and Hungary, a significant percentage of females are employed in regular part-time jobs. In the Netherlands, a third of all working age females are working part-time. In Belgium, Denmark, Luxembourg, the UK and Ireland a fifth or more of all females is working part-time.[6]

9.4.2 Part-time and Caring Obligations

There are basically two ways to assess the extent by which people who work part-time do so in order to be able to combine work with caring obligations and to improve their work–life balance: the so-called stated and revealed preferences method. With the 'stated preferences approach', one relies on the subjective answers to a question pertaining to the reason why respondents are working in part-time jobs. With the 'revealed preferences approach' one would look at the coincidence or association between variables indicating whether people actually work part-time and objective indicators for being engaged in caring obligations. In this section, we use both methods in turn.

Reason for working part-time
In the ECHP questionnaire respondents were asked for the main reason why they work part-time. Respondents could choose among six reasons. The information, however, is missing for the UK and Luxembourg, and the question for Germany only allows for choosing between two reasons. Unfortunately, no such information is available in the Hungarian panel. Note that the definition of part-time work used in the ECHP is slightly different from the one used here: the question was asked to everyone working less than 30 hours.

The main reason why males work part-time in Denmark and the Netherlands but also in Finland, Belgium, Germany, Austria and Ireland is, as they report so, because they are undergoing education or training, (Figure 9.3).

In France, Greece, Spain, Italy, but also in Portugal and Belgium, a significant percentage of males who are working part-time report do so because they are unable to find a full-time job. A part-time job seems to act as a second-best option due to the unavailability of a full-time job. In those countries, more than in others, males seem to be confronted with a constrained labour supply for they are unable to work the number of hours they prefer to work. With a view to these results, it must be concluded that caring obligations are not the main reason for males working part-time, not even in the Netherlands where only 10 per cent report this to be the main reason.

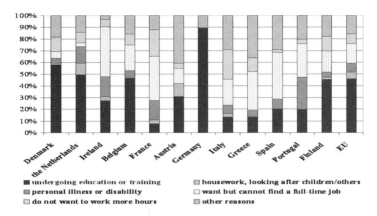

Source: ECHP, 1994–2001 (Eurostat).

Figure 9.3 Main reason for working part-time, males (18–64), 2001 (%)

The picture for females looks rather different (Figure 9.4). In most EU countries, the main reason why females work part-time is because of household activities or caring obligations either for children or other dependents in the household. But it is worthwhile to note some country specific differences. In Denmark and Finland the main reason why females work part-time is because they undergo education or training. There, the picture is not very different from that of males.

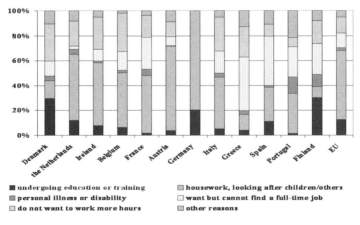

Source: ECHP, 1994–2001 (Eurostat).

Figure 9.4 Reason for working part-time, females (18–64), 2001 (%)

In most of the Southern European countries (Greece, Spain, but also Portugal), females – just like males – report they are constrained in their labour supply due to the unavailability of longer hours jobs. In France and Finland a fifth of the females working part-time also report they are unable to find a full-time job. When comparing Denmark and the Netherlands, it turns out that the share of females reporting housework as the main reason why they are working part-time is four times larger among Dutch females compared to Danish females.

Part-time and life course phase
In this part we discuss the relationship between labour market status and the life course stage of males and females. The labour market participation of males living in a couple appears to be larger than of single males (Figure 9.5). Associated with the presence of and care for children, they tend to participate more in the labour market. However, single males with caring obligations are, just as females, more likely to withdraw from the labour market and to become non-participants. Especially, when males living in a couple face the financial responsibilities of caring for children they tend to participate.

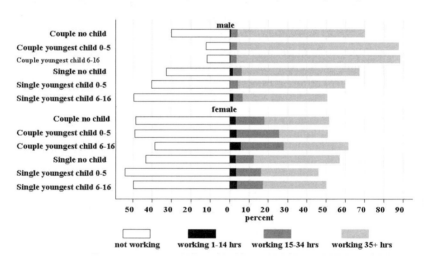

Source: ECHP, 1994–2001 (Eurostat); HHS, 1992–1997 (TARKI).

Figure 9.5 Labour market status and life course phase, males and females (18–64), 2001 (%)

Overall, we see that the life course phase, however, does not have much of an impact on the number of hours worked in the case of males. For females, however, the life course phase has a larger effect on their labour supply in terms of hours.

For single females with children and females in a relationship without children or with young children we indeed find that they are more likely to withdraw and to become non-participants. But when females participate and when they have a partner they more often work in a part-time or a small part-time job especially if they have children.

Transition rates

Over time people tend to change their employment position as socio-economic events (for example, unemployment, a job change or retirement) and socio-demographic events (for example, childbirth or marriage) require them to adapt their working time.

The changes in employment status over time are depicted in Table 9.3 for males and in Table 9.4 for females. In these tables we depict the transitions into another employment status after one, three and five years in the career.

Table 9.3 Transition rates in employment status after one year (t+1), three (t+3) and five years (t+5), males (18–64) (%)

	Status in $t+1$				
	Not working	1–14 hours	15–34 hours	35+ hours	Total
Status in t					
Not working	78	2	3	18	100
1–14 hours	34	28	12	26	100
15–34 hours	17	3	47	34	100
35+ hours	7	0	2	91	100
	Status in $t+3$				
	Not working	1–14 hours	15–34 hours	35+ hours	Total
Status in t					
Not working	65	2	4	30	100
1–14 hours	28	14	13	45	100
15–34 hours	21	2	33	44	100
35+ hours	11	0	2	86	100
	Status in $t+5$				
	Not working	1–14 hours	15–34 hours	35+ hours	Total
Status in t					
Not working	53	2	5	40	100
1–14 hours	27	6	11	56	100
15–34 hours	23	1	27	49	100
35+ hours	14	0	2	83	100

Source: ECHP, 1994–2001 (Eurostat); HHS, 1992–1997 (TARKI).

It is obvious from the tables that the status of full-time employment of the large majority of males (91 per cent) is pretty stable from year to year, and so is the status of non-employment (although the group is smaller in size). Part-time statuses are less stable at least for males. Less than half of all males in part-time jobs (15–34 hours) in a particular year are still working part-time one year later. A third of them have made a transition into full-time employment. Statuses in small part-time jobs are even less stable since only 28 per cent are still working in such a job one year later. A third has stopped working and a quarter has made a transition into full-time employment after one year.

The stability in non-participation is larger among females; 86 per cent remain out of the labour force between year *t* and the following year *t*+1. Female part-time employment (whether short or regular part-time) is also more stable than is the case for males: 47 per cent remain in their small part-time job and 69 per cent remain in their part-time job. This could mean that part-time employment is of a more persistent nature for females.

Table 9.4 Transition rates in employment status after one (t+1), three (t+3) and five years (t+5), females (18–64) (%)

Status in *t*	Status in t+1				
	Not working	1–14 hours	15–34 hours	35+ hours	Total
Not working	86	2	4	7	100
1–14 hours	26	47	19	8	100
15–34 hours	13	4	69	14	100
35+ hours	9	1	6	84	100
Status in *t*	Status in *t*+3				
	Not working	1–14 hours	15–34 hours	35+ hours	Total
Not working	78	3	7	11	100
1–14 hours	30	32	23	14	100
15–34 hours	20	4	57	19	100
35+ hours	16	1	9	74	100
Status in *t*	Status in *t*+5				
	Not working	1–14 hours	15–34 hours	35+ hours	Total
Not working	72	4	9	15	100
1–14 hours	32	24	27	17	100
15–34 hours	24	4	49	22	100
35+ hours	21	1	11	67	100

Source: ECHP, 1994–2001 (Eurostat); HHS, 1992–1997 (TARKI).

When the observation period is extended up to three or five years the working-time statuses on the labour market appear less stable because, as the years go by, there are more opportunities for people to adjust their labour supply on the labour market in accordance with their preferences or by adapting to external constraints. The differences between males and females appear to be larger as the observation period is extended up to three or five years. Significantly fewer females remain in full-time paid employment in the five years time horizon, and more of them make a transition out of employment.

However, as time passes, there are also more females who make a transition from part-time employment (whether small part-time or not) into full-time employment. Among females, the transition from part-time employment to full-time employment is least often occurring in the Netherlands and most often in Finland, Hungary, and Spain.

In Table 9.5, we report on the issue to what extent the transition for females from part-time employment to full-time employment is associated with the main reason why they work part-time.

Table 9.5 Transition rates in employment status after one year, three and five years for females (18–64) according to the reason why they work part-time in the current year (%)

Females reporting working part-time for other reasons than caring or free will					
	Status in *t*+1				
Status in *t*	Not working	1–14 hours	15–34 hours	35+ hours	Total
1–14 hours	34	39	17	10	100
15–34 hours	18	4	62	16	100
	Status in *t*+3				
Status in *t*	Not working	1–14 hours	15–34 hours	35+ hours	Total
1–14 hours	34	22	20	24	100
15–34 hours	26	3	50	21	100
	Status in *t*+5				
Status in *t*	Not working	1–14 hours	15–34 hours	35+ hours	Total
1–14 hours	31	15	27	28	100
15–34 hours	28	4	45	22	100
Females reporting working part-time because of caring obligations or free will					
	Status in *t*+1				
Status in *t*	Not working	1–14 hours	15–34 hours	35+ hours	Total
1–14 hours	25	51	19	5	100
15–34 hours	13	5	76	7	100
	Status in *t*+3				
Status in *t*	Not working	1–14 hours	15–34 hours	35+ hours	Total
1–14 hours	32	38	23	7	100
15–34 hours	20	5	64	11	100
	Status in *t*+5				
Status in *t*	Not working	1–14 hours	15–34 hours	35+ hours	Total
1–14 hours	35	31	26	8	100
15–34 hours	22	6	57	15	100

Source: ECHP, 1994–2001 (Eurostat).

Using the reasons as reported in Figure 9.4, we define a variable indicating whether or not females work less than full-time out of free will or because of caring obligations ('does not want to work more hours, works part-time because of household activities or caring obligations'), or because of other reasons (education, cannot find full-time job, personal illness or other reason).[7] On the one hand, Table 9.5 shows that transitions into full-time employment are more common for females reporting part-time employment for other reasons than caring obligations (or free will). This seems to be the case even in the medium-term (5 years) although the difference between the two groups is smaller than in the short-term (1 year). On the other hand, it is also illustrated that in the short-term, females not reporting care as the reason why they work part-time, are more likely to leave paid employment. However, the difference between the two groups is smaller in the medium term.

9.5 MODEL ESTIMATES

9.5.1 Model

Having described patterns of part-time employment in Europe and transitions across employment statuses, we now turn to modelling changes in the employment status over time. To do so, we estimate a multinomial logit model for the employment status after one, three and five years ($t+1$, $t+3$ and $t+5$), controlling for the number of hours worked in t and a number of covariates. As in the previous paragraph, the hours are categorised in non-participation, small part-time jobs (1–14 hours worked), part-time jobs (15–34 hours worked), and full-time jobs (working 35 hours or more). The multinomial logit model that is estimated distinguishes among these various employment statuses (see Box 9.1).

In order to test expectation 1, we consider part-time employment as the base category in the model. Furthermore, we set the reference category for the current employment status to full-time workers. In doing so, the estimated parameters can be interpreted as the difference in the probability of being employed full-time in the future for the workers who are currently not employed full-time.

Two variables that are specifically related to caring obligations enter the model: the variable indicating the life course phase and a dummy variable indicating whether or not one works less than full-time out of free will (does not want to work more hours, works part-time because of household activities or caring obligations).[8] Furthermore, the model controls for personal characteristics (age, educational level, health status, and past history of unemployment), as well as job characteristics (sector of activity, number of employees in the firm).[9] Year dummies are also included in order to capture economic cycle effects. Controlling for such background characteristics is important for workers in part-time jobs might be a selective group.

Box 9.1 The multinomial model

The probability of being in either state (non-participation, small part-time job, full-time), as compared to the reference state (regular part-time), is given by the following equation:

$$P(y = j) = \frac{\exp\left(\sum_{k=1}^{K} \beta_{jk} x_k + \gamma_j s_c\right)}{1 + \sum_{j=1}^{J-1} \exp\left(\sum_{k=1}^{K} \beta_{jk} x_k + \gamma_j s_c\right)}$$

with $J = 4$ (the four labour market statuses), j = part-time being the reference state and K the number of explanatory variables x. The variables included in the model are:

- Hours worked in t: non-participation, small part-time, regular part-time, full-time (reference);
- Household type: couple without child (reference), couple youngest child 0–5, couple youngest child 6–16, single no child, single youngest child 0–5, single youngest child 6–16;
- Part-time for caring: dummy for people who do not want to work more hours, or work part-time because of household activities or caring obligations;
- Age and age squared (/100);
- Education level: low, average (references), high;
- Bad health: dummy for people bad or very bad health;
- Public sector: dummy for people working in the public sector (coded 0 for people out of employment);
- Firm size: number of people working in the company (coded 0 for people out of employment);
- Past unemployment: dummy for people reporting unemployment in the past 5 years;
- Year dummies;
- Country dummies.
- Indicators for labour market opportunities: numerical flexibility and employment security.

9.5.2 Results

Employment status

The results of the estimation of the multinomial model are represented in Table 9.6.[10] They show that relative to full-time workers, part-time employees have a lower probability of being employed full-time one year later. The size of the effect shows that it does not matter much whether the part-time

Table 9.6 Results from model estimations on labour market participation one year later(t+1), three (t+3) and five years later (t+5) in the career, females (18–64 years) (coefficients from multinomial logit model)

	Hours worked in t+1			Hours worked in t+3			Hours worked in t+5		
	non-part.	small PT	full-time	non-part.	small PT	full-time	non-part.	small PT	full-time
Hours worked in t (ref: full-time)									
non-participation	1.817***	1.158***	-2.221***	1.287***	0.853***	-1.742***	1.029***	0.749***	-1.432***
small part-time	-0.305***	2.396***	-3.099***	-0.434***	1.520***	-2.247***	-0.529***	1.021***	-1.868***
part-time	-1.962***	-0.833***	-3.908***	-1.480***	-0.697***	-2.856***	-1.203***	-0.547***	-2.297***
Household type (ref: couple, no child)									
Couple youngest child 0–5	0.105**	0.073	-0.586***	0.115*	0.193*	-0.438***	-0.027	0.262*	-0.391***
Couple youngest child 6–16	0.020	0.156**	-0.193***	0.011	0.047	0.027	-0.096	0.014	0.21***
Single no child	-0.022	0.005	0.291***	-0.08	-0.288***	0.433***	-0.238***	-0.479***	0.411***
Single youngest child 0–5	0.151	0.024	-0.177*	0.009	-0.098	-0.122	-0.178	-0.185	-0.085
Single youngest child 6–16	-0.102	-0.101	0.117*	-0.171**	-0.402***	0.327***	-0.221**	-0.608***	0.481***
Part-time for caring	-0.314***	0.08	-0.793***	-0.103	0.093	-0.673***	-0.103	0.097	-0.639***
Age	-0.190***	-0.101***	-0.002	-0.215***	-0.098***	-0.024*	-0.229***	-0.083***	-0.025
Age squared (/100)	0.258***	0.127***	-0.022*	0.311***	0.135***	0.006	0.343***	0.126***	0.007
Educational level (ref: average)									
High	-0.274***	-0.154**	0.039	-0.218***	-0.165*	0.026	-0.137*	-0.088	-0.006
Low	0.213***	0.204***	0.01	0.245***	0.202**	-0.014	0.312***	0.293***	-0.075
Bad or very bad health	0.562***	-0.041	-0.048	0.624***	0.096	0	0.551***	-0.022	-0.123
Working in the public sector	-0.703***	-0.785***	-0.077**	-0.648***	-0.829***	-0.075	-0.685***	-0.866***	-0.069
Firm size	-0.086***	-0.098***	0.018***	-0.050***	-0.092***	0.008	-0.028**	-0.057*	0.006
Unemployed in the last 5 years	-0.013	-0.071	-0.157***	0.011	-0.087	-0.162***	-0.02	-0.074	-0.164***
Year dummies (ref: 1994)									
1995	0.006	-0.084	-0.011	0.031	0.07	-0.003	-0.008	-0.065	0.046
1996	0.024	0.024	-0.001	-0.003	-0.007	0.028	-0.140***	-0.092	0.033

Table 9.6 (Continued)

	Hours worked in t+1			Hours worked in t+3			Hours worked in t+5		
	non-part.	small PT	full-time	non-part.	small PT	full-time	non-part.	small PT	full-time
Year dummies (ref: 1994) (continued)									
1997	0.053	0.125	-0.011	-0.029	-0.036	0.067			
1998	0.017	-0.023	0.012	-0.140***	-0.072	0.044			
1999	-0.019	-0.053	0.033						
2000	-0.152***	-0.043	-0.035						
Country (ref: Denmark)									
the Netherlands	-0.434***	0.816***	-0.898***	-0.453***	1.076***	-1.114***	-0.436***	1.373***	-1.208***
Belgium	0.266***	0.068	-0.199***	0.365***	0.333*	-0.326***	0.410***	0.663***	-0.400***
France	0.474***	-1.011***	0.042	0.816***	-1.066***	0.023***	1.051***	-0.771***	0.077
Ireland	0.173***	0.354***	-0.319***	0.087***	0.560***	-0.491***	0.101	0.844***	-0.553***
Italy	0.551***	-1.035***	0.034	0.702***	-0.876***	-0.013***	0.822***	-0.648**	-0.019
Greece	0.568***	-0.619***	0.150***	0.722***	-0.386***	0.223***	0.865***	-0.191	0.283***
Spain	0.737***	0.320***	0.226***	0.833***	0.549***	0.306***	0.960***	0.837***	0.423***
Portugal	0.151**	0.361***	0.575***	0.251***	0.672***	0.711***	0.312***	0.976***	0.845***
Austria	0.145***	0.119	-0.109*	0.161*	0.304*	-0.24***	0.221*	0.754***	-0.290***
Finland	0.286***	-0.047	0.334***	0.388***	0.198	0.524***	0.447***	0.604*	0.559***
Germany	0.445***	0.876***	0.041	0.539***	1.232***	-0.06	0.643***	1.582***	-0.098
Luxembourg	0.253***	-2.338***	-0.287***	0.456***	-29.606***	-0.386***	0.440***	-30.277***	-0.462***
UK	-0.160***	0.595***	-0.388***	-0.029	0.919***	-0.334***	0.023	1.209***	-0.290***
Hungary	0.855***	-0.810***	0.694***	1.307***	-0.338	0.825***	1.774***	0.126	0.724***
Constant	3.661***	-0.331	3.146***	3.667***	-0.647	2.975***	3.678***	-1.406**	2.635***
R²	0.474			0.329			0.257		
N	270,447			167,876			86,450		

Note: * p < 0.10, ** p < 0.05, *** p < 0.01.

Source: ECHP, 1994–2001 (Eurostat); HHS, 1992–1997 (TARKI).

239

job is a short-hours or a regular job. Because all coefficients of the exit states of part-time employed females are negative, we can conclude that part-time is an absorbing state from which few people leave. This confirms the results from the descriptive part showing that the majority of females working part-time in a particular year remain in part-time employment one year later.

Furthermore, the results show that looking at the medium-term effects (after three and five years), we observe that the probability of part-timers being engaged in full-time jobs is still lower than that of full-timers but the 'scarring effect' is diminishing in size (from –3.908 for full-time employment after one year to –2.297 after five years). Whether or not we can speak of a true scarring effect depends on the extent to which being in part-time employment is the result of constraints on the labour market. If working part-time is out of free will, then we cannot speak of scarring. The estimates show that respondents who work part-time because of caring obligations or because they simply do not want to work more hours are less likely to be engaged in full-time employment in the future. This effect persists over time. Mothers with children between the ages of 6 and 16 are more likely to make a transition into full-time employment, probably because as children grow older, it becomes easier to combine full-time employment and caring obligations.[11]

Females who currently work part-time because of caring obligations or because of housework are significantly less likely to make a transition to full-time employment.[12] The effect does not slow down much as one looks ahead in the career one, three and five years later. On the one hand, this shows that working part-time offers females a relatively strong attachment to the labour market and that their strategy of working part-time is indeed associated with the stage of the life course they are in reflecting their need to combine work and care. On the other hand, the results show that the opportunities for full-time employment for caring mothers are still poor, even in the medium term.

In the medium term, Dutch females in particular are less likely to be engaged in full-time employment, but they are also less likely to exit to non-employment compared to Danish females (see also Fouarge and Baaijens, 2006). Engaging in a full-time job is also less likely to happen in Belgium, Ireland, Austria, Luxembourg and the UK. On the contrary, females in the Southern European countries (especially Portugal), Hungary and Finland are more likely than Danish females to be working in a full-time job in the medium-term. This reflects the cross-sectional evidence discussed above.

9.6 EFFECT OF CHILDBIRTH ON HOURS WORKED

The birth of a child is a major life course event that affects young parents' personal and social life. Such an event, however, has potentially also an impact on parent's working time. In particular, the new-born child and infants require additional care which might reduce the time available for labour market participation. In this section, we focus on the effect of childbirth on the labour supply of young parents. The analyses are performed on a sample that only included people from 18 to 45 years of age, as this is the most relevant group when it comes to childbirth.

In Figure 9.6, we use the pooled dataset to depict the average number of hours worked in the year of childbirth, as well as up to 3 years prior and after childbirth.[13]

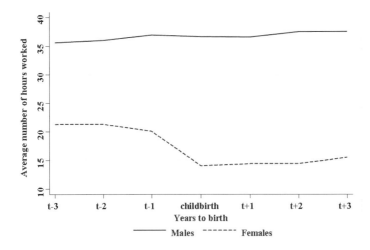

Source: ECHP, 1994–2001 (Eurostat); HHS, 1992–1997 (TARKI).

Figure 9.6 Average number of working hours of working males and females before and after childbirth, aged 18–45 years old

All respondents becoming parents are included, irrespective of their labour market status. Respondents who are not engaged in paid employment are assumed to work zero hours. Henceforth, the lines in the graph are the combined effect of (1) respondents reducing their number of hours, and (2) respondents withdrawing from the labour market.

As the figure shows, childbirth has no effect on the labour supply (working hours) of fathers. Mothers do adapt their labour supply with an average decrease in working hours that amounts to 5 hours per week. There seems to be an anticipation effect (with females already reducing their labour supply as childbirth approaches) and a small recovery effect (with a small increase in the labour supply three years after childbirth).

In order to better understand the total effect as depicted in Figure 9.6, we have computed the labour market status and working hours two years before and two years after childbirth. Moreover, the computation was done for females having their first child and for females who already had children before giving birth to another child. The results are represented in Figure 9.7.

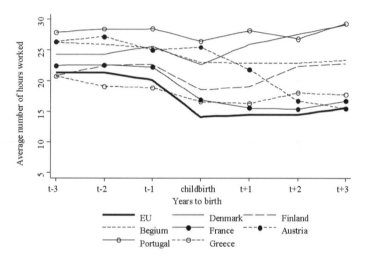

Source: ECHP, 1994–2001 (Eurostat); HHS, 1992–1997 (TARKI).

Figure 9.7 Labour market status of young mothers (18–45), 2 years before and 2 years after childbirth (percentages)

First it is important to note that the participation prior to and after childbirth is higher for females who gave birth to their first child. Moreover, females who already have children are more likely to work part-time. The reason for this is that having more than one child makes it even more difficult to combine caring obligations and employment. Second, as the figure shows, the reduction in the average number of hours worked as depicted in Figure 9.6 is due to two changes in the labour supply of females following birth. On the one hand, the largest part of the effect on average hours is due to females withdrawing from the labour market. This is the case for females giving birth to their first child – their participation rate drops significantly – but it is also the case for females giving birth to additional children. On the other hand, the drop in hours is also party explained by the reduction in the number of hours worked by females giving birth to their first child.

The effect of childbirth on the labour supply of young females (hours worked) varies significantly among countries. In Figure 9.8, we have plotted the average number of working hours before and after childbirth for countries where the effect of childbirth on working hours is below average in the EU.[14] Figure 9.9 contains the same plot for countries where the effect of childbirth on hours worked is above average in the EU.

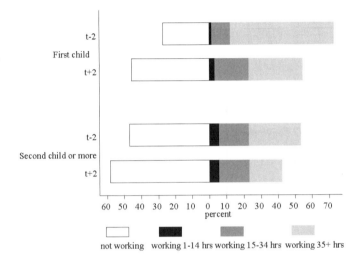

Source: ECHP, 1994–2001 (Eurostat); HHS, 1992–1997 (TARKI).

Figure 9.8 Average number of working hours of females (18–45) before and after childbirth in 7 countries (effect is below EU average)

In two countries, Portugal and Denmark, childbirth does not lead to a permanent decrease in the number of hours worked by females (see Figure 9.8). In Greece and Belgium, the reduction in working hours is relatively small whereas in Finland the reduction is only temporary while females return to their pre-birth level of working hours within two years following childbirth.

In the other group of countries (Figure 9.9), two countries show a remarkable pattern of pre- and post birth participation. In Germany and Hungary, the number of hours worked drops significantly in the year of childbirth because many females withdraw from the labour market. Participation only recovers slightly in the years following childbirth. In fact, the sharp decrease in the number of hours worked among German and Hungarian females following childbirth is the result of a significant withdrawal from the labour market. Generally speaking, where the labour market participation rate of young mothers is high prior to childbirth such as in Denmark, the Netherlands, Belgium and Portugal (major exceptions are Austria and Hungary), it tends to remain high even after childbirth. However, in Denmark, the Netherlands and Belgium this goes along with a significant increase in part-time employment, but not in Portugal. We might contend that the role of institutional support to working mothers for allowing them to keep on working and not to withdraw nearly fully is important in this respect. In countries where the level of institutional support is high such as in Denmark and the Netherlands women tend not to withdraw fully and to stay longer in part-time work than in countries where such support is lacking.

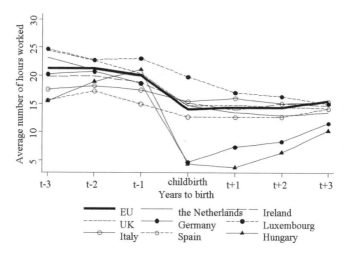

Source: ECHP, 1994–2001 (Eurostat); HHS, 1992–1997 (TARKI).

Figure 9.9 Average number of working hours of females (18–45) before and after childbirth in 8 countries (effect is above EU average)

9.7 INCOME AND SOCIAL TRANSFERS

9.7.1 Income in Various Stages of the Life course

In two studies of Anxo et al. (2005) and Klammer and Keuzenkamp (2005), the ECHP data were used to assess the impact of social transfers on household income. The conclusion then was that 'social security benefits are mainly concentrated in two phases of life: when people have children in the household and during retirement, when people are 60 years or older.' (Klammer and Keuzenkamp, 2005, p. 61; see also Anxo et al., 2005, p. 59–63).

Here, we focus on the composition of individual income of young females and find that social security benefits are especially important in the life phase in which females raise children, but especially when they have to do that alone as single mothers (Figure 9.10).[15]

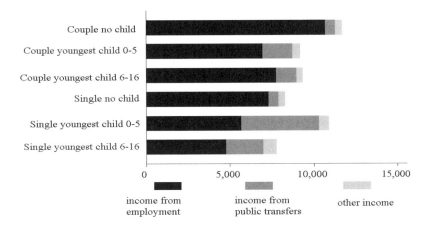

Source: ECHP, 1994–2001 (Eurostat); HHS, 1992–1997 (TARKI).

Figure 9.10 Composition of the personal income of young females (18–45) by household type in 2001 (in 2000 for PPP corrected euros)

Figure 9.10 reveals a similar static view on the life course as in the approach of Klammer and Keuzenkamp (2005) and Anxo et al. (2005). The evidence suggests that people go through the various life stages though respondents are only observed in one of these stages. To circumvent this problem, we have opted for a dynamic view on the life course by using real longitudinal data and by focusing on the effects over time of a particular but significant life course event (childbirth) on net personal income.

9.7.2 Income Effect of Childbirth

To assess the effect of (an increase in) caring obligations we computed pre- and post birth total net yearly personal income, the net yearly personal income from employment, and the net yearly personal income from public transfers. The yearly income from employment and from public transfers is zero when no income of such type is received by the respondent. The results are presented in Figure 9.11 for females aged 18 to 45 years and giving birth during the observation period.

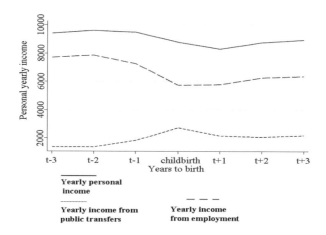

Source: ECHP, 1994–2001 (Eurostat); HHS, 1992–1997 (TARKI).

Figure 9.11 Pre and post birth yearly net personal income, all females aged 18–45 years (in 2000 for purchasing power parities corrected euros)

The figure shows that the yearly income from employment drops from some 8,000 euro in the years prior to childbirth to approximately 6,000 euro in the years following. This, of course is an average for all mothers and the income drop from employment is the combined effect of several things: (1) of the true evolution of the incomes of working females, (2) the reduction in female labour supply (see above) with a downsizing effect on the yearly wage, and 3) the withdrawal of females from the labour market (in which case the income drops to zero).

   For females who remain in employment, the effect is less dramatic (Figure 9.12) and the reduction is either the result of a reduction in the number of hours worked (which reduces yearly income), or the result of a change in hourly earnings after childbirth, or a mix of these two effects. Childbirth does result in a permanent lower level of income from employment on a yearly basis due to the permanent reduction in the number of hours worked per week as it was depicted in Figure 9.6. The reduction in labour income is only partly compensated by an average increase in the income from public transfers (see Figure 9.11). Henceforth, the total effect of childbirth on net personal income is negative but less negative than the effect on net labour income.

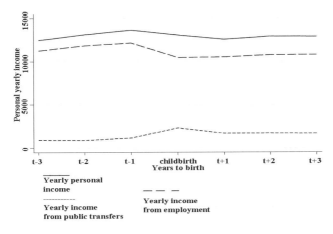

Source: ECHP, 1994–2001 (Eurostat); HHS, 1992–1997 (TARKI).

Figure 9.12 Pre and post birth yearly income, females aged 18–45 who remained employed (in 2000 for PPP corrected euros)

9.7.3 Modelling the Effect of Childbirth on Income

To assess the effect of childbirth on female labour income, we have then estimated a regression model on annual net personal labour income. We estimated a fixed-effects panel regression model that is explained in Box 9.2. The results are presented in Table 9.7.

Because of our focus on the effect of childbirth on female labour income, the model was estimated for females only who remained in paid employment and who did not drop out. Though increasingly so women tend to stay in employment after childbirth, the results are still not generally applicable to other females.[16] The estimates show that net of observed and unobserved time constant characteristics, childbirth has a significant negative effect on net yearly personal income from employment. The birth of a child reduces the net labour market income by some 5 per cent (–0.218/4.056).

The effect of childbirth on reducing the yearly wage income is rather strong as the first model shows. The second model with the country dummies included show that the childbirth effect is stronger in Austria and Finland than in the reference country Denmark, while the income loss is less than in Denmark in the Netherlands, Italy, Greece, Luxembourg and the UK. In Portugal, the yearly income after childbirth is larger than before childbirth. The reasons for these differences across counties are associated with the functioning of the labour market, the generosity of the transfer system and the

Box 9.2 The panel regression model

Our data contain information on the annual income of an individual i at each time point (year). Panel data techniques make use of this particular type of data structure and enable us to model the dependent variable (income) as a function of observed time varying characteristics in the data – such as the occurrence of a childbirth – and unobserved time constant characteristics of the respondents. The fixed-effects panel model estimated has the following form:

$$y_{it} = \alpha + \beta x_{it} + \mu_i + \varepsilon_{it}$$

where y_{it} is the annual income of individual i at time t, x_{it} is a set of time varying covariates, α is a constant term, μ_i is an individual specific unobserved effect, and ε_{it} is an error term with standard properties. μ_i can be identified because of the repeated measurement in the data, and it is not correlated to the error. Because we use a fixed effects specification we do allow for possible correlation between the fixed effects and other covariates in the model. Such a model better allows for a causal interpretation of the effect of childbirth on income than would a regular regression model do. The estimated parameter Sigma μ is an estimate of the standard deviation of the individual specific error, and Sigma ε stands for the standard error of the error term. The amount of error in the model that is due to individual unobserved variation in the data is represented by Rho (Sigma μ / ((Sigma μ)^2 + (Sigma ε)^2). It provides an indication for the relevance of applying such a model on the data. The variables included in the model are:

- A dummy for childbirth;
- A dummy for single mothers;
- Number of hours worked per week;
- Age and age squared (/100);
- Education level: low, average (reference category), high;
- Bad health: dummy for people having a bad or a very bad health;
- Public sector: dummy for people working in the public sector (coded 0 for people out of employment);
- Firm size: number of people working in the company (coded 0 for people out of employment);
- Past unemployment: dummy for people reporting unemployment in the past 5 years;
- Year dummies;
- Country dummies (that we also interact with the childbirth dummy).

Table 9.7 Fixed effects panel regression model on yearly income, females (18–45 years), 1994–2001 (beta coefficients)

	Yearly wage income	
Single	0.042	0.044
Hours worked per week (lag)	0.204***	0.211***
Age	0.174***	0.175***
Age squared (/100)	−0.169***	−0.170***
Educational level (ref: average)		
High	0.085**	0.086**
Low	−0.073*	−0.070*
Bad or very bad health	−0.087**	−0.085**
Working in the public sector	0.04	0.038
Firm size	0.067***	0.067***
Unemployed in the last 5 years	−0.103	−0.101
Year dummies (ref: 2000)		
1995	0.01	0.004
1996	0.022	0.019
1997	0.050***	0.050***
1998	0.01	0.012
1999	0.013	0.014
Childbirth	−0.218***	
Childbirth * Country (ref: Denmark)		−0.371***
Netherlands		0.321***
Belgium		0.188
France		0.145
Ireland		0.192
Italy		0.209*
Greece		0.363**
Spain		0.132
Portugal		0.486***
Austria		−0.786***
Finland		−0.314**
Germany		−0.1
Luxembourg		0.252*
UK		0.239**
Hungary		0.497
Constant	4.056***	4.032***
R^2	0.016	0.018
N	68,354	68,354
Sigma μ	1.868	1.865
Sigma ε	1.149	1.148
Rho	0.725	0.725

Note: * $p < 0.10$, ** $p < 0.05$, *** $p < 0.001$.

Source: ECHP, 1994–2001 (Eurostat); HHS, 1992–1997 (TARKI).

supporting role of families or social networks. According to Anxo et al. (2005) using cross-sectional data particularly in Sweden – more so than in the Netherlands or the UK – the transfer system appeared capable to compensate the earnings loss of women with young children (under seven) almost completely. The findings presented here point to the impact of institutional support mechanisms to cushion the earnings losses due to childbirth and caring duties.

The other variables included in the model show that investments in human capital pay off for women since the yearly wage income is higher for higher educated and lower for lower educated women. Women who keep on working long hours after childbirth obviously have a higher yearly wage income than women who reduce working hours more. Also the results by age confirm our predictions from the human capital theory: as experience (or age) increases, income also increases, but at a decreasing rate.

After some age threshold earnings tend to fall again probably while for older women it is harder to return into employment in longer hours jobs. For the same reason women reporting bad health end up with a lower yearly income, due to loss of productivity and hence of human capital. Women working in larger firms are either better paid, even after controlling for education level, age and health, or are capable of maintaining longer working hours because of which their earnings losses are lower. This might just reflect the better child care facilities in larger firms compared to smaller firms.

9.8 CONCLUSIONS

In this chapter, it is shown that the reasons why men and women choose to work part-time are rather different. The different reasons constitute one of the explanations why the share of part-time employment among males and females are markedly different. It also partly explains why the use of it is also very diverse across Europe. Females tend to use part-time employment for the purpose of combining employment with caring obligations, whereas males report very different reasons for working part-time showing their dissimilar work strategies compared to females. This is also shown in the transition rates out of part-time work. Females, more often than males, tend to remain in part-time employment whereas men tend to move to longer hours jobs. Therefore, the conclusion to be drawn is that males consider a part-time job to be a transitory state towards full-time employment and not a quasi-permanent state as it is for quite a number of women. This seems particularly the case in countries where part-time work tends to become the norm for women such as in the Netherlands where most women work part-time. If we observe the differences across Europe it turns out that overall in

Europe only 7.5 per cent of European male workers were employed in a part-time job, but more than a third of females. The percentage of females in part-time jobs however varies largely across Europe; it appeared lowest in Slovakia (4.1 per cent) and largest in the Netherlands (75 per cent).

We have examined several of our expectations associated with the so-called 'scarring' thesis. First of all, we expected part-time workers to have a lower probability to be in full-time employment later in the career than full-time workers; this is indeed confirmed, but this 'negative' effect becomes smaller as the observation period is extended. Second, we assumed that part-timers due to building up less human capital during their part-time career are more likely to make a transition into non-employment later in the career; this is also confirmed. Third, we contended that this effect becomes smaller over time and indeed the effect tends to diminish as we extend the period of observation. However, whether or not this point to a scarring effect of part-time work on the future employment career depends also on the fact whether part-time is considered an involuntary state for the occupants or not. In the case where it is voluntary, people choose for part-time work because if fulfils someone's preferences better. We examined the reasons why people opt for part-time work. Our analyses show that women who are working part-time because they report 'not wanting to work more hours' or 'because of caring obligations' are less likely to make a transition into full-time employment later in the career. This result appears robust even if we extend the time horizon. This corroborates again one of our expectations with respect to the role assigned to personal preferences for working part-time. Support for this is also found in the observation that when children grow older, the transition into full-time employment seems to become less unlikely. Obviously, people are better able by that stage in the life course to meet their preferences for working more hours although it might take some time to achieve that. However, working part-time is not only a matter of free choice. We also find that a significant proportion of females in Southern Member States, France, Belgium and Finland report to work part-time because of constraints in the labour supply.

Corresponding to our expectation, our analyses also show that childbirth has a sizeable effect on female labour market participation. The common pattern is that females who become mothers are more likely to drop out of the labour market. They are also more likely to reduce working hours and to work part-time before and after childbirth. However, our analysis reveals major country differences. In countries such as Germany and Hungary, but also in Austria, France and the UK, mothers are more likely to withdraw more or less fully from paid employment due to childbirth than in other EU countries. This might point to lack of institutional support to working mothers to allow them to stay in employment. In countries with more support for working mothers such as in Denmark and also the Netherlands we see that full withdrawal is less likely to occur but also that women tend to remain in part-time work and not to move into full-time employment.

The birth of a child is also associated with a reduction in labour market income or earnings. To some extent, this is the consequence of the fact that a portion of women withdraw from the labour market. The more they tend to withdraw and the less income support is available in a country, the higher the income consequences of childbirth are. But we find that even for women who remain in paid employment after childbirth, the yearly labour income is lower after childbirth than before. Public transfers seem to exert a cushion effect on the income reduction due to childbirth because of which the income shortfall due to childbirth is smaller. We estimated that the birth of a child reduces the yearly wage income by about 5 per cent as calculated over the eight year period. We also find that the income penalty differs strongly across countries; it appears lowest in the Netherlands, Luxembourg and the UK but also in the southern countries Italy, Greece and Portugal. The reasons might be very different for the various countries: in the UK it might be the efficiently functioning labour market allowing women to recover quickly from the initial drop in hours; in Sweden it might be the generous parental leave system (Anxo et al., 2005); in the Netherlands and Luxembourg it might be the generosity of the income transfer system and in the Southern countries it might be the family compensating for the initial earnings loss or the informal economy, but all this needs further scrutiny.

The overall conclusion seems to be that the role of institutions and policies in supporting working mothers through employment and income support plays a crucial role in avoiding scarring effects and in allowing women to realise their preferences for working part-time.

NOTES

1. The research was carried out in the framework of a research project sponsored by the European Foundation for Living and Working Conditions in Dublin. We gratefully acknowledge their invaluable support and contribution to the project. Some findings reported here were already published in the final report (Muffels et al., 2007). The data for the project were provided by Eurostat and used with their permission. However, the data provider bears no responsibility for the analyses or interpretations presented in this study. The data included for Sweden are cross-sections and are not used in this chapter.
2. The British Household Panel Study (BHPS) for the UK, the German Socio-Economic Panel (GSOEP) for Germany, and the Panel Socio-économique / Liewen zu Lëtzebuerg (PSELL II) for Luxembourg.
3. Note, however, that only a few respondents report such low number of hours in the case of Hungary.
4. This corresponds to findings based on other sources. See for example Eurostat Press Release of 10 September 2004.

5. Note that the percentages in the figure do not represent the share of part-time employment as such. The figure shows that around 50 per cent of females are employed in part-time jobs in the Netherlands, for example. The share of part-time employment in total employment, is of course much larger, approximately 75 per cent.
6. Note that for females our estimates for part-time employment (share of females in part-time employment) are similar to the Eurostat estimates (Figure 1), but we do overestimate the proportion of females in part-time jobs in Ireland, Greece, and to a lesser extent Hungary. For males, our estimate of the share of females working part-time is on average lower than the Eurostat numbers in Figure 9.1.
7. Obviously, the table does not include the countries for which the information is not available.
8. This dummy variable is coded 0 for the countries lacking this information (the UK, Luxembourg and Hungary). It is also coded 0 for people who work part-time according to our definition but for whom the reason why they work part-time is not known (remember that the question in the ECHP was only asked to people working less than 30 hours per week).
9. The health status and the number of employees in the firm are lacking for Hungary. Past unemployment (having been unemployed in the past 5 years) is missing for Hungary and Luxembourg. These variables are not modelled for those countries.
10. The models include variables that are only defined for people in employment (for example firm size, and the public sector dummy). These variables are only modelled for females in employment.
11. See Fouarge (2006) for similar evidence concerning the re-entry probability of non-working females in the Dutch labour market.
12. In the model, this is measured by a dummy taking the value for females reporting they work less than full-time because of housework or because they look after their children or because they do not want to work more hours (see Figure 9.7). This variable is code 0 for females reporting another reason for working part-time and in countries where the information is not available.
13. Childbirth is defined as a birth occurring between $t-1$ and t. This could be a first child or an additional child being born in a household.
14. In each graph, we depict the average effect of childbirth on hours worked in the EU.
15. All incomes measured in the ECHP and the Hungarian panel refer to last years' income.
16. Again, one should keep in mind that the analyses only apply to females who were and remained in paid employment prior to childbirth, in the year of childbirth and in the year after childbirth. Hence, the analyses does not account for self-selection into employment, neither do they account for the endogeneity of childbirth itself, that is, that the planning of childbirth might be dependent on the labour market position and the wage itself.

REFERENCES

Anxo, D., Boulin, J.-Y., Fagan, C. (2005), *Working time options over the life course: New work patterns and company strategies*, European Foundation, Luxembourg: Office for Official Publications of the European Communities, 145.

Becker, G. (1964), *Human Capital, A Theoretical and Empirical Analysis, with Special Reference to Education*, New York: National Bureau of Economic Research, Chicago, University of Chicago Press.

Becker, G. (1981), *A Treatise on the Family*, MA: Harvard University Press.

Blank, R. (1989), 'The Role of Part-Time Work in Women's Labor Market Choices Over Time', *American Economic Review,* **79** (1), 295–99.

Buddelmeyer, H., Mourre, G. and Ward-Warmedinger, M. (2005), *Part-Time Work in EU Countries: Labour Market Mobility, Entry and Exit,* ECB working paper series.

Dekker, R., Muffels, R.J.A. and Stancanelli, E. (2000), 'A longitudinal analysis of part-time work by women and men in the Netherlands', in Gustafson, S.S. and Meulders, D. (eds), *Gender and the labour market: Econometric evidence of obstacles to achieving gender equality*, New York: MacMillan/St. Martin's Press, 260–87.

Fouarge, D. (2006), 'Helpt kinderopvang de herintreding van moeders stimuleren?', *Tijdschrift voor Arbeidsvraagstukken*, **22** (3), 268–79.

Fouarge, D. and C. Baaijens (2006), *Changes of working hours and job mobility: the effect of Dutch legislation*, Amsterdam: TLM.Net working paper, see <www.siswo.uva.nl/tlm/>, 32.

Gornick, J., Meyers, M. and Ross, K. (1998), 'Public policies and the employment of mothers: a cross-national study', *Social Science Quarterly*, **79** (1), 35–54.

Kenjoh, E. (2003), *Women's employment around the birth of the first child in Britain, Germany, The Netherlands, Sweden and Japan*, ISER working papers, June 2003–16.

Klammer, U. and Keuzenkamp, S. (2005), *Working time options over the life course: Changing Social Security Structures*, European Foundation, Luxembourg: Office for Official Publications of the European Communities.

Muffels, R., Chung, H., Fouarge, D., Klammer, U., Luijkx, R., Manzoni, A., Thiel, A. and Wilthagen, T. (2008), *Flexibility and security over the life course*, Luxembourg: Office for Official Publications of the European Communities, 52.

O'Reilly, J. and Bothfeld, S. (2002), 'What Happens after Working Part Time? Integration, Maintenance or Exclusionary Transitions in Britain and Western Germany', *Cambridge Journal of Economics*, **26** (4), 409–39.

Román, A., Fouarge, D. and Luijkx, R. (2004), *Career consequences of part-time work: results from Dutch panel data 1990–2001*, Tilburg: OSA-rapport A206.

Uunk, W., Kalmijn, M. and Muffels, R. (2005), 'The Impact of Young Children on Women's Labour Supply: A Reassessment of Institutional Effects in Europe', *Acta sociologica*, **48**, 41–62.

Van der Lippe, T. (2001), 'The effect of individual and institutional constraints on hours of paid work of women: an international comparison', in Van der Lippe, T. and Van Dijk, L. (eds), *Women's employment in a comparative perspective*. New York: Aldine de Gruyter, 221–43.

10. Working Time Preferences, Labour Market Transitions and Job Satisfaction

Govert Bijwaard, Bram van Dijk and Jaap de Koning

10.1 INTRODUCTION

Compared to the previous chapter, the aim of this chapter is to acquire a deeper insight into the relationships between working time preferences and working time transitions (job moves) on the one hand and job satisfaction on the other. Due to the unavailability of data in other countries the analyses are limited to the Netherlands. The questions raised are to what extent do Dutch workers adjust the number of hours worked when they experience a discrepancy between the actual and the desired number of hours? and does such a discrepancy or a more general dissatisfaction with the current job leads worker to move to another job? Eventually, we deal with the question to what extent transitions reduce the discrepancy between actual and desired hours and increase job satisfaction.

The analysis is based on data obtained from the Dutch OSA household panel.[1] It is a broad survey covering almost all aspects of work like labour market status, number of hours worked, pay, type of employment, job satisfaction and many other topics. The data used in this chapter covers the period 1986–1998. In the meantime more recent data has become available, but there are good reasons to believe that adding more waves would not change the results significantly and would lead to similar outcomes. Visser and Van der Meer (2007) present OSA-data on transitions covering the period 1988–2002 and they find no sign of any trend break for their data after 1998.

According to the information in the panel approximately 20 to 25 per cent of the workers experience a discrepancy between the number of hours they actual worked and the number of hours that they consider desirable (De Koning et al., 2003). In some cases workers will be able to bargain with their employer about the number of hours worked and reduce the discrepancy between desired and actual numbers accordingly. In other cases, however, a job change might be necessary for a worker to realise their desired working hours. Job mobility then can play an important role in improving the situation for workers with respect to improving the match between desired and actual number of hours, which is likely to contribute to a better allocation of labour. However, it is also possible that job mobility is to a large degree triggered by shortages in labour supply during upswing periods of the business cycle. People's expectations about whether they will be able to realise their working time preference may simply rise by the fact that other people seek and find new employment opportunities. What people in reality achieve in this respect might be different from what they expected beforehand. Hence, we need to test whether job mobility is indeed caused by job dissatisfaction that arises from discrepancies in the number of hours and whether job satisfaction actually increases as a result of moving to another job. This is exactly what we attempt to do in this chapter.

Several policy reports in the past seven years (see for example Weehuizen, (2000), Leijnse (2001), WWR (2007)) suggest that nowadays women, but increasingly also men, are faced with more labour market transitions than before. For this development three societal trends are held responsible. First, the content of jobs changes rapidly and skills become more quickly obsolete due to an increased pace of the technological progress that is believed to be accelerated by ICT developments. The globalisation of the economy, the second factor, implies that economic activities at the country level are more affected nowadays by what happens abroad while they simultaneously are also more quickly transferred to other contexts. Finally, cultural factors such as processes of individualisation in society and women's emancipation are believed to be equally important. Preferences have therefore become more diverse than they used to be. The traditional household work pattern according to which men are mainly involved in paid work and women in non-market activities is (slowly) disappearing. Both men and women tend to participate in the labour process and both may wish to vary the number of hours worked during their career in response to changes in the family situation (see for example OECD, 2001, Chapter 4).

However, the available information does not seem to confirm a structural increase in job-to-job mobility; see Bergemann and Mertens (2002) for Germany, Graversen (2003) for the Nordic countries, Macaulay (2003) for the UK, Steward (2002) for the United States and, recently, Visser and Van der Meer (2007) for the Netherlands. It cannot be ruled out however that changes more frequently occur within the job, in the content of a job or in the number of hours worked, but within the context of a long lasting contract with one employer. In this chapter we test whether transition probabilities have increased structurally over time. By also taking within-job changes in working hours into account, we extend our analysis compared to studies analyzing changes in working hours associated with job-to-job mobility only. However, in this chapter the emphasis is on examining the issue to what extent job dissatisfaction has induced people to change their labour market position and whether the rise in the number of transitions people experience over their career also leads to increases in job satisfaction. Changes in a person's labour market position may involve a job change or a change in working hours or both.

Labour market transitions and changes in working time play a central role in the Transitional Labour Market concept. The original background of this concept is that full employment in its traditional meaning is not feasible anymore (Schmid, 1995). According to Schmid 'work for all' can only be guaranteed by work sharing strategies like an increasing use of part-time work and people altering periods of work with periods of non-participation devoted to education or caring activities. Later on, the Transitional Labour Market concept has been connected with the flexicurity concept (Schmid, 2006). Attention has been shifted to the fact that owing to changes in the economic context long-term relationships between workers and employers tend to become rather rare. However, although many workers will be confronted with temporary employment contracts they may still be permanently employed albeit not with the same employer all the time. Within the TLM framework it is important that workers make transitions at the right time, when such a move is appropriate, in order to prevent or to avoid unemployment. Training is for that reason important for as to make those kinds of transitions. So, when it comes to policy implications, the new TLM concept being more closely linked to the new notion of 'flexicurity', still has many similarities with the old idea of 'work sharing'.

Schmid views work sharing strategies as important solutions for guaranteeing work for all. However, individuals may not perceive for themselves as good what is considered good from a macro perspective. If everybody perceives his current work situation as optimal no change will occur unless a change will be imposed on the individual. Hence, it is important to investigate to what extent individuals experiences discrepancies between their current situation and their aspirations, whether these lead to changes in their work situation and whether these in their turn lead to a perceived improvement in the fulfilment of one's working time preferences. Ultimately, micro and macro perspectives have to be connected. Macro objectives can only realised if individuals behave in accordance with them and individuals can only meet their aspirations if the context allows them to do so. But this is beyond the scope of this chapter.

The chapter is structured as follows. Section 10.2 deals with theory. Then Section 10.3 presents the analyses in which we model labour market transitions and relate them to job satisfaction and other variables. In Section 10.4 we analyse to what extent transitions lead to improved job satisfaction. Finally, Section 10.5 makes some concluding comments.

10.2 THEORY

The issue of the discrepancy between the actual and desired number of hours worked constitute an important subject of this chapter. The discrepancy can be analysed with the help of a simple static utility maximising model. The existence of discrepancies implies that workers are rationed, which may induce them to leave one's job for another employer if adjustment is impossible in their present job. The search for a new job can be analysed within the framework of job search theory and human capital theory. People invest time and money to find a job that suits their preferences better then their present job. In some cases additional training may be needed for the new job. Assuming that they keep the new job for a certain period of time, the higher utility obtained from the new job over this period may outweigh the investment made. It is possible to analyse decisions concerning hours worked and job search with the help of a dynamic multi-period utility maximising framework, but that would require a more advanced mathematical treatment. Therefore, we will treat the different theories separately and explain how they are related in a qualitative way. The models treated are standard models (see for example Ehrenberg and Smith, 2003).

We assume that the individual's preferences can be described by a utility function according to which utility is positively dependent on income Y and leisure time L.

$$U = U(Y,L) \qquad \frac{\partial U}{\partial Y} > 0; \frac{\partial U}{\partial L} > 0 \qquad (10.1)$$

The individual is supposed to spend his income completely on consumption. Income consists of wage income and non-wage income

$$Y = wH + O \qquad (10.2)$$

where w denotes the hourly wage, H the number of hours worked and O non-wage income (HK). Total time is equal to the sum total of leisure time, hours worked and time spent on housekeeping (HK).

$$T = L + H + HK \qquad (10.3)$$

If (3) is substituted in (2) utility maximisation can be graphically depicted as in Figure 10.1. In the optimum the utility curve is adjacent to the budget curve. In the optimum Lopt hours are spent on leisure. An obvious case in which the worker experiences a discrepancy is when the number of hours worked is fixed by the employer at a level differing from T-HK-Lopt.

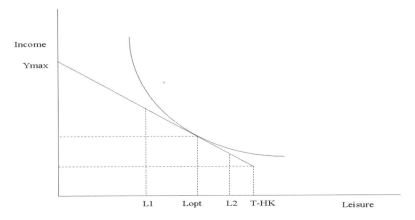

Figure 10.1 Working time discrepancies: a simple static utility maximising labour supply model

One might argue that such a model is unrealistic as it assumes that the number of hours worked can take any value and that people can freely choose the number of hours worked. Traditionally, hours are fixed to a certain number, the standard working time. However, during the last decades we have seen an erosion of the standard workweek. The emergence of part-time work has led to a considerable variation in working time. Workers will often not be completely free to choose the number of hours worked, though many will be able to change this number if they experience a discrepancy between the actual and desired number of hours. As we will show in the next section workers move from one class of working hours to the other, partly as a result of such a discrepancy.

Workers may accept a job in which the hours worked differ from the optimal number. Accepting such a sub-optimal job and continuing job search may yield a higher utility than prolonging the job search while staying unemployed. A job may not only be sub-optimal regarding the number of hours. Also the wage, type of contract (flexible and/or temporary) and the content of the job in relation to the person's skills may give rise to discrepancies. Job mobility may lead to the improvement on several of these dimensions, which will be evaluated jointly by the worker. In the next section dealing with the empirical analysis of transitions, discrepancies on several job aspects are taken into consideration as explanatory factors for mobility.

It is also possible that initially the number of hours was optimal, but that this is no longer the case owing to changing circumstances. There are two possible reasons why the optimum does no longer apply.

- Changes in the family household. If a child is born, the time spent on caring/house-keeping will increase. As a result workers will look for jobs with fewer hours. Its effect on the number of hours in the end will also depend on the partner's behaviour on the labour market.
- Changes in the labour market situation. When the labour market is tight it will be easier to find a job that yields a higher utility. Better payment, more or less working hours and a better job content may all contribute to such a utility improvement.

What matters is a higher utility attained with the new job. At least in theory the new job may still entail a discrepancy between the actual and desired number of hours, but at the same time it may yield a higher utility. It is even possible that a worker moves from a job that yielded an optimal combination of income and leisure to a job with higher utility but without the utility curve being adjacent to the budget curve. The reason could be that the new job is better paid, but does not allow the worker to work the number of hours he would prefer given the new hourly wage. The increased wage income could compensate for the fact that the number of hours worked differs from the preferred number. However, in all cases we would expect the change to lead to a higher utility assigned to the job. When deciding on taking a new job with a different employer the worker will also consider the search and transaction costs involved.

Changes in the family situation may be analysed through its consequences for the number of hours spent on caring/house-keeping. When a family has a child, the model predicts that both the hours worked and leisure time will decrease. When a person finds a partner, each one can spend less time on caring/house-keeping, implying that (s)he will increase both the hours worked and leisure time. However, decision-making in a family context may imply that the partners also weigh off the opportunity costs of non-working for each partner.[2] The results will also depend on the bargaining power each partner has in the decision-making, which will partly depend on existing norms and values.

The model is too simple when we want to analyse the role of the quality of the job or job content. In the model as presented so far, job content does not influence utility. Obviously, this is a not a realistic assumption. Dissatisfaction with the content of a job may well be a reason for workers to move to a different job. A possibility would be to include other job-related aspects in the utility function in addition to pay and leisure.

The model does not describe job mobility resulting from career shifts. Over time a worker's productivity will increase as a result of accumulated work experience during the execution of the various jobs he has held during his career. Furthermore, the person can increase his productivity by investing in training. Therefore, at different stages in his career the person may be able to switch to a higher paid job. A multi-period utility-maximising model including human capital investment could be used to describe such career steps. In such a model one could also take into account that preferences and household situation change with age.

So far, transitions are seen as the results of the decision-making of individuals. However, also the demand side of the labour market should be taken into account. The availability of jobs of different hours simply limits the opportunities for workers to realise their working time aspirations. Furthermore, particular types of transitions such as from employment to unemployment are not the result of free choice but are forced by the employer. Therefore, in explaining transitions we must also take into account of the general labour market context and firm's behaviour. However, the period to which our empirical analyses in the next sections applies (the mid 1980s until the end of the 1990s), is characterised by a considerable improvement in the labour market situation. At the end of this period, the unemployment rate had diminished to a very low level. We would expect, then, that during this period transitions are particularly supply-side induced.

Although we did not attempt to present one model covering all aspects relevant to explaining mobility in relation to working time discrepancies in the job, we think that the previous discussion gives some guidance as to the specification of the models we use in the next sections. It gives suggestions as to the types of explanatory variables to be included in the models. Furthermore, it helps us to interpret the results.

10.3 TO WHAT EXTENT DOES JOB SATISFACTION EXPLAIN LABOUR MARKET TRANSITIONS?

In this section we give a systematic and comprehensive analysis of labour market transitions in the Netherlands based on data from several waves of the OSA Labour Supply Survey (every two year between 1986 and 1998). Since 1986, the OSA has surveyed a sample of Dutch households every two years. A considerable percentage of households (and their partners) is surveyed in at least two consecutive waves of the survey. Therefore, it is possible to identify transitions on an individual level. The survey includes a large variety of personal and job characteristics, including: (changes in) discrepancies within the context of the job, changes in household composition, transitions and participation in training courses.

Against the background of the theoretical model shown in the previous sections an empirical model is developed that aims to explain the transitions on the labour market. However, not all mentioned determining factors are available in the data set. The data contain no information on labour demand. The search and transaction costs associated with transitions are also difficult to measure with the data available. The data however, contain ample information on characteristics of the individuals, the households they are part of and the job they hold. The data used for the analyses consist of those individuals in the OSA survey data who are employed at one of the seven interview moments[3] and for whom we have information on their labour market situation two years later. Thus, for each couple of consecutive interview moments we subtract the data for everybody who has been interviewed in both waves and who is employed at the first interview moment.

All these data are pooled and then analysed separately according to the number of working hours of each consecutive starting interview moment. This implies that some individuals have multiple entries in the data.[4] The range of working hours is grouped into three labour market situations: (i) small part-time job (0–24 working hours a week); (ii) big part-time job (24–34 working hours) and (iii) fulltime job (more than 34 working hours). From Table 10.1 we notice that the individuals with a big part-time job are the most mobile on the labour market; two years later only half of them are still in the same job with the same number of working hours.

Table 10.1 Transition rates by number of working hours in the starting year and two years later (in %)

At start	Two years later			UNE	NP	Other job			Total
	Same job								
	Small PT	Big PT	Full-time			Small PT	Big PT	Full-time	
Small part-time (0–24 hours)	63%	4%	3%	3%	10%	12%	3%	2%	2,537
Big part-time (24–34 hours)	10%	50%	13%	3%	7%	5%	6%	7%	1,159
Full-time job	1%	3%	75%	2%	4%	1%	1%	13%	8,615

Note: UNE = Unemployment; NP = Non-participation.

Source: OSA Labour Supply Survey, 1986–1998.

10.3.1 An Empirical Model of the Transition Probabilities

A structural model in which all the different types of transitions are the result of perceived utility differences between the various options is yet too cumbersome to estimate. Instead, we postulate a reduced form multinomial logit model[5] in which we examine the transition probability from being employed in a job with a certain number of hours at the date of interview to another position or job with the same or another employer two years later. The empirical model and the variables to be implemented depend on the available information in the OSA Labour Supply Survey on the employed people.

The models are aimed at identifying the factors that might induce an employed individual to change working time and/or a job. Undoubtedly, gender appears an important factor; women constitute the major group of small part-timers, while men mostly work full-time. Other factors are education level, age and the existence of children in the household. A change in the household situation (for example, childbirth) might be more important than having children per se. We also include job related factors in the models, such as contract type and business sector. Very crucial for the explanation of the transitions seem those factors that characterise, directly or indirectly, the labour market discrepancies. Possible indicators in the data set are job satisfaction, earnings satisfaction, whether somebody is looking for another job and the discrepancy between the preferred and actual number of working hours.

Over the years the OSA Labour Supply Survey questionnaire has been adjusted. Therefore, some interesting information is only available for a limited number of waves. For example, we only know how much time an individual spends per week on childcare and care for other household members from 1994 onwards. For the years that the question[6] was not asked we needed to impute the missing data. For continuous variables, such as time spent on childcare, a linear regression model was estimated using the available data (separate models were estimated for men and women). Based on these regression models we imputed the variable for the other years. For binary variables, such as whether the partner has a job or not, a logit model was estimated for the probability that the situation occurs (again different modls were estimated for men and women). Based on these logit models we put the variable for the missing years to one if the estimated probability exceeds a half.

10.3.2 Estimation Results

For each of the three different groups distinguished by number of working hours; a multinomial logit model was estimated with the starting position on the labour market in the base year acting as the reference category. Thus, for example, an individual currently in a small part-time job can be in eight different labour market states two years later (the next interview moment). If the individual remains in the same job (s)he may either work more hours, and move to a big part-time job or move to a full-time job, or work the same number of hours and thus remain in a small part-time job. If the individual moves to another job (s)he has, again, three possibilities: move to (another) small part-time job, move to a big part-time job or move to a full-time job. It is also possible that the individual becomes unemployed or leaves the labour market. The reference category for this individual is the same small part-time job.

Most of the included factors in the model are individual specific, X_i, but we also included time-varying variables that are the same for all individuals, Z_t, like a linear trend indicator and the national unemployment rate. The probability for individual i in period t to make a transition from the reference category, either a small part-time job, a big part-time job, or a full-time job, into one of the seven other labour market states is in a multinomial logit model equal to:

$$P_{ijt}(X_i, Z_t) = \frac{\exp(\beta_{0j} + \beta_j X_i + \gamma_j Z_t)}{1 + \sum_k \exp(\beta_{0k} + \beta_k X_i + \gamma_k Z_t)}, \tag{10.3}$$

The probability that this individual makes no transition is one minus the sum of the probabilities of the other seven transitions. We assume that each factor, X_i, has a different impact on each specific transition. Because we included around 30 different individual specific factors (differs among the three models), this implies that for each model we estimated a large number of parameters (up to 210).

In a standard linear model the parameters can be interpreted as the marginal effect of each covariate on the outcome. In a multivariate logit model even the sign of a parameter does not necessarily correspond to the sign of the marginal effect. In a multinomial logit model the marginal effects of the covariates are:

$$\frac{\partial P_{ijt}(X_i, Z_t)}{\partial X_i} = P_{ijt}(X_i, Z_t) \left[\beta_j - \sum_k P_{ikt}(X_i, Z_t)\beta_k \right], \tag{10.4}$$

Note that these marginal effects depend on (*i*) the value of all included factors, not just the value of the specific factor (*ij*) and on the parameters of the alternative transitions. The former implies that we could define many different marginal effects. The most common solution to this problem is to define the marginal effects at the average value of the factors. For binary factors, like the one 'prefers to work less', we follow an alternative, but also a rather common, approach and define the marginal effect as the difference between the value of the transition probability when the binary factor is one and the value of the transition probability when the binary factor is zero. Thus a marginal effect of 0.082 for the factor 'prefers to work 24–34 hours' for an individual in a small part-time job moving to a big part-time job (same job) implies that the probability to increase the number of working hours for this individual is 8.2 percentage-points higher than for an individual who stays there because it meets his preferences (see Table 10.3). The dependency of the marginal effect on the parameters of the other transitions may induce a positive marginal effect while the corresponding parameter is negative, and the other way round. This causes the parameters to be difficult to interpret, whereas the marginal effects are relatively easy to interpret. However, reporting all the marginal effects would result in an extremely large table containing possibly only a few interesting results. Therefore we have decided to present these marginal effects into six different blocks, separated according to the type of variables; (1) general characteristics (for example, the economic situation at the time of interview); (2) personal characteristics (age, gender and so on); (3) household characteristics (marital state, children and so on); (4) job characteristics; (5) job satisfaction and (6) working time preferences.

In Table 10.2 the marginal effects for the general background characteristics (economic situation) are given.

Table 10.2 Marginal effects of the general background variables based on the estimation of a multinomial logit model explaining yearly transitions in working hours

| | Two years later | | | | | | | |
| | Same job | | | UNE | NP | Other job | | |
At start	Small PT	Big PT	Full-time			Small PT	Big PT	Full-Time
Small part-time job								
Linear trend	0.025*	–0.001	0.000	–0.001	–0.009**	–0.012	–0.001	–0.001
Unemployment rate	0.049**	–0.001	0.000	0.002	–0.002	–0.037**	–0.009	–0.003*
Big part-time job								
Linear trend	0.003	0.037	–0.015	0.000	–0.011	–0.006	–0.006	–0.001
Unemployment rate	0.004	0.058	–0.018	0.001	–0.007	–0.008	–0.022	–0.008
Full-time								
Linear trend	0.001	0.002	0.004	0.000	–0.001	0.000	0.000	–0.006**
Unemployment rate	0.001	0.003	0.026**	0.003	0.000	–0.001	–0.001*	–0.030**

Notes: UNE = Unemployment; NP = Non-participation. ** is significant at 95%; * is significant at 90%.

Source: OSA Labour Supply Survey, 1986–1998.

Flexibility and Employment Security in Europe

The general unemployment rate seems to have a significant effect on a number of transition probabilities. A 1 percentage-point higher unemployment rate increases the probability to remain in the same small part-time job with almost 5 percentage-points. Furthermore, a positive trend can be observed in the probability to remain in small part-time jobs, while full-timers tend to move less to other full-time jobs. These results reflect the general tendency in the Netherlands to remain in a part-time job and not to shift to a full-time job.

Table 10.3 depicts the marginal effects of working time preferences on the transitions. As could be expected, the transitions into a different number of hours worked are usually in line with the preferences as expressed at the start of the two-year period. An individual in a small part-time job who prefers to have a big part-time job has a 7.2 percentage-point lower probability to remain in the same job with less than 24 hours of work a week.

Table 10.3 Marginal effects of working hours preferences on working time transitions as derived from the estimated multinomial logit model

	Two years later							
	Same job			UNE	NP	Other job		
At start	Small PT	Big PT	Full-time			Small PT	Big PT	Full-time
Small part-time								
Prefers to work 24–34 hours	-0.072^{**}	0.082^{**}	-0.002	-0.002	-0.008	-0.011^{*}	0.015^{*}	-0.001^{**}
Prefers to work full-time	-0.078^{**}	-0.007^{**}	0.097^{**}	-0.002	-0.009	-0.012^{**}	-0.003^{**}	0.014^{**}
Big part-time								
Prefers to work 0–24 hours	0.077	-0.052^{*}	-0.028^{**}	-0.002	-0.005	0.019	-0.005^{*}	-0.007^{**}
Prefers to work full-time	-0.028	-0.173^{**}	0.215^{**}	-0.004	-0.014	-0.012	-0.015^{**}	0.029
Full-time								
Prefers to work 0–24 hours	0.014^{**}	-0.003^{**}	-0.020	0.000	0.000	0.012^{**}	-0.001^{**}	-0.003
Prefers to work 24–34 hours	-0.001	0.021^{**}	-0.023	0.000	0.000	-0.000	0.007^{**}	-0.003

Notes and Source: See Table 10.2.

As mentioned before, such a preference increases the probability to increase the number of hours to big part-time in the same job with 8.2 percentage-points. The preference for a full-time job has a similar effect. The effect of these preferences on the probability to move to another job is lower, though significant. The preference for a working time change for part-timers working long hours is even larger. An individual with a large part-time job preferring a full-time job has a 22 percentage-point higher probability to increase his working hours within the same job, and a 17 percentage-point lower probability to remain in the same job with the same working time. The effect of a change in working time preference in the case of a full-time worker is lower but still significant.

In Table 10.4 the marginal effects of job satisfaction on working time transitions are given. General dissatisfaction with the job plays a significant role in explaining the transitions of small part-timers and full-timers.

Table 10.4 Marginal effects of job satisfaction on working time transitions as derived from the estimated multinomial logit model

At start	Two years later							
	Same job			UNE	NP	Other job		
	Small PT	Big PT	Full-time			Small PT	Big PT	Full-time
Small part-time								
Satisfied with job	0.178**	–0.008	–0.010	–0.030**	–0.060**	–0.050*	–0.010	–0.009**
Unsatisfied with wage level	–0.025	–0.012	0.004	0.009	–0.002	0.017	0.007	0.003
Looking for another job	–0.120**	–0.003	0.014	0.009	0.033	0.043	0.008	0.015**
Big part-time								
Satisfied with job	–0.012	0.070	0.073	–0.034	–0.019	–0.032	–0.021	–0.025
Unsatisfied with wage level	0.010	–0.111	–0.007	0.030	0.000	–0.020	0.033	0.065**
Looking for another job	–0.010	–0.143	0.005	–0.002	–0.001	0.034	0.075**	0.042**
Full-time								
Satisfied with job	0.000	–0.005	0.101**	–0.011**	–0.010	0.001	–0.007**	–0.070**
Unsatisfied with wage level	0.003	–0.002	–0.010	0.001	–0.002	0.001	0.001	0.009
Looking for another job	0.002	–0.007	–0.103**	0.007**	0.002	0.004*	0.001	0.093**

Notes and Source: See Table 10.2.

A satisfied small part-timer has an 18 percentage-point higher probability and a full-timer a 10 percentage-points higher probability to remain in the same job with the same working time. Only in the case of a large part-time job the dissatisfaction with the wage level seem to exert a significant effect on the transition rates. 'Looking for another job' is often significant, although one could argue that job search merely reflects the dissatisfaction with a job rather than exerting a separate substantive effect on the transitions probabilities.

In the next three tables a variable is only discussed when it has a significant marginal effect on, at least, one of the transition probabilities.

Table 10.5 Marginal effects of personal characteristics on working time transitions as derived from the estimated multinomial logit model

| | Two years later | | | | | | | |
| | Same job | | | UNE | NP | Other job | | |
At start	Small PT	Big PT	Full-time			Small PT	Big PT	Full-time
Small part-time job								
High educated	−0.008	0.027**	0.001	−0.001	−0.027	0.002	0.007	−0.001
Age (/10)	0.042	−0.015	−0.001	−0.006	0.01	−0.021	−0.006	−0.004*
Age (/10) squared	−0.034	−0.005	0	−0.003	0.044**	−0.003	0.001	0
Living in the North	0.032	−0.013	0	0.024**	−0.009	−0.025	−0.013	0.005
Course Taken	0.012	0	0.016	−0.006	−0.071**	0.041**	0.004	0.005
Big part-time job								
Age (/10)	0.006	0.035	−0.017	0.006	0.004	0.001	−0.014	−0.022*
Age (/10) squared	−0.003	−0.026	0.011	−0.003	0.022*	0.004	0.004	−0.009
Full-time job								
Female	−0.002	0.027**	−0.053**	0.007	−0.003	0.004	0.012**	0.008
Low educated	−0.003	0.003	0.017	0	0.002	0.001	−0.002	−0.017*
High educated	−0.002	0.009*	0.007	−0.004	−0.007	0.001	−0.001	−0.004
Age (/10)	−0.003*	0.001	0.039*	0.001	0.005**	0.001	−0.002*	−0.047**
Age (/10) squared	0.004**	0.005**	−0.019	−0.001	0.009**	0.002	0.002**	−0.002
Living in the North	0	0.007	0.013	0.006	0.001	0.002	−0.003	−0.025*
Course Taken	0.003	0.002	0.004	−0.005	−0.013**	−0.002	−0.001	0.021**
Ethnic minority	0	0	0.013	0.016**	0	0	0	−0.002

Notes and Source: See Table 10.2.

The insignificant results are not given here but were available upon request to the authors. Table 10.5 reports on the effect of important personal characteristics on working time transitions. Not surprisingly have full-time working females had a higher probability to move into a part-time job either by reducing their working hours in their current job or by the mobility into another job. Taking an education course reduces the probability to leave the labour market and, for full-time workers, increases the probability to move to another full-time job.

Table 10.6 presents the effects of household characteristics seemingly exerting a substantial effect on the transition probabilities.

Table 10.6 Marginal effects of household characteristics on working time transitions as derived from the estimated multinomial logit model

	Two years later							
	Same job			UNE	NP	Other job		
At start	Small PT	Big PT	Full-time			Small PT	Big PT	Full-time
Small part-time								
Child under 5 yrs	0.093	-0.047^{**}	0.001	-0.015	-0.002	-0.038	0.002	0.006
Childbirth	-0.053	-0.005	-0.005	0.004	0.036^{*}	0.025	-0.004	0.002
Big part-time								
Child under 5 yrs	0.022	-0.059	-0.042	0.003	-0.026	0.046	0.074^{*}	-0.018
Child birth	0.137^{**}	-0.189	-0.038	0.001	0.098^{*}	0.023	-0.013	-0.018
Full-time								
Hours care to household	0	0	0	0	0.001	0	0	-0.002^{*}
Hours childcare	0	0	-0.001	0	0	0	0	0.001^{*}
Not single	-0.001	0.005	-0.005	0.002	0.003	-0.007^{**}	0.002	0
Partner has a job	0.005	0.001	-0.02	-0.004	0	0.007^{**}	0.003	0.008
Female, not single	0.029^{**}	0.004	-0.024	-0.001	0.012^{**}	0.002	-0.001	-0.02
Female, child under 5 yrs	0.007	0.024^{**}	-0.132^{**}	0.072^{**}	0.004	0.004	-0.001	0.022
Female, child birth	0.064^{**}	0.014	-0.236^{**}	0.050^{**}	0.079^{**}	0.021	-0.003	0.01

Notes and Source: See Table 10.2.

Gender plays an important role in the transitions out of full-time employment. Females have a much lower probability to remain in their full-time job, especially when they have a child or when they have a child less than 5 years of age. A full-time working woman that recently gave birth has a 6 percentage-point higher probability to reduce her working time and to move into a small part-time job. She also has a 5 percentage-point higher probability to become unemployed and an 8 percentage-point higher probability to withdraw from the labour market. Not surprisingly, the probability to remain in her full-time job is likewise reduced by 24 percentage-points.

In Table 10.7 we present the findings on the effect of job characteristics that are considered important on working time transitions.

Table 10.7 Marginal effects of job characteristics on working time transitions as derived from the estimated multinomial logit model

| | Two years later | | | | | | | |
| | Same job | | | UNE | NP | Other job | | |
At start	Small PT	Big PT	Full-time			Small PT	Big PT	Full-time
Small part-time								
No tenure	-0.128^{**}	0.007	0.002	0.021	0.039^{*}	0.054^{**}	-0.003	0.007^{**}
Industry Sector	-0.089	0.003	0.01	-0.009	0.068^{**}		0.011	0.004
Public Sector	-0.023	0.035^{**}	0.015	-0.005	-0.008	-0.008	-0.006	-0.001
Long Tenure	-0.017	0.021^{*}	-0.004	-0.011	0.033	-0.018	-0.001	-0.003
Big part-time: None of the job characteristics have a significant marginal effect								
Full-time								
Log net income	0	0	-0.007	0.001	0.001	0	0.001	0.004^{*}
Long Tenure	0.001	0.007	-0.078^{**}	0.019^{**}	-0.001	0.002	0.004^{*}	0.045^{**}
Big company	0.001	0.005	0.018	-0.006	0.003^{*}	-0.001	0.001	-0.022^{**}
Industrial Sector	-0.003	-0.003	0.019	0.003	0.001	-0.002	-0.003	-0.013^{*}
Public Sector	0.002	0.015^{**}	0.032^{*}	-0.005	0.002	0.001	0	-0.047
Two jobs	0.009	0.018^{*}	-0.121^{**}	0.013	-0.007	0.009^{**}	0.012^{**}	0.067^{**}
Working overtime	0	-0.001	-0.044^{**}	-0.001	0	0	0	0.047^{**}
Commute > 30 min	0	0	-0.019	0	0	0	0	0.020^{*}

Notes and Source: See Table 10.2.

Tenure tends to keep workers in small part-time and full-time jobs but only when they move to another job. In the public sector there seem to be more opportunities to work in a part-time job as is reflected in a higher probability for people staying in the same job to remain either in a big part-time or a full-time job. Overtime work induces full-time workers to move to another job.

10.4 DO TRANSITIONS INCREASE JOB SATISFACTION?

In the previous section we concluded that dissatisfaction with the job and discrepancies between the actual and desired number of hours induce people to move from their job. But do these transitions also lead to an increase in job satisfaction? That is the question we want to address in this section.

Using the data from the same panel as we used for the analyses in the previous section, we can examine whether respondents experienced an increase or decrease in job satisfaction, or whether their job satisfaction remained the same. We use an ordered probit model to explain job satisfaction changes from a number of explanatory variables. One of these explanatory variables is the type of transitions. So we try to explain the change in job satisfaction between year t and year $t–1$ from, for example, a variable indicating whether the individual changed jobs between $t–1$ and t.

A complication is that by definition we do not measure the change in job satisfaction for those who leave employment. It may well be that dissatisfied workers have a higher chance of becoming unemployed than workers who are satisfied with their job. We model the change in job satisfaction under the condition that a person stays in employment. However, that could imply that we estimate the model on the basis of a selective group of workers, namely those who remain in employment. It is possible that unobserved factors are at play that both affect the degree to which workers improve their job satisfaction and the probability that they stay in employment. The motivation for work might be one example of such an unobserved factor. This implies that our model estimations of the change in job satisfaction (based on a single equation model) may yield biased estimates. Because the problem is caused by the fact that an econometric equation is estimated on the basis of a selective sample, it is often referred to as the sample selection bias problem.

This problem can be solved by jointly estimating the change-in-job-satisfaction equation and a discrete variable equation for staying in employment or not. If we measure job satisfaction as a continuous variable, Heckman's two-step estimation procedure could be used (see Greene, 2000 for an outline of this method). However, in our case we only observe whether job satisfaction has increased, whether it decreased or whether it remained the same. So, the dependent variable is measured as a discrete scale variable.

In Annex 10.1, the likelihood function of our simultaneous model is derived, which consists of an equation for the change in job satisfaction and the equation for remaining in employment or not. The parameters have been estimated by maximising this likelihood function. The source of bias is the correlation between the error terms of the two equations. Only if this correlation is zero, the bias is also zero. And only in that case we would be allowed to estimate the change-in-job-satisfaction equation individually.

For each working hours category (less than 24 hours, between 24 and 34 hours and more than 34 hours (or 'full-time') a model was estimated. The data used are from the 1992 to 1998 waves of the OSA Household panel. Owing to changes in the questionnaire, data from earlier waves could not be used for this analysis. Table 10.8 presents the outcomes for the two equations.

From the results obtained for the equation explaining the change in job satisfaction it appears that working time transitions (a labour contract becoming permanent or a change in job and/or employer) have a significant positive effect on the change in job satisfaction. Other explanatory variables that turn out to be significant or weakly significant in this equation are: the degree of job dissatisfaction in the base year and whether or not they are still searching for a new job two years later. Having followed a training course between two consecutive waves has a significant effect on job satisfaction for 'big' part-timers and full-timers, but not for 'small' part-timers. The same is true for age. The sector of employment in the base year is only significant for one of the three workers' categories. One obvious variable is not included, namely the change in the hourly wage rate since no reliable data for this variable were available. We expect that it is at least partly covered through the inclusion of age and education level. It should be noted that the constant term in the equation cannot be identified and is included in the threshold coefficients.

The results of the model estimation for staying in employment or not, can easily be interpreted. We concentrate on the equation for 'big' part-timers. Female workers have a higher chance of leaving employment, particularly when they have given birth to a child. Higher educated workers have a relatively low chance of leaving employment.

Workers with a temporary contract more easily leave employment. Both young and older workers have a relatively high chance of leaving employment; workers at the age of 28 years have the lowest chance.

Table 10.8 Estimation results of an ordered probit model on the change in job satisfaction, conditional on staying in employment between two consecutive waves from 1992 to 1998 (standard errors between brackets)

	Working hours at start		
Explanatory variables	<24	24–34	>34
Equation for change in job satisfaction (ordered probit model: 1 = increase; 0 = no change; –1 = decrease)			
Threshold 1	1.20 (0.116)	1.44 (0.269)	1.16 (0.067)
Threshold 2	3.35 (0.144)	3.55 (0.326)	3.36 (0.085)
Degree of dissatisfaction	1.20 (0.068)	1.29 (0.108)	1.23 (0.038)
Labour contract has become permanent	0.16 (0.094)	0.34 (0.151)	0.11 (0.062)
Change to other function and/or other employer	0.21 (0.089)	0.12 (0.121)	0.24 (0.048)
Found partner	1.32 (0.692)	–	–
In search of other job	–0.50 (0.117)	–0.79 (0.147)	–0.60 (0.059)
Training course followed		0.21 (0.121)	0.11 (0.046)
Age		0.004 (0.005)	
Aged between 31 and 50			0.13 (0.040)
Employed in the government sector	0.30 (0.098)		
Employed in health care	0.17 (0.008)		
Equation for staying in (0) or leaving employment (1): probit model			
Constant	2.12 (0.41)	–1.01 (1.174)	1.84 (0.331)
Age	–0.19 (0.019)	–0.074 (0.059)	–0.24 (0.016)
Age squared	0.0024 (0.002)	0.0013 (0.0007)	0.0034 (0.000)
Female		0.38 (0.185)	0.32 (0.096)
Secondary education, first stage, or lower	0.31 (0,097)		0.17 (0.080)
Higher education		–0.37 (0.213)	
Female, gave birth to child		0.64 (0.246)	1.09 (0.200)
Tenure >10 years	–0.46 (0.128)		–0.68 (0.096)
Temporary contract	0.20 (0.117)		
Employed in manufacturing industry	0.40 (0.159)	0.48 (0.195)	
Correlation between the error terms of the two equations	–0.23 (0.196)	–0.48 (0.29)	–0.01 (0.017)
Mean log likelihood	–0.999	–0.951	–0.873
Number of observations	1,356	647	4,289

Note: UNE = Unemployment; NP = Non-participation.

Source: OSA Labour Supply Survey, 1986–1998.

The correlation between the change in job satisfaction and the process determining whether a person stays in employment (0) or not (1), is only significant (at the 10 per cent level) for the 'big' part-timers. The correlation is indeed negative, indicating that those who leave employment would have had a relatively low change in job satisfaction if they had stayed employed. For full-timers the correlation is very low, indicating that the sample selection bias problem does not occur for this group. The 'small' part-timers hold an intermediary position. For this group the correlation is also relatively high (−0.23) but not significant. But we should also take into account that the number of observations is the smallest for this group. So, we can conclude that for part-timers (particularly for 'big' part-timers) the sample selection problem seems to be relevant, but not for full-timers.

10.5 CONCLUSIONS

A lot of attention is spent on the concept of transitional labour markets since its introduction by Schmid in the mid-1990s (1995). In particular Schmid's conjecture that transitions tend to increase over time has attracted much attention and debate. However, the analyses presented here render no supporting evidence for this proposition at least for the Netherlands; we observe no structural increase in the transition probabilities since the mid-1980s. Though an increase in job mobility has occurred, this can entirely be attributed to the improved labour market conditions.

It is important for the labour market to be sufficiently flexible to allow individuals to adapt their jobs to their preferences as much as possible. People may accept suboptimal working times in their jobs when they enter the labour market or when they are unemployed. Once, having obtained such a job, they might try to find a new one yielding a higher utility and a better match. A suboptimal situation in the job may also arise when the household situation changes. Furthermore, people may be able to improve their job match when they have acquired sufficient work experience, which allows them to take a new career step. A favourable labour market situation will, of course, make it easier to find a better job that meets one's working time preferences better. One could argue that a number of the workers who are rationed in their working hours and who are unable to change their situation accordingly, might withdraw entirely from the labour market. In that sense increases in working time flexibility may improve and even raise employment and hence, employment security.

From our longitudinal analyses it appears that the extent by which working time preferences are realised as indicated by the discrepancy between the actual and desired number of working hours significantly affects the probability of a working time transition. It is also more likely for a worker to make a transition when he is not fully satisfied with his job.

Changing jobs and working times tend on the other hand to lead to a significant reduction in that discrepancy and to a significant increase in job satisfaction.

A considerable part of the working population still cannot fulfil their working time preferences because they experience a discrepancy between the actual and desired number of hours worked. Some 15 to 20 per cent of the working population indicates that the number of hours worked differs from the desired number. This figure did not change much during the significant improvement of the labour market situation during the 1990s. Therefore, we conclude that the labour market in that period was not flexible enough to allow people to meet their working time preferences. People need to have more opportunities to adjust their situation to their preferences and aspirations. Since 2001, a Dutch law applies that gives workers the right to adapt the number of hours worked if they wish so. It is still too early to say what the impact of this law in practice is. The Dutch government has also introduced a so-called life course arrangement as of the beginning of 2007 that will make it possible for workers to save working time during the career, which they can then take up in the form of leisure time at some later point in the career for some specific purposes (education, caring, early retirement and so on). When a worker takes up the time (s)he saved to use it for education or other purposes, the government gives a premium to partially compensate for the loss of income. This may support workers to adjust the number of hours worked during the life course according to their preferences and constraints.

NOTES

1. The Dutch OSA Household Panel is a labour supply panel held by the Institute for Labour Studies at Tilburg University (OSA) every two years from 1984 up to 2007. The random sample is drawn from the Dutch population of 16 years and older containing on average 4000 persons each year.
2. For a review of the literature and a more general discussion of the basic model, see Ehrenberg and Smith (1997).
3. The information on the transitions between 1985 and 1986, the first and second interview moments, are removed from the analyses because this concerns a one-year period while all the other interviews are conducted every two years.
4. We realise that the transitions of one individual over time is highly correlated, but we do not, however, develop a dynamic model to account for this. Neither do we model the possible selective attrition of the individuals from the panel. A Huber-White sandwich estimate (Huber (1967) and White (1980)) is used to get more robust estimation of the variance-covariance matrix.
5. The multinomial logit model puts a heavy restriction on the interdependence of the probabilities. We also tried more general models like the nested multinomial logit (see Greene (1997) and the heteroscedastic 'Extreme Value' Model (see Bhat (1995). However, neither of these models did converge.
6. Other (partially) missing data were on the labour market situation of the partner (from 1992 onwards) and on tenure with the current employer (from 1994 onwards).

REFERENCES

Bhat, C.R. (1995), 'A heteroskedastic extreme value model of intercity travel mode choice', *Transportation Research B*, **29**, 471–83.

Bergemann, A. and Mertens, A. (2002), *Job Stability Trends, Layoffs and Quits – An Empirical Analysis for West Germany*, Paper for the 10th International Conference on Panel Data in Berlin.

De Koning, J., Bijwaard, G., Gelderblom, A. en Kroes, H. (2003), *Arbeidsmarkt-transities en aanboddiscrepanties* (Labour market transitions and supply side discrepancies),Tilburg: OSA publication A191, OSA.

Ehrenberg, G. and Smith, R. (2003), *Modern Labor Economics: Theory and Public Policy*, Boston, MA: Addison-Wesley.

Graversen, E.B. (2003), *Knowledge Circulation Imbedded in Job Mobility Indicators – Nordic Experience Based on Register Data*, Working Paper 2003/2, Analyse-institut for Forskning, Aarhus.

Greene, W.H. (2000), *Econometric analysis*, New Jersey: Prentice Hall.

Huber, P.J. (1967), 'The behavior of maximum likelihood estimates under nonstandard conditions', in Neyman, J. (ed.), *Proceedings of the fifth Berkeley symposium*, Berkeley: University of California Press, 221–33.

Leijnse, F. (2001), *Het nieuwe werken* (New work arrangements), Den Haag: Ministerie van Economische Zaken.

Macaulay, C. (2003), 'Job Mobility and Job Tenure in the UK', *Labour Market Trends*, 541–50.

OECD (2001), *Employment Outlook 2001*, Paris: OECD.

Schmid, G. (1995), 'Is full employment still possible? Transitional labour markets as a new strategy of labour market policy', *Economic and Industrial Policy*, **16**, 429–56.

Schmid, G. (2006), 'Social Risk Management Through Transitional Labour Markets', *Social-Economic Review*, **4**, 1–33.

Steward, J. (2002), 'Recent Trends in Job Stability and Job Security: Evidence from the March CPS', *BLS Working Papers No. 356*, US Department of Labor.

Visser, J. and Meer, M. van der (2007), 'Mobiliteit, interne arbeidsmarkten en arbeidsverhoudingen – naar een nieuwe dynamiek?' (Mobility, internal labour markets and labour relations – towards a new dynamics?), in Scheele, D., Theeuwes, J.J.M. and Vries, G.J.M. de (red.), Arbeidsflexibiliteit en ontslagrecht ('Labour flexibility and legislation concerning seperations'), Amsterdam: Amsterdam University Press.

Weehuizen, R.M. (red.) (2000), *Toekomst@werk.nl. Reflecties op economie, technologie en arbeid* (Future@work.nl. Reflections on economy, technology and labour), Den Haag:: Stichting Toekomstbeeld der Techniek.

White, H. (1980), 'A Heteroskedastic-consistent Covariance Matrix Estimator and a Direct Test for Heteroskedasticity', *Econometrica*, **48**, 817–38.

ANNEX 10.1 THE CONDITIONAL PROBIT MODEL

The model we used is a combination of a probit model and an ordered probit model. The probability of not having a job two years later is modelled as a probit model, and the change in job satisfaction is modelled as an ordered probit model. The two error terms are then modelled as a bivariate normal distribution with mean zero and variance 1 and correlation ρ. At the end of the two-year period a person can then be observed to belong to one of four states: not employed anymore, more satisfied with a job, equally satisfied with a job and less satisfied with a job. The four states can easily be viewed as being mutually exclusive. The model can be formalised as follows:

$$y_1^* = X\alpha + \varepsilon_1$$
$$y_2^* = X\beta + \varepsilon_2$$
$$y_1 = 1 \text{ if } y_1^* > 1, 0 \text{ otherwise}$$
$$y_2 = 1 \text{ if } y_2^* > S_2, 0 \text{ if } S_1 \le y_2^* \le S_2, -1 \text{ if } y_2^* \le S_1$$
$$\varepsilon_1, \varepsilon_2 \sim BVN(0, V)$$

where y_1 is the process of not having a job at the end of the period and y_2 is the process of the change in job satisfaction. The parameters are α, β, ρ, S_1 and S_2.

The log likelihood of a state is equal to:

$$\log\left(\Pr\left(Y_i = y_i\right)\right) = I_{y_i = nojob} \log\left(\Pr\left(\varepsilon_1 \le X\alpha\right)\right) +$$
$$I_{y_i = more} \log\left(\Pr\left(\varepsilon_1 \le -X\alpha, \varepsilon_2 > S_2 - X\beta\right)\right)$$
$$I_{y_i = equal} \log\left(\Pr\left(\varepsilon_1 \le -X\alpha, S_1 - X\beta \le \varepsilon_2 \le S_2 - X\beta\right)\right)$$
$$I_{y_i = less} \log\left(\Pr\left(\varepsilon_1 \le -X\alpha, \varepsilon_2 \le S_1 - X\beta\right)\right)$$

Estimation is done by maximum likelihood. We used the GAUSS programme to perform the estimation. The programme is available from the authors upon request.

PART III

'Best Policy Practices' in
Australia, Canada and Denmark

11. Labour Market Transitions in Australia: Employment, Flexibility and Security in a Liberal Welfare Regime

Stephen Ziguras and Peter Stricker

11.1 INTRODUCTION

11.1.1 The Australian Liberal Welfare Regime

During the 20th century, Australia developed a welfare state based on award coverage, compulsory arbitration and centralised wage fixing to provide a 'living wage' and protection from insecurity for workers, and tariff barriers to ensure profits and protection from competition for industry (Castles, 1988). Following World War II, this system was extended through a commitment to full employment policy and a minimalist social security system for those in temporary unemployment. Castles (1996) argued that the Australian welfare state – labelled the 'wage-earners' welfare state' – shared some features of Esping-Andersen's (1990) typology of a liberal regime, but was distinctive in that many welfare provisions were incorporated into the labour market. Specifically, the high minimum wage, a centralised bargaining, 'unfair dismissal' legislation, industry protection and full employment policies all provided workers with security, a high standard of living and a stable income distribution. This system ensured that, although the social security system was tightly targeted and provided low levels of financial support, few people had to rely on it for any length of time. From the 1980's on, though, the Australian wage earners' welfare state has changed in significant ways.

11.1.2 Economic Restructuring

From the early 1980s onwards, protectionism was replaced by a policy concern with greater integration of the Australian economy with international markets, based on the idea that economic growth would be increasingly determined through international trade. A common theme in changes over the following two decades was a shift from protection through risk prevention (tariff protection, centralised bargaining, and the breadwinner/family wage) to one of flexibility and adaptability. This was partly driven by neo-classical economic doctrines and Third Way variants (for example, Giddens, 1998). However, it is worth noting that policy makers during the 1980s were also influenced by the example of European countries such as Austria, Sweden and Norway which had adopted restructuring and active labour market policies, based on social democratic principles (Cass, 1988).

11.1.3 Labour Market Flexibility

Bargaining at the enterprise level largely replaced centralised bargaining over the 1990s, making wage rises conditional on productivity improvements, and detaching workers with less market power from the gains made by stronger unions (Buchanan and Watson, 2000). Economic policy became primarily concerned with economic growth with the assumption that increased employment would occur as a result.

The Australian economy, as for most Western countries, is now dominated in terms of output and employment by the services sector. Economic growth since 1960 has been strongly driven by rising levels of education (Chou, 2003), and demand for skilled workers is likely to continue (Keating, 2003). Growth over the medium term seems contingent on developing key technologies in the so-called 'knowledge industries': biotechnology, information and communications, but also in health, education and business services. This requires staff who are more highly educated and skilled, and who are willing to learn new skills in order to adapt.

At the same time, service industries have generated many low-skilled and low paid jobs, often part-time and casual (which means workers can be laid off without notice or compensation). The IT revolution has also created low-skilled low-paid positions (such as call centre workers) so it cannot be assumed that the knowledge economy will create only highly paid and skilled jobs. Overall, while many lower paid part time jobs have been created, if employment is measured in terms of total hours of work, there has also been strong demand for higher skilled occupations (Keating, 2003).

11.1.4 From Full Employment to Precarious Work

Australia enjoyed a brief period of 'full employment' (of between 1 and 2 per cent unemployment) during the 1950s and 60s, which meant, in effect male full-time employment but still exclusion of women from the labour market.

Over the last three decades the labour market has delivered mixed results: while there was a dramatic increase in labour force participation and increased female employment, the hours worked per head of the population remained fairly constant and the unemployment rate remained above 6 per cent until 2003. Under-utilised labour – the unemployed, those marginally attached to the workforce and those with part-time jobs who would like more work – is around double the unemployment rate (Australian Bureau of Statistics, 2004), and recent analyses put the rate of 'labour wastage' at 15 per cent of the labour force (Burgess, Mitchell and Preston, 2003).

The rise of casual, part-time and other non-standard employment over the same period has been well documented (for example, Borland, Gregory and Sheehan, 2001), and only around one quarter of the workforce is now engaged in full-time permanent jobs of 35–40 hours per week (Watson, Buchanan, Campbell and Briggs, 2003). There are multiple causes and both positive as well as negative impacts of this trend. Some non-standard employment is desired by workers, such as part-time jobs which suit many parents and students. Temporary jobs will continue to be necessary if entitlements to leave for study or caring are expanded, and after-hours jobs will be necessary as long as people wish to eat out at night!

For many, though, the rise of non-standard employment has heralded new forms of insecurity and risk. These include irregular or unpredictable income, uncertain working time and hours, poor access to training, reduced opportunities for participation in decision making, vulnerability to occupational health hazards, job insecurity and low pay (Macdonald and Holm, 2001, Standing, 2002, Watson et al., 2003). The trend towards casual contracts of employment appears to be driven by employers rather than employees, and some suggest this reflects a strategy to minimise labour costs and to devolve risks to workers (Watson et al., 2003).

11.1.5 The Polarisation of Household Employment

The fundamental demarcation between male (full-time) paid employment and female unpaid care and household work which lay at the heart of the old regime no longer applies. With increased female employment, gender inequality has been reduced substantially, although there has been little change in the domestic division of labour, leaving women to deal with the care crunch: the struggle to combine work and caring responsibilities. However, a new form of divergence is evident; that between 'work rich' households with two full-time (or one full-time and one part-time) wage earners and 'work poor' households with no-one in paid employment or with insufficient work (Dawkins, Gregg and Scutella, 2001). This trend has exacerbated the increase in income inequality due to the dispersion in wage income.

11.1.6 From Private to Public Income Transfers

One consequence of sustained unemployment and the growth of two-job and jobless households has been a shift in the means of income redistribution. Intra-family private redistribution of income from working husbands to non-working wives is being replaced by public transfers from working to non-working households, leading to growing expenditure on social security payments.

Although the social security system has been relatively effective in ameliorating poverty for low-income families with children, this trend has not been without cost. Greater targeting of government benefits for those of working age combined with an increasingly conditional and punitive approach, raise questions about the fairness and longer-term sustainability of current policies.

The Australian social security system is tightly targeted via steep means tests on income. While there is popular support for the pension and family payments, unemployment and sole parent payments are highly stigmatised. Middle class families increasingly resent paying taxes to subsidise the unemployed, as they see it, when they feel under great financial pressure themselves (Pusey, 2003). This trend has undermined the legitimacy of the social security system, and left it, and those relying on it, vulnerable to political attack. Since the mid-1990s, a range of changes to unemployment payments have been introduced; these include elements of workfare (Work for the Dole) first for young people and then for most others on unemployment payments, cuts to wage subsidy and training programs, and additional job search requirements. Most of these changes have emphasised the work-first approach to employment assistance rather than a skills development approach.

At the same time there has been an increase in less visible 'middle and upper class' welfare such as tax subsidies for housing investment, private health insurance and private pensions, relaxed income tests for the age pension, and greater funding for private schools (Australian Council of Social Service, 2003).

Australian taxpayer-funded flat-rate income support payments have been promoted as more financially viable than European social insurance defined-benefit schemes, which have to be supplemented with substantial government funding. However the downside is falling popular support and chronically inadequate levels of payment. Expansion of the range and scope of social assistance combined with some aspects of a social insurance approach (for example, tripartite funding from individuals, employers and government) may build greater social support for transfer payments.

11.1.7 Flexibility and Risk

The trends outlined above reflect the conclusions of Esping-Andersen's recent work (1999) on challenges facing various welfare state regimes. As traditional forms of protection have been dismantled and Australia has progressed further towards a pure liberal model, risks have been increasingly individualised. The economy has generated both demand for high skilled workers and numerous low skill service jobs and while increased flexibility has led to jobs growth, it has also allowed under-employment and precarious work to flourish. Since the protection enshrined in the labour market has been wound back, more people have to rely on the social security system and are forced to live on very low incomes, sometimes complemented with part-time or casual work taxed at very high marginal rates.

Previous Australian research has argued that these risks require new forms of protection, which will involve greater adaptability and flexibility combined with more concern for support and redistribution towards those at greatest risk (Ziguras, Considine, Hancock and Howe, 2004). This reflects a similar debate in Europe on the flexibility–security nexus (Muffels, Wilthagen and Van den Heuvel, 2002).

11.1.8 Transitional Labour Markets

Schmid's (2000, 2002, 2006) notion of transitional labour markets (TLMs) has been proposed as one way of responding to the changes described above (Ziguras et al., 2004). TLMs describe phases in people's life cycle during which they move between full-time work and other activities such as caring, education and retirement. Schmid's TLM approach involves policies which combine the flexibility and adaptation which are the hallmarks of the active labour market approach, with an aspiration for a fairer distribution of paid employment. European researchers have also identified TLMs as a useful framework for new directions in employment policy (De Gier and Van den Berg, 2006).

In effect, Schmid proposes that active labour market policies be expanded to allow people to move both in and out of paid employment more easily. TLMs require an 'activating approach' in that they should both provide not only financial support but other assistance (such as for training and caring for others) for people to make transitions between employment roles, such as between (permanent) employment and precarious employment or unemploy-ment and between employment and other activities: caring, education or retirement. They should embody the principle of increased capacity building central to activating labour market policies, but are also directed to create bridging activities for people who wish to move out of work, as well as for those who are unemployed. The TLM framework can be thought of as both normative and descriptive. It can be used to describe the current operation of the labour market, and also to design policies to change the way the labour market is structured.

11.2 RESEARCH AIMS

This chapter aims to investigate the extent to which labour market transitions of the type described by Schmid exist in Australia, and to document the characteristics of those most at risk of labour market exclusion (or 'exclusionary transitions') following the breakdown in the wage-earners' welfare state. The chapter is divided into three main sections; description of current transitions, analysis of exclusionary transitions and preference for hours of work.

In the first section we explore whether TLMs provide a useful lens for viewing the Australian labour market, by investigating transitions on the Australian labour market as mentioned before. In particular, we are interested in the annual frequency of these transitions and how they varied by sex and age. Since part-time work has grown dramatically during the 1990s, we explore transitions between full-time employment, part-time work combined with other activities (focusing on caring and education), unemployment, and other activities outside the labour market (caring, education and retirement).

The second section of the chapter investigates the risk factors for exclusion. Schmid (1998) argues that TLMs can also be used as a normative device to describe the quality of transitions. Cebrián, Lallement and O'Reilly (2000) suggest it may be possible to distinguish three types of transitions; integrative, maintenance and exclusionary. Integrative transitions would allow people not in paid employment, such as the unemployed, students and carers, to move into full-time employment via part-time work. Maintenance transitions would allow people in employment to maintain 'employment continuity by moving between different working time regimes' (Cebriánet al, 2000, p. 4). Finally, exclusionary transitions would be represented by periods of part-time or temporary work within a longer pattern of unemployment or non-employment. This would effectively mean transitions only between the peripheral labour market and non-work.

Muffels et al, 2002) defined total exclusion as working for no period over three years, and partial exclusion as working less than fifty per cent of the time. For reasons described, in this chapter, we define exclusionary transitions having spent less than 50 per cent of the year in employment. For this analysis we include only those in the labour market or who are marginally attached to the labour market. We therefore do not count people voluntarily out of work as excluded. We explore which people are at risk of poor transitions, by examining risk factors for flows into and out of unemployment and a broader measure of exclusion from paid work.

The third part of the chapter explores the potential in Australia of Schmid's proposal that TLMs could restore full employment by redistributing paid employment. We investigate the incidence of over-work and under-work as measured by whether those employed preferred to work more, less or the same number of hours (see also Chapter 10 in this book dealing with the Netherlands). Finally, we present the implications of our results for policy, specifically around preventing transitions into unemployment, and to support transitions back to work.

11.3 METHOD

11.3.1 Data

This analysis uses data from the Household, Income and Labour Dynamics of Australia (HILDA). HILDA is a longitudinal study of a stratified random sample of the Australian population. The data used in the analysis was collected in the first two waves in 2001 and 2002. In 2001, 13,969 adults over the age of 15 were included. In 2002, 85.9 per cent of these were included, an attrition rate of 14.1 per cent which is fairly low by international comparison (Watson and Wooden, 2002). This leaves data on 11,993 persons.

11.3.2 Analysis

We used Schmid's framework to classify respondents into nine situations according to their employment status and other activities. We distinguished between full-time work, three categories of part-time work, unemployment, unpaid caring, study, retirement, and not being in the labour force but not studying or caring. Since part-time work has grown significantly, and appears to be a key factor in transitions, we distinguished between people studying or caring with part-time work from those in these categories not in the labour force. Care here means caring for a dependent child under 16 years of age in the same household, but does not include caring for a relative with a disability.

In the case of part time work, we created three categories based on the main reason people stated they were working part-time. Part-time work (caring) indicates they were caring for a child under 16 years of age, and part-time work (study) means they were undertaking post-secondary education. Part-time work (other) includes people working part-time because of a disability, who were seeking full-time work, who preferred part-time work, or were undertaking part-time work for other reasons not stated. The last category – not being in the labour force (other) includes those people who were not in the labour force according to conventional definitions, were not caring or studying and who had not retired permanently from paid employment.

11.4 RESULTS

11.4.1 Labour Market Transitions and Flow Rates in Australia

Transitions and flow rates
Table 11.1 indicates the proportion of respondents in each of the nine labour market states in 2001 and the number and proportion of those who changed their activities between 2001 and 2002.

In Table 11.2, for those who changed, we depict the percentage of people moving from a particular origin into a particular destination state.

Table 11.1 Labour market transitions and flow rates, 2001–2002

	No. in 2001	No. changing between 2001–02	No. unchanged between 2001–02	Per cent changing 2001–02 (flow rate)
Full-time work	4,981	583	4,398	11.7
Part-time work (care)	750	325	425	43.3
Part-time work (study)	510	212	298	41.6
Part-time work (other)	1,100	499	601	45.4
Unemployed	488	344	144	70.5
Not in the labour force (care)	734	246	488	33.5
Not in the labour force (study)	426	244	182	57.3
Not in the labour force (retired)	1,411	200	1,211	14.2
Not in the labour force (other)	1,593	979	614	61.5
Total	11,993	3,632	8,361	30.3

Source: Panel data on Household, Income and Labour Dynamics of Australia (HILDA), 2001–2002.

Table 11.2 Proportions of persons changing between 2001–02 from various origins to various destinations (%)

	Full-time work	Part-time work (care)	Part-time work (study)	Part-time work (other)	Un-employed	Not in the labour force (care)	Not in the labour force (study)	Not in the labour force (retired)	Not in the labour force (other)
Full-time work	n.a	12.3	5.1	39.6	13.7	6.9	2.7	8.1	11.5
Part-time work (care)	25.5	n.a	1.2	43.4	4.3	18.8	0.9	1.8	4.0
Part-time work (study)	44.8	1.9	n.a	23.6	9.9	0.5	16.5	0.0	2.8
Part-time work (other)	43.3	14.4	4.0	n.a	6.0	3.0	1.0	14.0	14.2
Unemployed	32.0	2.3	10.5	18.0	n.a	9.3	6.1	3.8	18.0
Not in the labour force (care)	8.9	34.1	0.4	9.8	12.2	n.a	4.9	10.6	19.1
Not in the labour force (study)	18.0	0.0	31.1	11.1	19.7	4.9	n.a	1.2	13.9
Not in the labour force (retired)	4.5	1.5	0.0	16.5	2.5	5.5	0.0	n.a	69.5
Not in the labour force (other)	5.9	1.9	1.0	6.0	5.6	6.6	2.2	70.6	n.a

Source: Data from the panel on Household, Income and Labour Dynamics of Australia HILDA), 2001–2002.

It can be seen for example, that 4,981 people were in full-time work in 2001, and of these, 4,398 or around 88 per cent were still in full-time work a year later (but not necessarily in the same job, or for the whole year). Around 69.7 per cent of the sample was in the same labour market situation at both times, and around 30 per cent made a transition to another situation. Around one third of transitions were outside the labour market, for example, ceasing to care for a child but not entering the workforce. Two thirds of all transitions (corresponding to 20 per cent of all adults) were either within the labour market (for example, from unemployment to full-time work) or either into or out of the labour market (for example, from studying and not working to studying and working part-time). In other words, around one fifth of the adult population went through some type of labour market transition over the year 2001–2002.

The most common transitions were:

- From full-time work to part-time work (other) (6.3 per cent of all transitions).

- From part-time work (other) to full-time work (5.9 per cent).
- From part-time work (caring) to part-time work (other) (4.0 per cent).
- From unemployment to full-time work (3.0 per cent).
- From part-time work (study) to full-time work (2.6 per cent).
- From full-time work to unemployment (2.3 per cent).

The labour market status with the highest flow rate is unemployment: 70.5 per cent of those who were unemployed in 2001 were no longer unemployed in 2002. People in part-time work were also highly likely to make a transition, with up to 50 per cent of these changing over the one-year period.

Labour market transitions by gender

Table 11.3 shows flow rates by gender. One clear gender difference was that 37 per cent of women underwent a transition compared to only 23 per cent of men. Men were more likely to move from full-time work to retirement or unemployment whereas women moved into caring roles with part-time or no

Table 11.3 Flow rates of those changing labour market status between 2001–2002 by gender (%)

2001	2002	Full-time work	Part-time work (care)	Part-time work (study)
Full-time work	Males	n.a	4.5	4.2
	Females	n.a	18.9	6.0
Part-time work (care)	Males	43.3	n.a	3.3
	Females	23.7	n.a	1.0
Part-time work (study)	Males	45.5	–	Na
	Females	44.4	3.2	Na
Part-time work (other)	Males	56.3	1.7	4.0
	Females	36.3	21.2	4.0
Unemployed	Males	40.8	–	7.6
	Females	21.9	5.0	13.8
Not in the labour force (care)	Males	22.7	9.1	–
	Females	7.6	36.6	0.4
Not in the labour force (study)	Males	21.9	–	29.8
	Females	14.6	–	32.3
Not in the labour force (retired)	Males	8.2	1.6	–
	Females	2.9	1.4	–
Not in the labour force (other)	Males	9.6	0.3	1.4
	Females	3.9	2.9	0.8

Note: 'n.a' = not applicable, '–' indicates no data.

Source: Data from the panel on Household, Income and Labour Dynamics of Australia (HILDA), 2001–2002.

work. Men were also more likely to move from part-time work to full-time whereas women were more likely to cease caring and retain part-time work or move out of the labour force completely. The pattern suggests a preference by women for part-time work, regardless of caring status. We explored gender differences for three particular transitions in more detail; from full-time employment, part-time work and caring, and unemployment. 42 per cent of the adult population was in full-time work in 2001, and of these, 12 per cent changed their situation during 2001–02.

Figure 11.1 shows the transition from full-time work in 2001 to other activities in 2002. The dominant destination for both genders was part-time work with neither caring nor studying orientation.

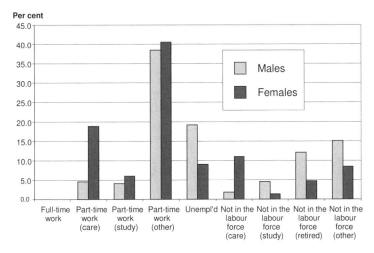

Figure 11.1 Flow rates from full-time employment in 2001 to other activities in 2002 by gender

Women were more likely than men to move to part-time work with caring responsibilities (19 at 4.5 per cent), and more likely than men to leave the labour force in order to undertake caring duties (11 at 1.9 per cent). More men than women moved into unemployment (19.2 at 9.1 per cent) and men were also more likely to switch from full-time work to retirement and other non labour force activities. Only about 6.3 per cent of the population was working part-time and caring in 2001, with 95 per cent being women. 43 per cent changed labour market status over the year to 2002.

Figure 11.2 shows the destinations of those who changed. Men were much more likely to move to full-time work (43.3 per cent) than women (23.7 per cent) and men were also more inclined to retire altogether (10.0 at 1.0 per cent).

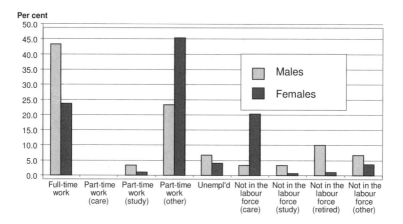

Figure 11.2 Flow rates from part time work and caring in 2001 to other activities in 2002 by gender

Women were more likely than men to change to other activities in conjunction with part time work (45.4 at 23.3 per cent males) – probably a large proportion of these kept working part-time after their youngest child turned 16, so they were not classified as caring in our definition. Women were also more likely than men to move out of the labour force altogether while retaining their caring responsibilities (20.3 at 3.3 per cent).

In 2001, 4.1 per cent of the adult population were unemployed (or 6.2 per cent of the labour force), of whom 71 per cent changed situations by the following year (Figure 11.3).

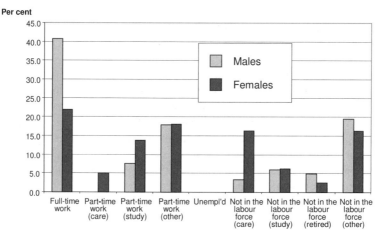

Figure 11.3 Flow rates from unemployment in 2001 to other activities in 2002 by gender

Men were twice as likely as women to move to full time work (41 against 22 per cent). Women more likely than men to take up caring either with part-time work (5 per cent of women compared to no men) or outside the labour force (16.3 against 3.3 per cent), and were also more likely to move to a combination of study and part-time work.

Labour market transitions by age
We explored labour market transitions for three age groups; 15–24 year old, 25–44 year olds and 45–64 year olds. Those in the youngest age group were more likely to undergo a transition (43.6 per cent) compared to the 25–44 group (25 per cent) and 45–64 age group (27 per cent). More detailed tables by age are available upon request from the authors.

The rate of movement out of full time work was low for all age groups. Only 16.7 per cent, 10.2 per cent and 12.1 per cent of full-time workers for these age groups respectively moved out of full-time work.

Flow rates out of full-time work are shown in Figure 11.4. It can be seen that young people were more likely to move from full-time work to unemployment or to study (either solely or with part-time work). The middle age group was more likely to move into caring activities (either solely or with part-time work), while the 45–64 year olds were most likely to move into part-time work (other), or out of the labour market completely.

Per cent

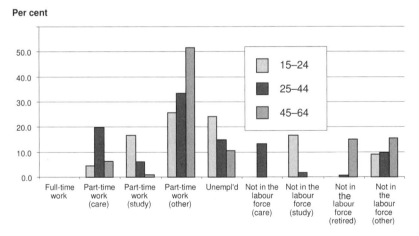

Figure 11.4 Flow rates from full-time work in 2001 to other activities in 2002 by age group

The 15–24 year olds group was more likely to be unemployed in 2001 (9.7 per cent at 4.1 per cent of total), but there was little difference in the rate of transition out of unemployment in the three age groups (from youngest to oldest 71.8 per cent; 69.6 per cent and 69.9 per cent made the transition during the year). Figure 11.5 shows flow rates out of unemployment; the transitions into the various destinations show some similar patterns to those out of full-time work. Young people were more likely to move into study, middle aged people into full-time work or caring roles, and the oldest age group to move into part-time work (other) or out of the labour market altogether.

Per cent

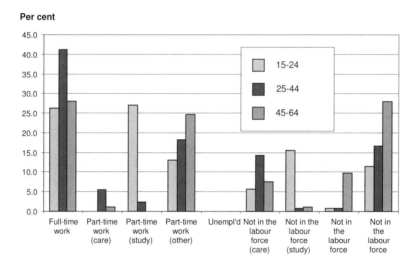

Figure 11.5 Flow rates from unemployment in 2001 to other activities in 2002 by age group

In summary, younger people were more likely to be involved in transitions around study, part-time work and unemployment. Those in the 25–44 age range were more likely to be moving between full-time work, part-time work and caring roles, and the 45–64 age group moved into part-time work with no other activities or out of the labour market altogether.

11.4.2 Predictors of Labour Market Participation and Exclusion

From the flow rates presented in the first part of this chapter, it is clear that there is considerable dynamism in the Australian labour market and that a significant section of the population goes through some type of transition each year. This leads to the question as to whether some transitions are better than others, and who is at risk of low quality or 'exclusionary' transitions. We operationalised exclusion in two ways. The first was flows into unemployment. However, since unemployment is basically a measure of point in time exclusion, we also examined the proportion of the year spent in paid work. This latter figure is a better measure of long-term exclusion. Given these definitions, this section focuses on three key questions:

- What are the key determinants of participation in paid employment?
- Of those in the labour market, which groups are most likely to move into unemployment?
- Of those unemployed, which groups are least likely to move back into paid employment?

Predictors of employment

This analysis examined the factors which were correlated with labour market participation in the year 2001–02. The sample included people below retirement age in 2002 and who were either in the labour market in 2001 or marginally attached to the labour market, leaving a sample size of 8,373 people. Those not in the labour force but marginally attached were included since they express a desire to work, and are often likely to enter the workforce given favourable circumstances. Inclusion of this group allows us to investigate involuntary exclusion from employment.

The HILDA dataset includes a derived variable which estimates the percentage of time in the previous year spent in paid employment (full-time or part-time). This variable is specified as a continuous variable with values ranging from 0 to 100 per cent of the year. However, 10 per cent of the sample spent no time in paid work and another 75 per cent spent 100 per cent of the year in work. Since these two categories accounted for 85 cent of the total sample, it is apparent that the data violated the assumptions of a normal distribution required for standard multiple regression analysis. The variable was recategorised into a dichotomous variable with the values of 0 (50 per cent or more of the year spent in employment) and 1 (less than 50 per cent of the year spent in employment).

Of the sample for this analysis, 7,001 people (84 per cent) worked fifty per cent or more of the 2001–02 year with the remaining 1,372 (16 per cent) spending less than half the year in work (we refer to this category in the text as 'excluded' since the majority appeared to be working not at all).

Logistic regression was used to estimate the risks of labour market exclusion. The independent variables included in the analysis are shown below. Some categorical variables with more than 2 categories (education, marital status, region) were dummy coded into two separate variables as described:

- Age.
- Age squared.
- Sex (female versus male).

- Marital status (divorced, widowed or separated; never married; comparison group is married people).
- Level of education (less than Year 12; Year 12 but less than a degree; the comparison group consists of people with tertiary degrees or higher levels of education).
- English proficiency (poor English versus other).
- Aboriginal or Torres Strait Islander status (Indigenous versus other).
- Dependent children (Children under 5 years versus other).
- Choice in participation (Involuntary exit from employment in last 10 years versus other).
- Region (Major urban area; regional area; the comparison group is rural and remote areas).

The results of the analysis are shown in Table 11.4. The model predicted 85 per cent of cases correctly (Nagelkerke R Square = 0.25).

Table 11.4 Predictors of exclusion from employment

Predictor	Odds ratio
Involuntarily lost job in last 10 years	5.24***
Less than Year 12 education	3.39***
Long-term health problems	2.89***
Migrant with poor English proficiency	2.84***
Has children under 5 years of age	2.66***
Female	2.51***
Indigenous	2.40***
Divorced, separated or widowed	1.76***
Never married	1.64***
Year 12 education but less than degree	1.58***
Age squared	1.00***
Age	0.83***
Major urban region	0.96 ns
Regional area	0.90 ns

Note: *** $p < 0.001$; ns = not significant.

Source: Data from the panel on Household, Income and Labour Dynamics of Australia (HILDA), 2001–2002.

The odds ratios shown in column two indicate the relative risk of working less than fifty per cent of the year for the predictor in column one (compared to the reference group for each category). In other words, this analysis indicates those who worked from among the population which could be considered the extended labour force.

The results show that people who had been involuntarily unemployed in the last 10 years were five times more likely to work less than 50 per cent of the time over the year and hence, to be excluded form work, those with less than year 12 education, with long term health problems or with poor English proficiency were about three times more likely to be excluded from work and individuals with children under five years of age, women and Indigenous people were about two and a half times more likely to be excluded from work. People who were separated or never married had about a two-thirds higher risk of exclusion from work. Region had no relationship with levels of employment, but this may be because very broad categories were used. Further analysis showed that, although single status did contribute to less likelihood of employment, the greatest effect was for single people with young children (that is, sole parents).

Inflows to unemployment

The second question was related to risks of unemployment. We were interested in exploring the factors which contributed to greater risk of unemployment in 2002 of those who, in 2001, were in the labour market or marginally attached to the labour market (unemployed). Again, logistic regression was conducted which results are presented in Table 11.5.

Table 11.5 Predictors of unemployment in 2002

Predictor	Odds ratio
Involuntarily lost job in last 10 years	6.45***
Unemployed in 2001	5.74***
Divorced, separated or widowed	2.17***
Indigenous	2.17***
Less than Year 12 education	1.82**
Never married	1.67**
Long-term health problems	1.54**
Migrant with poor English proficiency	1.38 ns
Year 12 education but less than degree	1.20 ns
Female	1.16 ns
Age squared	1.00 ns
Age	0.97 ns
Has children under 5	0.97 ns
Major urban region	1.10 ns
Other urban region	0.98 ns
Was working in wave 1 but wanted less work	0.95 ns

Note: *** $p < 0.001$, ** $p < 0.01$, * $p < 0.05$; ns = not significant.

Source: Data from the panel on Household, Income and Labour Dynamics of Australia (HILDA), 2001–2002.

The model included the same independent variables as in the former model with the addition of two other independent variables. One variable indicated that the person was working in wave 1 but wished to reduce their hours, and the second whether the person was unemployed at wave 1. The outcome variable was being unemployed or not at wave 2. The model predicted 95.2 per cent of cases correctly (Nagelkerke R Square = 0.26). The odds ratios in column two indicate the relative risk of unemployment in wave 2.

It can be seen that the most significant factors affecting the likelihood of unemployment in 2002 were: having been retrenched in the previous 10 years, being unemployed in 2001, being separated or never married, being of Indigenous background, having less than Year 12 education or having a long-term health problem. These results are broadly similar to the results of the previous analyses of flows into unemployment (for example, Le and Miller, 2001).

Outflows from unemployment
The third question concerned the factors associated with employment following a period of unemployment. This analysis included those who were unemployed in 2001 (488) and excluded those who reached retirement age in wave 2 (5 people) leaving the number of persons to 483.

Figure 11.6 shows the transitions made by unemployed people between 2001 and 2002.

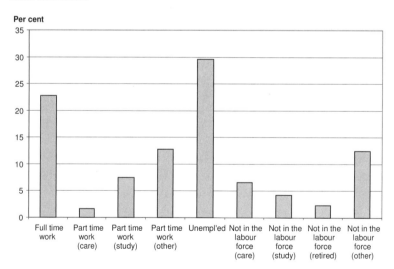

Figure 11.6 Employment destinations in 2002 of people who were unemployed in 2001

It shows that 143 people (30 per cent) were still unemployed and 340 (70 per cent) had moved into another labour market status. However, as can be seen from Figure 11.6, those who did move out of unemployment, moved either into work or out of the labour market. Around 45 per cent of those unemployed in Wave 1 moved into employment in wave 2 (roughly half into full-time and half into part-time work), about 30 per cent stayed unemployed and 26 per cent moved out of the labour market. Of those who moved, about two thirds moved into work and a third out of the labour market altogether.

We investigated factors associated with participation in paid work following unemployment. Logistic regression was conducted using the same variables as for the previous analysis (excluding the question about wishing to reduce working hours which only applied to those working in wave 1). The outcome variable was working fifty per cent or more of the year or less than fifty per cent. The results are shown below in Table 11.6. The odds ratios indicate the relative risk of working less than fifty per cent of the 2001–02 year and represent the difficulty faced re-entering the workforce following a period of unemployment.

Table 11.6 Predictors of labour force exclusion following unemployment

Predictor	Odds ratio
Long-term health problems	2.61***
Divorced, separated or widowed	2.61*
Never married	1.92*
Female	1.68*
Age squared	1.00*
Age	0.90*
Indigenous	2.46 ns
Has children under 5	1.97 ns
Less than Year 12 education	1.71 ns
Major urban area	1.65 ns
Regional area	1.64 ns
Year 12 education but less than degree	1.16 ns
Migrant with poor English proficiency	0.82 ns
Involuntarily lost job in last 10 years	0.81 ns

Note: *** $p < 0.001$, ** $p < 0.01$, * $p < 0.05$; ns = not significant.

Source: Data from the panel on Household, Income and Labour Dynamics of Australia (HILDA), 2001–2002.

The main predictors of exclusion were the presence of: long-term health problems, being separated or never married, and being female. With age, people were less likely to be excluded. Since the sample for this analysis was much smaller than in the previous two analyses, odds ratios of the same magnitude were less likely to be statistically significant: those with young children had almost a doubled risk of exclusion but this was not quite statistically significant at p = 0.065. Indigenous people had a much higher probability of exclusion (two and a half times) but this was not statistically significant, probably because of the small number of Indigenous people in the sample (n = 26).

11.4.3 Preferred and Actual Working Hours

This final analysis examines preferences for more, less or the same working hours. TLMs are proposed as a way of redistributing paid employment more equitably (Schmid, 1998), by establishing transitions whereby those who would prefer to work less can reduce their hours, and those who would prefer to work more, can increase hours. This raises the question – to what extent are Australians happy with their current working hours and do they want to change them?

Respondents were asked several questions in HILDA about their actual and preferred working hours. Of those working in 2001, 28.7 per cent said they would prefer to work less hours (taking the effect on income into account), 54.9 per cent preferred working about the same hours and 16.3 per cent more hours. Almost half those working would have preferred different working hours, implying that the current distribution of work is not optimal as far as the workforce at that time is concerned.

Using the weights built into the sample to obtain population estimates, it can be estimated that there were around 2,631,000 people in Australia who wanted to work less hours in 2001, and on average, this group preferred to work about 13.9 hours less per week. Around 1,496,000 people already in work (that is, not counting the unemployed or those not in the labour force) wanted to work an average 11.6 hours more per week. On average, those in work preferred to work 2.3 hours less per week. These figures are similar to those found by Drago, Tseng and Wooden (2004) also using HILDA wave 1 data. They found that in 2001 those in work worked on average 38.5 hours per week, but preferred to work 36.2 hours per week.

Overall, taking these preferences into account, people employed in 2001 would have preferred working a net of 19 million hours less per week. This figure equates to the number of hours which would be worked by 500,000 people in full time jobs, which is roughly the number of people unemployed, most of whom want full time work.

The proportions wanting fewer, the same, or more hours remained roughly the same in 2002. While some people moved closer to their ideal hours, others had moved further away, and overall the picture remained the same.

For example, of those who were happy with their hours in 2001, about one third preferred to work either more or less hours a year later.

These results suggest that the current infrastructure does not operate to enable people to work their desired hours. Policies to support a closer match between preferred and actual working hours could, under certain circumstances, provide the opportunity for those currently excluded from work to increase their working hours.

11.5 CONCLUSIONS

The results of this study show that the Australian labour market is a very dynamic one, with around 20 per cent of the adult population each year making a transition into, out of or within employment combined with other activities such as study or caring. Part-time work plays an important role in many transitions. The transitional labour market framework is therefore a useful analytical tool for studying Australian working conditions. Kruppe (2002) reporting on the period 1994–95 for European union countries, found around 16 per cent of the population went through a transition each year, but this is not directly comparable due to different categories of transitions used. However, he reports that around one third of transitions took place outside the labour market, a similar figure to that found here.

Women were more likely to undergo a transition during the year than men, again reflecting results from European countries (Kruppe, 2002). Women are far more likely to care for a young child (around 95 per cent of carers either working part-time or not working at all are women) and to move into and out of caring roles combined with part-time work. Women appear to have a general preference for part-time work, whereas men appear to prefer full-time work. For example, of those working part-time and caring for a young child, 45 per cent of women who changed their labour market position stayed in part-time work but ceased caring for a child, but around the same proportion of men moved to full-time jobs.

Younger people are more likely to be involved in transitions around study, part-time work and unemployment. Those aged between 25 and 44 years are more likely to be moving between full-time work, part-time work and caring roles, and the 45–64 age group are likely to move into part-time work with no other activities or out of the labour market.

Research on European welfare states regimes (Muffels et al., 2002) found that Liberal regimes (UK and Ireland in that study) combined a high level of labour mobility and flexibility with a low level of work security. Although the figures are again not directly comparable due to different time periods of the studies, our results certainly appear to support the contention that

Australia reflects this pattern. Further work to develop measures of transitions consistent with European studies would be useful to allow greater comparative analysis.

There are clearly some groups at much greater risk of exclusion from employment. These include those who have been retrenched within the last decade, those with less than year 12 education, people with long-term health problems, migrants with poor English, parents with children under five years of age (especially sole parents), women and Indigenous people. These findings reflect similar results from previous studies (for example, Le and Miller, 2001) and overseas evidence (Campbell, 2001).

It is possible that the higher risk for these groups represent the result of screening practices by employers rather than a lack of capacity to undertake employment. This is probably true in the current situation of a large supply of under-utilised labour. However, some of these factors also represent reduced capacity to work if labour demand increased; for example migrants with poor English would probably be unable to undertake a wide range of jobs.

Since these groups are either already in the labour market or marginally attached, we can assume that they would like to work given the right circumstances, and they are therefore involuntarily excluded from employment. The results suggest some broad policy directions consistent with the TLM framework which would lead to greater participation in employment of those who are currently excluded. These include:

- Retraining/placement policies for retrenched workers (since previous retrenchment appears to have a long-term scarring effect).
- Better labour market programs for long-term unemployed people, probably linked to work experience and formal qualifications.
- Better funding for disability/chronic health services linked to labour market programs.
- Youth transitions policies targeting young people at risk of early school leaving.
- More resources for improving English skills for migrants.
- Better access to and affordability of childcare for parents with young children, especially sole parents.
- Affirmative action policies for indigenous people.

These suggestions follow Esping-Andersen's argument that combining flexibility and security requires a 'mobility guarantee' to ensure that some groups are not permanently excluded or marginalised (1999). He also emphasises the importance of education and training as part of this guarantee. Some of these approaches have been trialled at welfare agencies in Australia (for example, the Brotherhood of St Laurence (BSL), a welfare agency located in Melbourne), which provides a range of employment services for marginalised people. It acts as a policy testing ground by developing new programs which may be able to be replicated more widely in national policy.

Two examples of these programmes directly relevant to the TLM model are its work with young people at risk of early school leaving (MacDonald, 1999) and with long-term unemployed public housing tenants in inner Melbourne (Temby, Housakos and Ziguras, 2004). These programmes provide intensive support and case management, have a strong vocational training component, and take a 'human capital' rather than a 'work-first' approach, combined with a significant degree of personal support to overcome barriers such as health problems. They appear to be relatively successful in re-integrating those at greatest risk, and have some similarities to the principles proposed for the Neighbourhood Renewal program in the UK (Campbell, 2001). However other approaches will also be needed, especially attention to retraining retrenched workers (where there is a very large policy gap) whereby many older workers end up on disability pensions and early involuntary retirement.

A misdistribution in hours of work was also evident, with substantial proportions of the workforce expressing a desire for either more or less hours. If these preferences were met, there would be a net increase of around half a million full-time jobs, equivalent to the number of people unemployed. Policies to support a closer match between preferred and actual working hours could, under certain circumstances, provide the opportunity for those currently excluded from work to increase their working hours.

This chapter has shown that the TLM framework is a useful one for describing the current labour market in Australia. We also see, however, systematic risks of exclusion for a significant number of people under the current policy settings, suggesting a need for new directions in managing flexibility and risk, and the TLM approach appears to have great potential for conceptualising new models to ensure that citizens are able to make beneficial and productive transitions.

REFERENCES

Australian Bureau of Statistics (ABS) (2004), *Australian labour market statistics, April 2004*, Cat. No. 6105.0, Canberra: ABS.

Australian Council of Social Service (2003), *Budget waste and well-off welfare ACOSS INFO 345*, Strawberry Hills, NSW: Australian Council of Social Service.

Borland, J., Gregory, B. and Sheehan, P. (eds) (2001), *Work rich, work poor: inequality and economic change in Australia*, Melbourne: Centre for Strategic Economic Studies, Victoria University.

Buchanan, J. and Watson, I. (2000), 'Beyond the wage earner model', in Hancock, L., Howe, B. and O'Donnell, A. (eds), *Reshaping Australia social policy: changes in work, welfare and families,* Growth, Melbourne: CEDA, 48.

Burgess, J., Mitchell, W. and Preston, A. (2003), 'The Australian labour market in 2002', *The Journal of Industrial Relations*, **45** (2), 125–50.

Campbell, M. (2001), *New deal for communities: national evaluation scoping phase (worklessness evidence review),* Department for Transport, Local Government and the Regions, available at: <www.renewal.net/Nav.asp? Category=:worklessness>, accessed 19 October 2004.

Cass, B. (1988), *Income support for the unemployed in Australia: towards a more active system,* Canberra: Australian Government Publishing Services.

Castles, F. (1988), *Australian public policy and economic vulnerability: a comparative and historical perspective,* Sydney: Allen and Unwin.

Castles, F. (1996), 'Needs-based strategies of social protection in Australia and New Zealand' in Esping-Andersen, G. (ed.), *Welfare states in transition,* London: Sage.

Cebrián, I., Lallement, M. and O'Reilly, J. (2000), 'Introduction', in O'Reilly, J., Cebrián, I. and Lallement, M. (eds), *Working-time changes: social integration through transitional labour markets*, Cheltenham, UK and Northampton, MA, USA: Edward Elgar.

Chou, Y.K. (2003), 'The Australian growth experience, 1960–2000: human capital, R&D, or steady-state growth?', *Australian Economic Review*, **36** (4), 397–414.

De Gier, E. and Van den Berg, A. (2006), *Managing social risks through transitional labour markets: towards an enriched European Employment Strategy*, Appeldoorn, Antwerpen: Het Spinhuis.

Dawkins, P., Gregg, P. and Scutella, R. (2001), *The growth of jobless households in Australia,* Melbourne Institute Working Paper No. 3/01, Melbourne: Melbourne Institute for Applied Economic and Social Research.

Drago, R., Tseng, Y.-P. and Wooden, M. (2004), *Family structure, usual and preferred working hours, and egalitarianism in Australia,* Working Paper No. 1/04, Melbourne: Melbourne Institute of Applied Economic and Social Research.

Esping-Andersen, G. (1990), *The three worlds of welfare capitalism*, Cambridge, UK: Polity Press.

Esping-Andersen, G. (1999), *Social foundations of postindustrial economies,* Oxford: Oxford University Press.

Giddens, A. (1998), *The Third Way: renewal of social democracy*, Cambridge, UK: Polity Press.

Keating, M. (2003), The labour market and inequality, *Australian Economic Review*, **36** (4), 374–96.

Kruppe, T. (2002), 'The dynamics of employment in the European Union: an exploratory analysis', in Schmid, G. and Gazier, B. (eds), *The new dynamics of full employment: social integration through transitional labour markets*, Cheltenham, UK and Northampton, MA, USA: Edward Elgar.

Le, A.T. and Miller, P.W. (2001), 'Is a risk index approach to unemployment possible?', *Economic Record*, **77** (236), 51–70.

Macdonald, F. and Holm, S. (2001), 'Employment for 25- to 34- year olds in the flexible labour market: a generation excluded?', in Hancock, L., Howe, B, Frere, M. and O'Donnell, A. (eds), *Future directions in Australian social policy: new ways of preventing risk,* Growth 49, Melbourne: CEDA.

MacDonald, H. (1999), *Bridging the gap: assisting early school leavers to make the transition to work*, Fitzroy: Brotherhood of St Laurence.

Muffels, R.J.A., Wilthagen, T. and Heuvel, N. van den (2002), *Labour market transitions and employment regimes: evidence on the flexibility–security nexus in transitional labour markets,* Berlin: Wissenschaftszentrum Berlin.

Pusey, M. (2003), *The experience of middle Australia: the dark side of economic reform,* Port Melbourne: Cambridge University Press.

Schmid, G. (1998), *Transitional labour markets: a new European employment strategy,* Discussion paper FS I 98–206, Berlin: Social Science Research Centre Berlin, <www.wz-berlin.de/default.en.asp>, accessed 5 September 2003.

Schmid, G. (2000), 'Transitional labour markets: a new European employment strategy', in Marin, B., Leulders, D. and Snower, D.J. (eds), *Innovative employment initiatives,* Aldershot, UK: Ashgate Publishing.

Schmid, G. (2002), 'Towards a theory of transitional labour markets', in Schmid, G. and Gazier, B. (eds), *The Dynamics of full employment: social integration through transitional labour markets,* Cheltenham, UK and Northampton, MA, USA: Edward Elgar.

Schmid, G. (2006), Transitional labour markets: experiences from Europe and Germany, *Australian Bulletin of Labour,* **32** (2), 114–38.

Standing G. (2002), *Beyond the new paternalism: basic security as equity,* London: Verso.

Temby P., Housakos, G. and Ziguras, S. (eds) (2004), *Helping local people get jobs: Insights from the Brotherhood of St Laurence experience in Fitzroy and Collingwood,* available at: <www.bsl.org.au /main.asp? PageId=132>.

Watson, I., Buchanan, J., Campbell, I. and Briggs, C. (2003), *Fragmented futures: new challenges in working life,* Sydney: The Federation Press.

Watson, N. and Wooden, M. (2002), *The Household, Income and Labour Dynamics in Australia (HILDA) Survey: Wave 1 survey methodology,* Melbourne: Melbourne Institute of Applied Economic and Social Research.

Ziguras, S., Considine, M., Hancock, L. and Howe, B. (2004), *From risk to opportunity: labour markets in transition,* Melbourne: Centre for Public Policy, University of Melbourne, available at: <www.public-policy.unimelb.edu.au/ research /TLMs background_paper.pdf>.

12. From Unemployment to Employment Insurance: Towards Transitional Labour Markets in Canada?

Axel van den Berg, Claus-H. von Restorff, Daniel Parent and Anthony C. Masi

12.1 INTRODUCTION

When considering the nature and effects of Canadian (Un)Employment Insurance it is important to keep in mind some of Canada's peculiarities as compared to most other Western countries.[1] Canada is not only a vast country, but it is also quite varied in terms of industrial structure and economic conditions. In particular, local unemployment rates vary enormously from region to region, and chronically so, with rates traditionally high in the Maritime Provinces and Québec, intermediate in British Columbia and much lower in Ontario and the Prairie Provinces. Second, and not entirely unrelated, seasonal occupations such as mining, logging, fishing and hunting are quite prominent in some regions, again, especially the Maritimes, Québec and British Columbia. Third, Canada has one of the most decentralised federal governmental structures in the world, with many policy domains related to labour market policy, especially education and training, firmly under provincial jurisdiction.

In 1996/1997 the Canadian federal government undertook a major reform of the Unemployment Insurance regime. To underline the seriousness of the intended change in aims and policies, the new system was dubbed the Employment Insurance program. Advocates of the reform have hailed it as 'the most sweeping reform since the UI (unemployment insurance) Act of 1971' (Gray, 2004, p. 1), and an unprecedented move from passive to active labour market policies, designed to reduce spells of unemployment and increase the ease with which the unemployed and new entrants find jobs (for example, Fedorovitch, 2001). The newly created Canada Employment Commission calls it 'the most fundamental restructuring of the Unemployment Insurance program in 25 years' (Canada Employment Insurance Commission, 2004a). Critics, on the other hand, have described the reform as a thinly disguised cost-cutting measure 'motivated most importantly by a desire to reduce expenditures within the program as part of the government's overall strategy of deficit reduction' (McIntosh and Boychuk, 2000: 90), this being done at the expense of the unemployed by means of tightening eligibility rules and reductions of benefit levels and periods (see for example, Campeau, 2001; Martel, Laplante and Bernard, 2005; Canadian Labour Congress, 2003).

There is no question that the reform was intended to be a bit of both, quite explicitly so in fact.[2] In order to monitor the effects and effectiveness of the reform and its several subsequent modifications, the Canada Employment Insurance Commission was created with the specific mandate of producing an annual report based on the latest in-house and independent research. The Commission's instructions are quite clear in treating cost saving as every bit as important a criterion of success as providing the temporarily unemployed with adequate earnings replacement and active support in finding (new) employment.[3]

12.2 THE EMPLOYMENT INSURANCE REFORM: A BRIEF OVERVIEW

The 1996 Reform was the culmination of three converging forces. After a decade of rather exuberant expansion beginning with the passing of the 1971 Unemployment Insurance Act (see McIntosh and Boychuk, 2000, pp. 85–7), the federal UI system came under increasingly severe criticism during the 1980s. Two weighty Royal Commissions, the Royal Commission on the Economic Union and Development Prospects for Canada (the Macdonald Commission) and the Commission of Inquiry on Unemployment Insurance (the Forget Commission) strongly criticised the system for encouraging chronic dependence on UI benefits, providing too little incentive for the unemployed to accept suitable employment and thus for inhibiting the proper functioning of the labour market (Canada, 1985; 1986; McIntosh and Boychuk, 2000, pp. 87–8; Martel, Laplante and Bernard, 2005, pp. 248–9). Similar criticisms were voiced by economists (for example, Grubel, 1988). Second, and not wholly unrelated, the desirability of emphasising 'active' rather than 'passive' (income-supporting) labour market policies became increasingly accepted across the political spectrum, as it did elsewhere in the advanced economies. This led to a series of much-publicised but short-lived new initiatives which particularly stressed the need to (re-)train the labour force in view of the rising skill requirements of the new 'knowledge economy' (see, for example, Mahon, 1990; Miller, 1994; Van den Berg, Furåker, and Johansson, 1997, pp. 39–40; Van den Berg and Smucker, 1992; Yates, 1995). Third, and according to some critics by far most important, the federal government embarked on a massive cost-cutting campaign from the early to mid-1990s on, with the aim of eliminating the annual deficit and reducing the federal public debt (McIntosh and Boychuk, 2000, pp. 90–92; Miller, 1994; Haddow, 1998).

After several years of unsatisfactory tinkering with the existing Unemployment Insurance system by successive governments (see Lin, 1998; Van den Berg and Smucker, 1992), the government passed Bill C-12, the Employment Insurance Act, in 1996. The Act consisted of two distinct thrusts, one to implement a series of changes in the structure and eligibility rules of the unemployment benefit system and the second to introduce a new, more coherent organisation of active labour market policies intended to enhance the efficiency and flexibility of the Canadian labour market and to strengthen Canadians' labour force attachment.

12.2.1 The Reform Part I: Changing Benefits Rules

The benefits rules changes implemented by Bill C-12 were meant, on the one hand, to tighten the rules of eligibility for unemployment insurance benefits so as to reduce what were seen to be inappropriate uses and abuses of the system as well as to reduce costs. But it also contained a number of measures, particularly with respect to part-time workers and parental leave schemes, which were intended to increase levels of and accessibility to earnings replacement benefits. The main reforms were the following:

- Hours-based eligibility. Eligibility for benefits is based on the total number of hours worked rather than on the number of weeks of 15 hours worked or more. Instead of having to have worked between 12 and 20 weeks of 15 hours or more during the 52 weeks preceding the claim, claimants need to have worked, and contributed insurance premiums, between 420 and 700 hours before being able to claim benefits.[4] This effectively makes EI benefits accessible to part-time workers working less than 15 hours a week as well as workers with irregular but particularly intense work patterns, such as some seasonal workers. On the other hand, it increases the total minimum number of hours one has to have worked to qualify for benefits from between 180–300 hours to 420–700 hours.
- More demanding eligibility requirements for New Entrants or re-entrants. New entrants or re-entrants, defined as those with less than 490 hours of insurable employment during the year preceding the

claim, are required to work for 910 hours before being eligible for EI benefits.[5]

- Reduced benefit period. The maximum benefit entitlement period has been reduced from 50 to 45 weeks. The maximum benefit period also varies by EI region, depending on local levels of unemployment (see fn. 3 above), so that effective maximum benefit periods actually vary from 14 to 45 weeks.

- Reduction of maximum insurable earnings (MIE). The MIE is reduced by more than 10 per cent from $845 (€605) a week to $750 (€535) and has remained frozen at this level ever since. As a result, given the 55 per cent replacement ratio (see below), the maximum benefit rate payable is reduced to $413 (€280) per week from $465 (€335).

- Tightened benefit calculation. Benefits are calculated by dividing the earnings received over the 26-week period preceding the claim by the weeks of work or the minimum 'divisor' ranging from 14 to 22 (depending on EI region, see footnote 4 above), whichever is greatest, multiplied by the 55 per cent replacement ratio.[6] The 'divisor' is two above the number of weeks of work required as the minimum entrance requirement and is intended to give claimants a strong incentive to work at least 2 weeks longer than the minimum necessary before claiming benefits.

- Tightened repayment of benefits rule ('clawback'). The earnings threshold after which recipients must pay back up to 30 per cent of benefits received was lowered by 20 per cent for those who have received 20 weeks or less of benefits during the past 5 years and by 40 per cent for those who have received more than 20 weeks of benefits. The maximum repayment rate varies from 50 to 100 per cent, depending on the number of weeks of benefits received. But the more-than-20-weeks rule was abolished again in 2000, while first-time benefit claimants were exempted from the clawback rule and the maximum repayment rates were reduced somewhat.

- Intensity rule. In order to discourage multiple use of EI benefits as a regular income supplement, the regular benefit rate (that is, 55 per cent of insured earnings) is reduced by one percentage-point for each 20 weeks of benefits collected in the previous five years up to a maximum reduction of five per cent, potentially reducing the rate to 50 per cent of ensured earnings. However, after disappointing results with this new restriction, this rule was rescinded again in 2000.

- Family supplement. Claimants with dependent children and annual net family incomes of two-thirds of the MIE or less are entitled to a top-up of basic insurance benefits, raising the maximum replacement rate to 65 per cent in 1997 and eventually to 80 per cent in 2000. This change involves a switch from an individual-earnings to a family-income eligibility criterion as well as a significant increase in benefit level.

- Maternal and parental benefits enhanced. In 2000 Bill C-32 expanded the maternity and parental leave program. Whereas the maximum benefit period for maternal leaves for mothers of newborn and adopted children remained at 15 weeks, the maximum period for parental leave (tenable by either parent) was lengthened from 10 to 35 weeks and the entrance requirement was reduced from 700 to 600 insurable hours of work. In 2002 the total number of 'special benefit' weeks allowed (sickness, maternal and parental) was increased to a maximum of 65 weeks.[7]

Table 12.1 shows overall expenditures on income claims from the EI program for the fiscal year 2005–06 as well as trends since 1995–96, the last full fiscal year before the EI Reform took effect, in numbers of claims, average weekly benefits and total amounts paid.

*Table 12.1 Post-reform EI program activity compared to the last full year of UI**

Fiscal year (Ending March 31)	1995–96	1997–98	1999–00	2001–02	2003–04	2005–06
Number of new claims (in 1000)	1,818	1,498	1,361	1,480	1,493	1,350
Total amount of benefits (in 1000 dollars)	9,527	7,717	7,026	8,008	8,769	8,054
Average weekly benefits (dollars)	276	277	283	305	312	324

Note: *EI benefits and expenditures associated with Employment Benefit and Support Measures (EBSMs) are not included.

Source: Gray, 2004. Updated using 2006 Monitoring and Assessment Report (Canada Employment Insurance Commission, 2007).

12.2.2 The Reform Part II: 'Active' Labour Market Programs.

'Part II' of the Reform consists of a whole collection of programs and initiatives in which all so-called 'active EI clients', individuals who are unemployed with a current EI benefits claim, and 'former EI clients', those who had such a claim ending during the preceding three years, are eligible to participate.[8] The most important ones can be summarised as follows:[9]

Employment Benefits Programs

- Targeted Wage Subsidies are intended to provide work experience for the unemployed by providing a wage subsidy to employers hiring insured participants whom they would not normally hire in the absence of a subsidy.
- Targeted Earnings Supplements are meant to encourage 'EI clients' and especially the longer-term unemployed, to accept low-wage jobs by temporarily topping-up earnings from such jobs.
- The Self-Employment Program provides financial assistance and business planning advice to EI-eligible participants to help them start their own businesses, covering personal living expenses and other expenses during the initial stages of the development of their business.
- Job Creation Partnerships projects fund the creation of jobs in the community and local social economy sector to permit participants to gain work experience that will lead to ongoing employment.
- Skills Development provides financial assistance and guidance to help participants to obtain skills relevant to employment through additional schooling and apprenticeships. Apprentices receive ordinary EI benefits during their apprenticeships and may also obtain help in covering additional expenses such as travel costs.

Support Services

- Employment Assistance Services include counselling, training in job search skills, job finding clubs, job placement services and the provision of labour market information.
- Labour Market Partnerships provide funding to help partners, which can be employers, employees, employee and/or employer associations or communities, to implement labour force adjustments in industries or sectors in distress. It primarily involves helping to plan adjustments in cases of large (impending) lay-offs such as those in the forestry industry in British Columbia and automobile manufacturing in Ontario.
- The Aboriginal Human Resources Development Strategy (AHRDS) consists of agreements with Aboriginal organisations granting them the authority to design and deliver employment programs and services that reflect and serve the needs of Aboriginal people at the community level.[10]

For 2005–06 expenditure levels for these various programs and services, see Table 12.2.

Table 12.2 Expenditures on employment benefits and support measures (EBSM) for fiscal 2005–06

In $ 1000s by Intervention in 2005–06	
Employment Benefits[*]	
Targeted Wage Subsidies	96,580
Self-Employment	145,873
Job Creation Partnerships	60,283
Skills Development	919,257
Total Employment Benefits	1,221,993
Support Measures (Services)[1)]	502,787
Other Support Measures[1)]	138,630
Total EBSMs-Regular	1,863,410

Note: *Includes expenditures ($8.5 million) for Aboriginal groups in Nova Scotia, Ontario and British Columbia.

12.3 THE REFORM IN ACTION: ACTIVATION OR JUST COST-CUTTING?

There have by now been a large number of studies conducted, both at the behest of the Canada Employment Insurance Commission (CEIC) and by independent academics, of the effects of many of the reforms implemented under the new EI system. Here we will summarise only the portion of their findings relating more or less directly to the issues of labour market flexibility as well as to access to benefits and their (re-)distributive aspects. Although relatively generous after the major reforms of the 1970s (Lin, 1998), the Canadian UI system has been gradually tightened up in terms of eligibility restrictions and benefit levels over the years, in response to persistent political concerns about allegedly widespread overuse and the danger of fostering labour market rigidities through the supposed disincentives produced by an 'overly generous' benefit system. While the Canadian labour market certainly never exhibited the level of apparent rigidity experienced in some of the European countries, particularly with respect to long-term (12 months and more) unemployment, the chronically higher levels of unemployment in Canada than in the US have been routinely blamed on Canada's 'excessively' generous UI rules (for example, Grubel, 1988). The overall result of the gradual tightening up of the Canadian system have brought it closer into line with what is now often referred to as the

'Anglo-Saxon Market Model', one that is considerably more restrictive, punitive and less generous than the various versions of the 'European Social Model' found in most countries on the European Continent.

The contrast usually drawn between the two 'models' is one between an allegedly 'free market' approach emphasising minimal interference with market mechanisms versus a more interventionist approach emphasising security and equity. The former is widely held to produce more flexible and efficient labour markets but at the cost of high levels of inequality and poverty as it forces workers to accept whatever (low-paid) work is available whereas the latter is claimed to be more equitable but possibly at the cost of greater rigidities. However, some advocates of the European Model have long argued that a combination of generous, redistributive benefits and well-designed 'active' labour market policies aimed at reintegrating the unemployed and low-skilled into the workforce and at facilitating labour force entry for those currently outside, is capable of producing the best of both worlds: equity and security as well as labour market flexibility (see, for example, Van den Berg, Furåker and Johansson, 1997, Chapter 4; see also Chapter 6 by Muffels and Luijkx in this book). The underlying concern of the research inspired by the Transitional Labour Market approach is to precisely find out when, where and how this is in fact the case.

As can be seen from the summary overview presented in the previous section, the Canadian EI Reform contains elements of both. On the one hand, it contains a number of new restrictions and reductions that, from a European standpoint, may appear almost punitive, but on the other it also introduces a considerably expanded emphasis on an array of active policies. But note that, even among the active policies there are some – most strikingly the Targeted Wage Subsidies program – which explicitly seeks to encourage workers to accept low-paid jobs where available, that appear more in line with the restrictive Anglo-Saxon approach than with the European Social Model. Be this as it may, when considering the effects of the reform it is of obvious importance to examine both the effects on accessibility to benefits and the effects on labour market mobility.

12.3.1 Effects on Access to Benefits

By OECD standards, income inequality in Canada is about halfway between the most and the least unequal countries. Moreover, unlike other Anglo-Saxon countries that have energetically pursued policies of labour market deregulation in recent years (the US, Great Britain, New Zealand) the rise in income inequality in Canada since the beginning of the 1990s has been relatively modest (see, for example, Alderson and Nielsen, 2002; Atkinson, 2003; Smeeding, 2002; Smith, 2002). This appears to have much to do with the redistributive effects of Canadian labour market and welfare state programs (Smeeding, 2005; Haddow, 2000, pp. 46–47). Critics have warned, however, that this compensatory effect may be significantly reduced as a result of the EI Reform and concurrent reductions in social assistance benefits in the mid-1990s (Haddow, 2000, p. 47; McIntosh and Boychuk, 2000).

At first sight, the effects of the Reform might appear to be fairly dramatic. Table 12.3 compares a number of activity indicators for the EI program with figures for the UI program in the last full fiscal year preceding the reform, that is, 1995–96. On the face of it, the Reform succeeded remarkably well in cutting the cost of the unemployment benefits program. Overall expenditures on 'regular' benefits – that is, excluding benefits paid to participants in 'active' programs and 'special' benefits such as those for maternity, parenting, sickness and the fishery industry – fell by 19 per cent between 1995–96 and 1997–98, from 9.5 to 7.7 billion dollars. This reduction appears to have been primarily the result of a reduction in the number of new claimants, which dropped by 18 per cent over the same period, while average weekly benefits remained virtually unchanged. Can we conclude, then, that the new, more restrictive eligibility and benefit level rules of the EI program have succeeded in engineering a cost saving for the Canadian Federal government of some $1.8 billion by excluding close to one fifth of formerly eligible unemployed workers from access to insurance benefits?

Things are not quite so simple. Note that all three categories of claimants dropped considerably in number and that the smallest drop, proportionately, occurred for 'frequent claimants', precisely the group targeted most clearly by the EI reform. This suggests that some considerable part of the reduction in numbers of claimants may be due to conditions in the labour market rather than changes in the rules governing access to insurance benefits. In fact, the years in question were characterised by rapid employment growth in much of the Canadian economy. As a result, the numbers of recently laid-off workers who were most likely to be eligible for EI benefits, declined sharply while the number of new entrants into the labour market grew as the prospects of finding work brightened, leaving a relatively larger proportion of unemployed workers not eligible because they quit voluntarily, did not have a previous job or had been unemployed for more than 12 months. Based on an analysis of detailed monthly statistics on unemployed regular EI beneficiaries, the 1998 'Employment Insurance Monitoring and Assessment Report' concludes that at most one third of the reduction in the number of EI beneficiaries between 1995–96 and 1997–98 could be the result of the EI Reform, while somewhere between one third and one half of the overall expenditure reduction might be attributed to the Reform, the remainder being due to changes in labour market conditions (CEIC, 1998, pp. 59–61).

It is perhaps also worth dwelling briefly on the trend in frequent claimant numbers shown in Table 12.3. Recall that the 'intensity rule' was introduced as part of the EI Reform specifically to discourage this category of claimants. But as can be seen from the Table, the rule apparently had little or no effect. In fact, the percentage of frequent claimants as a proportion of all regular claimants actually increased somewhat, from 38.8 per cent in 1995–96 to 41.1 per cent in 1997–98 and then declined back to the earlier level again by 1999–2000. Quite likely, this disappointing result was the reason why the intensity rule was repealed again in 2001. But note that from 2000–2001 onwards, the proportion of frequent claimants began to decline and even more so in the two years after that, that is, after the repeal of the intensity rule.

Table 12.3 Post-reform EI program activity compared to the last full year of UI (numbers x 1000)

Fiscal year (ending 31 March)	1995–96	1997–98	1998–99	1999–00	2000–01	2001–02	2002–03	2003–04
Number of new claimants	1,818	1,498	1,488	1,361	1,372	1,480	1,428	1,493
Frequent claimants	706	616	585	526	500	500	492	510
Occasional claimants	623	475	470	431	442	475	465	485
First time claimants	490	407	433	405	430	505	471	499
Total amount of benefits (x 1000 dollars)	9,527	7,717	7,754	7,026	6,834	8,008	8,206	8,769
Average weekly benefits (dollars)	276	277	282	283	297	305	309	312

Notes: EI benefits and expenditures associated with Employment Benefit and Support Measures (EBSMs) are not included. Frequent claimants in the year of observation are defined as those having filed separate EI claims in three of the past five years, while occasional claimants are defined as those having filed separate EI claims in one or two of the past five years, exclusive of first-time claimants.

Source: Gray, 2004, Annual EI Monitoring and Assessment Reports, Annex 2, Table 2.3 ('Regular Benefits').

The reason for this were undoubtedly the major leaps in the numbers of first-time and occasional claimants which occurred during this period which was characterised by a sudden economic slowdown. As Gray (2004, p. 2) has suggested, this may well have been the result of the buoyant labour market of

1999–2000 that may have helped many more or less marginal workers and relatively new entrants to qualify for EI benefits before the sudden subsequent downturn.

A question still remains, however, how exactly the EI Reform could have reduced the number of regular claimants by a third, as claimed in the 1998 Report. The only other group of potential claimants, besides the aforementioned frequent claimants, for whom access to benefits became more restricted under the new system were new entrants and re-entrants into the labour force, referred to in the jargon as 'NEREs'. Recall, however, that the Reform also expanded access to benefits by replacing the 15-hour week-based eligibility criterion with one based on total hours worked. This change might be expected to have benefited NEREs in particular since a disproportionate number of them are likely to be marginal or part-time workers who might not have been able to qualify under the old weeks-based system. Consequently, it is no easy task to try and estimate the overall effect of the EI Reform on their access to benefits.

Several carefully conducted statistical analyses have tried to discern the effects of these two seemingly opposed factors (Kapsalis, 2000; Phipps and McPhail, 2000). Their conclusion seems to be that the net effect on NEREs' access to EI benefits has been small. The tightening of eligibility rules for NEREs does seem to have had a significant effect in rendering a considerable proportion (up to 7 per cent, see Kapsalis, 2000) who would have been eligible for UI benefits ineligible for benefits under the EI system affecting young workers in particular (Audas and Murell, 2000, pp. 21–23). On the other hand, much of this reduction appears to have been counterbalanced by two opposite forces. First, as expected, the switch to an hours-based system of eligibility assessment does appear to have benefited entrants so that the net reduction of numbers of eligible entrants as a result of the EI Reform turns out to have been quite small (Phipps and McPhail, 2000). In addition, however, an ongoing study of NEREs commissioned by the CEIC (Audit and Evaluation Directorate, 2004) has found that there was a significant increase in the number of hours worked by those NEREs who just barely qualified for EI benefits, which had the result, together with the switch to an hours-based system, of virtually neutralising the effect of the tightening of the rules on the numbers of NERE claimants. Thus, the working population appears to have adjusted its labour market behaviour rather effectively to the new eligibility rules in this respect. Furthermore, new and re-entrants were overwhelmingly concentrated among youth. It should be kept in mind, however, that the period covered was one of exceptional and sustained growth in employment, with the exception of the brief slowdown of 2001–2002, and that demographic trends undoubtedly play a major role in producing these findings as well.

The conclusion that the changes in rules have had only modest effects on access to EI benefits is confirmed by other studies of the effect of the switch to hours-based eligibility. These studies suggest that, if anything, the net effect has been to slightly increase the access to insurance benefits, by a little over 2 per cent of all job separators (Sweetman, 2000). This appears to have especially affected seasonal workers working, or being able to work, long hours during a relatively short number of weeks (Green and Riddell, 2000).

Can we conclude, then, that the EI Reform has had little or no negative effect at all on access to insurance benefits for Canadian workers who have lost their jobs? According to one of the studies commissioned by the CEIC (Bertrand et al., forthcoming), 88.4 per cent of Canadian workers would be eligible for EI benefits if they lost their jobs, the remaining 11.6 per cent being new or re-entrants without the number of working hours required to qualify. Only some of these latter non-eligibles are likely to have been affected by the new, more restrictive rules on eligibility. Thus, the degree of coverage of the target labour force would seem to have remained quite high even after the Reform. The 'Employment Insurance Coverage Survey' conducted since 1997 by Statistics Canada shows that in 2006, 82.7 per cent of the unemployed target population (those who had lost or quit their jobs with 'just cause' in the preceding 12 months) were eligible for EI benefits (Statistics Canada, 2007). But at the same time, the actual beneficiary-to-unemployed (B/U) ratio was only 45 per cent in 2006. The Canadian Labour Congress (CLC, 2003) views the sharp decline in the B/U ratio since the late 1980s (see Figure 12.1) as evidence for a dramatic decline in unemployment insurance coverage as a result of a series of increasingly restrictive changes in the eligibility rules inspired by a neoliberal policy agenda, including the 1996 Reform.

Some caveats are in order here, however. First, as several careful analyses have pointed out, the B/U ratio has a number of important flaws as a measure of EI coverage. The most important of these has to do with the fact that its numerator and denominator cover somewhat different populations and that the denominator lumps together an enormously heterogeneous population of individuals, many of whom would not qualify for unemployment benefits under any insurance system (for example, new entrants, those who have exhausted their benefits, those not making claims for one reason or another; see Jones, 2004; Gray and Sweetman, 2004; Shillington, 2004; Applied Research Branch, 1998).

Second, as can be seen from Figure 12.1, the bulk of the decline took place between 1989 and 1996, that is, before the EI Reform could have had any major effect. Third, a declining B/U ratio could also be caused by independent changes in the labour market, such as the (re-)entry of large numbers of workers without previous work experience, producing a rise of the number of unemployed who are not eligible for such benefits.

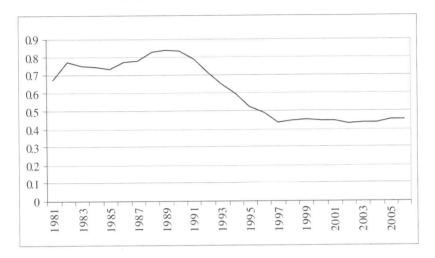

Figure 12.1 Beneficiary to unemployed (B/U) ratio

A study conducted by HDRC's Applied Branch (1998) estimates that less than half of the decline of the B/U ratio may be attributed to program changes in the UI/EI program, the remainder being due to changes in the composition of the unemployed population (see also CEIC, 2005, pp. 55–59; CEIC, 2007, p. 48).[11] Of course, the large reduction in regular unemployment benefits expenditures after the EI Reform could be due at least in part to the reduction in the level of average weekly benefits and/or the reduction in the average number of weeks during which those benefits are received that the Reform sought to produce as well. But since, as Table 12.1 shows, the average weekly benefit level actually increased gradually since 1995–96, reflecting rising insured wage levels rather than any changes in the rules, this cannot have been a major factor. Nor can the average duration account for much of the reduction in expenditure. According to one study, the effective average benefit entitlement period was reduced by at most 0.3 weeks as a result of the Reform (Sweetman, 2000). Yet the actual average benefit period actually went up slightly, by about half a week, for claimants starting their benefit period in 1997–98 as compared to 1995–96 claimants (CEIC, 1998, p. 60) and it has hovered between 20 and 22 weeks ever since (Gray, 2004, p. 3). At the same time, results of more sophisticated econometric studies are contradictory, some suggesting that EI did have a slightly downward effect on overall average benefit reception spells (Lacroix and Van Audenrode, 2000), others showing no effect (Jones, 2000). Here, too, it is likely that we have the combined effects of improving labour market conditions and the counteracting tightening and loosening provisions of the EI Reform.

But such figures do not directly address the question of whether and to what extent the expenditure cuts were achieved at the cost of greater hardship for the unemployed, as critics have predicted. A better measure of this would be the degree to which the unemployed find it necessary to use up the benefits to which they are legally entitled. One indicator of this is the proportion of maximum entitlements used up by the average benefits recipient. Surprisingly, several studies have found that the proportion of total entitlements used up by the average regular claimant actually declined from 64.1 per cent in 1995–96 to around 60 cent, even during the 2001 economic downturn. Similarly, if anything the proportion of claimants using up all the benefits they are entitled to has decreased, from 36.5 per cent in 1995–96 to less than 30 per cent in 2004–05 (CEIC, 2007, pp. 56–7).

Another way of trying to determine the amount of hardship that may have been caused by the Reform is to look at the proportion of job losers who are forced to resort to social assistance within 12 months after the loss of their jobs. Again, somewhat surprisingly, two studies suggest that this proportion declined from slightly over 6 per cent in 1995–96 to less than 4 per cent even during the recession of 2001 (see CEIC, 2005, p. 69; Audit and Evaluation Directorate, 2003a; Audit and Evaluation Directorate, 2001; Grey, 2002). This finding should be particularly surprising in light of the dire predictions that some have made about the likely effect of the EI Reform on poverty levels (Haddow, 2000, p. 47; McIntosh and Boychuk, 2000). However, this too, is undoubtedly in part a case of improving labour market conditions drowning out whatever negative effects the EI Reform might have had.[12] In addition, it may well reflect the fact that eligibility rules and benefit rates of provincial social assistance plans have also been tightened for budgetary reasons during this period (McIntosh and Boychuk, 2000, pp. 75–81, 101–3).

Yet another measure of potential hardship is loss of consumption power after job loss. According to another of the HRSD studies (Audit and Evaluation Directorate, (2003b) no more than 12 per cent of those who had lost their jobs experienced a decrease in consumer spending one year after. The average drop of consumption spending for this group was nevertheless a significant 24 per cent of monthly household income. Single-earner families and especially single parents were, for obvious reasons, most vulnerable to a drop of spending capacity due to job loss. We do not know, however, whether this is a deterioration or an improvement relative to the pre-Reform situation. But again, this result must be interpreted in view of the generally favourable labour market during the period under study as well as the prevalence of multiple-earner families and even the willingness to maintain spending levels in spite of earnings losses by using credit and other forms of debt. This, too, is an area in which much research still needs to be done.

One recent study (Martel, Laplante and Bernard, 2005) has tried to compare the time it takes families to regain their pre-unemployment income (not consumption spending) after an unemployment spell of one of their members before and after the Reform using the SLID panel dataset. It concludes that this period was shortened somewhat after the Reform, even as the odds of receiving benefits after becoming unemployed are significantly reduced under the new regime. While the authors interpret their findings as suggesting that the less generous EI system forces the unemployed into accepting possibly less desirable jobs more quickly than was the case under the UI system, it could equally be the result of relatively more favourable economic conditions. The more rapid recovery of pre-unemployment family income after the Reform does not, at any rate, constitute direct evidence of greater economic hardship caused by the Reform.

The other changes in the benefit rules implemented are less controversial since their budgetary importance is modest and they are generally measures that increase rather than restrict access to benefits. We can briefly summarise their major effects here. Some 155,000 claimants (out of a total of 1,827 million) received the Family Supplement for families with low incomes during the most recent reporting period for which data are available (2005–06). While the average top-up was a modest $43 (€30) per week, this still adds up to some $2200 (€1500) worth of additional annual income. Initial studies suggest that the new system does improve the degree to which low-income families are targeted by the family income criterion, but raise questions about the possible negative effects on women's dependence on their husbands' earnings. Given the modesty of the benefits and the fact that much poverty is linked to lack of labour force attachment and thus ineligibility for any kind of EI benefits, the effect of the supplement on overall poverty levels remains very small (Cheal and Kampen, 2000; Phipps, MacDonald and McPhail, 2000).

Access to and take-up of maternal and parental benefits appears to be quite high. Among Canadian women with children aged 12 months or younger who had earned insurable income, some 86 per cent received maternal and/or parental benefits in 2005–06. Women collected around 30 weeks of benefits on average. While men have increasingly made use of parental leave benefits, their relative numbers remain small and they tend to take much shorter leave (14.9 weeks on average; see CEIC, 2007, pp. 53–4; Marshall, 2003). Calculated in a slightly different way, around 90 per cent of mothers who left their employment to take care of new-born children reported receiving maternity and/or parental benefits both before and after the EI Reform (HRDC, 2001c). The introduction of an hours-worked eligibility rule did not have a dramatic effect on working women's access to maternity leave, as a relatively large proportion of women with children in Canada work full-time or nearly full-time. The extension, in 2000, of the maximum leave period, on the other hand, did have an immediate and dramatic effect, pushing up the median length of maternal/parental leaves from 25 to 50 weeks within a year (Audit and Evaluation Directorate, 2005; see also Perusse, 2003). Since 2001, Canada compares relatively favourably to other advanced countries in terms of the total duration of benefit-supported parental leaves, but the level of benefits remains rather low, especially when compared to the Nordic countries (Phipps and Lethbridge, 2005).

12.3.2 Impact on Labour Force Transitions

As for the effects of the Canadian EI system on labour mobility and labour market flexibility, and in particular on the ability and willingness of Canadian workers to undertake a variety of labour market transitions, the picture is considerably more complicated. First, there are the two distinct components of the EI system to consider, the 'passive' regular and special benefits programs and the 'active' programs covered by 'Part II' of the EI Act. A primary goal of both has been to enhance labour force attachment. In fact, as noted, the main purpose of the reform of the benefits system was 'to strengthen the link between work effort and benefits' (CEIC, 2004, p. 56). Obviously, then, the Reform intended to promote particularly one type of transition, the transition from unemployment to employment. Nevertheless, the system does contain a number of 'special' benefits, especially for parents of young children, that do enable beneficiaries temporarily to withdraw from market-paid employment. An important question with respect to these benefits is whether they have increased or decreased the beneficiaries' labour force attachment.

Effects of the new benefits rules

The question of greatest practical and theoretical concern is whether the Reform has effectively helped to accelerate the rate at which the unemployed find new jobs. In theory at least, the changes made to the unemployment insurance system were meant to induce changes in job search behaviour which should lead to shorter unemployment and benefit claiming spells (Jones, 2000, p. 1). The most sophisticated econometric studies have tried to assess the effects of the EI Reform as a whole on the duration of unemployment spells, other things being equal, that is, controlling for a host of other factors including changes in labour market conditions, demographic composition, occupational structure, season, and so on. In other words, they do not explicitly distinguish between the effects of changes in the benefits system as opposed to the greater emphasis on 'active' labour market policies. Nevertheless, in view of the still relatively modest numbers involved in those 'active' measures (see below), the tacit assumption is that most of the effects uncovered in these large-scale statistical analyses must be due to the changes in the benefits system.

The few available econometric studies agree more or less in their results (Lacroix and Van Audenrode, 2000; Jones, 2000; Shen, 2004). They find that the shift to the EI regime did have a statistically significant, albeit modest, effect in shortening average unemployment spells. By one estimate, the 'hazard' of exiting from unemployment to a job has increased, as a result of the Reform, by between 10 and 20 per cent at any one time during the spell of unemployment (Jones, 2000), which would have a significant, but small effect on overall average spells. Somewhat surprisingly, however, the implementation of the EI Reform seems to have affected adult (that is, older than 25 years of age) males more than females and it appears to have had little or no effect on the labour market behaviour of young workers. This is particularly puzzling in view of the importance of the greater restrictions imposed on new entrants and re-entrants in terms of eligibility criteria by the EI Reform, which should have affected women and young workers disproportionately. Also, according to the findings of Martel, Laplante and Bernard (2005, p. 259), the Reform appears to have had no significant effect on the search behaviour of the unemployed, which, once again, suggests that factors other than the Reform itself may have been more important in producing the above results.

Other aspects of the labour market that the EI Reform was designed to affect have been examined by a handful of studies many of which were commissioned by the Department of Human Resources Development Canada. The main purpose of the switch from the weeks-based (of 15 hours or more) to an hours-based calculation of benefit eligibility was to eliminate the possible distorting effect that the old system might have had on hours worked. In particular, the old UI system was thought to have led employers to split jobs so as to create more jobs of less-than-15 hours per week so as to be able to avoid having to pay unemployment insurance premiums, and seasonal workers to spread their seasonal jobs over the maximum number of weeks of 15 or more hours. It turns out, however, that the effects on overall eligibility for benefits of this switch are quite varied and complicated, depending on overall hours and numbers of weeks worked and the level of local unemployment (see Friesen and Maki, 2000, pp. 3–5). Nevertheless, several studies of the likely effect of the switch on (the distribution of) hours worked agree that it has been more or less as predicted: the proportion of jobs of less than 15 hours per week has declined somewhat whereas the proportion of jobs with very long hours (over 40) has increased, especially in the

Atlantic provinces and among seasonal workers (Green and Riddell, 2000; Friesen and Maki, 2000; Sweetman, 2000). Moreover, the switch also seems to have been of benefit to many multiple job-holders who were likely to be uninsured for at least one of their part-time jobs under the old UI system. There is some evidence that suggests that multiple job-holding did in fact increase significantly (by between 5 and 6 per cent) in response to the switch (see HRDC, 2001a; Sweetman, 2000, p. 7–8).

A particularly sensitive issue in Canada, both politically and economically, is whether and to what extent the regional variation in eligibility criteria has produced a dependency on UI/EI transfers in regions with chronically high levels of unemployment and seasonal employment, especially the Atlantic Provinces (Newfoundland, New Brunswick, Nova Scotia and Prince Edward Island). Critics have long held that the excessive 'generosity' of the system in these provinces has encouraged a 'culture' of dependency, helped artificially to sustain inefficient industries and jobs and inhibited migration out of these provinces to provinces with labour shortages (see, for example, Canada, 1986; Kaufman et al., 2003; Audas and Murell, 2000; Day and Winer, 2001; May and Hollet, 1995; Vincent et al., 2003). But since the regional variation in eligibility rules has remained unaffected by the EI Reform, one would not expect major changes in EI-claiming behaviour in the Atlantic provinces. The only noticeable effect may be the lengthening of the work week in seasonal employment due to the switch to hours-based eligibility rules, as already noted (see also HRDC, 2001b). On the other hand, the so-called 'intensity rule' was explicitly meant to discourage frequent claims and may have had some modest discouraging effects in the Atlantic provinces (Audas and Murell, 2000), but, as noted, it was repealed again in 2000.

On the question of the effects of EI on mobility and migration, expert opinion appears to be divided. While critics insist that the mobility-deterring effects of UI were substantial and that they have not been adequately addressed by the EI Reform (Kaufman et al., 2003; May and Hollet, 1995), studies of labour mobility tend to show that the effects of UI were minimal at worst (Day and Winer, 2001) and that there is no compelling evidence of any direct relationship at all between the EI program and mobility (Audas and McDonald, 2003). The rate of inter-community mobility appears to be quite high, particularly among EI claimants (Canadian Employment Insurance Commission, 2004, p. 40), and, as might be expected, it appears to have been unaffected, one way or the other, by the introduction of the Reform measures (Audit and Evaluation Directorate, 2004a).

The introduction of the so-called 'divisor' to calculate benefits payable was intended to affect the labour market behaviour of potential benefits claimants in a quite specific manner: it should give them a strong incentive to work two weeks beyond what is necessary to be eligible so as to maximise the benefits they are entitled to. This new rule appears to have had exactly the intended effect: the proportion of claimants who did not work at least two weeks beyond the minimum eligibility requirement dropped by more than half, from 6 per cent prior to the EI Reform to 2.5 per cent at the end of 1997, and has remained below 4 per cent ever since, in spite of the ups and downs in labour market conditions since then (CEIC, 2007, p. 59).

As mentioned, the rate of take-up of maternal and parental benefits by working parents (that is, mostly mothers) of new-born and adopted children has been quite high under both the old UI and the new EI systems. From the transitional labour market perspective the most important question is whether and to what extent these kinds of benefits have enhanced or weakened the beneficiaries' attachment to the labour force. In other words, are these benefits used primarily to support a temporary absence from paid employment, as they were intended to? One study addresses this question for the period immediately before and after the Reform (HDRC, 2001c). It reports that under both systems about 9 per cent of maternal/parental benefits recipients had not (yet) returned to paid employment by the 75th week after the initial job separation. Of those returning to paid employment, around 85 per cent returned to the same job. The study reports that 'there has been no apparent impact of the switch from UI to EI on the probability of an early return to paid employment'.

These findings are perhaps not that surprising since no major changes were made to these programs until the major extension of benefit periods introduced in December 2000. An important question from the point of view of transitional labour markets is whether and how these extensions, which effectively increased the maximum number of weeks of 'special' (maternal, parental and sickness) benefits for the sake of taking care of new-born or adopted children from 40 to 65 weeks, affected the labour market behaviour of the beneficiaries. Did it loosen or strengthen their eventual attachment to the labour force? Two CEIC-commissioned studies come to the firm conclusion that the new extended benefits have, if anything, increased the probability of an eventual return to paid employment by beneficiaries (CEIC, 2005, Annex 5, pp. 5.22–23; Ten Cate, 2004). Thus, the maternal and paternal leave component of the EI system appear to have had the intended effect of strengthening the labour force attachment of mothers while allowing them to take leave to stay home with their newborn or newly adopted children. Interestingly, other studies have found that legal job protection rather than the amount of benefits obtainable are the crucial factor in determining women's decisions to take a leave while remaining attached to the labour force (Phipps, Burton and Lethbridge, 2001; Ten Cate, 2003).

According to some critics the modest increase in support for low-income families by means of the new Family Supplement could undermine the work incentive. What little evidence there is, however, suggests that there has been no such effect; between 1994 and 2002 the average number of weeks that recipients of the Supplement were on EI benefits actually declined by a week (Canada Employment Insurance Commission, 2005, pp. 67–68 and Annex 5, pp. 5.18–19).

Do 'active' policies really activate?
While, over the years, Canadian federal governments have launched a series of reforms which were supposed to show their commitment to 'active' labour market policies, the rhetoric has generally been far ahead of the actual practice. Canada has been and remains among the most modest spenders on active labour market policies in relative (proportion of GDP) terms among the OECD countries (see, for example, Martin, 2000; Van den Berg and Smucker, 1992; Van den Berg, Furåker and Johansson, 1997, Chapter 2; OECD, 2007, Chapter 5). However, there is no question that the EI Reform did include a substantial increase in the amount spent on measures, services and programs grouped together under Part II of the legislation. From fiscal year 1995–96 to 1998–99, expenditures on so-called Employment Benefits and Support Measures (EBSMs) rose by 45 per cent from a little over 1.8 to 2.5 billion dollars and have remained between about 2.3 and 2.5 billion ever since (CEIC, 1999, p. 36; CEIC, 2002, p. 28; CEIC, 2004, pp. 24–5 and Annex 2, Table 2.11; CEIC, 2007, Annex 3). This trend is also reflected in the fairly steep rise in the total number of EBSM interventions undertaken between 1995–96 and 1998–99 from around 440,000 to 650,000 interventions. A large part, perhaps half, of this increase is accounted for by the inclusion of 'former EI clients' who would not have been eligible for participation in comparable programs under the old UI system. Unlike expenditures, the number of interventions took another jump in 2001–02, reaching over 950,000 in 2005–06. Virtually all the growth in the numbers of interventions is due to increases in so-called 'short-term' or employment services interventions. These consist mostly of counselling and other employment-seeking assistance services. The numbers of interventions through the so-called 'long-term' employment programs, which include skills development, apprenticeships, wage subsidies, and so on, have actually declined by about one fifth, from around 260,000 to around 170,000 since fiscal year 1998–99 (see CEIC, 1999, p. 35; CEIC, 2002, p. 25; CEIC, 2005, pp. 26–28, Annex 3, Table 3.6; CEIC, 2007, Annex 3, Table 3.6). All other things being equal, a shift from long-term interventions to job search assistance would occur naturally in periods when employment prospects are relatively good. But the greatest shift towards relatively more short-term

services actually occurred in 2001–02, in the wake of a brief recession. It is therefore hard to escape the impression that there has been a longer-term shift underway from the most to the least 'active' labour market programs.

One might think that such a shift was a response to disappointing results of the 'long-term' interventions. But this is unlikely, for the simple reason that little is known so far about the relative effectiveness, let alone cost effectiveness, of any of these active labour market programs. To be sure, the Canada Employment Insurance Commission reports in its annual Monitoring and Assessment Report on the numbers of clients who returned to employment after having undergone one or more interventions and on the amounts of benefits dollars thus 'saved'. And these figures certainly seem quite impressive. Thus, the Commission's 2006 report announces that close to 200,000 EBSM clients returned to work during the 2005–06 fiscal year and that these returns saved the system almost $807 (€575) million in 'unpaid benefits' (CEIC, 2007, p. Annex 3, Tables 3.14 and 3.15).

But these results look decidedly less impressive when put in their proper context. For one thing, the number of returns to work was only about one third of the total number of 'clients' served that year, which was close to 456,000 (ibid., Table 3.5). Second, the 'unpaid benefits' are calculated as the proportion of the maximum benefits that a 'client' was entitled to but which remained unused. But, as we have already mentioned, the average 'client' only uses up about two thirds of this maximum. Moreover, short of carefully designed matched-sample studies there is no way of knowing how much improved labour market conditions – rather than the 'activating' interventions – contributed to these successful returns to employment. Third, as the Commission itself notes, the apparently favourable results of the Apprenticeship Program are largely due to the fact that apprenticeships are often linked to existing jobs for which the apprentices are being trained (CEIC, 2005, p. 34).[13] The Commission is aware of these problems, of course, and rightly cautions against drawing any serious conclusions as to program effectiveness from the figures it reports (ibid., p. 33).[14]

Given these problems, the CEIC has the mandate to commission thorough-going 'summative evaluations' in all (provincial) jurisdictions. A panel of private sector evaluators and independent academics has been convened to develop a methodological framework meeting the highest standards of scientific rigour to study the net impacts of EBSMs, in terms of employment, skills gains, job quality and increased self-sufficiency. By 'net' impact, we mean the incremental impact on 'clients' over and above what would have occurred without the assistance of the program in question, as measured by an appropriately defined and sampled comparison group. The methodologies used include large-scale surveys of 'clients' and members of comparison groups and a variety of qualitative methods including key informant interviews, focus groups, case studies, panels of experts, and so on (see CEIC, 2005, pp. 77–78 and Annex 5, pp. 5.26–5.27).

So far, these summative evaluations have been completed in six jurisdictions: British Columbia, Alberta, Ontario, Quebec, Nunavut and Newfoundland and Labrador. Their results are already proving to be of some interest, particularly when compared to evaluations of similar results in other countries (see Martin, 2000; Martin and Grubb, 2001). Based on the findings so far, the CEIC concludes that 'EBSMs appear to yield mixed results, and where these results are positive, they are modest in their net impact on participants', depending on the type of intervention, client type and jurisdiction (CEIC, 2007, p. 64). The main outcome variables studied were employment and earnings up to 24 months after the intervention and subsequent use of provincial social assistance. The Skills Development program turned out to have modest positive net effects on employment chances and earnings in some jurisdictions for 'active clients' but there was no clear trend discernible for 'former clients'.[15] Rather surprisingly, the Targeted Wage Subsidy turned out to have fairly little impact for the former but positive impacts were found for the latter. The Job Creation Partnership program had either a mixed, no or even a negative impact where it was evaluated. The Self-Employment program also showed a mixture of some positive and some non-significant results. Finally, participation in an EBSM seemed to have quite mixed effects on subsequent EI or social assistance use. The latter, however, may either mean that EBSM participation has somewhat reduced the need to have recourse to social assistance, or it could be the effect of tightened eligibility rules in the provincial social assistance programs (for all these results, see CEIC, 2004, pp. 58–63 and Annex 5, pp. 5.16–17; CEIC, 2005, pp. 77–81 and Annex 5, pp. 5.26–27; CEIC, 2007, pp. 64–67).[16]

It is well known from the international literature on the subject that the evaluation of the net effects of these kinds of policies is fraught with problems relating to the choice of comparison groups, potential self-selection of participants and much more (Martin, 2000). But the variety and kinds of methodologies employed in these 'summative evaluations' certainly do not compare unfavourably with what is currently considered the state of the art in the labour market policy evaluation field and their findings so far appear to be largely in line with those found elsewhere in the literature which also tend to show relatively modest positive effects of an array of 'active' labour market policies in a variety of national and regional settings (see, for example, Martin, 2000; Martin and Grubb, 2001; De Gier and Van den Berg, 2005).

12.4 THE CANADIAN REFORM IN COMPARATIVE PERSPECTIVE

The past couple of decades have witnessed the emergence of something of an international 'post-Keynesian' consensus which has helped to spur similar reforms in labour market policies in a number of otherwise quite different countries (see, for example, De Gier and Van den Berg, 2005, pp. 42–47; Barbier, 2004). The main elements of this consensus are a growing reluctance to rely on government-induced macroeconomic stimuli to increase employment, particularly in the form of deficit spending, and an increasing emphasis on 'active' rather than 'passive' labour market policies.[17] But the way these general goals have been pursued has differed significantly between countries, depending on the pre-existing institutional context, political power constellation and welfare state traditions. Canada has traditionally been in the 'conservative' camp (Haddow, 2000, pp. 48–9; Van den Berg and Smucker, 1992), in particular when compared to the Nordic social democratic countries with which left-leaning critics have tended to compare it (Haddow, 2000; Campeau, 2001; McIntosh and Boychuk, 2000; see also Van den Berg and Smucker, 1992). A brief comparison with the recently implemented labour market policy reforms in Australia and Denmark, the two other case studies presented in this volume, might be instructive.

Australia and Canada undoubtedly to some degree share the Anglo-Saxon settler society's 'rugged individualism' with its attendant suspicion of abuse of 'the dole'. Both certainly have taken a decidedly 'residual' approach to the provision of social welfare. But while Canada, with the significant exception of Québec, has had a relatively weak labour movement, Australia has been famously dubbed a 'wage-earners' welfare state', characterised by relatively strong unions, centralised and state-sanctioned collective bargaining, strong job and industry protection and government commitment to maintaining full employment (Castles, 1994; Harbridge and Bagley, 2002, p. 181; Ziguras and Stricker in this volume). Recent reforms in the two countries appear to reflect these differences in welfare and industrial relations traditions.

During the early 1990s, there were some striking similarities between the two countries' governments' attempts to move in the direction of more emphasis on 'active' labour market policies. In 1994, the Australian Labour government initiated a series of programs under the Working Nation banner which were very similar in design and intent to the Canadian Jobs Strategy introduced in Canada by the Tory government in the late 1980s. Both programs sought to deal with the growing problems of youth and long-term unemployment by seeking to 'reactivate' target groups through intensified labour market assistance, training and job subsidies. Both programs also met with relatively disappointing results and an early demise as the governments initiating them were voted out of office.

It is with these changes of government, from Progressive Conservative ('Tory') to Liberal in Canada in 1993 and from Labour to Liberal-National in Australia in 1996, that the two countries' directions in labour market policies started to diverge. While the new, slightly less conservative Canadian government continued to declare itself committed to more active labour market policy, in practice, as we have seen, deficit reduction and raising eligibility requirements to unemployment benefits became at least as important in the implementation of the 1996 EI Reform. In the end, the much-heralded Reform turned out to be fairly modest in its actual effects in terms of both access reduction and activation. By contrast, the new, more conservative Australian government appeared more intent on fundamental change. It introduced the Work for the Dole scheme, requiring benefit recipients to accept full or part-time work or training or face cuts in their allowances – what is known in North America as 'Workfare'. It introduced privatised employment services and it passed the 1996 Workplace Relations Act with the explicit intent of decentralising the collective bargaining system and deregulating the labour market. While these reforms appear to have had some success in terms of their self-declared aims, they remain controversial (Harbridge and Bagley, 2002, pp. 186–191).[18] While some predict that these reforms will lead to increasing earnings inequality and the precariousness of employment in Australia, the evidence that such trends are actually underway and that they can be wholly or in part attributed to the reforms in question is still lacking.

By contrast, Denmark's celebrated 'flexicurity' model is currently the toast of policy makers and researchers in Europe and beyond (Madsen, 2006, p. 8).[19] Conventionally Denmark is classified as being squarely in the 'social democratic' camp. However, it is probably better characterised as a 'hybrid' case combining features from the liberal as well as the Scandinavian types of welfare state, providing an interesting contrast to the Australian case (Madsen, 2005, p. 280).[20] The Danish system combines a very generous social welfare and unemployment benefits system and a strong commitment to active labour market policies with a highly flexible labour market based on the near absence of restrictive employment protection, putting it close to Canada, the UK and the USA in the OECD rankings of employment protection strictness (see Madsen, 2004, p. 192, 2006, p. 14).

All three major components are, as Madsen points out (2005, pp. 281–284), features of long standing in the 'Danish model'. Yet they have not always produced the remarkable combination of high employment and low unemployment rates, healthy economic growth and low inflation that Denmark is now so widely admired for. As recently as the early 1990s,

Denmark posted unemployment rates close to 10 per cent and long-term (more than 1 year) unemployment rates of around 25 per cent. It was at that time that the Social Democratic government embarked on a major overhaul of the labour market policy system. Instead of reducing the generosity of the benefits, however, the Danish reforms focused on shortening the maximum benefit periods in which beneficiaries would not be required to participate in activation measures to eventually (in 1999) 1 year (from the original 4), increasing the pressure on benefit recipients to seek employment or training, decentralisation of delivery of employment services, and abolishing the 'revolving door' system whereby participation in 'active' programmes counted towards building up eligibility for future unemployment benefit claims. The Conservative–Liberal government that came to power in 2001 implemented its own reforms in 2003, but these were largely in line with the direction set out by the Social Democrats, rationalising the programme structure and increasing the pressure on the long-term unemployed to accept employment and mobility. Most notably, however, not even the Conservative–Liberal government was able to bring down the benefit levels or their accessibility, meeting a united opposition from unions and employers.[21]

The Danish approach appears to have achieved a measure of 'flexicurity', a combination of high labour market mobility and high levels of social security, but it does come at a price (see Madsen in Chapter 13). Whereas Canada spends around 1.2 per cent of GDP on active and passive labour market policies combined, Denmark spends as much as 4.6 per cent (Madsen, 2006, p. 18). Moreover, evaluations of the effects of the various active programmes have produced mixed results, much as they have in Canada and elsewhere. Where job counselling appears to be effective it is hard to distinguish the impact of counselling services from that of a favourable economic climate (the availability of jobs). Assessments of the various kinds of labour market training echo those conducted elsewhere: private sector, especially on-the-job training appears to have positive effects on employability but the effects of other forms (publicly provided training, educational leaves) are weak or unclear (see De Gier and Van den Berg, 2005, pp. 37–42). At the same time, even sceptical observers appear to agree that the reforms of the 1990s have made some contribution towards increasing the flexibility and mobility of Danish labour markets by increasing the willingness of the (long-term) unemployed to be 'reactivated' into training and/or employment (Madsen, 2006, pp. 19–26).

But whether or not the Danish 'hybrid' approach is to be preferred to the more stringent Canadian 'liberal' approach is not a question that can be answered entirely by more and better information about the effectiveness of these programs. For in the end, whether the additional 3.4 per cent of GDP spent by the Danes is justified depends on how one evaluates their effects, which in turn is ultimately a question of basic political values.[22] The stylised facts of the matter are relatively straightforward. Canada's unemployment rates tend to be a couple of percentage-points higher than Denmark's, but the Danes have considerably more long-term unemployment (20 per cent versus 10 per cent of the unemployed having been so for one year or more in recent years). In terms of mobility the two countries appear to be relatively similar. Both have also had reasonably good overall economic growth performances in recent years. At the same time, the unemployed, especially those with below-average earnings and occupations, are better off in Denmark than in Canada, and there is less income inequality and less poverty in the former than in the latter. Conversely, given that macroeconomic conditions have been particularly favourable during the past decade which witnessed the 'Danish miracle', whether the Danish system, even after its recent reforms, can fiscally weather a serious recession remains an open question.

12.5 CONCLUSION

By comparison the Canadian EI system is likely to hold up relatively well when the next recession hits.[23] This is in part due to the fact that the much-heralded transformation of Canada's old unemployment insurance program into a brand-new Employment Insurance system designed to meet the new demands of a modern, knowledge-based economy was not quite as sweeping as it was made out to be. Much of the EI Reform involved tightening of benefits access rules and lowering of obtainable benefits intended as much to produce significant cutbacks in expenditures as to influence labour market participation behaviour. Nor was the conversion to greater emphasis on 'active' labour market policies quite as spectacular and thorough-going as the rhetoric of the time suggested. Nevertheless, there was some shift towards more emphasis and expenditure on active labour market policies and some components of the EI Reform were intended to facilitate certain labour market transitions, including temporary leaves for the sake of childcare. But this hardly adds up to a conversion to labour market flexibilisation along the lines of Transitional Labour Market theory or the European Social Model. Contrary to the latter two approaches, the Canadian reforms remained firmly wedded to the typically 'Anglo-Saxon' assumption that overly 'generous' unemployment benefits necessarily undermine labour market flexibility. At the same time, the Reform did increase access to and the level of certain specific benefits, in particular for new parents and poor families and some part-time workers, in the apparent belief that these benefits would not undermine labour market participation and flexibility. And what little evidence exists on the matter suggests that this latter assumption was correct.

But overall the Canadian unemployment benefits regime remains one of the most restrictive among the OECD countries.

But however disappointing by European standards, the EI Reform did implement some major changes in Canada's labour market policy regime and these changes present valuable opportunities to researchers to study the impacts of different policies in roughly the same labour market and institutional setting with important implications for labour market policies elsewhere. One important issue in the debate over the relative merits and shortcomings of the Anglo-Saxon as opposed to the European Models is whether there is a necessary trade-off between inequality (and hence relative poverty) and employment. The Canadian case offers opportunities to shed further light on this vexed issue. In particular, it will be of much interest to delve further into the exact causes of the successful expenditure reductions after the transition to the EI system. Did it effectively occur by excluding (poor) unemployed people whom the advocates of the European Social Model would wish to include in the social safety net? Or was it primarily achieved by redirecting resources away from uses of the benefits system that merely serve to undermine labour market flexibility?

For similar reasons, there is probably a great deal to be learnt from taking a closer look at the reasons for the somewhat puzzling long-term decline in the ratio of insurance beneficiaries to unemployed mentioned earlier. While the decline has been the subject of much political argument, we actually know very little about its exact causes. Is it the long-term result of ever more restrictive benefits rules or are there other factors having to do with the changing composition of the labour force and other secular trends that account for it? And whichever it is, is there a case to be made for remedial action?

One important question that tends to arise in discussions of unemployment insurance reform in Europe does not appear to have any counterpart in the Canadian case: the degree to which older workers (and their employers) should be allowed to use the unemployment insurance system as a way to subsidise early retirement from jobs and industries that are in relative decline. This difference is not hard to explain prima facie: given the strictly limited periods for which unemployed workers can receive unemployment insurance benefits at all in Canada, particularly in low-unemployment regions, it is not easy to use the benefit system to help bridge the period to full retirement for workers 55 years and up, as some of the European systems have done. But this does not make the difference any less interesting and worthy of further examination. After all, Canada has had its share of traditional, mature manufacturing industries, employing disproportionate numbers of middle-aged men, that have been in relative decline over the past decades. The interesting question is: has there not been the same kind of pressure for special arrangements for these workers through the UI/EI system and if not, why not? Certainly, a close look at the treatment and fate of workers in this age group in the UI and later the EI system could provide analysts and policy makers with important clues concerning the possible ways of dealing with this increasingly pressing issue.

Many more questions regarding various components of the Canadian system and the EI Reform are in need of more careful analysis. Certainly the overall effects of the (changes in) benefits rules are still far from fully understood. While the currently available 'summative evaluations' commissioned by the CEIC have begun to examine the effects of Employment Benefit and Support Measures much work still remains to be done in this area. But given the almost unique intermediate position that Canada occupies in many respects between the European Social Model on one side and the supposedly most extreme version of the 'Anglo-Saxon Model' to its south, the results of such more detailed studies are likely to have important implications for the issues that fuel the ongoing debates between their respective proponents.

NOTES

1. The research on which this paper is based was funded by the Social Sciences and Humanities Research Council of Canada. We thank John Burnett, Carol Ann McGregor, Natalka Patsiurko, Jonathan DeWolfe and Kevin Daley for their able assistance in gathering the literature and information used.
2. Throughout the 1998s and 1990s *both* cost containment *and* a more active approach to labour market policy have been consistently presented as the main motivations for UI reforms (see McIntosh and Boychuk, 2000, pp. 87–8).
3. Section 3(1) of the *Employment Insurance Act* states that the Commission 'shall monitor and assess: a) how individuals, communities and the economy are adjusting to the changes made by this Act to the insurance and employment assistance programs under the *Unemployment Insurance Act*; b) whether the savings expected as a result of the changes made by this Act are being realised; and c) the effectiveness of the benefits and other assistance provided under this Act, including (i) how the benefits and assistance are utilised by employees and employers; and (ii) the effect of the benefits and assistance on the obligation of claimants to be available for and to seek employment and on the efforts of employers to maintain a stable workforce'.
4. The actual number depends on what 'EI region' the claimant lives in. Canada is divided into 58 EI regions according to their current (average annual) levels of unemployment. The higher the level of unemployment relative to the national average, the lower the eligibility requirements for EI benefit claimants and the lower the so-called 'divisor' are used to calculate benefits payable (which raises the level of benefits). Currently, the minimum work requirement of 420 hours, or 12 weeks of full-time (35 hours per week) work, obtains in EI regions with unemployment rates of 12–13 per cent or more, while the maximum of 700 hours is required in regions with rates of about 2 per cent below the national average (which was 7.6 per cent in 2003–2004).
5. This amounts to an increase from the previous 20 weeks of full-time (35 hour) work required for new and re-entrants under the old UI Act to 26 weeks.
6. Since the mid-1970s, when the maximum replacement ratio was 75 per cent, the ratio has been gradually reduced until it reached 55 per cent in 1994 (see Lin, 1998, p. 47).

7. In addition, made effective from January 2004 up to six weeks of 'Compassionate Care' benefits can be claimed to provide care for a gravely ill family member.

8. Unemployed individuals who are neither active nor former EI clients are considered 'non-insured' and are eligible only for those employment services provided by the National Employment Service, involving counselling, labour market information and so on.

9. The following overview relies primarily on Annex 3, Tables 3.2 and 3.3 of the *2003 Monitoring and Assessment Report* (Canada Employment Insurance Commission, 2004).

10. Given the jurisdictional divisions of the Canadian federal system of government the federal government has had to conclude Labour Market Development Agreements (LMDAs) through which responsibilities are shared to varying degrees between federal and provincial agencies to be able to implement many of these programs.

11. The proportion of the decline in the B/U ratio attributable to program change rather than change in the labour market varies dramatically across provinces, however, causing considerable interprovincial and federal-provincial friction (see McIntosh and Boychuk, 2000, pp. 93–7).

12. Previous research does seem to confirm that, ceteris paribus, tightening of UI eligibility rules and benefit levels tends to result in greater use of social assistance support (see, for example, Fortin, Lacroix and Thibault, 1999).

13. This does, however, confirm the importance of close linkage between training and existing jobs, a well-known finding in the labour market policy evaluation literature (see Martin, 2000, pp. 91–3, 96; De Gier and Van den Berg, 2005, pp. 37–42).

14. This *does* raise the question, of course, as to why these figures are gathered and reported at all, no doubt at a considerable expense of tax-dollars.

15. An 'active client' is someone who is entitled to current EI benefits; a 'former client' is an unemployed person whose benefit period has ended during the preceding 36 months (see CEIC, 2005, p. 77, fn. 62)

16. For a review of the literature on the interaction between UI/EI and social assistance claims until 1997, see McIntosh and Boychuk (2000, Appendix G, pp. 139–45).

17. Although, as Barbier (2006 Chapter II) exhaustively shows, there are several quite different philosophies and approaches that employ the same 'activation' terminology and rhetoric.

18. After encountering persistent problems in finding ways to monitor and steer the new quasi-markets in employment services there now appears to be a move towards some forms of reregulation afoot (Considine, 2005).

19. 'Barroso champions the Nordic approach to growth', *Financial Times*, January 25, 2006. See also Barbier (2006, pp. 36–38).

20. This brief summary primarily relies on the authoritative accounts by Per K. Madsen (2002a, 2002b, 2004, 2005, 2006) but see also De Gier and Van den Berg (2005, pp. 31–34, 61). See Barbier (2006, Chapter III) for a much more detailed analysis of the current state of the Danish 'activation' system.

21. Interestingly, Danish employers have traditionally supported high benefit levels as a way to ward off union demands for more restrictive employment protection (Madsen, 2006, pp. 27–28). With an economy dominated by small and medium-sized firms, Danish employers are particularly dependent on their ability to flexibly adjust to market conditions.

22. This is effectively also Barbier's conclusion of his in-depth comparison of recent French, British, Danish and German efforts to introduce a stronger element of labour market 'activation' in their policies (2006, pp. 169–182).

23. In fact the so-called 'EI Account' has been running large surpluses as the government has refused to heed calls for premium reductions while cutting back expenditures, causing a great deal of political controversy (see McIntosh and Boychuk, 2000, pp. 91–97).

REFERENCES

Alderson, Arthur S. and Nielsen, François (2002), 'Globalization and the Great U-Turn: Income Inequality Trends in 16 OECD Countries', *American Journal of Sociology*, **107** (5), 1244–99.

Applied Research Branch, HDRC (1998), *An Analysis of Employment Insurance Benefit Coverage*. Ottawa: Human Resources and Development Canada, <www11.hrsdc.gc.ca/en/cs/sp/hrsdc/arb/publications/research/1998–000128/page00.shtml>.

Atkinson Anthony B. (2003), 'Income Inequality in OECD Countries: Data and Explanations', *Sifo Economic Studies*, **49** (4), 479–513.

Audas, Rick and Murell, David (2000), *Beyond a Hard Place: The Effects of Employment Insurance Reform on Atlantic Canada's Economic Dependency*, Halifax, NS: Atlantic Institute for Market Studies.

Audas, Rick and McDonald, James (2003), *Employment Insurance and Geographic Mobility: Evidence from SLID,* Ottawa: Social Research and Demonstration Corporation.

Audit and Evaluation Directorate (2001), *Did the Social Assistance Take-up Rate Change After EI Reform for Job Separators?,* Ottawa: HRSD.

Audit and Evaluation Directorate. (2003a), *Did the Exhaustion of UI/EI Benefits and the Take-up of Social Assistance Change After EI Reform?,* Ottawa: HRSD.

Audit and Evaluation Directorate (2003b), *To What Extent is Household Spending Reduced as a Result of Unemployment?,* Ottawa: HRSD.

Audit and Evaluation Directorate (2004a), *EI Reform and Community Mobility,* Ottawa: HRSD.

Audit and Evaluation Directorate (2004b), *EI Reform and New Entrants/Re-Entrants (NEREs) to the Labour Market*, Ottawa: HRSD.

Audit and Evaluation Directorate (2005), *Evaluation of EI Parental Benefits,* Ottawa: HRSD.

Audit and Evaluation Directorate, (forthcoming*), The Qualification for Maternity Benefits and EI Reform,* Ottawa: HRSD.

Barbier, Jean-Claude (2004), 'Activation Policies: A Comparative Perspective', in Serrano, Pascual A., (ed.), *Are Activation Policies Converging in Europe? The European Employment Strategy for Young people*, Brussels: ETUI, pp 47–84.

Barbier, Jean-Claude (2006), *Analyse comparative de l'activation de la protection sociale en France, Grande Bretagne, Allemagne et Danemark, dans le cadre des lignes directrices de la stratégie européenne pour l'emploi,* Rapport de recherche pour la DARES, Ministère du travail, avec deux contributions de Ndongo Samba Sylla et Anne Eydoux, Paris: Centre d'Études de l'Emploi.

Bertrand, Jean-François, Ten Cate, Adrienne, Kapsalis, Constantine and Tourigny, Pierre, (forthcoming), *EI Eligibility of Employed Canadians in 2001 Using the Survey of Labour and Income Dynamics (SLID),* Ottawa: HRDC and Data Probe Economic Consulting Inc.

Campeau, Georges (2001), *De l'assurance-chômage à l'assurance-emploi: L'histoire du régime canadien et de son détournement,* Montréal: Les Éditions du Boréal.

Canada (1985), *Royal Commission on the Economic Union and Development Prospects for Canada, Report, Vol. III,* Ottawa: Supply and Services Canada.

Canada (1986), *Commission of Inquiry on Unemployment Insurance, Report,* Ottawa: Supply and Services Canada.

Canada Employment Insurance Commission (2007), *Employment Insurance 2006 Monitoring and Assessment Report,* Submitted to the Minister of Human Resources and Skills Development Canada, Ottawa: HRSDC.

Canada Employment Insurance Commission (2005), *Employment Insurance 2004 Monitoring and Assessment Report,* Submitted to the Minister of Human Resources and Skills Development Canada, Ottawa: HRSDC.

Canada Employment Insurance Commission (2004), *Employment Insurance 2003 Monitoring and Assessment Report,* Submitted to the Minister of Human Resources and Skills Development Canada, Ottawa: HRSDC.

Canada Employment Insurance Commission (2002), *Employment Insurance 2002 Monitoring and Assessment Report,* Submitted to the Minister of Human Resources and Skills Development Canada, Ottawa: HRSDC.

Canada Employment Insurance Commission (1999), *Employment Insurance 1999 Monitoring and Assessment Report,* Submitted to the Minister of Human Resources and Skills Development Canada, Ottawa: HRSDC.

Canada Employment Insurance Commission (1998), *Employment Insurance 1998 Monitoring and Assessment Report,* Submitted to the Minister of Human Resources and Skills Development Canada, Ottawa: HRSDC.

Canadian Labour Congress (2003), *Falling Unemployment Insurance Protection for Canada's Unemployed*, Ottawa: Canadian Labour Congres/Congrès du travail du Canada, Social and Economic Policy Department.

Castles, Frances (1994), 'The Wage Earners' Welfare State Revisited: Refurbishing the established model of Australian social protection', *Australian Journal of Social Issues*, **29** (2), 120–45.

Cheal, David and Kampen, Karen (2000), *The EI Family Supplement and Relative Income in Two-earner Families with Children,* Ottawa: HDRC.

Considine, Mark (2005), 'Steering, Efficiency and Partnership: The Australian Quasi-Market for Public Employment Services', in Bredgaard, Thomas and Larsen, Flemming (eds), *Employment Policy from Different Perspectives*, Copenhagen: DJØF Publishing, 191–210.

Day, Kathleen M. and Winer, Stanley L. (2001), *Policy-induced Migration in Canada: An Empirical Study,* Ottawa: HRDC.

De Gier, Erik and Van den Berg, Axel (2005), *Making Transitions Pay! Towards a European Employment Insurance Strategy (EEIS)*, Final Policy Report of the EU Thematic Network on Managing Social Risks through Transitional Labour Markets (TLM.NET), Amsterdam: SISWO/Social Policy.

Fedorovitch, Nancy (2001), 'Moving from Unemployment to Employment Insurance: The Case of Canada', in Weinert, Patricia, Baukens, Michèle, Bollérot, Patrick, Pineschi-Gapènne, Marina and Walwei, Ulrich (eds), *Employability: From Theory to Practice*, New Brunswick, NJ: Transaction Publishers, 177–89.

Fortin, Bernard, Lacroix, Guy and Thibault, Jean-Francois (1999), 'The Interaction of UI and Welfare, and the Dynamics of Welfare Participation of Single Parents', *Canadian public policy,* **25**, S115–32.

Friesen, Jane and Maki, Dennis (2000), *The Effect of Bill C-12 on Weekly Hours of Work,* Ottawa: HRDC.

Gray, David (2004), *Employment Insurance: What Reform Delivered,* C.D. Howe Institute Backgrounder, No. 82, Toronto: C.D. Howe Institute.

Gray, David and Sweetman, Arthur (2004), *Review of the Employment Insurance Coverage Measures,* Ottawa: HRDC.

Green, David A. and Riddell, W. Craig (2000), *The Effects of the Shift to an Hours-Based Entrance Requirement,* Evaluation Report, Ottawa: HRDC.

Grey, Alex (2002), *Employment Insurance and Social Assistance: Evidence on Program Interaction*, Ottawa: HRDC, Applied Research Branch.

Grubel, Herbert H. (1988), Drifting Apart: Canadian and US Labor Markets, *Contemporary Policy Issues*, **VI** (1), 39–55.

Haddow, Rodney (1998), 'How Ottawa Shrivels: Ottawa's Declining Role in Active Labour Market Policy', in Pal, Leslie A. (ed.), *How Ottawa Spends 1998–1999: Balancing Act: The Post-Defecit Mandate*, Oxford: Oxford University Press, 99–128.

Haddow, Rodney (2000), 'The Political and Institutional Landscape of Canadian Labour Market Policy-Making', in McIntosh, Tom (ed.), *Federalism, Democracy and Labour Market Policy in Canada*, Montreal: McGill-Queens' University Press, 29–64.

Harbridge, Raymond and Bagley, Prue (2002), 'Social Protection and Labour Market Outcomes in Australia', in Sarfati, Hedva and Bonoli, Giuliano (eds), *Labour Market and Social Protection Reforms in International Perspective: Parallel or converging tracks?*, Aldershot: Ashgate, 173–97.

HRDC (2001a), *EI Reform and Multiple Job-Holding*, Ottawa: HRDC.

HRDC (2001b), *An Evaluation Overview of Seasonal Employment*, Ottawa: HRDC.

HRDC (2001c), *Unemployment Insurance-Employment Insurance Transition: An Evaluation of the pre-2001 Maternity and Parental Benefits Program in Canada*, Ottawa: HRDC.

Jones, Stephen R.G. (2000), *EI Impacts on Unemployment Durations and Benefit Receipts*, Ottawa: HRDC.

Jones, Stephen R.G. (2004), *Review of the Employment Insurance Coverage Measures*, Ottawa: HRDC.

Kapsalis, Constantine (2000), *The Impact of Bill C-12 on New Entrants and Re-Entrants*, Evaluation Report, Ottawa: HRDC.

Kaufman, Martin, Swagel, Phillip and Dunaway, Steven (2003), *Regional Convergence and the Role of Federal Transfers in Canada*, IMF Working Paper WP03/97. Washington, DC: International Monetary Fund.

Lacroix, Guy and Van Audenrode, Marc (2000), *An Assessment of Various Components of Bill C-12 on the Duration of Unemployment Spells*, Ottawa: HRDC.

Lin, Zhengxi (1998), 'Employment Insurance in Canada: Policy Changes', *Statistics Canada Perspectives*, 42–47.

Madsen, Per Kongshøj (2004), 'The Danish model of 'flexicurity': experiences and lessons', *TRANSFER. European Review of Labour and Research*, **10** (2), 187–207.

Madsen, Per Kongshøj (2005), 'The Danish road to flexicurity: Where are we. And how did we get there?', in Bredgaard, Thomas and Larsen, Flemming (eds), *Employment Policy from Different Angles*, Copenhagen: DJØF Publishing, 269–89.

Madsen, Per Kongshøj (2006), 'How can it possibly fly? The paradox of a dynamic labour market in a Scandinavian welfare state', in Campbell, John L., Hall, John A. and Pedersen, Ove K. (eds), *National Identity and a Varity of Capitalism: The Case of Denmark*, Montreal: McGill University Press.

Mahon, Rianne (1990), 'Adjusting to Win? The New Tory Training Initiative', in Graham, Katherine A. (ed.), *How Ottawa Spends 1990–1991: Tracking the Second Agenda*, Ottawa: Carleton University Press.

Marshall, Katherine (2003), 'Benefitting from Extended Parental Leave', *Perspectives on Labour and Income*, **15** (2), 5–11.

Martel, Édith, Laplante, Benoît et Bernard, Paul (2005), 'Chômage et stratégies des familles, de l'assurance-chômage à l'assurance emploi', *Recherches sociographiques*, **46** (2), 245–80.

Martin, John P. (2000), 'What Works Among Active Labour Market Policies: Evidence from OECD Countries' Experiences', *OECD Economic Studies*, **3** (I), 79–113.

Martin, John P. and Grubb, David (2001), 'What Works for Whom: A Review of OECD Countries' Experiences with Active Labour Market Policies', *Swedish Economic Policy Review*, **8**, 9–56.

May, Doug and Hollet, Alton (1995), *Between a Rock and a Hard Place: Atlantic Canada and the UI Trap*. Toronto: CD Howe Institute.

McIntosh, Tom and Boychuck, Gerard W. (2000), 'Dis-covered: EI, Social Assistance and the Growing Gap in Income Support for Unemployed Canadians', in McIntosh, Tom (ed.), *Federalism, Democracy and Labour Market Policy in Canada*, Montreal and Kingston: McGill-Queen's University Press, 64–158,

Miller, Riel (1994), 'Education and Training in the Knowledge Economy: Prospects and Missed Opportunities', in Phillips, Susan D. (ed.), *How Ottawa Spends 1994– 1995: Making Change*. Oxford: Oxford University Press.

OECD (2007), *Employment Outlook 2007,* Paris: OECD.

Perusse, Dominique (2003), 'New Maternity and Parental Benefits', *Perspectives on Labour and Income,* **15** (2), 22–25.

Phipps, Shelley and Lethbridge, Lynn (2005), *International Comparison of Maternity/Parental Benefits,* Ottawa: HRDC.

Phipps, Shelley, Burton, Peter and Lethbridge, Lynn (2001), 'In and Out of the Labour Market: Long-Term Income Consequences of Child-Related Interruptions to Women's Paid Work', *Canadian Journal of Economics*, **34**, 411–29.

Phipps, Shelley, MacDonald, Martha and MacPhail, Fiona (2000), *Impact of the Family Supplement,* Ottawa: HDRC.

Phipps, Shelley and McPhail, Fiona (2000), *The Impact of Employment Insurance on New-entrants and Re-entrant Workers*, Evaluation Report, Ottawa: HRDC.

Shen, Kailing (2004), *How Were Canadian Labour Market Transitions Affected by the 1996 Employment Insurance Reform?,* paper presented at the 38th Annual Meeting of the Canadian Economics Association, Toronto.

Shillington, Richard (2004), *Measuring the Effectiveness of Employment Insurance,* Ottawa: HRDC.

Smeeding, Timothy M. (2002), 'Globalisation, Inequality, and the Rich Countries of the G-20: Evidence from the Luxembourg Income Study (LIS)', in D. Gruen, D., O'Brien, T. and Lawson, J. (eds), *Globalisation, Living Standards, and Inequality, Recent Progress and Continuing Challenges*. Sydney: Reserve Bank of Australia and Australian Treasury, 179–206.

Smeeding, Timothy M. (2005), 'Public Policy, Economic Inequality, and Poverty: The United States in Comparative Perspective', *Social Science Quarterly*, Supplement to Volume, **86**, 955–83.

Smith, Michael R. (2002), 'Income Inequality and Economic Growth in Rich Countries: A Reconsideration of the Evidence', *Current Sociology*, **50** (4), 573–93.

Statistics Canada (2007), *Employment Insurance Coverage Survey,* Ottawa: Statistics Canada.

Sweetman, Arthur (2000), *The Impact of EI on Those Working Less than 15 Hours Per Week,* Evaluation Report, Ottawa: HRDC.

Ten Cate, Adrienne (2003), *The Impact of Provincial Maternity and Parental Leave Policies on Employment Rates of Women with Young Children in Canada,*

Working Paper 2003–03, Department of Economics, Hamilton, Ontario: McMaster University.

Ten Cate, Adrienne (2004), *Determinants of Mothers' Time at Home after Childbirth: The Role of Maternity and Parental Leave Policy,* Paper presented at the Canadian Economics Association Meetings, Toronto.

Van den Berg, Axel and Smucker, Joseph (1992), 'Markets and Government Interventions: A Comparison of Canadian and Swedish Labor Market Policies', *International Journal of Contemporary Sociology*, **29** (1/2), 9–46.

Van den Berg, Axel, Furåker, Bengt and Johansson, Leif (1997), *Labour market Regimes and Patterns of Flexibility: A Sweden-Canada Comparison,* Lund: Arkiv.

Vincent, Carole, De Raaf, Shawn and Kapsalis, Costa (2003), 'Seasonal work and Employment Insurance Use', *Perspectives on Labour and Income*, **15** (4).

Yates, Charlotte (1995), Job Ready, I Ready; Job Creation and Labour Market Reform in Canada, in Phillips, Susan D. (ed.), *How Ottawa Spends 1995–1996: Mid-Life Crises*, Oxford: Oxford University Press.

Ziguras, Stephen and Stricker, Peter (2008), 'Labour Market Transitions in Australia: Employment, flexibility and security in a liberal welfare regime', in Muffels, R. (ed.), *Flexibility and Employment Security in Europe: Labour Markets in Transition*, Cheltenham, UK and Northhampton, MA, USA: Edward Elgar.

13. The Danish Road to 'Flexicurity': Where are we Compared to Others? And How Did We Get There?

Per Kongshøj Madsen

13.1 INTRODUCTION

The successful development of the Danish economy and labour market in recent years has stimulated ideas about the existence of a particular Danish model of the employment system characterised by:

- A flexible labour market with a high level of external numerical flexibility indicated by high levels of worker flows in and out of employment and unemployment; the high degree of numerical flexibility is made possible by a low level of employment protection, allowing employers to freely adapt the workforce to changing economic conditions.
- A generous system of economic support for the unemployed.
- Active labour market policies aimed at upgrading the skills of those unemployed that are unable to return directly from unemployment to a new job.

Originally these special traits were pointed at in a report of the Danish Ministry of Employment (Arbejdsministeriet, 1999). They have later been the subject of a number of academic articles and papers and also emphasised by the OECD (2004).[1] Furthermore, the analysis of the 'Danish model' has been linked to the growing international literature on 'flexicurity', where the Danish approach is seen as a variant that fits into this broader concept (see Wilthagen and Tros, 2004). In this perspective, the flexibility–security nexus found in Denmark is a combination of a high numerical flexibility and a correspondingly high level of income security for the unemployed in the form of generous and long-lasting benefits. In addition, the Danish model includes an additional strong element of employment security stemming from active and resourceful labour market policy. Finally, in a comparative perspective, it should be noted that the Danish model is characterised by an encompassing flexicurity approach covering all employees, in contrast to models where flexicurity is limited or specific to subgroups on the labour market.

This chapter builds on earlier work from the author that looked in detail to the various elements of the Danish employment system and the interplay between them (Madsen, 2002, 2003, 2004, 2006). The purpose of this chapter is to place the Danish version of flexicurity into perspective in two ways. Firstly, the aim is to compare in more detail the Danish employment system with the situation in two other European countries that are conventionally seen as representatives of a liberal Anglo-Saxon and a Scandinavian or Nordic welfare state, respectively. Secondly, the intention is to broaden the understanding of the Danish model by looking at the historical preconditions of the Danish version of flexicurity. What were the economic, social and political forces that created the system in its present form?

13.2 THE DANISH MODEL OF FLEXICURITY AND THE 'GOLDEN TRIANGLE'

The Danish model is often portrayed in the form of a 'golden triangle' of flexicurity (Figure 13.1). The arrows in the model indicate flows of persons between different positions within work, welfare and active labour market programmes. The two arrows linking the flexible labour market and the generous welfare system indicate that between 20 and 25 per cent of the Danish workforce is affected by unemployment every year, but that the majority of the unemployed returns to employment after only a short spell of unemployment. Active labour market programmes support those who do not quickly return into employment, before re-entering a job.

The dotted eclipse indicates the basic flexibility–security nexus combining a high level of numerical external flexibility (linked to a low level of employment protection) and a generous system of economic support (income security) for the unemployed. The main role of active labour market policy is to support the mobility flows from unemployment back into employment by upgrading the skills of the unemployed. This reflects the element of employment security in the Danish model.

Furthermore, in recent years increased emphasis has been put on the motivation – or threatening – effect of mandatory activation (Rosholm and Svarre, 2004). The effect is caused by the aversion of the unemployed towards taking part in the active programmes and to search more eagerly for work, when the deadline for activation is approaching.

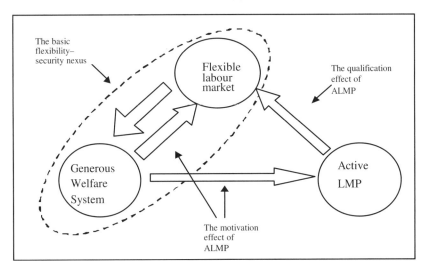

Figure 13.1 The Danish model of 'flexicurity'

Hence, the Danish experience seems to convey supporting evidence to the economic feasibility of a 'hybrid employment system' combining on the one hand the virtues of a liberal labour market with few restrictions on the employment contract and on the other, a reasonable level of income protection of the individual wage earner. The Danish model therefore does not seem to support the idea of a necessary 'trade-off' between a highly flexible labour market and a high level of income protection as is usually presumed: it combines a very flexible employment relation with a highly protective social protection system and active labour market programmes, which protect the individual worker from the potential costs of a low level of employment security.[2] In this respect, the model represents a genuine alternative to the common idea of making the individual employer responsible for safeguarding income and employment security by establishing a high level of the individual workers' employment protection at the company level.

13.3 THE DANISH EMPLOYMENT SYSTEM IN A COMPARATIVE PERSPECTIVE

The interpretation of the Danish model of combining the traits of a liberal labour market system with those of a Scandinavian or Nordic welfare state justifies a closer comparison with countries that are traditionally seen as representative for the liberal Anglo-Saxon and the Scandinavian models, respectively.[3] In the present context, Sweden and the UK are chosen for this comparative exercise. Table 13.1 provides the basic information about the core indicators for the flexicurity triangle in the three countries.

Table 13.1 Basic indicators of the 'flexicurity triangle' for Denmark, Sweden and the United Kingdom

	Unit of measurement	Year	Denmark	Sweden	United Kingdom
Average tenure	Years	2000	8.3	11.5	8.2
Employment protection of regular employment	Index (0–6)	2003	1.5	2.9	1.1
Net replacement Rates	Per cent	1999	81	79	69
ALMP expenditure as share of GDP	Per cent	2000	1.58	1.37	0.37

Source: For average tenure: Auer and Casez (2000), Table 2.1; for employment protection: OECD (2004), Employment Outlook 2004, Table 2.A2.1; for net replacement rates: OECD (2002), Benefits and Wages, Table 3.10; for ALMP: OECD (2004), Employment Outlook 2004, Table H.

The hybrid character of the Danish model becomes evident from Table 13.1. When it comes to average tenure and the employment protection index, Denmark is close to the United Kingdom. However, with respect to the net replacement rates of the unemployment benefits and the expenditure on active labour market policies, Denmark seems much more like its Scandinavian counterpart.

The following sections take the analysis further by looking more closely at the determining factors behind the performance of these three countries on the basic indicators.

13.3.1 Average tenure and employment protection

Firstly, the available sources allow for a more detailed look at the level of numerical flexibility measured here by average tenure but disaggregated by short and long duration, age, gender, business sector and education level. A high level of average tenure is taken to be indicators of a low level of numerical flexibility but also a high level of long tenure points to a low level of numerical flexibility. Table 13.2 provides an overview of the data.

Basically, when it comes to the extent of numerical flexibility, the disaggregated data in Table 13.2 confirms the existence of a dividing line between Denmark and the United Kingdom on the one hand and Sweden on the other. Actually, by some indicators, numerical flexibility seems even higher in Denmark than in the UK. The share of employees with tenure at less than 1 year is highest in Denmark. Also the share of employees with long tenure is lower in Denmark than in the UK.

Table 13.2 Average tenure by duration, sex, age, business sector and education level, 2000

	Unit of measurement	Denmark	Sweden	United Kingdom
All	Years	8.3	11.5	8.2
Tenure under 1 year	Per cent of labour force	23.0	15.7	19.3
Tenure 10 years and over	Per cent of labour force	31.1	46.7	33.3
Sex				
Men	Years	8.8	11.3	8.9
Women	Years	7.5	11.5	7.4
Age				
15–24 years	Years	1.6	1.9	2.0
25–44 years	Years	6.2	8.6	7.4
45 years or more	Years	13.6	16.8	12
Business sector				
Agriculture	Years	12.4	15.9	11.6
Manufacturing	Years	8.8	12.3	9.2
Construction	Years	7.9	11.9	9.0
Trade	Years	7.0	9.6	7.0
Financial sector	Years	8.2	8.5	7.1
Public sector	Years	8.3	12.7	8.9
Education level				
Low	Years	7.6	14.8	8.2
Medium	Years	8.7	11.3	8.0
High	Years	9.0	10.9	8.2

Source: Auer and Casez (2003), Table 2.3.

The similarity between Denmark and the United Kingdom is moreover found, when looking at the tenure data for men and women, separately. In both cases the lowest tenure is found for women, while Sweden shows the opposite pattern. By age we found that for two out of three age groups, Denmark has the lowest tenure. By business sector we see that the cross-sectoral pattern is similar for all three countries, but again with Denmark having the lowest tenure levels in most groups, followed by the UK. In particular one should note that the tenure for public sector employees in Denmark is similar to the average level for all wage earners – and lower than tenure is in manufacturing. Thus, the perception of the public sector as having a relatively low numerical flexibility is not supported in the Danish case.

Finally, when it comes to tenure data by education level, one finds different patterns in the three countries. In Denmark tenure increases with education level, whilst in Sweden tenure levels are lower for higher education – and in the UK no relation is found. Again Denmark and Sweden are not following the same pattern.

One obvious candidate for explaining the different levels of numerical flexibility are the differences in the national regimes with respect to the dismissal protection rules for individual employees. More easiness in the firing rules of the individual employee should make numerical flexibility a more attractive strategy for the employer than for instance functional flexibility (within firm mobility) or working time changes (internal numerical flexibility).

As indicated by the aggregated data in Table 13.1, the overall protection of the individual employee seems to be the lowest in the UK, followed closely by Denmark and with Sweden being a category of its own. The data presented here are taken from the latest OECD-survey of employment protection legislation (OECD, 2004, Chapter 2).[4] That study adopted a detailed approach in assigning quantitative scores to many aspects of the employment protection legislation. In a next step they aggregated these scores and transformed them into a few general indices. In order to get a better understanding of the causes of the different index-levels assigned to the three countries in question, Table 13.3 presents the underlying data for the assessment of the level of protection of the individual employee against dismissal. The basic indicators in Table 13.3 cover three main areas of employment protection:

1. Procedures for dismissals with respect to notification (oral statement, written statement and involvement of third parties) and delay.
2. Conditions under which dismissals can be justified or unjustified (considerations with respect to lack of work, individual worker qualifications, social considerations, obligation to attempt retraining).
3. Relation between notice period or severance pay and length of tenure of the employee.

Concerning the first two categories of indicators, the similarity between Denmark and the United Kingdom in their dismissal regulations and the difference with Sweden are the most striking. In both Denmark and the UK an employer can dismiss an individual worker within short notice using a written statement and without the involvement of a third party. Trial periods are long and compensation for unfair dismissal is about one quarter of the Swedish level. Only when it comes to notice and severance pay, the picture is more mixed, with Sweden having less restrictive regulations than Denmark in two out of the six chosen indicators.

Table 13.3 Indicators for the strictness of employment protection regulation for regular employees, 2003

	Unit	Denmark	Sweden	UK
Basic indicators				
1.1 Procedures	Scale 0 to 3	1	2	1
1.2 Delay to start of notice	Days	1	14	2
2.1 Definition of unfair dismissal	Scale 0 to 3	0	2	0
2.2 Trial period before eligibility arises	Months	10.5	3	12
2.3 Unfair dismissal compensation at 20 years of tenure	Months	9	32	8
2.4 Extent of reinstatement	Scale 0 to 3	1	1	1
3.1 Notice period after 9 months	Months	1.8	1	0.24
3.2 Notice period after 4 years	Months	3	3	0.9
3.3 Notice period after 20 years	Months	4.25	6	2.8
3.4 Severance pay after 9 months	Months	0	0	0
3.5 Severance pay after 4 years	Months	0	0	0.5
3.6 Severance pay after 20 years	Months	1.5	0	2.4
Summary scores by main area				
1. Regular procedural inconveniences	Index 0 to 6	1	3	1
2. Difficulty of dismissal	Index 0 to 6	1.5	4	1.3
3. Notice and severance pay for Individual dismissal	Index 0 to 6	1.9	1.6	1.1
Overall strictness of protection against dismissals	Index 0 to 6	1.5	2.9	1.1

Source: OECD (2004), Table 2.A2.1.

However the overall picture is unmistakable. The overall level of employment protection of the individual employee is clearly lower in Denmark and the United Kingdom than in Sweden. In the former countries, the employment contract is seen essentially as an individual economic agreement between an employer and an employee, which can be terminated at will from both sides, without the involvement of third bodies. Therefore the concept of unfair dismissal plays a limited role in those countries, although limitations may exist for instance, due to bans on ethnic and other forms of discrimination. Other limitations may refer to pregnant women. But on the whole, the employment contract takes few social or other considerations into account concerning the employees' rights in the event of dismissal.

While this may be in line with the traditional perception of a liberal labour market, it is more surprising to find such a regime within the framework of the Danish society, which is normally seen as belonging to the family of Scandinavian welfare states. One clue to understanding this apparent anomaly is to look closer at the income security provided in the three countries compared. This is the subject of the following section.

13.3.2 Income security in Denmark, Sweden and the United Kingdom

Based on the above description of the Danish labour market as providing a rather insecure environment for the individual wage earner, one could suspect that Danish employees would regard their working life as unsafe and risky. The paradox is however that the vast majority of studies of working-life satisfaction (and life-satisfaction in general) come to the conclusion that Danes are among the populations that express the highest level of job-satisfaction and sense of stability in their working lives.

Thus, in a survey conducted in 1996, the proportion of Danish workers *not* strongly agreeing with the statement 'my job is secure' was about 45 per cent, and therefore considerably lower than in all the other countries in the sample. This feeling of job security was found among all subgroups of workers (OECD, 1997, Table 5.2). Although this may also reflect the positive labour market situation at the time of the survey, there are no clear indications that Danish workers are reacting to the high level of numerical flexibility with a strong feeling of insecurity. Furthermore, similar results are found in a more recent survey (The European Foundation for Working and Living Conditions, 1999) and in a study by Auer and Cazes (2003, Figure 1.1). The data from 1994 published in Gallie and Paugam (2000, p. 292) also showed that the economic well-being of the Danish unemployed was the highest among the European countries in the sample and that the difference in economic well being between employed and unemployed was the lowest.

One plausible explanation for the sense of security and economic well being among the Danish working population is the generous safety-net, which is provided during both short and long spells of unemployment.

Numerous studies have looked into the interplay between social security benefit levels (including support to the unemployed) and the income distribution in different welfare regimes (see for instance Gallie and Paugam, 2000). It is also well known that international comparisons in this area are difficult due to differences in the specific institutional set-up at the national level. For example the benefits paid to an unemployed person will in general differ with respect to previous income, but may also be influenced by the family situation and the interplay with other forms of social assistance and with the tax system. Also the duration of the eligibility period will differ. Therefore summary indicators of (for example) replacement rates may give a misleading impression of the actual situation.

The aim of the present section is therefore to dig a bit deeper into the design, level and targeting of the income security arrangements in the three countries under scrutiny here. The descriptions rules and regulations are based on a recent comparative study (Werner and Winkler, 2004). The quantitative information is taken from the OECD's benefits and wages database (OECD, 2002).

Concerning the design of the unemployment insurance systems,[5] the Danish system is based on private, but mainly state-funded, unemployment insurance funds with close ties to the trade unions. Benefits are calculated as 90 per cent of the earned income during the previous 12 weeks with a maximum of around 400 Euro per week. There is no waiting period. The maximum duration of benefits is four years, and the recipient must take part in training programmes, which are typically offered after one year of unemployment. For the unemployed not eligible to unemployment benefits, cash benefits are available, but on a means-tested basis only. The duration of such benefits is unlimited. The level of cash benefits will vary with the family situation. All benefits are taxed. Taking part in labour market training will not make the unemployed eligible for an extension of the benefit period.

In Sweden the benefit system is managed by a number of unemployment insurance funds supported with government subsidies. The income related unemployment benefit amounts to 80 per cent of previous wages with a maximum of around 350 Euro per week. There is a five-day waiting period. The maximum duration is 60 weeks for persons under 57 years of age. Persons who are not members of an unemployment insurance fund receive a basic unemployment benefit of around 150 Euro per week. All benefits are taxed. Training will also qualify for further benefits.

Finally, in the UK, unemployment benefits are part of the mandatory social security system for all employees. Employers and employees pay contributions. The system makes a distinction between contribution based unemployment benefits and income-based benefits, where the former call for a minimum number of contributions. The contribution-based benefit amounts to about 90 Euro per week for adults, while the income-based benefits are means-tested and depends on the family situation and so on. There is a three-day waiting period. The maximum duration of contribution based benefits is

182 days, while income-based benefits have unlimited duration. The former is taxable and the latter is not.

Based on this brief comparison, the clear differences that stand out are the following.

- Both the Danish and the Swedish systems provide relatively high levels of compensation, although with a maximum.
- The duration of benefits is long in Denmark and short in the UK; for Sweden the potential duration is influenced by the fact that training may qualify for further benefits.
- Both in Sweden and in the UK, there is a waiting period before benefits may be collected.

In Table 13.4 a quantitative comparison is made, using data provided by the OECD and taking the earnings-level of the average production worker (APW) as the starting point.

Table 13.4 Net replacement rates for two income levels and four family types for a short and a long unemployment period, 1999 (in per cent)

	APW-level				2/3 of APW-level				Average
	Single	Mar-ried couple	Couple with 2 chil-dren	Lone parent, 2 chil-dren	Single	Married couple	Couple with 2 chil-dren	Lone parent, 2 chil-dren	
				1st month of benefit receipt					
Denmark	63	63	73	78	89	89	95	96	n.a
Sweden	71	71	78	85	82	82	90	93	n.a
UK	46	46	49	49	66	64	54	55	n.a
				60 months of unemployment					
Denmark	60	69	80	79	85	96	102	97	81
Sweden	54	73	85	59	79	102	110	70	79
UK	46	57	80	71	66	80	88	81	69

Note: APW-level indicates the income of the 'average production worker'.

Source: OECD (2002): Benefits and Wages. OECD Indicators, Table 3.2, Table 3.5 and 3.10.

The main impression from the data in Table 13.4 is that the countries fall into two groups with Denmark and Sweden having rather similar – and high – levels of net replacement rates, while the UK has much lower levels.

This finding is especially evident in the case of short-term unemployment, which is the most relevant case when assessing the level of income security in relation to the level of numerical flexibility. Here the net replacement rates for the UK are less than 50 per cent at the APW-level and around 60 per cent for a low-income worker. For both Denmark and Sweden the net replacement rates are in the range of 63 to 85 per cent at the APW-income-level and between 82 and 96 per cent for a low-income earner.

The comparison of the income effects in the case of short-term unemployment for Denmark and Sweden, show a more mixed picture. At the level of the APW the Danish set-up is less favourable due to the relatively low fixed maximum level of the unemployment benefit. On the other hand, the Danish level of compensation is generally higher than the Swedish for low-income workers with net compensation rates close to 100 percent for families with children.

In the case of long-term unemployment the differences between the three countries become less distinct, although the ranking is largely unaffected. But based on these data, it seems that the UK benefit system is relatively more generous in the long than in the short term.

13.3.3 Active labour market policy and employment security

The interpretation of the 'flexicurity triangle' in Section 13.2 was that the nexus between numerical flexibility and income security should be considered central to the Danish model. However, and even more so in the 1990s and 2000s, it should be reminded that active labour market policy has entered the scene. Two important functions are attributed to active measures. Firstly, they shall enhance the employability of those unemployed that have not been able to return directly to employment after a short unemployment spell. Secondly, they serve as a means to check the availability for work of the unemployed acting as such as an incentive to job search – the so-called threatening or motivation effect of active measures. Especially through improving the qualifications of the unemployed and thus their prospects for getting reemployed, one can value active labour market programmes as adding an element of *employment security* to the model.

Table 13.5 presents some basic data about active labour market policies in the three countries. The table illustrates first of all the huge difference in spending on active measures between Denmark and Sweden on the one hand and the UK on the other. Apart from youth measures, the spending in the UK on active programs is almost negligible.[6] Denmark and Sweden are more similar, but one may note the high level of spending on labour market training in the Danish case. These measures are mainly serving the unemployed and reflect as such the relatively strong role that in the Danish version of flexicurity has been assigned to employment protection measures.

Table 13.5 Public expenditures on labour market programmes, 2000

Per cent of GDP	Denmark	Sweden	UK
PES and administration	0.12	0.3	0.13
Labour market training	0.86	0.29	0.04
Youth measures	0.1	0.02	0.15
Subsidised employment	0.17	0.26	0.02
Measures for the disabled	0.34	0.5	0.02
Total active measures	1.59	1.37	0.36
Unemployment compensation	1.37	1.31	0.44
Early retirement for labour market reasons	1.67	0.06	0
Total passive measures	3.04	1.37	0.44
Total expenditures on labour market policy	4.63	2.74	0.8

Source: OECD (2004): Employment Outlook 2004, Table H.

13.3.4 Summing up: The label 'hybrid' is appropriate

The purpose of this section is to dig somewhat deeper into the question of whether the characterisation of Denmark as being a hybrid case between a liberal-Anglo-Saxon and a Scandinavian-Nordic type of welfare state is appropriate, when it comes to the interplay between flexibility on the labour market and the income support to the unemployed. The conclusion is clear. The available indicators of numerical flexibility and employment protection legislation reveal a close similarity between Denmark and the UK, with Denmark in some cases being even the most liberal one. On the other hand, when one looks at the support provided to the unemployed, the Danish welfare state provides a safety net, which matches the level of the Swedish system, and in some cases turns out to be even more generous.

With reference to the growing literature on the 'Varieties of Capitalism' (VOC) approach, Denmark provides a very interesting variety, which does not fit well with the theoretical regime clustering either of the liberal market economy (LME) or the coordinated market economy type (CME) (Hall and Soskice, 2001). From the VOC-perspective, Denmark would be seen as having an unstable configuration of institutions and being on the move in the direction of one of the two clusters. However, when looking at the historical roots of the Danish model of flexicurity, the main evidence is that the model has been developed through a long time period and underpinned by stable institutions and continuous class compromises. In the following section the focus will be on the further analysis hereof.

13.4 THE HISTORICAL DEVELOPMENT OF THE DANISH MODEL OF FLEXICURITY

Basically, the model should be seen not as the result of a well-defined grand scheme, but as the outcome of a long historical development involving a multitude of negotiations and social compromises in different policy areas. Hence, the high level of workers' mobility supported by a low level of employment protection appears to be a long-term feature of the Danish labour market. The present version of the system of income support to the unemployed dates back to the last large reform of the unemployment benefit system in 1969. Finally, the present system of active labour market policy dates back to programmes introduced in 1979, which were subject to a large-scale overhaul in the years 1993–94.

However, the recent interest in the Danish employment system has largely been caused by the reform of labour market policy in 1993–94 and the spectacular reduction in unemployment during the 1990s. Therefore, examinations of the Danish model often confuse the reasons for this latest success story with the more persistent traits of the employment system. This is especially tempting, because of the coincidence of the labour market reform and the decline in unemployment rates. But by focusing on the development in the 1990s one takes a too narrow perspective on the historical foundations of the present situation. And of course, one also faces the risk of losing sight on the merits of the Danish model, once unemployment starts to rise again.

Against this background, two different, but related, research questions will be dealt with in this section. The first looks at the basic and long-term traits of the Danish employment system, which has been able to sustain a high and rising level of employment during the post-war period leading to a level of the employment rate, which is among the highest found in the OECD-countries. The second question focuses on the more spectacular part of Danish employment history, which is the remarkable – and inflation-free – reduction in unemployment in recent years.

Both these questions will be dealt with in an attempt to disentangle the longer-term positive development of the Danish employment system from the noticeable success during the late 1990s and the 2000s and to discuss the historical development of the different components of the Danish version of flexicurity.

Finally, it should be mentioned that the author elsewhere has provided more detailed descriptions and analysis of the different elements of the Danish model: workers' mobility, employment protection, compensation rates and labour market policies (see Madsen, 2003, 2004, 2006). Such documentation has therefore been omitted here.

13.4.1 The historical foundations of the Danish model

As already indicated, the Danish 'model of flexicurity' is not the result of a well-defined grand scheme, but the outcome of a long historical development with strong elements of path-dependency.

Hence, the high level of worker mobility supported by a low level of employment protection appears to be a long-standing feature of the Danish labour market, although further research is still needed to identify concisely the historical process, by which this situation has come about.

In the form of hypothesises one can however point to the historical dominance of small and medium sized firms in the Danish economy. From the instrumental point of view it has therefore been less functional to put a burden of strict employment protection on the individual firms. Furthermore, the low level of employment protection reflects the long-lasting liberal tradition of the Danish welfare state, which has its social and political foundation in a close co-operation between the agrarian and the labour movement.[7]

The present version of the system of income support for the unemployed dates back to the last large reform of the unemployment benefit system in 1969, where the state took over the responsibility for financing the extra costs of unemployment benefits that were caused by the increases in unemployment (the principle of public financing 'at the margin'). The members of the unemployment insurance funds would therefore only be obliged to pay a fixed membership contribution, independent of the actual level of unemployment. As shown by Kærgaard and Hansen (1994), the average compensation rate of unemployment benefits almost doubled during the late 1960s and 1970s. Data from the databank of the macro-econometric model ADAM indicate that the level of compensations then levelled out around 60 per cent. During the 1990s the average rate of compensation has slowly fallen to around 50 per cent. By international comparison, the rate is compensation is still high and actually in 2003 the highest among the OECD-countries (OECD, 2002).

A further observation can be made concerning the present foundation of the model. The relationship between the liberal regime of employment protection and the well-developed state-funded system of unemployment compensation is strongly supported by both trade unions and employers' organisations. This support becomes manifest every time political proposals for restrictions in the access to unemployment benefits are put forward. In such cases a strong alliance between trade unions and employers' organisations is formed, where the employers' organisations point to the risk of claims for improving the level of employment protection in the case of deterioration of the benefit system.

A definite illustration of the strength of this alliance was given in August 2003, when the Minister of Employment, as part of the negotiations for the budget for 2004, put forward a proposal to reduce unemployment benefits by a number of reforms, including the introduction of a longer waiting period for high-income earners. Originally the aim of this and related proposals was to reduce public expenditures by around 100 million Euros. Immediately the proposals met strong resistance from the trade unions, especially in the construction sector. Longer terms of notice were called for, if the rules were changed. Then the employers' organisations moved in and supported the views of the trade unions referring to the lower flexibility that would be the outcome of the cutbacks in the benefit-system. At first the protests lead to a reduction in the intended savings to around 20 million Euros, and in the end the Minister had to drop the proposal all together.[8]

The third element in the triangle, active labour market policy, is also the outcome of a long tradition of public interventions into the functioning of the labour market. When it comes to the setting of the wage bargain, the September Compromise in 1899 is often taken as the starting point, because this agreement between the social partners also laid the foundation for the state's role as mediator in collective agreements. Ik, 1907 the first law on Unemployment Insurance Funds was passed and in 1913 a public employment service was established. In 1942 the Ministry of Labour was established as a separate Ministry. Hence, labour market policy in Denmark has a long political legacy, although it only developed into a distinct policy area in the mid-1950s (Jørgensen and Larsen, 2002, pp.171–75). Being partly based on a system of private unemployment insurance funds which were affiliated with the trade unions and traditionally also on a large number of tri-partite bodies responsible for labour market training and other institutions, Danish labour market policy seems a prime example of the negotiated economy, as is stated in the following quote:

> The September Compromise provided the foundation for labour market regulation that emphasized negotiation early on, and organizational representation in government committees, boards and commissions has remained strong ever since. The state has learned to delegate authority to the labour market organizations, and they almost always assist in the design of initiatives. The organizations also have a strong sense of 'ownership' of the post-war labour market policy (Jørgensen and Larsen, 2002, p. 171).

Also the reforms of labour market policy in the 1990s were the outcome of a carefully prepared compromise, which was struck in the early 1990s in a special tri-partite committee (the Zeuthen Committee). The committee hammered out the foundation of the active and de-central profile of the Danish labour market policies in the years to come. The background for the Zeuthen Committee was the increasing level of dissatisfaction with the general framework of labour market policy, which had been the outcome of the last reform in 1979. Also, the dramatic rise in unemployment rates in the early 1990s pushed the need for reform high on the political agenda.

Recent studies of the political processes behind the reform of labour market policy in 1993 and its successors have pointed to a number of factors behind this development (see the various contributions in Madsen and Pedersen, 2003).

- The changes in the discourse in which active labour markets programmes were increasingly argued as being an important instrument to lower structural employment which received support from both proponents of workfare-oriented and human-capital oriented strategies (cf. also Torfing, 2004).
- The need of the newly elected government led by the Social Democrats to demonstrate its ability to 'break the curve' of unemployment.
- The broad public support for reforms, including the various leave schemes.
- While the social partners had a dominant role during the work in the 'Zeuthen Committee', their function in the subsequent adjustments has been somewhat ambiguous. In some years especially in 1998 they played an important part, while the Government took the lead in other situations, thus shifting between different political channels for decision making (see Winter, 2003).

However most observers will agree that the corporatist structure plays an important role in explaining the development and robustness of the particular Danish version of 'flexicurity' (Mailand and Due, 2003; Jørgensen and Larsen, 2002). At face value, the above observations also fit well with Katzenstein's view on 'small state democratic corporatism' in the sense that the Danish version of 'flexicurity' allows for flexible adaptation of the level and composition of employment to a changing international environment with ongoing shifts in the demand for goods and services (Katzenstein, 1985). In a slightly different context, Auer (2000) has also pointed to the importance of a strong system of corporatist governance as an explanatory factor for the success of a number of small European countries, including Denmark.

13.4.2 Basic traits and specific causes for success in the 1990s

Concerning the question of the relationship between the longer-term traits of the Danish labour market and the specific developments of the 1990s, it is therefore important to note that neither the flexibility–security nexus nor a well-performing employment system (indicated by a high employment rate) is something new. To the contrary, and in spite of the difficult years of the first and the second oil crisis, the post-war economic and social history of Denmark must be seen as having undergone in many respects a successful transformation from an agrarian into a modern society, and because of which it has kept its place in the top league of nations measured by most indicators of economic and social performance. Table 13.6 aims at summing up both the basic traits and the more recent developments of the Danish model of flexicurity.

Viewing firstly the political environment, we should recall what has been described earlier about the strong corporatist structure and the long-lasting, but implicit social contract on the way in which the balance between security and flexibility must be retained. The development in the 1990s was then initiated by the 'problem window', which was opened by the steep increase in unemployment in the late 1980s and early 1990s. Also the many years of often unsuccessful experiments with various forms of programmes for the unemployed had created a widespread feeling that policy changes had to be introduced. The concept of activation entered the discourse (Torfing, 2004). Furthermore, the social partners had already in 1987 issued a joint declaration stating their willingness to accept the responsibility for the macro-economic development and to include that in the bargaining process about work and pay conditions. Finally, a new government headed by the Social Democrats came into power in 1993 that strongly committed itself to reducing unemployment and to enact reforms of labour market policies.

Looking at the macro-economic developments, a successful transformation from an agrarian to an industrial, and later to a service economy, characterised Denmark during the 20th century. Gradually, the economy became more integrated in the international economic system and more sensitive to the fluctuations of the world economy. The oil crises of the 1970s and 1980s rendered a major lesson. Therefore, the increased awareness of the need to sustain the international competitiveness of the Danish economy was the major factor behind the above-mentioned declaration of the social partners in 1987. Also, deficits on both the internal and external trade balance limited the use of active fiscal policies.

Table 13.6 An overview of the Danish system of 'flexicurity'

	Basic traits of the Danish system of 'flexicurity'	Specific developments in the 1990s
Political environment	Strong corporatist structures. Implicit social contract concerning balance between security and flexibility.	Broad political support for reforms of labour market policies. Acceptance by social partners of the need for wage restraints. New government headed by the Social Democrats.
Macroeconomic environment	Changing international economic conditions. Active fiscal policy, but constrained by external balance.	Strong internal demand. Favourable external balance. Lower level of international inflation.
Employment situation	High employment rate (around 75 percent). Shifting levels of open unemployment. Rising share of persons receiving transfer income.	Significant reduction in both open and gross unemployment. Reduction in structural unemployment.
Worker mobility (external numerical flexibility)	High by international standards.	High by international standards.
Employment protection	Weak	Weak
Unemployment benefits	Significant increase in compensation rate with reform in the late 1960s. Cash benefits for non-insured unemployed.	Slow decline in compensation rate, but still high by international standards. Reduction in duration, especially for passive benefits.
Active labour market policy	High expenditures on LMP in general. Incremental policy adjustments since 1979.	Decentralised, individualised rights and duties to early activation.

Source: Compiled by the author. For a more detailed discussion, see Madsen (2006).

A steady improvement in the cost competitiveness of the Danish industry and the loosened constraints from the external trade balance allowed for a shift into an expansionary fiscal policy in 1993–94 supplemented by a reform that eased the household's access to cheap mortgages. A strong increase in internal demand was the immediate outcome.

Concerning employment, high employment rates of 70 to 75 per cent have characterised the Danish employment system at least since the early 1960s. While unemployment rates have fluctuated over the years, and were strongly influenced by the oil crisis, a further long-term trend has been a growth in the share of the adult population living on various forms of transfer income – from about 7 per cent in 1960 to around 25 per cent in the 1990s. The main change in the 1990s was therefore a dramatic reduction in the unemployment rates, which over a few years fell back to the level of the 1970s. Since this reduction took place without any outburst of wage inflation, it rendered clear indications that structural unemployment had fallen as well.

Turning then to the three corners of the triangle depicted in Figure 13.1, one can point to the following historical developments.

As already mentioned, the low level of job protection and the high level of worker mobility is a long-lasting feature of the Danish employment system. Available empirical evidence does not indicate any significant shift in the level of numerical flexibility from the 1980s up to the 1990s. Also, the unemployment benefit system retained, in the 1990s and 2000s, the basic characteristics, which were introduced in 1969. The most important change was the abolishment of the rule that let the unemployed regain their right to benefits due to their participation in active measures. From 1993 onwards, only regular work would qualify a person to receive unemployment benefits. This implied a fixed limit to the length of time that a person could receive unemployment benefits.[9]

Thus the basic flexibility–security nexus of the Danish model has remained stable for several decades now.

By contrast, important changes took place with respect to the third corner of the triangle: active labour market policy. Traditionally Denmark has had a high level of public expenditures for active and passive measures together. However, the labour market reform of 1993 – and the subsequent reforms in the following years – marked a shift into a more active, decentral and flexible Danish labour market policy approach.

Therefore, the element of employment security in the Danish model was significantly strengthened during the 1990s and early 2000s.

13.5 SUMMING UP: THE ROAD TO 'FLEXICURITY' IN DENMARK

The above analysis of the historical development of the Danish version of flexicurity can be summarised in three steps.

Firstly, one can identify a high level of workers' mobility (external numerical flexibility) as a structural characteristic of the Danish labour market. An important explanatory factor for this situation is the liberal regime of employment protection as it is adopted in the Danish labour market policy context.

Secondly, the high level of numerical flexibility is made acceptable for the trade unions and, more broadly, became legitimate within the framework of the traditional value system of a Scandinavian type welfare state by the development of a state supported unemployment insurance system supplemented by cash benefits for the uninsured unemployed. These two elements constitute the basic flexibility–security nexus, which in its current version has been present since the late 1960s.

Thirdly, during the 1990s, a more ambitious active labour market policy was added to it by incorporating stronger motivation and qualification effects to stimulate the flows of workers between employment and unemployment because of which the element of employment security has even been reinforced.

Therefore, one must stress that the Danish model of 'flexicurity' is the outcome of a long historical process involving a series of negotiations and compromises between the social partners, the evolution of the welfare state and – in recent years – a gradual development of a more active profile of labour market policy. The model is thus a prime example of the specific Danish version of the negotiated economy.

Therefore it should be taken as a source of inspiration for new ideas about alternative configurations of flexible labour markets and economic security for the individual – not as a simple scheme, which is ready for immediate export.

If one should point to a specific lesson, which may inspire policy makers from other national backgrounds, it could be the awareness of the positive effects of a low level of individual employment protection on the dynamism of the labour market. If a liberal regime of employment protection is combined with institutions that support income (and employment) security, one can obtain a competitive employment system and social welfare combined. The challenge is to achieve the level of thrust between the social partners, which allows for employment protection to be reduced, while security mechanisms are being created.

NOTES

1. For recent academic work on the subject, see for example, Madsen (2002, 2003, 2004, 2006). For a more detailed empirical presentation and analysis of the Danish employment system, reference is made to these publications.
2. For a further development of this idea of trade-offs between different configurations of numerical flexibility and social protection, reference can be made to Auer and Cazes (2003), Chapter 1.
3. One should add that the author's previous studies of the Danish model have also taken a comparative approach, but mainly by presenting and comparing basic statistical information for several OECD-countries on employment protection, labour mobility etc (see for instance

Madsen, 2003). In the present context, the aim is to delve somewhat deeper into the comparison of a more limited selection of countries.

4. The OECD-study covers the protection of both regular employment, temporary employment and the employees in case of collective dismissals. Since the focus in the present context is on numerical flexibility related to the individual employment contract, the other elements in the study are not included here.
5. The description of the national systems refers to the situation in 2004.
6. One can add that the impression of a low spending level for the UK is supported by the evidence given in the 'European Social Statistics on Labour Market Policy: Expenditure and Participants', 2002, from Eurostat. Although there are some differences between this source and the OECD-data, the magnitude is about the same.
7. For a broad introduction to the historical development of the Danish welfare state, reference can be made to Jørgensen (2002), Chapter 2.
8. The final blow was delivered when copies were broadcasted of a statement by the Prime Minister, who during the election campaign had announced that no cutbacks in the benefit system would take place, if he came into power.
9. For a more detailed description of the benefit system and other institutional factors, see Madsen (2002, 2003).

REFERENCES

Arbejdsministeriet (1999), *Arbejdsmarkedsreformerne – ét statusbillede,* Copenhagen: Ministry of Labour.

Auer, P. (2000), *Employment revival in Europe. Labour market success in Austria, Denmark, Ireland and the Netherlands,* Geneva: International Labour Organization.

Auer, P. and Cazes, S. (eds) (2003), *Employment stability in an age of flexibility. Evidence from industrialized countries*, Geneva: International Labour Organization.

European Foundation for the Improvement of Working and Living Conditions (1999), *Employment options of the future*, Luxembourg: Office of Official Publications of the European Community.

Gallie, D. and Paugam, S. (2000), *Welfare regimes and the Experience of Unemployment in Europe*, Oxford: Oxford University Press.

Hall, P.A. and Soskice, D. (2001), *Varieties of Capitalism: The Institutional Foundations of Comparative Advantage,* Cambridge: Cambridge University Press.

Jørgensen, H. (2002), *Consensus, Cooperation and Conflict: The Policy Making Process in Denmark*, Cheltenham, UK and Brookfield, US: Edward Elgar.

Jørgensen, H. and Larsen, F (2002), 'Labour market policies', in Jørgensen, H., *Consensus, Cooperation and Conflict: The Policy Making Process in Denmark,* Cheltenham, UK and Brookfield, US: Edward Elgar, 167–89.

Katzenstein, P.J. (1985), *Small States in World Markets. Industrial Policy in Europe,* London: Cornell.

Kærgaard, N. and Hansen, H. (1994), Den danske arbejdsløshed 1903–1990, *Samfundsøkonomen* (6), 9–13.

Madsen, P. Kongshøj (2002), 'The Danish model of flexicurity: A paradise – with some snakes', in Sarfati, H. and Bonoli, G. (eds), *Labour market and social protections reforms in international perspective: Parallel or converging tracks?*, Aldershot, UK, Ashgate Publishing, 243–65.

Madsen, P. Kongshøj (2003), 'Flexicurity' through labour market policies and institutions in Denmark', in Auer, P. and Cazes, S. (eds), *Employment stability in an age of flexibility. Evidence from industrialized countries,* Geneva: International Labour Organization, 59–105.

Madsen, P. Kongshøj and Pedersen, L. (eds) (2003), *Drivkræfter bag arbejdsmarkedspolitikken,* København: Socialforskningsinstituttet 03: 13.

Madsen, Per Kongshøj (2004), The Danish model of 'flexicurity': experiences and lessons, *TRANSFER. European Review of Labour and Research,* **10** (2), 187–207.

Madsen, Per Kongshøj (2006), 'How can it possibly fly? The paradox of a dynamic labour market in a Scandinavian welfare state', in Campbell, J.A. Hall J.A. and Pedersen, O.K. (eds), *National Identity and the varieties of Capitalism: THE DANISH EXPERIENCE,* Montreal: McGill-Queen's University Press, 321–55.

Mailand, M and Due, J. (2003), 'Partsstyring i arbejdsmarkedspolitikken – perspektiver og alternativer', in Madsen, P. Kongshøj and Pedersen, L. (eds), *Drivkræfter bag arbejdsmarkedspolitikken,* København: Socialforskningsinstituttet 03: 13, 202–33.

OECD (1997), *Employment Outlook,* Paris: OECD.

OECD (2002), *Benefits and wages. OECD Indicators,* Paris: OECD.

OECD (2004), *Employment Outlook,* Paris: OECD.

Rosholm, Michael and Michael Svarer (2004), Estimating the Threat Effect of Active Labour Market Programmes, IZA Discussion Paper, No. 1300.

Torfing, J. (2004), *Det stille sporskifte i velfærdsstaten, Magtudredningen,* Aarhus Universitetsforlag.

Wilthagen, T. and Tros, F. (2004), 'The concept of 'Flexicurity': A new approach to regulating employment and labour markets', *TRANSFER,* **10** (2), 166–86.

Werner, H. and Winkler, W. (2004), 'Unemployment Compensation Systems – A Cross-Country Comparison', *IAB topics,* No. 56, Institute for Employment Research of the Federal Employment Services, Germany <www.iab.de>.

Winter, S. (2003), 'Kanalrundfart eller Zapning? – Om kanaler og arenaer i den aktive arbejdsmarkedspolitik', in Madsen and Pedersen (eds), *Drivkræfter bag arbejdsmarkedspolitikken,* 268–317.

14. Conclusion. Flexibility and Employment Security in Europe: a Siamese Twin?

Ruud Muffels

14.1 RESEARCH QUESTIONS AND CONCEPTUAL MODEL

Transitional labour markets and flexicurity

The now very popular debate on 'flexibility' and 'security' in European academic and policy circles mirrors the classical economic issue as to how policies can maintain or even improve the balance between efficiency and equity on the labour market. Flexibility is understood in this volume in economic terms as the degree to which the labour market is capable of creating opportunities for employers and employees to meet their demands for qualified workers and jobs. A flexible labour market implies an efficiently operating labour market exhibiting high levels of mobility on the internal (functional flexibility) as well as the external labour market (numerical flexibility). It means that employers have more leeway either due to lack of institutional constraints or to opportunities offered by the terms of law to adapt the workforce to changes in demand. For workers and the unemployed it means that they rapidly acquire the job they are looking for and for which they are qualified, but also that they can adapt their labour input according to their needs throughout the life-course (Schmid, 1995b). The meaning of equity and security is rather straightforward and boils down to assuming that properly working labour markets safeguard equal opportunities or chances to maintain fair levels of income and employment security to all workers over the entire career. To the extent that countries are capable to maintain a balanced mix of flexibility and security, this volume tries to answer the 'why' question as to what are the main explanatory factors for the observed mix in a country but also the 'how' question, as to which policies and institutions can be held responsible for the relative 'success and failure of the different policy regimes' or 'pathways' in Europe in attaining a balance between the two.

In Chapter 1, we formulated a heuristic framework or conceptual model that allowed us to put the various contributions into an analytical and theoretical perspective. The core of the conceptual model is constituted by two main socio-economic approaches, which have an analytical as well as a normative, policy associated part, and which are known under the headings of the 'Transitional Labour Market' (TLM) and 'flexicurity' approach (Schmid, 1995a; Wilthagen and Tros, 2004). Each of the two strands in the literature refers to broader theoretical underpinnings in the realm of economics, sociology and political science.

The conceptual model as explained in Chapter 1 builds on these two main approaches by examining labour market transitions, how they are affected by the institutional set-up and how they shape the attained levels of flexibility and security in society. We formulated two competing hypotheses known as the trade-off and the flexicurity thesis. The first, for various reasons, argues for a negative or trade-off relationship between flexibility and security. One major reason is related to how labour markets adjust to economic shocks and to the need for more flexibility associated with the internationalisation of the economy, either through adapting the size ('numerical flexibility') or the organisation of the labour force ('functional flexibility') or through adapting prices and wages ('wage flexibility'). Due to the strong employment protection and wage setting institutions, European labour markets have little leeway and confront either low productivity or high unemployment levels, and/or a large segment of lower-paid and less secure 'non-standard contracts' to which, because of the knowledge economy especially the low-skilled workers are likely to be assigned (Blau and Kahn 2002; DiPrete, et al. 2006). The second argues for a positive relationship between flexibility and security because the 'employment relationship' itself has shifted due to globalisation forces and the alleged flexibilisation process. This shift can be delineated as a change from 'lifetime employment' to the 'boundary-less career' (Stone, 2001, 2005a). Following this view the workplace is changing significantly due to the ongoing shifts, replacing the old employment relationship based on job security and lifetime employment by a new one, sometimes called the flexible employment relationship, according to which job security is put in place by employability security and lifetime employment by the 'boundary-less career' (Stone 2005b). This shift went along with the 'erosion of internal labour markets' (Gazier, 1998; Grimshaw et al., 2001; Schmid and Gazier, 2002) because of which workers have to change jobs more frequently thus weakening the ties with their employer. Job security tends to be replaced by employability security that will offer employees more opportunities to develop their human capital that in turn will allow them to maintain employment on the external labour market. From a policy perspective the 'flexicurity' thesis boils down to stressing the synergy that may arise from particular policies aiming at increasing flexibility as well as security by reducing labour market rigidities and increasing worker's 'employability' through investments in human capital, training or life-long learning programmes (European Commission, 2006, 2007a; Wilthagen and Tros, 2004). In the empirical parts I and II of the book as well as in the policy part III we try to gain a better understanding of the relationship between flexibility and security and to discover whether this relationship is indeed symbiotic due to a high level of flexibility which is considered a prerequisite for affording a high level of employment security and vice versa. In the title of this chapter we therefore used in a metaphorical sense the term 'Siamese twin' to delineate the very close relatiosnship between the two notions.

Whereas the empirical evidence to date only provides static snapshots of the country's levels of flexibility and security, the contributions collected in this volume use a dynamic approach to examine in-work transition patterns during the 1990s and how they impact upon the flexibility–security nexus. Particular interest has been devoted to the impact of labour market institutions and socio-economic policies on that relationship.

Outline
In sections 14.2 to 14.4 we discuss the contributions dealing with the three parts of the book: 14.2. Labour market mobility and in-work transitions, 14.3. Scarring effects of unemployment and non-standard employment and 14.4. Best policy practices in Australia, Canada and Denmark. In the concluding Section 14.5 we draw some policy lessons from the findings and we formulate some ideas for future research.

14.2 LABOUR MARKET MOBILITY AND IN-WORK TRANSITIONS

'Stepping-stones' versus 'dead-end' thesis
The focus in this part is on the transitions from non-standard into standard jobs. The major issue dealt with concerns the roles that non-standard jobs fulfil in modern labour markets: do they act as 'stepping-stones' bridging the gap between open-ended contracts and unemployment or do they act as 'employment traps' into low-paid, low level jobs from which workers rarely escape, known as the so-called 'dead-end' jobs. If the actual situation in Europe supports the 'dead-end' thesis, non-standard jobs are indeed to be considered 'precarious' as the French word 'precarité' for these type of jobs alludes to as explained in the contribution of Barbier in Chapter 2. He made

an inventory of the French and international literature providing an in-depth review of the academic debate on this notion of 'precarité'. He refers among other things to the work of the sociologist Robert Castel who drawing on the 'regulationist' literature describes the rise of new forms of labour in the last decennia as the erosion of the classical wage-earner relationship ('la societé salariale') or wage–labour nexus in the Fordist era. Just like Castel who considers these new employment forms among the clearest manifestations of this erosion, Barbier argues that precarious work is one of, if not, the most important feature of this erosion but it also affects the core labour force. He mentions the word précarisation in the French language, that is, the process whereby society as a whole becomes more and more precarious, and becomes basically destabilised, resembling the notion of the 'risk society' (Beck, 1992; Giddens, 2007). Job précarisation is therefore seen by him as part of the dynamics of modernisation. Barbier eloquently shows that the term 'precarious jobs' has no legal equivalent in other contexts than the French with the exception maybe of some Southern countries such as Spain and Italy. Barbier mentions therefore that in a European-wide research project at the conceptual level there was a strong disagreement between researchers on the notion of 'precarité'. He argues that underlying the different conceptual notions a more or less implicit, normative debate takes place in Europe about the consequences of the current trends of labour market flexibilisation.

For that reason he prefers the broader notion of 'job quality' that in the national context will also be affected by normative interpretations and value orientations but that seems a much more useful concept in comparative perspective. Barbier is not alone in his critical account of these new employment contracts, as also the American sociologist DiPrete supposes that the majority of workers engaged in these fixed-term contracts are low-skilled workers who through a process of 'creaming-off' and lack of sufficient demand for low-skilled people are not able to find a permanent job (DiPrete et al., 2006).

Evidence presented earlier and from some European surveys in the 1990s showed that a substantial number of non-standard jobs are indeed of low quality in terms of pay, working conditions and job security. In the Employment in Europe 2001 report, the Commission calculated the number of 'dead-end' jobs on two-thirds of all fixed-term contracts (that is, 8 per cent of 12 per cent) in 1996 in the 14 European countries under scrutiny. However, the Commission used a static definition as either a fixed-term or a short-term contract, or a job without formal contract in non-supervisory functions, that do not offer any further employer-provided training (European Commission, 2001).

The evidence also suggests that with respect to the quality of these jobs there is a North–South divide with low quality, badly paid jobs with poor conditions in the South but better quality jobs in the North. In a recent report (Philips and Eamets, 2007) it was shown that although in Eastern transition countries the prevalence of time-limited contracts is much lower, the quality in terms of pay level, poverty risk and training opportunities was similarly poor to that in the South but worse compared to the North.

Some evidence on the quality of temporary jobs is given by Debels in Chapter 3 in this volume. She shows that temporary workers bear higher risks on poverty than permanent workers but less so than unemployed workers. She also showed that these risks very much depend on the institutional context; in Northern countries with more generous benefit systems the poverty risks of temporary workers are much lower than in the UK, France or the Southern countries with rather ungenerous benefits, suggesting that the income consequences of temporary employment are cushioned in the Northern welfare states by generous income transfers. She also showed that the household context matters a lot; if there are other workers and incomes earned in the household the poverty risks for temporary workers are strongly reduced. This holds true especially for the Northern countries as well as for France and the UK but not for the Southern countries. The explanation for the unanticipated findings for the Southern countries is that it is due to a selection effect associated with self-selection of young people with relatively high personal income into households without other workers. This remarkable finding is associated with the well-known fact that young people tend to stay rather long in their parent's home in Southern countries unless the level of their personal income is sufficiently high to afford a living on their own (Aassve et al., 2001). It also implies that a move from a temporary job into a permanent job might in the Southern countries involve, when it is accompanied with leaving the parent's home, an increase in poverty instead of a decrease as it generally does. She also found that such a transition in the UK has no significant effect on the individual poverty risk, possibly due to the low wages paid to these temporary workers.

One might also assume that these jobs allow particular categories of workers to fulfil their very specific working-time preferences which arise from caring duties or family responsibilities (Anxo et al., 2006; Dekker, 2007). Non-standard jobs might also grant workers more time to search for the best job on the labour market (for example, school-leavers) and might render workers more flexible working times which are better tuned to the caring obligations of female workers therewith improving the work–life balance. Evidence from the Employment in Europe 2001 report shows that about 35 per cent of all workers in temporary contracts is involuntarily employed in these contracts and 40 per cent of those in part-time work (European Commission, 2001). It shows that for the majority of these non-standard workers, employment in such jobs is not enforced but based on free choice suggesting that such jobs meet their working-time preferences better than standard jobs. Hence the picture about the role these non-standard jobs fulfil for people's working lives and careers appears mixed.

One of the contributions (Chapter 4 by Hernanz et al.) looked more specifically into the involuntary nature of temporary work and whether it impacts upon the chance to move into a permanent job in two Southern countries. They compared Italy with Spain using the national Labour Force Surveys and showed that respectively 40 and 70 per cent of workers are involuntarily engaged in such jobs but that in Italy and even in Spain there are no significant differences in transition rates between involuntary and voluntarily temporarily employed workers after controlling for a set of personal or family and labour market characteristics. They also showed that the transition rates into permanent employment are higher for temporary workers than for the unemployed especially in Spain. For Italy they found that after correction for self-selection through estimation of a bivariate probit model – unemployed workers having more opportunities to get a permanent job seem to prefer to stay unemployed and not to move into a temporary job – the difference in transition rates between temporary and unemployed workers is much lower than in Spain. They show again that it very much depends on the institutional context to what extent a temporary job is a substitute for the unavailability of a standard job or a means to fulfil someone's working time preferences.

Mobility into permanent jobs

The results of Debels in Chapter 3 indicate that if temporary workers find a permanent job they might indeed enter the ranks of job-secure workers but they still are confronted with low demanding jobs offering few opportunities for training, low pay and also poor income and wage prospects.

These findings might explain why Booghmans et al. in Chapter 5 of this volume drawing from evidence on mobility patterns and career paths of various categories of Belgian workers found higher mobility rates among workers with low wages, among part-time working women and among young people and those entering employment for the first time. These categories are overrepresented in the population of non-standard workers. Because of the lower security involved in a substantial part of the non-standard jobs the mobility rates are inherently higher than in standard jobs. On the other hand these jobs are attractive to particular categories of workers exactly because of their weaknesses in terms of the flexibility and security involved allowing the beholders more leeway to manage their careers and life-courses in particular stages. For this very reason they are just seen as an intermediate step in the career. With respect to the evidence presented on career paths they also point to generation effects, because over time the careers of younger generations of workers tend to become more volatile as they experience more episodes of non-work due to unemployment, career breaks or care leaves which Schmid has called 'transitional phases' in the career. A similar conclusion is drawn in a recent study for the Netherlands and the UK also based on sequence data analyses of which the results are given in a report of the European Foundation (Muffels et al., 2008).

They further sketched the vulnerable career paths of older workers and immigrants. The first group tends to have more stable careers with much less volatility, but also much lower re-entry chances once they get unemployed, whereas the latter group experience much more volatility during their careers but similar to older workers higher exit rates into unemployment or inactivity and lower re-entry chances.

Trade-off or synergy
These results suggest that dependent on the institutional context there is a trade-off between mobility on the one hand and employment/income security on the other (Muffels and Luijkx, 2008). A high mobility into permanent jobs as is the case in the liberal, unregulated or uncoordinated British labour market seems to offer in the end little guarantees to these temporary workers on employment and income security. This is also shown in a recent comparative study for the Netherlands, Germany and the UK by Dekker (2007). These trade-offs are even more evident in the strongly regulated labour markets of the South where a low level of external numerical flexibility due to strong employment protection rules for the 'insiders' is geared to lenient regulation with respect to fixed-term contracts entailing low levels of employment and income protection to the non-standard workers, the 'outsiders'. But the evidence presented here also shows that such trade-offs do not need to exist since in some of the Nordic welfare states a low level of employment protection seems to go along with a high level of mobility within standard jobs and between temporary and permanent jobs. When these high mobility rates are geared towards activating labour market policies, regular skills-upgrading efforts and generous social security systems, high levels of income and employment security are to be achieved even in the longer run which is delineated by the European Commission as the 'flexicurity' pathway.

The results also show that there is no definite answer to the question whether non-standard jobs act as stepping-stones or as 'dead-end' jobs. It seems fair to say that due to the large heterogeneity of these jobs they act for some categories of workers as stepping-stones and for others as 'dead-end' jobs though much of their positive or adverse consequences are mediated through the institutional and labour market context. In countries with strong institutional support to safeguard the employment as well as the income security attached to working in a temporary job, it emerges that these jobs are much more similar in terms of the income and employment security they provide over the entire career than in countries where there is lack of such institutional support and the conditions of work and pay are ruled by the market such as in the UK. Institutions do seemingly matter to explain the dissimilar mobility patterns and outcomes across countries. However, to arrive at more robust conclusions about which perspective is more dominant in Europe we also have to take the longer-term or career effects into account.

14.3 SCARRING EFFECTS OF UNEMPLOYMENT AND NON-STANDARD WORK ON THE CAREER

Trigger events and scarring

The results so far seem to provide evidence for the thesis that the process of social stratification in modern societies can partly be explained by the occurrence of 'trigger events' such as unemployment or employment in a low-level and low-paid temporary or part-time jobs (Gangl, 2006). Trigger events can be defined as life-course events having potentially strong adverse or 'scarring' effects on the future career and life-chances of people (job loss, childbirth, marriage). In this part we investigate to what extent trigger events such as temporary work, self-employment, unemployment and part-time work have indeed lasting 'scarring' effects on the future employment position and career of different categories of workers. The main question dealt with is to what extent the institutional context might help to mitigate the longer-term 'scarring' effects of these trigger events. The long-term focus is important because in the end what matters to people more is not so much their current status but their prospects also. If indeed working in a temporary or a part-time job has a lasting 'scarring' effect on the career, just like unemployment might have, one might question why national and European policies should indeed support the creation of such jobs. It might also be that it very much depends on the institutional setting or on prevailing social norms what effects non-standard jobs entail for employment and income security.

For looking into this issue in more detail, Muffels and Luijkx in Chapter 6 first examine the effects of the institutional context on occupational and contract mobility and income and employment security using comparative data on male workers for the 1990s. They elaborated some institutional and dynamic outcome indicators for mobility/flexibility and income and employment security after which they mapped the countries according to their performance in safeguarding simultaneously high levels of mobility/flexibility and security. The results confirm the findings from the contributions in Part I that the Anglo-Saxon and Nordic welfare regimes outperform the regulated Continental and Southern countries in terms of the attained levels of mobility and security. They show that the unregulated Anglo-Saxon countries seem to pay a small price for their high mobility not through lower levels of employment security, which are better than expected, but through reduced income security due to poor benefits and a low safety net. In the same vein they show that the Nordic countries, performing much better with a view to safeguarding income security, pay a small price though in terms of a lower mobility. The results especially with a view to the performance of the regulated Southern countries provide a warning against too much regulation leading to a segmented labour market protecting insiders at the expense of outsiders and therewith endangering the levels of mobility or flexibility as well as of security. These results therefore confirm the conjectures of the 'Varieties of Capitalism' literature that there is a sharp divide between unregulated and regulated market economies with respect to, for example, skill formation, wage setting and industrial relations (Hall and Soskice, 2001; Albert, 1991).

The mapping of the countries based on these dynamic indicators show no largely different results compared to the classifications in the Employment in Europe 2006 and 2007 reports which were based on institutional as well as static outcome indicators for external and internal flexibility and for income, employment and work–life balance security (European Commission, 2006; 2007). The evidence from these reports and from Chapter 6 shows that the regime clustering resembles to a large extent the renowned but amended classification of Esping-Andersen but also that whatever indicator set used (static versus dynamic and external numerical only versus internal and external numerical and functional flexibility) the results are fairly robust.

The findings on the estimation of some explanatory regression models – in particular multinomial logit models – on occupational and contract mobility convincingly show that although institutional differences clearly play a part in explaining the differences across countries, common structural factors such as human capital endowments and occupational class still exert a major impact explaining the process of mobility and stratification in society. The authors found, not surprisingly, strong support for the role of human capital investments and the 'knowledge economy' on occupational and contract mobility patterns in Europe. The low-educated worker seems more likely to experience downward moves into lower-level jobs on the labour market than the higher skilled worker. They also found that the low-educated worker is less likely to move from a temporary job into a permanent job compared to the worker at intermediate education level. Remarkably the same though unanticipated effect was found for the high educated worker. This might again point to the selection effect found in the Hernanz et al. study in Chapter 4 where they showed that high educated workers tend to stay unemployed instead of accepting a temporary job due to their perceived better chances to find a permanent job. The high educated workers occupying a temporary job are therefore likely to be a selective group of high educated people with reduced chances to acquire a permanent job for other reasons associated with for example, health impairments or very specific working-time preferences which permanent jobs cannot fulfil. The same unanticipated effect for the high educated was found by Dekker in his comparative study for the UK, the Netherlands and Germany (Dekker, 2007).

Unemployment and temporary employment scarring
In the contribution of Gangl in Chapter 7 some more evidence on the scarring thesis is given but for unemployment acting as the trigger event. He applied a non-parametric treatment or matching technique using panel data for the US and Europe to estimate the causal effects of unemployment experience on subsequent employment and wage histories. His findings show that unemployment in both the US and Europe represents a veritable career risk to workers because unemployment entail serious economic costs in terms of diminished employment prospects and reduced post-unemployment earnings. He also compared the 'scarring' effects of unemployment in the unregulated American labour market with the 'scarring' in the strongly regulated labour markets in Europe. He found that in the US, employment prospects tend to recover fairly quickly, yet the post-unemployment earnings losses remain in the order of 10 per cent even after three years of subsequent employment. Remarkably though, the same results were obtained in very different institutional and labour market contexts in Europe and seemingly also hold true for British and French workers, but even for German workers who faced more difficulties to recoup from the initial employment losses through finding stable employment. He observed a large heterogeneity in the 'scarring' effects in Europe signalling much lower economic costs of unemployment in the Nordic and Southern countries. With respect to post-unemployment earnings the Nordic regimes perform best because the average post-unemployment earnings in Denmark and Finland are, during the 1990s, a full 8 per cent above the average earnings in the unregulated regimes of the UK, Ireland and the US (as reported in Gangl, 2006). In the same study he even observed for the continental countries Germany, France, Austria and Belgium a 5 per cent earnings advantage for the unemployed worker compared to the Anglo-Saxon countries.

He also argued that labour market institutions may have a significant role to play but the interesting twist of the story is that only those countries do well in recovering the 'scarring' effects that rely on either employment protection regulation or on generous unemployment benefits to protect the earnings capacity across spells of unemployment but not on both. Evidently, employment protection tends to lower scarring in countries with weak unemployment benefit systems but sharply increases scarring in countries with strong unemployment insurance systems. In parallel with this he concludes that generous unemployment insurance benefits reduces scarring in flexible or unregulated labour markets but increases it in more regulated ones. The regimes in continental Europe combining a strong labour market regulation with fairly generous benefits show no less unemployment scarring than the unregulated Anglo-Saxon labour markets lacking extensive worker protection through regulation or insurance.

A similar conclusion on the size of scarring effects across regimes was drawn in a recent study also using the European Community Household panel but not for the unemployed but for workers employed in fixed-term contracts (Muffels et al., 2008). In the same study drawing evidence from the longer running national panel data sets of the UK, the Netherlands and Germany they show that scarring effects for workers in these contracts tend to persist longer over time in Germany and the Netherlands than in the UK. In the UK workers seem to have more opportunities to catch up and to recover from the initial wage drop signalling the more efficiently operating labour market.

The findings on unemployment scarring tempted Gangl in another study to suggest that the employment protection legislation (EPL) and unemployment insurance (UI) institutions seem to affect the wage setting and labour market segmentation on the labour market. Unemployment insurance might improve overall labour market matching because it enhances the permeability of occupational and industrial boundaries in the labour market suggesting that it reduces therewith segmentation. On the other hand UI and EPL seem to reduce between-firm wage dispersion in identical occupations and industries which also reduces the likelihood that workers end up accepting relatively bad jobs for reemployment (Gangl, 2006). This supports the well-known thesis that UI and EPL also fulfil a role in improved job matching on the labour market, because they render employers and employees more time to search for the best match.

Some more evidence on the impact of EPL and UI on in-work transitions is given in another study (Muffels, 2007). That study shows that the tighter EPL is, the lower downward and upward occupational mobility is. The stricter these rules are, the more employers and employees seek for more flexible options as a way to circumvent these rules, which also explains the larger share of temporary or non-standard contracts in more regulated countries. This also explains why the more lenient the EPL for temporary workers is to compensate for the strict rules for standard workers, the lower occupational mobility rates are. With respect to contract mobility it is shown that the less strict the EPL in a country is for standard workers, the more likely for temporary workers to move into a permanent job. The UI seems to exert neither a significant effect on occupational mobility nor on contract mobility, except for the negative effect on the move from a temporary job into self-employment and inactivity. The results of these studies certainly beg for further scrutiny into the effects of UI and EPL on labour market mobility.

Self-employment scarring

In Chapter 7, Meager proceeds on investigating the scarring effects of another important trigger event, that is, a spell of self-employment (SE) in the UK. There is much less evidence on the scarring of self-employment spells because of which his treatment renders a noteworthy insight into the scarring that self-employed people face in the unregulated British labour market that is traditionally featured by a high share of non-salaried workers. His review of the previous UK evidence (up to the late 1980s) on the impacts of self-employment spells on the careers and income-levels in the short term and over the life-course supplemented with more recent work using UK panel data shows no firm evidence that such spells in the unregulated UK labour market make a positive contribution to employment and wage career development. The findings also call for some scepticism regarding the promotion of SE as a policy tool within the transitional labour market framework. The self-employed constitute a very heterogeneous group of people with highly polarised and dispersed wage and income levels. Once other factors are controlled for they face higher life-course risks in terms of ending into the lowest income deciles group. Short-term scarring effects are likely to be limited since transitions into regular employment do not seem to impair the income prospects compared to those who had not experienced such spells.

The longer-term scarring effects seem however a serious threat to those who consider a start-up into self-employment since having had spells of self-employment during the life-course is a predictor of very low incomes in later life. This latter effect is associated with lower built-up resources by the self-employed compared to their counterparts in paid employment due to the high costs involved in drawing up savings for UI and pension entitlements.

He estimated logit models of self-employment entry and exit and multinomial models of entry and exit by three occupational groups, professional workers, skilled and unskilled workers. The findings reveal strong gender effects in self-employment patterns; women are less likely to enter into self-employment and to survive in self-employment compared to men. By occupational group it is shown that the gender penalty for entry is significant across all groups but clearly lowest for flows to professional self-employment whereas it is significant and highest for exit out of professional self-employment. A similar striking difference might be observed between the young and the old: young people are less likely to enter self-employment and to maintain in self-employment than older people though after some age threshold older people are less likely to enter and more likely to exit.

Meager is therefore very pessimistic about self-employment as a vehicle for social and occupational upward mobility. The most striking results in his view are that despite the growth in self-employment in the UK, and the greater dynamism of self-employment, having had a self-employed parent remains one of the strongest and statistically significant predictors of entry to, and success in (survival in) self-employment. Disaggregating by occupation shows unambiguously, that this process of inter-generational transmission of self-employment propensities applies particularly to the self-employed in semi- and unskilled occupations. For the higher skilled worker (professional occupations), it is not so much parental self-employment background per se but parental occupational status that impacts upon entry in self-employment.

This renders a warning against too optimistic voices in policy circles about facilitating transitions into self-employment as a means to improve the 'employability' as well as the income and employment security of workers who otherwise have few chances to make a successful career. In the last part of his contribution he went into the role of activating labour market policies by comparing a supported self-employed sample of 2,000 persons between 18 and 30 years old with a matched comparison group of non-supported self-employed persons of 1,600 persons in the same age group in the UK during the early 2000s. He used a matching technique to estimate the causal effect of the treatment, in this case of the young self-employed persons being supported by the State to facilitate their business start-up. Though the matching was based on a large number of characteristics, unobserved heterogeneity due to differences in ability, attitudes and motivation might have affected the outcomes even though some self-reported attitudinal variables dealing with risk-taking were taken account of. Some sort of selection bias might therefore have the effect that the impact of the support scheme (the treatment) is overestimated because differences in outcomes are attributed to the scheme whereas in reality it reflects the higher level of motivation among the scheme participants (that is, the treated). Therefore it is more notable that the support scheme seems to have had any significant effect on subsequent employment or earnings chances over the three wave observation window in the early 2000s. Rather the results suggest that the scheme participants were worse off compared to the comparison sample (the non-treated) while they were in self-employment and no better off (or possible worse off) after the self-employment spell.

Meager shows in his contribution that these illuminating results for the UK are also confirmed for another unregulated or liberal welfare state being the US, rendering little support to the idea that facilitating self-employment might be a vehicle for activating labour market policies. The evidence presented provides little ground to expect that self-employment entry contributes to improving the employability of particular groups on the labour market such as the young (unemployed) people and women who after a career-break due to childbirth want to return into employment. To what extent these results also hold for other labour market contexts than the unregulated liberal labour markets of the UK and the US remains an open question but certainly for further research.

Scarring effects of part-time work and childbirth
A part-time employment spell is another trigger event but one that is often preceded by an even more important life-course event, childbirth. In Europe, 7.5 per cent of males and one third of women work part-time though in some countries like the Netherlands the percentage is much higher, that is, 75 per cent. Part-time work forms part of our definition of non-standard labour for which it is argued that it might have lasting 'scarring' effects on the future career of especially women. In Chapter 9, Fouarge and Muffels looked into the scarring effects of part-time work for the future employment and wage career. They also tried to gauge the differential impacts of supporting institutions on the change in working time owing to the career break that followed childbirth in 13 countries. Further to that, they examined the quickness in which especially women tend to recoup from the initial reduction in working time due to the caring duties involved. The authors showed that women much more than men tend to stay in part-time work and are not so likely to move like men do, into longer working hours and full-time jobs. Women tend to have a lower probability to end up in full-time employment after the career break than men though the negative effect becomes smaller the longer ago the event took place. Part-timers are more likely to end up in unemployment due to their lower human capital as a result of the interrupted career, though again the effect becomes smaller over time. Whether these effects point to scarring depends on whether the entry into part-time work and the change in hours is voluntary or not. They examined the reasons for women to change working time and they found that part-time working women who do not want to work more hours because of caring obligations are less likely to make a transition into full-time employment which results are robust for longer time periods since the event happened. This confirms that a large share of part-time work is voluntary reflecting differences in working-time preferences.

Childbirth indeed seems to reduce working hours in all countries but to a largely different extent. In continental countries such as Germany, France and Austria but also in the transition country Hungary and the UK, women tend to withdraw almost fully from the labour market after childbirth. According to the authors this might signal differences in institutional support to help mothers to retain employment since in countries with more institutional support such as in Denmark and the Netherlands full withdrawal from the labour market is less likely to occur as a result of childbirth and women also tend to stay longer in part-time work after childbirth. These differences might partly also signal the role of social norms in society in such a way that in countries where the norm is to work part-time for working mothers such as in the Netherlands, women tend to adhere to these norms by withdrawing only partially and by staying in part-time work during the following career whereas when the norm is to work full-time like in the UK women tend to withdraw fully from the labour market and to recoup into full-time employment later on.

Withdrawal from the labour market or reducing working hours also leads to a reduction in earnings and the more so the more women tend to reduce hours and the less income support is available in a particular country. But even for women who remained in paid employment, post-childbirth earnings tend to be markedly lower though the availability of public transfers seems to cushion the adverse income shortfall due to childbirth. The authors calculated the earnings penalty to be 5 per cent on average for all the countries each year for the five-year time period following the childbirth event. The income penalty however appears relatively lower in the Netherlands and the UK and in the Southern countries. The reasons for this might be very different across the countries: in the UK it might be the efficiently operating labour market allowing women to recoup quickly from the initial drop in working hours; in the Netherlands it might be the generosity of the income transfer system and in the Southern countries the family or the informal economy compensating for the initial earnings losses. The authors eventually conclude that the role of supporting institutions and policies to help working mothers to quickly recoup from the working time and earnings losses play a crucial role in avoiding scarring effects and in allowing women to meet their working time preferences and to improve their work–life balance.

In the following contribution Bijwaard, Van Dijk and De Koning dealt again with part-time work and the role played by working time preferences but their focus was not on the scarring effects of part-time work nor on the role of institutions but on the salient effects a transition in the labour market might have to fulfil one's working time preferences. They focused on the relationship between the discrepancy people experience between desired and actual working-time and subsequent transitions on the labour market and whether these transitions then indeed reduce the initial discrepancy and increase job satisfaction. They only had panel data for the Netherlands but since part-time work is widespread among females and increasingly also among males in the Netherlands, the study is interesting. The findings are especially relevant against the backdrop of more and more people expressing difficulties to meet the time pressures they face during the so-called 'rush hour' of life, the stage in the life-course where people are between 35 and 50 years of age and work, education and caring duties cumulate. A marked share of 20 to 25 per cent of the Dutch workers, apparently felt such discrepancy between actual and desired working hours. The relevant issue is whether the discrepancy can be resolved by the subsequent decision to make a transition or to change job and whether indeed it has the salient effects of improving job satisfaction and the work–life balance. They used a simple utility maximising framework and estimated multinomial logit models to examine the two-yearly transitions between a small part-time job, a big part-time job and a full-time job. The authors firstly note that there is a trend in the Netherlands to remain in a part-time job and not to move to full-time jobs exactly for reasons related to their working time preferences and work–life balance. The results further confirm the conjecture that the extent by which working time preferences are realised in one's job measured by the discrepancy between actual and desired hours significantly affects the likelihood of a working time transition later in the career irrespective of whether it involves a job change or not. Such a transition appears more likely when the beholder of a job is unsatisfied with his job.

In the second part of their contribution they moved on to the issue whether a working time transition helps to increase job satisfaction. However, in order to deal with selectivity bias because people who are dissatisfied with their job are more likely to leave employment and to drop out of the sample, they tried to correct for that by estimating a conditional probit model using maximum likelihood in a two step procedure. The results made convincingly clear that changing jobs or making a working time transition leads to a significant reduction in the perceived discrepancy and to lead to a significant increase in job satisfaction. More generally, we might conclude that the findings provide support to the idea that the more the labour market is capable to offer a wide range of working time options the better workers are able to meet their working time preferences and the more satisfied they will be with their job and work–life balance.

14.4 BEST POLICY PRACTICES IN DENMARK, CANADA AND AUSTRALIA

In part III of the volume the focus shifted from empirical analyses to analysing 'best policy practices' with a view to TLM and flexicurity in three country cases: Australia, Canada and Denmark.

Australia

In Chapter one we mentioned that the authors of Chapter 11 Ziguras and Stricker argued that Australia went through a major shift of its welfare state from a typical 'wage earners' welfare state' in the 1980s and early 1990s into a pure liberal welfare state in the late 1990s and early 2000s like the UK or the US. Also for other reasons Australia is a dynamic welfare state with more than 20 per cent of the population changing position within employment each year compared to 16 per cent on average in Europe in the mid 1990s. The authors show that this shift has occurred due to traditional forms of protection being dismantled and social risks increasingly being individualised. The social security system became tightly targeted through steep means tests on income. Since the mid 1990s a range of measures were introduced such as including elements of workfare for young people (Work for the Dole scheme), and then for all unemployed, cuts to wage subsidy schemes and training programs, privatised employment services and additional job search requirements At the same time there has been an increase in 'middle and upper-class' welfare such as tax subsidies for housing, private health insurance and private pensions, and greater funding of private schools. Most of these measures have emphasised the 'work-first' approach to employment assistance rather than a 'skills development' approach. The protection enshrined in the labour market has been wound back and while increased flexibility has led to job growth (mostly in the service sector for both, high and low skilled workers), it has also allowed under-employment and precarious work to flourish forcing workers to live on very low incomes, sometimes complemented with part-time or casual work taxed at very high marginal rates.

They show evidence on which particular groups are faced with high risks on being excluded from the labour market using Australian panel data for the early 2000s. The usual suspects turned up in the analyses: the involuntarily unemployed, the low educated, people with long-term health impairments, migrants with poor English, (single) parents with young children, women and indigenous people. The risks for women are particularly related to their working time needs allowing them to combine work and caring duties during the 'rush hour' of life where needs are however not easily met. The authors argue that these risks require new forms of protection which will involve greater adaptability and flexibility combined with concern for better support and redistribution towards those at greater risk reflecting the debate in Europe on 'transitional labour markets' and 'flexicurity'. More concretely, they support the ideas in the TLM-framework for a 'mobility guarantee' to ensure that the aforementioned groups are not permanently excluded. They report on successful practices in some local areas in Australia in the early 2000s with innovative policy programs based on intensive support and case management; vocational training and human capital investments rather than work-first measures.

The authors leave the question open as to what extent their sketch of the Australian development during the 1990s and 2000s of increasing risks on social exclusion has to be attributed to the endogenous process of internationalisation and flexibilisation of the labour market or that the trend can also be attributed, at least partially, to the reforms itself.

Canada

In the next chapter Van den Berg, Von Restorff, Parent and Masi report on the most sweeping reform as their advocates has hailed it of the Canadian (Un)Employment Insurance in the late 1990s which was seen as a major shift from unemployment to employment insurance and from passive to active labour market policies to increase the ease with which unemployed and new entrants find jobs. As we argued in Chapter 1 already, the Canadian reform might teach us about the salient effects of 'employment insurance' compared to the classical 'unemployment insurance' since the transitional labour market advocates claim that the first improves the effectiveness of labour market policies.

The Reform consisted of two main parts, a gradual tightening-up of the unemployment benefits to bring it closer in line with the more restrictive, punitive and less generous 'Anglo-Saxon Market Model' and the set-up of a collection of programs and initiatives for the activation of the 'Employment Insurance' clients consisting of two main parts: the Employment Benefits Program and the Support Services. The Employment Benefits Program implied the creation of targeted wage subsidies and earnings supplements schemes (top-up on earnings of the long term unemployed to facilitate acceptance of low-wage jobs), the self-employment (financial assistance to start-ups) and job creation partnership programmes and the skills development scheme (financial assistance for apprenticeships). The support services implied the creation of employment assistance (counselling, job placement, and mediation), labour market partnerships (funding for smoothening labour force adjustments and collective layoffs) and the Aboriginal human resources development strategy (based on agreements with the Aboriginal organisations to deliver employment programs and services).

The conclusion the authors draw from their in-depth review of the evidence on the success of the reforms was that in the end the transformation of Canada's old unemployment insurance scheme into a brand-new Employment Insurance system, designed to meet the new demands of the modern, knowledge-based economy, was not that sweeping as it made out to be. Much of the reform as the authors argue involved tightening of benefits access rules and lowering of benefits intended as much to produce significant cutbacks in expenditures as to create incentives for changing behaviour. Though there was some shift to activation this hardly adds up to a coherent and comprehensive endeavour along the lines of the TLM approach. In the end, the authors conclude, the much heralded reform turned out to be fairly modest in its actual effects on access to benefits reduction and activation to work. The reform seems to resemble more the classical 'make work pay' logic of the Anglo-Saxon approach rather than the 'make transitions pay' logic of TLM, presuming that overly generous unemployment benefits necessarily create disincentives to work and undermine labour market efficiency even though the reform also intended to raise the maternity and parental leave benefits for new parents and the family supplement benefits to poor families which do not have that adverse effect.

The authors drawing some comparisons with Australia argue that basically Canada shares with Australia the Anglo-Saxon's settler society's 'rugged individualism' with its attendant suspicion of abuse of 'the dole'. They also share the residual approach to the provision of social welfare but while Canada has a weak labour movement, Australia has been famously dubbed a 'wage earners' welfare state, with a strong labour movement, strong job protection, fair minimum wages, and public commitment to full employment. Comparing the reforms in both countries during the late 1980s and early 1990s however, they also note the similarity in the way labour market policies shifted into a more 'active' stance. But while Canada remained on that path after the shift from a progressive conservative ('Tory') to a Liberal government in 1993, though with a proviso with respect to the actual effects of the intended reforms, the Australian change of government from Labour to Liberal-National in 1996, implied a move to a more restrictive, punitive and less generous system as reported in the contribution by Ziguras and Stricker (Chapter 11 in this book).

Viewing the reforms and the evolution of the Canadian and Australian systems over time as convincingly documented in the previous two contributions however, the similarity in the development of both systems are more striking than the differences. Whatever reforms and institutional changes the various governments intended to implement during the 1990s and early 2000s, in the end both countries' policies stay essentially on their national and historical roads resembling their Anglo-Saxon roots. A general conclusion might therefore be that due to institutional inertia policy pathways tend to remain on their original tracks implying that fundamental changes in the features of particular pathways are very unlikely to occur. This also means that there is little reason to support the convergence thesis according to which national systems tend to become more akin while they are subject to the same processes of modernisation (Inkeless, 1981). This holds true even though the similarity of the Canadian and Australian reforms with the reforms in the European context within the domains of labour market and social policies during the same period is rather striking suggesting that structural patterns of individualisation and economic internationalisation are equally important as institutional changes induced by governments to explain the policy processes and outcomes in the various countries. The results of both exercises also show that the two country cases certainly do not fulfil the conditions for qualifying them as 'best practices'. For that reason Van den Berg et al. (see Chapter 12) state that the 'toast of policy makers and researchers in Europe' nowadays seem to be the Danish 'flexicurity' model.

Denmark

In the last chapter therefore, Madsen goes into more detail into the Danish road to 'flexicurity' or the 'golden triangle' of a flexible labour market with weak employment protection, a generous system of economic support for the unemployed and activation policies rooted in upgrading of skills of the unemployed. The version of flexicurity found in Denmark is according to Madsen in terms of Wilthagen's nexus featured by a high numerical flexibility combined with a high level of income security safeguarded through generous and long-lasting benefits and a strong element of employment security stemming from active and resourceful labour market policies.

The chapter compares the Danish employment protection regulations with the Swedish and British one in detail and concludes that Denmark has rather low levels of employment protection equivalent to the UK in many respects (lenient procedures for dismissal, long trial periods, short notice period and low level of compensation) though not in all (severance pay). Madsen therefore concludes that the individual labour contract in Denmark is likewise to the UK to be seen as an economic agreement which can be terminated at will by both sides without the involvement of a third party. The concept of unfair dismissal seems therefore to play a limited role in both countries. He also compared the three countries using indicators on tenure, expenditures on active labour market policies and benefit generosity (replacement rates).

Despite the low level of employment protection, Danish people, according to Madsen, express the highest level of job satisfaction and sense of stability in their working life. The reason might be that lack of security in terms of job security seems compensated by high levels of income security and employment security attained through generous benefits and especially through investments in skills-upgrading of the unemployed and therewith improving their 'employability'. Denmark in some respects seems even more liberal than the most liberal country in the EU, that is, the UK, but the support provided to the unemployed created a safety net equivalent to the much heralded Swedish one and in some respects even more generous. For that reason Madsen labels Denmark as a hybrid case sharing the characteristics of a liberal labour market through high levels of numerical flexibility with a Scandinavian tradition of generous benefits and active labour market policies.

Madsen accentuates that the three components of the 'golden triangle' are the outcome of a long historical development of neo-corporatist consensus building in which the relationships between the State and the social partners on the one hand and between the labour Unions and the Employers' organisations on the other were gradually formed and extended. The main thrust of Denmark seems therefore its high levels of consensus and trust in the social arena enabling the government to trade a high level of flexibility and hence a low level of job security against high levels of income and employment security. Madsen for an explanation, further refers to the impact of the unemployment scheme reforms by the newly elected Social-Democratic government in the early 1990s for which there was strong public support. Eventually, he refers to Katzenstein's view on 'small state corporatism' pointing to the impact of strong 'corporatist governance' in a small and therefore very flexible country. Van den Berg et al. in their contribution (Chapter 12 in this book) adds that in the early 1990s, when Danish unemployment rates were close to 10 per cent, the Social Democratic government embarked on a major overhaul of the unemployment benefit system. This was pursued not by strongly reducing the benefits but by shortening the maximum drawing period of benefits in which recipients would not be required to participate in activation programmes to eventually – in 1999 – 1 year instead of 4. This increased the pressures on the unemployed to seek employment or training explaining at least partly the larger levels of labour market mobility in Denmark (Van den Berg et al. in Chapter 12 of this volume). According to Madsen, Denmark's social history can certainly be viewed as a successful example of modernisation; the transformation of an agrarian into a modern society. It has brought Denmark in his view to the top league of nations, measured by most indicators of economic and social performance, for which reason it has been labelled the 'Danish miracle' though it remains to be seen whether they can repeat that success story in the nearby future when the next recession sets in. Madsen sees the Danish approach more as a source of inspiration to acquire new ideas about alternative pathways of welfare regimes rather than a simple roadmap ready for immediate transfer to other contexts.

De Gier and Van den Berg (2005) in their study convincingly argue that the Danish success was not a deliberate long-term strategy but a 'somewhat lucky outcome of a confluence of developments and circumstances that are in many respects peculiar to Denmark and may not be readily transferred to countries with different institutions and traditions' (p. 31). Denmark is an obvious case for 'policy learning' and transferability of 'best practices' but a 'copy and paste' approach is likely to be inadequate while policy interventions tend to be effective only insofar that they do not depart too much from the national path-dependent roads.

14.5 POLICIES AND FUTURE RESEARCH

Labour market mobility and in-work transitions
The lessons to be learned from the contributions in this volume are manifold. A first lesson deals with the question we posed in the first part of the volume of whether the 'stepping-stone' or 'dead-end' thesis holds with a view to the mobility from non-standard into standard jobs. We concluded that, as usual, the evidence is mixed and that it very much depends on the economic and institutional context. A North–South distinction seems at stake with a better quality of non-standard jobs with a view to the security and wage prospects involved in the North than in the South, while these jobs in the North provide better mobility chances into permanent jobs and also better pay and income prospects. The contribution of Barbier showed that we should not forget or deny the 'quality of work' dimension. Also Debels in her contribution showed that the mobility into permanent jobs is deemed insufficient in Southern countries where the wages for these workers are too low to allow the poor temporary workers to pass the poverty threshold. The 'quality of work dimension' also contributes to explaining the Danish miracle that seems associated with the very demanding work environment, the highly productive workforce and the large autonomy in work (European Commission, 2007a).

The main lesson to be drawn is that segmented and strongly regulated labour markets perform worse in reintegrating workers in these contracts into permanent jobs and flexible, unregulated labour markets best. The key to success seems to be either a high turnover facilitated through low levels of employment protection such as in the unregulated labour markets or activating policies based on investments in the employability of workers in the regulated ones. In the unregulated labour markets, the policy of sustaining a high flexibility should be geared to fair income support and safety nets for people with fewer endowments to allow them to bridge spells of unemployment and to prevent poverty (see the contribution of Debels in this volume). In the regulated labour market, employability policies should be geared to incentives-sustaining benefit systems avoiding overly generous benefits and too lenient access conditions to benefits and activation services to prevent 'revolving door' problems and welfare dependency. Another option in this pathway would have been to embark on deregulation policies to render employers more options to adapt the work force to changes in demand and at the same time to create more employment opportunities to workers.

The scarring effects of unemployment and non-standard jobs

The policy implications of the evidence presented in the second part are derived from the finding that the size and persistence of scarring effects are very much determined by the institutional context and, as we contended, by the existing social norms and social norm behaviour in society. The evidence of both Gangl and Muffels and Luijkx show a large heterogeneity in the scarring effects of unemployment and fixed-term contracts respectively across Europe, corroborating the contended impact of the institutional context. Overly generous benefits and strict regulation in regulated regimes and ungenerous benefits and lenient regulation in unregulated regimes tend to increase scarring. This implies that in strongly regulated regimes the combination of a weakening of the employment protection rules for standard workers and an improvement of the protection of temporary workers might be a viable option to reduce segmentation and to resolve, at least partly, the insider-outsider problem whereas in weakly regulated regimes the recipe should be to create adequate income support systems and fair safety nets to prevent income insecurity and poverty.

The findings with respect to part-time work shows again how important the institutional context and particularly the ruling social norms are to understand primarily the labour market behaviour of women. We concluded that in countries with strong institutional or legal support for part-time jobs these jobs seem much more similar to standard jobs in the way that they provide for income and employment security. This was explained by referring to the important role played by social norms and social norm behaviour. If there is strong political and popular support to work part-time as in the Netherlands, employers as well as employees tend to behave in such a way that part-time work is set on an even par with standard work. Policies to support part-time work are likely to contribute to making the jobs more accepted in society and therefore to improve its attractiveness also in terms of their wage career prospects. Though social norm behaviour seems important, it cannot be ruled out that women work part-time because there are no full-time jobs available to them.

The evidence from the former contribution and from that of Bijwaard, Van Dijk and De Koning (Chapter 10) suggests that part-time work is important while it meets the preferences of especially women. Bijwaard et al, not surprisingly, also show that if people move to another job in order to better meet their working time preferences, job satisfaction also increases. In countries where the norm is to work full-time and when there is a lack of support for working mothers to work part-time, especially in Anglo-Saxon and Southern countries, the quality of part-time jobs in terms of pay and wage prospects is worse compared to countries where part-time work is strongly supported. The findings on the labour supply effects of part-time work suggest that policies aimed at creating improved working time options have a better record in keeping women at work after childbirth. A second lesson in this respect is that income support policies are important to cushion the adverse income effects of the reduction in hours due to childbirth, suggesting that income support policies are truly critical to mitigate the scarring effects on income or on reducing working hours prior to and after childbirth.

Finally, Meager's contribution on the scarring effects of self-employment provides important warnings to policies while he remains very sceptical and pessimistic about the salient effects of self-employment for upward career mobility and of policy interventions to facilitate start-ups. Finding rather strong scarring effects in the unregulated British and also American labour market, he renders a warning to too-optimistic voices in policy circles about facilitating start-ups as a means to improve the chances of people who otherwise would have had few chances to make a successful career. Inter-generational transmission of skills seems a more reliable predictor of success in self-employment careers than purposeful actions of benign governments to support the unemployed. He adds a proviso though since it remains unclear whether this conclusion holds true also in other institutional contexts.

'Best practices' and policy learning

From the contributions in part three a first policy lesson we might draw deals with the experiences of the Canadian and Australian reforms in the 1990s and early 2000s. We concluded that these regimes whatever reforms they inten-ded originally, in the end returned to their original residual Anglo-Saxon tracks for which reason it tempts us to question the convergence thesis. The implication also is that the idea of pathways that the European expert group on flexicurity headed by Wilthagen proposed in their study and the Commis-sion apparently adopted in its latest communication on flexicurity, might indeed be a realistic way to proceed (European Commission, 2007b). The rationale for it is also the large heterogeneity of policies in the enlarged EU27 and the lack of competence the EU still has in the social domain. For these various reasons the Commission is also unwilling to engage in a 'naming and blaming' exercise where very successful pathways such as the Danish are pro-moted and the other less successful ones are blamed for their lack of success. Policies which seem to be a success now might not be it anymore tomorrow because regimes might fail to adapt successfully to changing conditions. The Commission therefore does not opt for a 'one-size fits-all' approach.

We already discussed the much heralded flexicurity model of Denmark that is praised while it is a prototype of a 'high-performance' labour market featured by high levels of employment and productivity and low levels of unemployment. Except in fairy tales though, there are hardly ever winners only and the question as to who are the losers remains an important one that should not to denied or withered away. In the Danish case but maybe in general, the losers are the weaker groups on the labour market, in particular the handicapped workers who are unable to catch up with the work demands in the highly advanced and demanding economy. The 'miracle' is that workers do not complain, not about their hard work since they appear rather satisfied with their job and not about their work–life balance that they even judge better as in most other countries. The trigger for the first is likely to be that they have many opportunities to invest in training and skills-upgrading and that they have a large autonomy in their work. The trigger for the good work–life balance seems to be the rather high level of public child care and of working time flexibility implying that workers have many options to be engaged in flexible working time schedules, in maternity and parental leave or in career breaks and sabbaticals. Evidence from the European Commission (2007b) also shows that not only the incidence of use of flexible working time arrangements is much higher in the Scandinavian countries but also the free choice involved for the worker to determine their working hours.

Pathways

To conclude, we argue that although the Commission might have had other and more political-strategic reasons to speak about pathways rather than about regimes, the notion of pathways is attractive while it has an academic rationale too. 'Ideal-types' of regimes in their 'pure' form in reality rarely exist and regimes due to institutional inertia tend to depart little from their original roots and stay on their historical paths. Many regimes share features of the others and no one fits entirely into a single 'ideal-type'. The Danish case is considered a representative of the Scandinavian regime but one that shares many features of the Continental and Anglo-Saxon regime types. That also holds for the other pathways, but whatever pathway the Commission has in mind for a particular country, due to the OMC principles, the way and speed in which they will be implemented is fully left to the authority of the member states.

In July 2007 the communication on flexicurity has been released and in November 2007 the Member States already agreed on the common principles. Even though there might be a general agreement on these principles in the EU, the consequences for some individual member states to transform these principles into concrete policies at the national level might be one bridge too far. The debate on the 'green paper' concerning a reform of European labour law in 2007 already made clear that the notion of flexicurity is not uncontested and that some see it as a sort of 'Trojan horse' into existing labour law in some member states (Jørgensen and Madsen, 2007).

The implementation of concrete 'flexicurity' policy measures at the national level is still in its infancy and need to be started up by the countries themselves. That process will certainly take a longer time but the terms of success are likely to be determined by the political will and economic conditions in the years to come. The more unfavourable the economic conditions are, the less room governments have to embark on policies sustaining high levels of employment and income security when simultaneously there are strong pressures to adapt to rising flexibility demands. The demise of flexicurity policies would be that governments lack the political will to act otherwise and indeed would follow this road by increasing flexibility at the expense of security levels whereas the real challenge in such a context would be to sustain high security levels while creating more room for flexibility needs.

Future research
Though the volume provides ample evidence on a variety of topics related to labour market dynamics and the relationship between flexibility and security, some issues could not be dealt with and had to be left out of scope. Partly, this has to do with practical considerations of space and time, and partly it is related to the lack of data on the main subject of the volume, in-work transitions. We only had European-wide comparable and longitudinal employee or supply data but lacked European-wide company or demand panel data. For that reason we miss out the company's perspective implying also that internal functional flexibility and employability issues are not satisfactorily captured. For the same reason we had to leave out the company's policies on the balance between flexibility and security. That issue is left for further scrutiny in future research when company level data, such as matched employer–employee panel data, will become available for a larger number of countries.

The results on the impact of institutions on occupational and contract mobility could have been more robust if we had more countries than the European Community Household Panel contained. For the near future especially SILC (Statistics on Income and Living Conditions) covering nearly all EU countries from 2005 onwards, though with a shorter time horizon, might allow us to test the impact of a larger variety of regimes, pathways and policy measures on mobility flows and outcomes in Europe. Another way to progress would be to examine the existing longer-running panel data for a limited number of countries (UK, Germany, the Netherlands, Belgium and Luxembourg) and to look at the country level into the impact of specific policy measures on flexibility and security outcomes and to the occurrence and causation of regime shifts over time. We also have not used life course data which tend to become increasingly available in countries such as Germany, Belgium, Sweden, the Netherlands, Italy and the United

Kingdom. The use of life course data would allow us to view the real long-term career effects of working in non-standard jobs. In a recent report for the European Foundation (Muffels et al., 2008) life-course data were used for the United Kingdom, Germany and the Netherlands to look at the life course career effects of childbirth and part-time work. Life course data potentially provide a rich source for research in the way in which the individualisation and diversification of life courses affect people's interactions and hence the social and economic outcomes of policy regimes and welfare state approaches. In future research we seek to use these data sources more.

Some aspects and dimensions of the relationship between flexibility and security were only partly covered such as the gender and the quality of work dimension though they deserve a more matured treatment. Especially, the 'quality of work' dimension has to date not been sufficiently addressed in the literature on the subject nor in this volume, even though it is beyond doubt that to tackle it in research would be a way forward in our understanding of the relationship between flexibility and security.

Final remarks
Globalisation and individualisation trends are held responsible for a shift from lifetime and permanent employment to a situation of more job insecurity, labour volatility and interrupted career patterns. Though the available evidence on tenure suggests that the majority of careers is still shaped on rather durable employment, an increasing number of people tends to experience more volatile employment in temporary, part-time or flexible contracts or are confronted with career interruptions due to childbirth, unemployment or education. These shifts are also delineated as a move into the 'new employment relationship' or the 'boundary-less' career but empirical analyses into the size and consequences of these alleged shifts is still rather scarce or scattered. This book attempts to contribute to the literature on the subject by providing a broad comparative picture of the empirical evidence and the consequences of in-work transition patterns, in particular the mobility from temporary to permanent contracts, from part-time to full-time employment and from unemployment to self-employment. It also examines the role policy regimes and specific welfare state institutions play in the way they affect the levels of flexibility and security in society. The book further documents the effects of major policy reforms in three country case studies which were believed to represent 'best practices' for transitional labour market and flexicurity policies. From the outcomes, important lessons are to be drawn for future research and for the challenges national and European policies face in the decades to come. It goes beyond the scope of this book to debate in detail the challenges and responses welfare states confront but Streeck's prediction some years ago that indeed attempts to reconstruct social

cohesion around 'competive solidarity' (read 'flexicurity') will be the dominant force in reforms of the welfare state tends to become more and more realistic (Streeck, 2000; see for a comprehensive overview Leibfried and Mau, 2008).

We sincerely believe that the book can contribute to inspire policies which indeed wish to take up the challenge to define new ways to create a wealthy and fair society with high levels of income and employment security and sufficient room to accommodate to rising flexibility needs.

REFERENCES

Aassve, A., Billari, F.C. and Ongaro, F. (2001), 'The impact of income and employment status on leaving home: evidence from the Italian ECHP sample', *Labour: Review of Labour Economics and Industrial Relations,* **15** (3), 501–29.

Albert, M. (1991), *Capitalisme contre capitalisme*, Paris: Editions du Seuil.

Anxo, D., Boulin, J.-Y. and Fagan, C. (2006), *Working time options over the life course: New work patterns and company strategies*, Luxembourg: Office for Official Publications of the European Communities.

Beck, U. (1992), *Risk Society: Towards a New Modernity*, London: Sage Publications.

Blau, F.D. and Kahn, L. M. (2002), At Home and Abroad: US Labor Market Performance in International Perspective, New York: Russell Sage Foundation.

De Gier, E. and Van den Berg, A. (2005), *Making Transitions Pay! Towards a European Employment Insurance Strategy (EEIS),* Amsterdam: Amsterdam School for Social Science Research, 87.

Dekker, R. (2007), *Non-standard employment and mobility in the Dutch, German and British labour market*, Ridderkerk: Ridderprint.

DiPrete, T. A., Goux, D., Maurin, E. and Quesnel-Vallee, A. (2006), 'Work and pay in flexible and regulated labor markets: A generalized perspective on institutional evolution and inequality trends in Europe and the US', *Research in Social Stratification and Mob ility*, **24**, 311–32.

European Commission (2001), *Employment in Europe 2001: recent trends and prospects,* Luxembourg: Office for Official Publications of the European Communities.

European Commission (2006), *Employment in Europe 2006*, Luxembourg: Office for Official Publications of the European Communities.

European Commission (2007a), *Employment in Europe 2007*, Luxembourg: Office for Official Publications of the European Communities.

European Commission (2007b), *Towards Common Principles of Flexicurity: More and better jobs through flexibility and security,* Brussels: European Commission.

Gangl, M. (2006), 'Scar Effects of Unemployment: An Assessment of Institutional Complementarities', *American Sociological Review*, **71** (December), 986–1013.

Gazier, B. (1998), *Transitional Labour Markets and Labour Market Segmentation: A Preliminary Discussion,* Paris: CNRS.

Giddens, A. (2007), *Europe in the Global Age*, Cambridge: Polity Press.

Grimshaw, D., Ward, K.G., Rubery, J. and Beynon, H. (2001), 'Organisation and the Transformation of the Internal Labour Market', *Work, Employment and Society*, **15** (1), 25–54.

Hall, P. and Soskice, D. (eds) (2001), *Varieties of capitalism: the institutional foundations of comparative advantage*, Oxford: Oxford University Press, 560.

Inkeless, A. (1981), 'Convergence and Divergence in Industrial Societies', in Attir, M.O., Holzner, B. H. and Suda, Z. (eds), Boulder, CO: Westview Press, 3–38.

Jørgensen, H. and Madsen, P. K. (2007), *Flexicurity and Beyond. Finding a new agenda for the European Social Model*, Copenhagen: DJØF Publishing Copenhagen.

Leibfried, S. and Mau, S. (2008), *Welfare States, Construction, Deconstruction, Reconstruction*, Cheltenham, UK and Northampton, US, Edward Elgar.

Muffels, R. (2007), 'Roads of 'Flexicurity' in Europe: How un(equal) are they?', in Jørgensen, H. and Madsen, P.K. (eds), *Flexicurity and beyond. Finding a new agenda for the European Social Model*, Copenhagen: DJØF Publishing, 215–43.

Muffels, R., Chung, H., Fouarge, D., Klammer, U., Luijkx, R., Manzoni, A., Thiel, A. and Wilthagen, T. (2008), *Flexibility and security over the life course*, Luxembourg: Office for Official Publications of the European Communities, 52.

Muffels, R. and Luijkx, R. (2008), 'The Relationship between Labour Market Mobility and Employment Security for Male Employees: Trade-off or Flexicurity?', *Work, Employment and Society*, **22** (2), 221–42.

Philips, K. and Eamets, R. (2007), Approaches to flexicurity: EU Models, Luxembourg: Office for Official Publications of the European Communities: European Foundation, 51.

Schmid, G. (1995a), 'Institutional Incentives to Prevent Unemployment: Unemployment Insurance and Active Labor Market Policy in a Comparative Perspective', *Journal of Socio Economics*, **24** (1), 51–103.

Schmid, G. (1995b), 'Is Full-Employment Still Possible – Transitional Labor-Markets as a New Strategy of Labor-Market Policy', *Economic and Industrial Democracy*, **16** (3), 429–56.

Schmid, G. and Gazier, B. (2002), *The dynamics of full employment: social integration through transitional labour markets*, Cheltenham, UK and Brookfield, US: Edward Elgar.

Stone, K.V.W. (2001), 'The new psychological contract: Implications of the changing workplace for labor and employment law', *Ucla Law Review*, **48** (3), 519–661.

Stone, K.V.W. (2005a), 'Procedural justice in the boundaryless workplace: The tension between due process and public policy', *Notre Dame Law Review*, **80** (2), 501–21.

Stone, K.V.W. (2005b), *Rethinking Labor Law: Employment Protection for Boundaryless Workers*, UCLA Schoool of Law, 1–33.

Streeck, W. (2000), 'Competitive Solidarity: Rethinking the 'European Social Model'', in Hinrichs, K., Kitschelt, H. and Wiesenthal, H. (eds), *Kontingenz und Krise: Institutionenpolitik in kapitalistischen und postsozialistischen Gesellschaften*, Frankfurt am Main: Campus, 245–61.

Wilthagen, T. and Tros, F. (2004), 'The Concept of 'Flexicurity': A new approach to regulating employment and labour markets', *Transfer, European Review of labour and research*, **10** (2), 166–86.

Author Index

Subject Index